Understanding State Constitutions

Understanding State Constitutions

G. Alan Tarr

PRINCETON UNIVERSITY PRESS

PRINCETON, NEW JERSEY

Copyright © 1998 by Princeton University Press
Published by Princeton University Press, 41 William Street, Princeton, New Jersey 08540
In the United Kingdom: Princeton University Press, Chichester, West Sussex

Library of Congress Cataloging-in-Publication Data

Tarr, G. Alan (George Alan)
Understanding state constitutions / G. Alan Tarr.
p.   cm.
Includes bibliographical references and index.
ISBN 0-691-01112-5 (cloth : alk. paper)
1. Constitutional law—United States—States.   2. Constitutional
history—United States—States.   I. Title.
KF4550.Z95T37   1998   342.73'02—dc21   98-12782

This book has been composed in Sabon

Princeton University Press books are printed on acid-free paper and meet the guidelines
for permanence and durability of the Committee on Production Guidelines for Book
Longevity of the Council on Library Resources

http://pup.princeton.edu

Printed in the United States of America

10   9   8   7   6   5   4   3   2   1

For Susan

Contents

Understanding State Constitutions

Introduction

AMERICANS live under a system of dual constitutionalism, but one would hardly know it. Leading constitutional-law texts—even those that proclaim as their subject the generic "constitutional law" or "American constitutional law"—focus exclusively on the United States Constitution and its interpretation.[1] So too do most contemporary constitutional commentaries and constitutional histories.[2] Legal scholars announce constitutional theories that actually encompass only the federal Constitution—the rough equivalent of propounding a literary theory that pertains to a single novel.[3] Small wonder, then, that almost half the

[1] See, e.g., William B. Lockhart, Yale Kamisar, Jesse H. Choper, and Steven H. Shriffrin, *Constitutional Law: Cases—Comments—Questions*, 7th ed. (St. Paul: West, 1991); Walter F. Murphy, James E. Fleming, and Sotirios A. Barber, *American Constitutional Interpretation*, 2d ed. (Westbury, N.Y.: Foundation Press, 1995); and even Ralph A. Rossum and G. Alan Tarr, *American Constitutional Law*, 4th ed. (New York: St. Martin's, 1995).

[2] Leading constitutional commentaries with an exclusively federal focus include Lawrence Tribe, *American Constitutional Law*, 2d ed. (Mineola, N.Y.: Foundation Press, 1988); and Richard J. Rotunda, John E. Nowak, and J. Nelson Young, *Treatise on Constitutional Law* (St. Paul: West, 1986). Major constitutional histories that share this federal focus include Leonard W. Levy, *American Constitutional History* (New York: Macmillan, 1989); Alfred H. Kelly, Winfred A. Harbison, and Herman Belz, *The American Constitution: Its Origin and Development*, 7th ed. (New York: Norton, 1991); and Kermit L. Hall, *Major Problems in American Constitutional History*, 2 vols. (Lexington, Mass.: D. C. Heath, 1992). A somewhat broader perspective is found in Paul W. Kahn, *Legitimacy and History: Self-Government in American Constitutional Theory* (New Haven: Yale University Press, 1992); and in Stephen M. Griffin, *American Constitutionalism: From Theory to Politics* (Princeton: Princeton University Press, 1996).

[3] Illustrative of the early constitutional-theory literature, with its exclusively federal focus, are Ronald Dworkin, *Taking Rights Seriously* (Cambridge: Harvard University Press, 1977); John Hart Ely, *Democracy and Distrust: A Theory of Judicial Review* (Cambridge: Harvard University Press, 1980); Michael J. Perry, *The Constitution, the Courts, and Human Rights* (New Haven: Yale University Press, 1982); and Sotirios Barber, *On What the Constitution Means* (Baltimore: Johns Hopkins University Press, 1984). Most of the more recent contributions to the literature continue the federal focus: Sanford Levinson, *Constitutional Faith* (Princeton: Princeton University Press, 1988); Mark V. Tushnet, *Red, White, and Blue: A Critical Analysis of Constitutional Law* (Cambridge: Harvard University Press, 1988); Bruce Ackerman, *We the People: Foundations* (Cambridge, Mass.: Belknap Press, 1991); and Earl M. Maltz, *Rethinking Constitutional Law: Originalism, Interventionism, and the Politics of Judicial Review* (Lawrence: University Press of Kansas, 1994).

For an initial attempt to elaborate the implications of the constitutional-theory literature to state constitutions, see G. Alan Tarr, "Constitutional Theory and State Constitutional Interpretation," *Rutgers Law Journal* 22 (summer 1991): 841–61.

respondents in a recent survey did not even realize that their state had a constitution.[4]

Why have state constitutions been so neglected? One obvious reason is that scholars have tended to gravitate toward "where the action is," and for most of the twentieth century that has been the national political arena, as the federal government and the federal Constitution have increasingly dominated American public life. In addition, the success of the federal Constitution has endowed it with a normative dimension. As Carol Rose tartly observed, "[T]he federal Constitution has the status of what might be called the 'plain vanilla' brand—a brand so familiar that it is assumed correct for every occasion. This Constitution is the standard by which we understand and judge other constitutions, as for example those of states and localities."[5] This likewise has discouraged research on state constitutions; for to those enamored of the federal model, most state constitutions appear decidedly "nonconstitutional." State constitutions juxtapose broad statements of principle with provisions on subjects as mundane as ski trails and highway routes, public holidays and motor vehicle revenues.[6] This apparently haphazard lumping together of the fundamental and the prosaic in a single document has prevented many scholars from taking state constitutions seriously. Indeed, one recent critic charged that a people that would constitutionalize a "liberty to ski" is "simply a frivolous people who are unable to distinguish between things that are truly important and things that are not."[7] Finally, whereas

[4] In a 1991 survey, 52 percent of respondents knew that their state had its own constitution, 11 percent believed that it did not, and 37 percent did not know or gave no answer. These results are reported in *Changing Public Attitudes on Governments and Taxes, 1991* (Washington, D.C.: Advisory Commission on Intergovernmental Relations, 1991), 14, table 15. A similar question in 1988 produced even fewer respondents who were aware of their state constitution. See *Changing Public Attitudes on Governments and Taxes, 1988* (Washington, D.C.: Advisory Commission on Intergovernmental Relations, 1988), 6, tables 5 and 6.

The problem is not limited to the general public. An eminent public-law scholar began a recent book review in the *American Political Science Review* with the confession, "I barely have a clue as to what my state constitution provides. I will bet that most persons who read this book review are in the same foggy state of mind about their own state constitution's provisions." See Bradley C. Canon, review of *Constitutional Politics in the States, American Political Science Review* 91 (March 1997): 200.

[5] Carol M. Rose, "The Ancient Constitution vs. the Federalist Empire: Anti-Federalism from the Attack on 'Monarchism' to Modern Localism," *Northwestern University Law Review* 84 (1989): 74.

[6] On ski trails, see New York Constitution, art. 14, sec. 1; on the routes of highways, see Minnesota Constitution, art. 14, sec. 2; on the establishment of Huey Long's birthday as a state holiday, see Louisiana Constitution of 1921, art. 19, sec. 22; and on motor vehicle revenues, see California Constitution, art. 19.

[7] James A. Gardner, "The Failed Discourse of State Constitutionalism," *Michigan Law Review* 90 (February 1992): 819–20.

the durability and relative unchangeability of the federal Constitution inspire reverence, the frequent amendment and replacement of state constitutions have precisely the opposite effect for both scholars and the general public.[8]

Yet the disdain for state constitutions is unfortunate; for one cannot make sense of American state government or state politics without understanding state constitutions. After all, it is the state constitution—and not the federal Constitution—that creates the state government, largely determines the scope of its powers, and distributes those powers among the branches of the state government and between state and locality.[9] It is likewise the state constitution that structures political conflict within the state and provides mechanisms for its resolution. And it is the state constitution that arguably embodies the aims and aspirations of the state's citizenry.[10] Efforts during the 1990s to devolve additional responsibilities on state governments mean that these governments—and their constitutions—are likely to assume increased importance.

State constitutions are as significant for what they reveal as for what they prescribe. They comprise a crucial scholarly resource for historians and political scientists, because political disputes in the states have often had a constitutional dimension, and the texts of state constitutions record those conflicts and their outcomes. As Lawrence Friedman has noted, "An observer with nothing in front of him but the texts of these constitutions could learn a great deal about state politics, state laws, and social life in America."[11] Moreover, because the states have regularly

[8] On the reverence accorded the federal Constitution, see Levinson, *Constitutional Faith;* and Max Lerner, "Constitution and Court as Symbols," *Yale Law Journal* 46 (June 1937): 1290–1319. The mystique of the Constitution and its framers distinguishes the federal Constitution not only from American state constitutions but also from the constitutions of most other countries. See Robert A. Goldwin and Art Kaufman, eds., *Constitution Makers on Constitution Making: The Experience of Eight Nations* (Washington, D.C.: American Enterprise Institute, 1988). The difference in popular attitudes toward the relatively unchanged federal Constitution and the frequently altered state constitutions recalls James Madison's comments on the inadvisability of frequent referral of constitutional issues to the people. See *The Federalist* no. 49.

[9] See Donald S. Lutz, "The Purposes of American State Constitutions," *Publius* 12 (winter 1982): 27–44. It must be admitted that the federal Constitution, by assigning certain powers to the national government and denying some powers to the states, helps determine what powers state governments may exercise. Chapter 2 deals with the influence of the federal Constitution on state constitutions in greater detail. However, state constitutions primarily determine what powers state governments can exercise.

[10] Daniel J. Elazar, "The Principles and Traditions Underlying American State Constitutions," *Publius* 12 (winter 1982): 11–25. For dissenting views, see Gardner, "Failed Discourse," 824–27; and Paul W. Kahn, "Interpretation and Authority in State Constitutionalism," *Harvard Law Review* 106 (March 1993): 1159–60.

[11] Lawrence M. Friedman, *A History of American Law,* 2d ed. (New York: Simon and Schuster, 1985), 120.

amended and replaced their constitutions, successive versions of a state constitution mirror the political and social changes that have occurred in the state. Comparison of state constitutions over time and among states thus reveals patterns in American political development. Or as James Bryce put it almost a century ago, state constitutions are "a mine of instruction for the natural history of democratic communities."[12]

It might even be suggested that some of the factors that have discouraged scholarly inquiry into state constitutions should actually have invited it. The differences between state constitutions and the federal Constitution, as well as between the state and federal constitutional experiences, raise intriguing questions that go to the heart of American constitutionalism. Why has constitutional change in the states occurred largely through the formal mechanisms of amendment and revision, while federal constitutional change has occurred primarily outside these formal channels? If the nation in fact reveres the federal Constitution, why have state constitution-makers rejected major elements of the federal model and embraced quite different constitutional models? Why should a distinctive constitutional tradition have developed at the state level at all, and why has it persisted over time despite the nationalization of much of American political life? Finally, how should the distinctive elements of state constitutions affect how one understands and interprets those documents?

Explaining the distinctiveness of the state constitutional experience and assessing its implications both for state constitutional interpretation and for understanding American constitutionalism are the tasks of our book. Chapter 1 identifies the distinctive features of American state constitutions and state constitutional development. Chapter 2 critically assesses various explanations that have been proposed to account for these distinctive features. Chapter 3 undertakes a more detailed examination of state constitutions and state constitution-making during the late eighteenth century. Chapters 4 and 5 continue this examination for the nineteenth and twentieth centuries. These chapters reveal that state constitutional politics has been dominated by three recurring issues. One is the distribution of political power among groups and regions within the individual states, reflected in conflicts over apportionment and the franchise. A second is the scope of state governmental authority, particularly what sorts of substantive or procedural limitations should be imposed on state

---

[12] James Bryce, *The American Commonwealth*, 2 vols. (Chicago: Charles H. Seagal, 1891), 1:434. One enthusiastic turn-of-the-century commentator went even further, claiming: "One might almost say that the romance, the poetry, and even the drama of American politics are deeply embedded in the many state constitutions" (James Q. Dealey, *Growth of American State Constitutions from 1776 to the End of the Year 1914* [Boston: Ginn and Company, 1915; rpt. New York: Da Capo, 1972], 11).

legislatures. A third is the relation of the state to economic activity, including both the extent of direct governmental support for enterprise and the appropriate balance between promotion and regulation of economic development. In tracing the development of these and other issues peculiar to particular states or eras, these chapters clarify how understandings of politics and of constitutionalism in the states have changed over time. They also identify patterns in state constitutionalism and clarify the dynamics of state constitutional change. Chapter 6 examines the implications of these findings for the practice of state constitutional interpretation. More particularly, it considers how the distinctive development and design of state constitutions pose problems for those interpreting them, assesses the usefulness of contemporary constitutional theory for addressing those problems, and sketches an approach to state constitutional interpretation.

My research on state constitutions began almost two decades ago, and over the course of that period a number of persons and organizations have encouraged and supported my work. For much of this period, the Rutgers University Research Council has underwritten my research on state constitutions with timely grants. In 1987 the National Endowment for the Humanities awarded me a Fellowship for College Teachers that enabled me to pursue research on state constitutions, and in 1996 it again awarded me a Fellowship, enabling me to devote a year to completing my research and writing this book. For over a decade and a half, I have benefited immensely from discussions with two friends and collaborators, Mary Cornelia Porter and Robert F. Williams. They have read earlier versions of this manuscript in its entirety and have offered both thoughtful suggestions and encouragement. I have also benefited over the years from discussions with numerous other scholars, among them Daniel Elazar, Susan Fino, Christian Fritz, Richard Harris, Russell Harrison, Dick Howard, Ellis Katz, John Kincaid, and Earl Maltz. From 1993 to 1997, I participated in the Delaware Valley Constitutional Seminar, organized by Daniel Elazar, and the discussions on state constitutions at these meetings were a great help in clarifying my thoughts and suggesting new avenues to explore. Colleagues and administrators at Rutgers University–Camden have provided a vibrant intellectual atmosphere for conducting research, and the secretary of the Department of Political Science, Karen McGrath, has been an unfailing source of assistance. Two students, Nancy Leso and Jay Keesler, have provided helpful research assistance. My wife, Susan, and my sons, Bob and Andy, have made all the work worthwhile.

The Distinctiveness of State Constitutionalism

IN 1982, five years before the nation celebrated the bicentennial of the federal Constitution, Georgia abandoned its constitution of six years duration and adopted a new constitution. The 1982 replacement, the state's tenth constitution, was over four times as long as the federal Constitution. Within a decade it had been amended more times than the federal Constitution has been in over two hundred years.[1] Georgia's experience, though extreme, is hardly unique. Whether one examines the structure of state constitutions, the range of topics they address, the level of detail they encompass, the changes they have undergone, or the political perspectives underlying them, the conclusion remains the same: state constitutions are different. These differences reveal that the United States has not just a system of dual constitutionalism but dual constitutional traditions. This chapter documents differences in constitutional design and constitutional practice that have developed at the state and national levels. Its survey of the structure and substance of state constitutions lays the groundwork for chapter 2, which assesses various explanations that have been proposed to account for this state constitutional distinctiveness.

STATE CONSTITUTIONAL DESIGN

Power and Purpose

Because it furnishes what has become the standard account of American constitutionalism, *McCulloch* v. *Maryland* provides a convenient starting point for identifying what is distinctive about state constitutionalism.[2] In upholding the congressional creation of a national bank and striking down a state tax on it, Chief Justice John Marshall acknowledged that the federal Constitution granted only limited powers to the national government. But this limited delegation did not restrict Congress to only those powers expressly granted to it; for it was probably impossible and certainly undesirable to provide "an accurate detail of all the subdivisions of which [the Constitution's] great powers will admit, and of all the

---

[1] Information on Georgia's constitutional experience is drawn from Melvin B. Hill Jr., *The Georgia State Constitution: A Reference Guide* (Westport, Conn.: Greenwood Press, 1994).

[2] *McCulloch* v. *Maryland*, 17 U.S. (4 Wheat.) 316 (1819).

means by which they may be carried into execution." To do so would require that the Constitution "partake of the prolixity of a legal code," which was inappropriate for a charter of government. Rather, it was sufficient that the Constitution's "great outlines be marked, its important objects designated, and the minor ingredients which compose those objects be deduced from the nature of the objects itself."[3] Put differently, because the federal Constitution was created to achieve certain broad ends, its grants of power were to be interpreted as carrying with them the subsidiary powers necessary for the achievement of those ends. If there were any doubts on this score, the grant to Congress of implied powers through the necessary and proper clause effectively removed them. Thus, in *McCulloch* the failure specifically to grant to Congress the power to create a bank did not determine the bank's constitutionality, because the Constitution's language, as well as its overall character, bespoke a willingness to permit Congress broad discretion in determining how the Constitution's aims were to be achieved. As Marshall concluded: "Let the end be legitimate, let it be within the scope of the constitution, and all means which are appropriate, which are plainly adapted to that end, which are not prohibited, but consist with the letter and spirit of the constitution, are constitutional."[4]

What is striking about Marshall's constitutional analysis is how little of it applies to American state constitutions. Whereas Marshall recognized that the federal government could exercise only those legislative powers granted to it by the federal Constitution, state governments have historically been understood to possess plenary legislative powers—that is, those residual legislative powers not ceded to the national government or prohibited to them by the federal Constitution. As the Kansas Supreme Court has observed: "When the constitutionality of a statute is involved, the question presented is, therefore, not whether the act is authorized by the constitution, but whether it is prohibited thereby."[5] State governments are not restricted in the purposes for which they can exercise power—they can legislate comprehensively to protect the public welfare—and because of this, state constitutional interpretation cannot

[3] 17 U.S. (4 Wheat.) 316, 405 and 407 (1819).
[4] 17 U.S. (4 Wheat.) 316, 420.
[5] *State ex rel. Schneider v. Kennedy,* 587 P.2d 844, 850 (Kan. 1978). The plenary character of state legislative power has long been recognized: see Thomas M. Cooley, *Constitutional Limitations: A Treatise on the Constitutional Limitations Which Rest upon the Legislative Power of the States of the American Union,* 8th ed. (Boston: Little, Brown, 1927), 175–79 for discussion and a listing of supporting cases. For indications that the situation may be more complicated than it initially appears, see Robert F. Williams, "State Constitutional Law Processes," *William and Mary Law Review* 24 (winter 1983): 178–79; and Walter F. Dodd, "The Functions of a State Constitution," *Political Science Quarterly* 30 (1915): 205.

proceed in terms of a state government's "important objects" and "minor ingredients."[6] Furthermore, whereas Marshall viewed grants of power as carrying with them subsidiary powers, what appear as grants of power in state constitutions typically do not operate in that fashion. The state provisions may be included for emphasis, indicating powers that the state government can exercise, without enlarging those powers.[7] Or they may direct state legislatures to exercise powers that they command.[8] Or they may serve to overrule judicial decisions limiting legislative power, to eliminate questions of authority where state power was doubtful, or to indicate exceptions to constitutional prohibitions on the legislature.[9] Most often, however, these apparent "grants of power" function as limitations. For in a constitution of plenary legislative powers, an authoriza-

[6] That state governments possess the "police power"—the power to protect the health, safety, welfare, and morals of their citizens—has long been recognized in judicial rulings, both federal and state. Pertinent federal rulings include *Hammer* v. *Dagenhart*, 247 U.S. 251, 276 (1918); *United States* v. *E. C. Knight Co.*, 156 U.S. 1, 11 (1895); and *Munn* v. *Illinois*, 94 U.S. 113, 123, 135 (1877). Illustrative state rulings include *Commonwealth* v. *Alger*, 7 Cush. 53 (Mass. 1851); *Hingham and Quincy Bridge and Turnpike Corp.* v. *County of Norfolk*, 88 Mass. 353 (1863); and *Commonwealth* v. *Strauss*, 191 Mass. 545 (1906). The scope of state legislative activity under the police power is surveyed in William J. Novak, *The People's Welfare: Law and Regulation in Nineteenth-Century America* (Chapel Hill: University of North Carolina Press, 1996).

Even legal commentators eager to restrain state legislative power have recognized the breadth of the police power; see Cooley, *Constitutional Limitations*, 829–32. However, for an argument that the concept of the police power has no place in state constitutional law because—despite its breadth—it implies limitations on a plenary state legislative power, see Hans A. Linde, "Without 'Due Process': Unconstitutional Law in Oregon," *Oregon Law Review* 49 (February 1970): 125–87.

[7] See, for example, the Illinois Constitution, art. 8, sec. 2(b), recognizing the authority of the General Assembly to appropriate funds.

[8] See, for example, the New Jersey Constitution, art. 8, sec. 4, par. 1, directing the legislature to provide a "thorough and efficient education" for all students.

[9] Examples of amendments designed to overrule judicial decisions include California Constitution, art. 1, sec. 27, which instituted capital punishment after it was outlawed in *People* v. *Anderson*, 493 P.2d 880 (Cal. 1972); California Constitution, art. 1, sec. 7a, forbidding the use of busing to achieve racial balance in public schools in the absence of prior intentional discrimination, partially overturning *Crawford* v. *Board of Education*, 551 P.2d 28 (Cal. 1976); and Massachusetts Constitution, part 1, art. 26, reinstituting capital punishment in the wake of *District Attorney for the Suffolk District* v. *Watson*, 411 N.E.2d 1274 (Mass. 1980).

New Jersey furnishes a prime example of a provision designed to eliminate doubt about the scope of legislative authority. After the state supreme court upheld a bus transportation program for parochial students in *Everson* v. *Board of Education*, 44 A.2d 333 (N.J. 1945), a provision was added to the state constitution (New Jersey Constitution, art. 8, sec. 4, par. 3) to prevent the judiciary from later reversing or limiting its holding.

For an example of a provision crafting an exception to a prohibition on the legislature, see Idaho Constitution, art. 7, sec. 5, which requires uniformity in taxation but authorizes the legislature to create exemptions as are "necessary and just."

tion to pursue one course of action may by negative implication serve to preclude pursuing alternative courses that were available in the absence of the "grant," under the familiar legal canon of *expressio unius est exclusio alterius*.[10]

Length and Detail

Although Chief Justice Marshall cautioned that a constitution should avoid the prolixity of a legal code, state constitution-makers have largely ignored his counsel of constitutional minimalism.[11] Indeed, for those unfamiliar with state constitutions, probably their most striking feature is their length. State constitutions, particularly those adopted during the late nineteenth century, are replete with "constitutional legislation," provisions that in their length and detail are indistinguishable from statutes but that nonetheless have been elevated to constitutional status.[12] During the twentieth century, state constitutional reformers have attacked the proliferation of constitutional legislation as the primary flaw in state constitutions and campaigned to prune their state charters of such provisions. In several states these reformers have prevailed, although in none did they succeed in reducing the state constitution to the dimensions of the federal Constitution. Even a reform constitution such as New Jersey's, adopted in 1947, is three times as long as its federal counterpart. Moreover, in other states constitutional reform has proceeded slowly— Louisiana's constitution of 1921 ballooned to over 250,000 words before it was finally replaced in 1974—or has failed altogether.[13] Finally, those states that have the constitutional initiative have found their consti-

[10] See the discussions in Frank P. Grad, "The State Constitution: Its Function and Form for Our Time," *Virginia Law Review* 54 (May 1968): 928, 967–68; and Williams, "State Constitutional Law Processes," 178–79 and 202–3. Some recent state constitutions have attempted to forestall this interpretation of the "grants" they contain. For example, the Alaska Constitution, art. 12, sec. 8, states: "The enumeration of specified powers in this constitution shall not be construed as limiting the powers of the State."

[11] It should be noted that Marshall's view of what was appropriately included within a constitution and what was more appropriate for a statute was hardly idiosyncratic. James Madison, for example, in responding to a complaint that the Philadelphia convention had not secured the common law, argued that they could not have done so without importing antirepublican and even ecclesiastical doctrines and that "if they had undertaken a discrimination [as some of the states had done], they would have formed a *digest of laws, instead of a Constitution*" (James Madison to George Washington, Oct. 18, 1787, in Galliard Hunt, ed. *The Writings of James Madison*, 12 vols. [New York: G. P. Putnam's Sons, 1900–1910], 5:14; emphasis added).

[12] As of 1997, more than half the states—twenty-six in all—were operating under constitutions adopted during the second half of the nineteenth century.

[13] Lee Hargrave, *The Louisiana State Constitution: A Reference Guide* (Westport, Conn.: Greenwood Press, 1991), 16.

tutions increasing in length, particularly during the late twentieth century, as groups have used the initiative to circumvent the legislature and enact legislation via constitutional amendment. Currently, the unamended text of the typical state constitution remains over three times as long as that of the federal Constitution, and state constitutions on average contain over 120 constitutional amendments.[14]

To some extent this greater length of state constitutions can be attributed to the plenary character of state legislative power. Because legislative power exists in the absence of constitutional limitations and because state courts have characteristically interpreted such limitations narrowly, many state constitution-makers have believed it necessary to detail the limitations they sought to impose on their state legislatures. To some extent, too, this greater length derives from the inclusion of elements not found in the federal Constitution. Donald Lutz has argued that the brevity of the federal Constitution and the length of state constitutions are related.[15] According to Lutz, the federal Constitution is an "incomplete constitution," which depends for its operation on state constitutions that "complete" and consequently form a part of the national constitution. For example, the original federal Constitution did not need to define voting qualifications because state constitutions had already done so. Even today, it can say nothing about education and local government—to choose but two examples—because state constitutions deal with such matters.

Yet neither the plenary character of the state legislative power nor the incompleteness of the federal Constitution fully explains the length of state constitutions.[16] For if these shared features were decisive, then all state constitutions would be roughly similar in length. But in fact they vary widely. The longest current state constitution (Alabama's) is more than twenty-six times as long as the shortest (Vermont's), and nine state constitutions contain over forty thousand words, while eleven contain less than fifteen thousand.[17] Furthermore, state constitutions within individual states have varied enormously over time in both their length and

[14] Data on contemporary state constitutions are drawn from Janice C. May, "State Constitutions and Constitutional Revision, 1992–93," in *The Book of the States, 1994–95* (Lexington, Ky.: Council of State Governments, 1994), 19, table 1.1.

[15] Donald S. Lutz, "The United States Constitution as an Incomplete Text," *Annals of the Academy of Political and Social Science* 496 (March 1988): 23–32. In making this claim, Lutz draws upon a long tradition of constitutional analysis. Even the strongly nationalist justice Joseph Story observed that "the state governments are, by the very theory of the constitution, essential parts of the general government. They can exist without the latter, but the latter cannot exist without them" (Joseph Story, *Commentaries on the Constitution of the United States* [1833; Durham: Carolina Academic Press, 1987], sec. 258).

[16] Chapter 2 considers other explanations for the length of state constitutions.

[17] May, "State Constitutions, 1992–93," 19, table 1.1.

their contents. Many state constitutions during the nation's first half-century resembled the federal Constitution in their length and absence of policy prescriptions, but post–Civil War constitutions grew to enormous lengths. For example, the revised constitutions in Maryland (1867), Arkansas (1874), and Missouri (1875) all exceeded their predecessor constitutions by over ten thousand words.[18] More substantively, whereas nineteenth-century constitutions included lengthy provisions dealing with local government and financial matters, most recent constitutions have eschewed their predecessors' detailed treatment of those topics.

Structure and Substance

Since at least the late nineteenth century, most state constitutions have shared a more or less uniform structure and have dealt with a common set of issues (while differing in the detail of their treatment of those issues and in the range of other issues addressed). In certain structural features these state constitutions resemble their federal counterpart. All fifty state constitutions have eschewed a parliamentary system, established a tripartite division of governmental power, provided for regular elections, and guaranteed a range of fundamental rights, while all but Nebraska's have created a bicameral legislature. However, closer inspection of the structure and substance of state constitutions highlights many features that distinguish them from the federal Constitution.[19]

RIGHTS GUARANTEES

In contrast to the federal Constitution, the initial article of the state constitution (following the preamble) is typically a declaration (or bill) of rights.[20] This ordering of rights and powers dates from the earliest state

---

[18] Sister M. Barbara McCarthy, *The Widening Scope of American Constitutions* (Washington, D.C.: Catholic University of America, 1928), 25.

[19] As Daniel J. Elazar has noted, "There are scientific principles involved in the making of constitutions, as the fathers of the United States Constitution of 1787 demonstrated in their reliance on the 'new science of politics,' which had discovered such vital principles of republican regimes as separation of powers, federalism, and the institution of the presidency. But the combination of those elements and their adaptation to the constituency to be served is an art." See Daniel J. Elazar, "Constitution-Making: The Pre-eminently Political Act," in Keith G. Banting and Richard Simeon, eds., *Redesigning the State: The Politics of Constitutional Change* (Toronto: University of Toronto Press, 1985), 232.

The examination of the structure of state constitutions that follows does not address provisions on elections and suffrage, which are discussed in detail in chapters 3–5, nor various minor features of state constitutions such as the delineation of state boundaries and the schedule for transition from one constitution to the next.

[20] Preceding the initial article is a preamble, which indicates the general purposes for which the people established the constitution. However, the preamble does not create

constitutions, some of which expressly divided their basic law into a declaration of rights and a constitution, or frame of government (although they typically contained provisions emphasizing that the declaration was part of the constitution and hence obligatory). Many of the early bills of rights included provisions that would not be understood as rights guarantees today. Virginia's famous Declaration of Rights, for example, mandated a separation of powers and admonished citizens to treat each other with "Christian forbearance, love, and charity."[21] Pennsylvania's Declaration of Rights recommended that the legislature "consist of persons most noted for wisdom and virtue" and urged citizens to "pay particular attention to these points in electing officers and legislators."[22] And the Massachusetts Declaration of Rights required local governments to "make suitable provision" for "the support and maintenance of public Protestant teachers of piety, religion, and morality in all cases where such provision shall not be made voluntarily."[23] Due to the widespread interstate borrowing that has characterized state constitution-making, both the precedence given to rights and the inclusion of "nonrights" material have been carried over to constitutions in other states.

Although some states have retained their original constitutional language, over time state bills of rights have come to resemble more closely the federal Bill of Rights.[24] Still, important differences remain. Many state guarantees are more specific than their federal counterparts. For example, in addition to prohibiting governmental establishment of religion, nineteen states specifically bar religious tests for witnesses or jurors, and thirty-five prohibit expenditures for "any sectarian purpose."[25] Sev-

---

powers or confer them on the state government. Some states do include short articles before their declaration of rights. Article 1 of both the Arizona and Arkansas constitutions, for example, give the state boundaries. But few state constitutions have followed the federal practice of appending the declaration of rights to the end of the constitution. Interestingly, the preambles of nineteenth-century state constitutions differ from those of earlier state constitutions in including an acknowledgment of God's existence and beneficence. The implications of this reference to the Deity for the interpretation of state guarantees of religious liberty are explored in G. Alan Tarr, "Church and State in the States," *Washington Law Review* 64 (winter 1989): 87–88.

[21] Virginia Constitution of 1776, art. 1, secs. 5 and 16.

[22] Pennsylvania Constitution of 1776, art. 1, secs. 7 and 14.

[23] Massachusetts Constitution of 1780, Declaration of Rights, art. 3.

[24] It may be more correct to say that the federal Bill of Rights resembles state protections. As Donald S. Lutz observes, "Almost every one of the twenty-six rights in the U.S. Bill of Rights could be found in two or three state documents [i.e., declarations of rights], and most of them in five or more" (Lutz, "The State Constitutional Pedigree of the U. S. Bill of Rights," *Publius* 22 [spring 1992]: 28). For an encyclopedic overview of state constitutional guarantees and their interpretation, see Jennifer Friesen, *State Constitutional Law: Litigating Individual Rights, Claims, and Defenses,* 2d ed. (Charlottesville, Va.: Michie, 1996).

[25] See Ronald K. L. Collins Jr., "Bills and Declarations of Rights Digest," in *The Ameri-*

eral state constitutions not only forbid cruel and unusual punishments but also ban unnecessary rigor in punishments, require that penalties be proportionate to the offense, and/or establish rehabilitation as an aim of punishment; while others expressly authorize capital punishment.[26] In addition, many state bills of rights contain protections that have no federal analogue. Thus, thirty-nine states guarantee access to a legal remedy to those who suffer injuries, and eleven expressly protect a right to privacy.[27] Furthermore, in contrast with federal practice, states have not treated their bills of rights as sacrosanct but have amended them with some frequency. From 1986 to 1993, for example, the states adopted fifty-two amendments to their declarations of rights.[28] Some of these amendments served to expand rights—for example, fourteen states added "little ERAs" to their constitutions between 1971 and 1976.[29] Other served to curtail them—Texas, for instance, has amended its bill of rights to restrict the right to bail and California to permit the use of illegally obtained evidence in criminal proceedings.[30] Finally, although the federal Bill of Rights only protects against governmental invasions of rights, some state guarantees prohibit private violations of rights as well. A few, like the Louisiana Constitution's ban on private discrimination, do so expressly.[31] Other guarantees leave themselves open to extension to private action by not specifying that they are directed against governmental violations. A case in point are those state free-speech guarantees that affirmatively protect freedom of speech without specifying against whom. These provisions have been used to protect speech rights on private property open to the public, such as shopping malls.[32]

---

can Bench, 3d ed. (Sacramento: Reginald Bishop Forster and Associates, 1985–86), 2500–2501; and Tarr, "Church and State," 93–100.

[26] Collins, "Bills and Declarations Digest," 2510.

[27] On the state constitutional right to a remedy, see David Schuman, "The Right to a Remedy," *Temple Law Review* 65 (winter 1992): 1197–1227; state provisions are listed at 1201 n. 25. On the state constitutional right to privacy, see Ken Gormley and Rhonda G. Hartman, "Privacy and the States," *Temple Law Quarterly* 65 (winter 1992): 1279–1323; state provisions are listed and discussed at 1282–83.

[28] May, "State Constitutions, 1992–93," 7, table B.

[29] On state guarantees of gender equality, see G. Alan Tarr and Mary Cornelia Porter, "Gender Equality and Judicial Federalism: The Role of State Appellate Courts," *Hastings Constitutional Law Quarterly* 9 (summer 1982): 953, table A.

[30] The Texas amendment restricting the right to bail is Texas Constitution, art. 1, sec. 11(a). The California amendment, adopted in 1982, is California Constitution, art. 1, sec. 28, part (d).

[31] Louisiana Constitution, art. 1, sec. 12.

[32] Altogether, forty-four states have such provisions. The Kansas Constitution, art. 1, sec. 11, is representative: "The liberty of the press shall be inviolate; and all persons may freely speak, write or publish their sentiments on all subjects, being responsible for the abuse of such rights." State free-speech provisions have spawned considerable litigation

GOVERNMENTAL INSTITUTIONS AND THE DISTRIBUTION OF POWER

The Separation of Powers. Both federal and state courts recognize the separation of powers as a constitutional principle, but from the outset several states were not content to leave the principle to implication.[33] Currently, forty state constitutions expressly mandate a separation of powers, rejecting dual office-holding and restricting each branch to the powers appropriate to it. At the same time, many of these constitutions anticipate that the state may not maintain a strict separation of powers, permitting departures from it if authorized elsewhere in the constitution. Wyoming's article 2 is representative:

> The powers of the government of this state are divided into three distinct departments: The legislative, executive, and judicial, and no person or collection of persons charged with the exercise of powers properly belonging to one of these departments shall exercise any power belonging to either of the others, except as in this constitution expressly directed or permitted.[34]

The inclusion of such separation-of-powers provisions in state constitutions serves to illustrate the interesting questions that arise in interpreting state charters. Federal courts enforce a separation of powers even without an explicit constitutional mandate, as do some state courts, treating the requirement as implicit in the constitutional design.[35] What,

---

concerning speech rights on private property. These cases are surveyed and discussed in G. Alan Tarr, "State Constitutionalism and 'First Amendment' Rights," in Stanley Friedelbaum, ed., *Human Rights in the States* (Westport, Conn.: Greenwood Press, 1988); John A. Ragosta, "Free Speech Access to Shopping Malls under State Constitutions: Analysis and Rejection,"*Syracuse Law Review* 37 (1986): 1–42; and Todd F. Simon, "Independent but Inadequate: State Constitutions and Protection of Freedom of Expression," *University of Kansas Law Review* 33 (winter 1985): 305–43. For more general discussions of whether federal state-action requirements are relevant to the interpretation of state constitutions, see Daniel D. Devitt, "State Action in Pennsylvania: Suggestions for a Unified Approach," *Emerging Issues in State Constitutional Law* 3 (1990): 87–114; and Robert Skover, "The Washington Constitutional 'State Action' Doctrine: A Fundamental Right to State Action," *University of Puget Sound Law Review* 8 (winter 1985): 221–82.

[33] Whereas the federal Constitution's separation of powers derives from the vesting of powers in the various branches in Articles 1–3, several of the original states expressly constitutionalized the separation of powers in their initial constitutions. As James Madison documented in *Federalist* no. 47, however, this constitutionalization did not necessarily betoken a willingness to maintain such a separation.

[34] Wyoming Constitution, art. 2. For a discussion of the variations among state separation-of-powers provisions, see John Devlin, "Toward a State Constitutional Analysis of Allocation of Powers: Legislators and Legislative Appointees Performing Administrative Functions," *Temple Law Review* 66 (winter 1993): 1236–41.

[35] Representative federal cases include *Youngstown Sheet and Tube Company* v. *Sawyer,* 343 U.S. 579 (1952); *Morrison* v. *Olson,* 487 U.S. 654 (1988); and *Mistretta* v. *United States,* 488 U.S. 361 (1989). State cases in the absence of an express constitutional require-

then, is the effect of constitutionalizing the separation of powers? Some state courts, loath to hold that the constitutional language has no effect, have suggested that the state provisions must impose a more stringent separation than is established by the federal Constitution. Thus, the West Virginia Court of Appeals has insisted that the requirement "must be strictly construed and closely followed," holding that "the plain language of [the separation-of-powers provision] calls not for construction, but only for obedience."[36] Other courts, reluctant to attribute a different meaning to the principle of the separation of powers at the state and federal levels, have read the state provisions as mere truisms and generally rejected constitutional challenges raised under them.[37] However, even these courts have been obliged to recognize that the provisions impose some restrictions on the range of legislative powers that can be exercised by the state's executive and judicial branches.[38] A further question arises: if constitutionalizing the separation of powers has an effect on constitutional interpretation, what is the effect of not constitutionalizing it? Or, put differently, given the inclusion of separation-of-powers provisions in many state constitutions, what implications—if any—should be drawn from the fact that a state's constitution-makers chose not to include such a provision?

These questions reveal some of the complexities involved in interpreting a state constitution in the context of other constitutions that have treated the same issue.

State Governmental Institutions. The next three articles found in state constitutions typically establish the legislative, executive, and judicial branches of the state's government.[39] Like Articles 1–3 of the federal

---

ment of a separation of powers include *State v. A.L.I.V.E. Voluntary,* 606 P.2d 769 (Alas. 1980), and *State ex rel. Stephan v. House of Representatives,* 687 P.2d 622 (Kan. 1984).

[36] *State ex rel. Quelch v. Daugherty,* 306 S.E.2d 233, 235 (1985). For a review of one set of pertinent cases, see L. Harold Levinson, "The Decline of the Legislative Veto: Federal/State Comparisons and Interactions," *Publius* 17 (winter 1987): 115–32.

[37] Thus, in *Brown v. Heymann,* 297 A.2d 572, 577 (N.J. 1972), the New Jersey Supreme Court denied that the inclusion of an express requirement of a separation of powers made any difference: "There is no indication that our State Constitution was intended, with respect to the delegation of legislative power, to depart from the basic concept of distribution of powers of government embodied in the Federal Constitution. It seems evident that in this regard the design spelled out in our State Constitution would be implied in constitutions which are not explicit in this regard."

[38] See G. Alan Tarr and Russell Harrison, "Legitimacy and Capacity in State Supreme Court Policymaking: The New Jersey Supreme Court and Exclusionary Zoning," *Rutgers Law Journal* 15 (spring 1984): 541.

[39] Some state constitutions—for example, California's and Georgia's—insert an article dealing with voting and elections before the discussion of the three branches. Chapters 3–5 deal with state constitutional provisions on these matters.

Constitution, these articles create offices and prescribe the qualifications, terms, and mode of selection for their occupants. However, the state articles differ in important respects from their federal counterparts.[40] Article 1 of the federal charter grants a set of enumerated powers to Congress; but state constitutions do not delineate state legislative powers, because (as noted previously) state legislative power is considered to be plenary. This has important implications for state constitutional interpretation. In determining the distribution of powers among the branches of state government, the underlying premise must be that the powers of the executive and judicial branches are defined by the constitution, whereas the legislature's are not, so all powers not clearly granted to those branches are reserved to the legislature. Thus, under state constitutions implied powers reside in the legislature rather than the governor or the courts.[41] In addition, in contrast with federal constitutional interpretation, which historically has focused on the implied powers of Congress, the fundamental interpretive issue under state constitutions is the implied limitations (if any) on state legislative power.[42]

The legislative article in state constitutions focuses primarily on the limitations on the state legislature's powers. Some of these limitations are substantive. State legislatures are enjoined from undertaking various actions, such as lending the credit of the state, or adopting laws on certain topics, such as lotteries.[43] They are also prohibited from enacting certain

[40] For more detailed discussions of distinctive aspects of the states' division of powers among the three branches, see Devlin, "Toward State Constitutional Analysis"; Harold H. Bruff, "Separation of Powers under the Texas Constitution," *Texas Law Review* 68 (June 1990): 1337–67; Scott M. Matheson Jr., "Eligibility of Public Officials and Employees to Serve in the State Legislature: An Essay on Separation of Powers, Politics, and Constitutional Policy," *Utah Law Review* 1988:295–377; and John V. Orth, "Forever Separate and Distinct: Separation of Powers Law in North Carolina," *North Carolina Law Review* 62 (October 1983): 1–28.

[41] As the Rhode Island Supreme Court has observed: "Since the adoption of the constitution, this court has consistently held that the powers of both the Crown and Parliament reside in the Legislature, unless that power has been subsumed by the Constitution of the United States, or has been removed from the General Assembly by the Constitution of the State of Rhode Island. . . . .Because the General Assembly does not look to the State Constitution for grants of power, we have invariably adhered to the view that the General Assembly possesses all powers inherent in the sovereign other than those that the constitution textually commits to the other branches of state government (*City of Pawtucket v. Sundlun*, 662 A.2d 40, 44 [R.I. 1995]). For further elaboration of the character of state legislative power, see Michael Besso, "Connecticut Legislative Power in the First Century of State Constitutional Government," *Quinnipiac Law Review* 15 (spring 1996): 1–56; and Robert F. Williams, "Comment: On the Importance of a Theory of Legislative Power under State Constitutions," *Quinnipiac Law Review* 15 (spring 1996): 57–64.

[42] Walter F. Dodd, "Implied Powers and Implied Limitations in Constitutional Law," *Yale Law Journal* 29 (December 1919): 137–62.

[43] See, for example, New Jersey Constitution of 1947, art. 4, secs. 6 and 7.

types of special laws—the list can be very long—such as laws granting divorces or changes of name, and from passing special laws when more general enactments are possible.[44] Other limitations on state legislatures are procedural, regulating the process of legislation in order to ensure a more open and orderly deliberative process. These procedural require-ments have no counterpart in the federal Constitution. For example, many state constitutions prescribe the form that bills must take, limit the range of subjects a single bill can encompass, and specify the procedures by which a bill is to be considered and adopted.[45] These requirements might prove onerous if they were consistently enforced. However, state courts usually have allowed state legislatures to police their own obser-vance of these requirements, and thus the requirements have seldom impeded the legislative process.[46]

Like Article 2 of the federal Constitution, the state executive article enumerates the powers of the executive. However, unlike their federal counterpart, most state executive articles establish a nonunified execu-tive. Only New Jersey has no elected executive-branch officers beyond the governor, and many states have several independently elected execu-tive officers who undertake important administrative responsibilities and who need not share the governor's political affiliation. As late as 1920, over three-quarters of the states elected their secretary of state, state audi-tor, and attorney general; and even today, more than two-thirds of the states have at least four independently elected executive officials.[47] State executive articles therefore must delineate the sphere of authority of each executive officer and the division of responsibility among them, as well as the extent to which the governor or other officials can exercise authority over their fellow executive officers. The executive article may in addition attempt to ensure administrative rationality by limiting the number of executive departments in state government.[48] Finally, state executive arti-cles may create and independently empower executive agencies: Florida's Game and Fresh Water Fish Commission is a prime example.[49] This con-

[44] See, for example, Nebraska Constitution of 1875, art. 3, sec. 15.

[45] Michael W. Catalano, "The Single Subject Rule: A Check on Anti-Majoritarian Logroll-ing," *Emerging Issues in State Constitutional Law* 3 (1990): 77–86; Millard H. Ruud, "No Law Shall Embrace More Than One Subject," *Minnesota Law Review* 42 (January 1958): 389–452; and Robert F. Williams, "State Constitutional Limits on Legislative Procedure: Legislative Compliance and Judicial Enforcement," *Publius* 17 (winter 1987): 91–114.

[46] Williams, "State Constitutional Limits," 106–12. This contrasts with state courts' willingness to intervene in the process of constitutional amendment, discussed later in this chapter.

[47] McCarthy, *Widening Scope,* 52–55; and "The Executive Branch," *Book of the States, 1996–97* (Lexington, Ky.: Council of State Governments, 1996), 35, table 2.10.

[48] See, for example, New York Constitution, art. 5, sec. 2.

[49] Florida Constitution, art. 4, sec. 9.

stitutionalization of executive agencies obviously limits the alternatives available in reorganizing the state's executive branch. It also creates a rather anomalous situation in which rules adopted by the agencies in pursuance of their constitutionally granted authority are superior to statutes enacted by the legislature.[50]

Finally, in contrast with Article 3 of the federal Constitution, several states have chosen to set up their entire judicial system by constitutional prescription rather than by statute. The judicial articles in these states establish all state courts, specify each court's jurisdiction, delineate the boundaries of the districts in which the courts shall operate, and provide for the selection of judges to serve on them. State judicial articles may also institute an administrative office of the courts, create judicial discipline commissions, and provide for officials such as court clerks, prosecuting attorneys, coroners, and sheriffs.[51] For some state constitutions, no detail appears too minor for inclusion. The New York Constitution specifies the quorum for its Court of Appeals, the Nevada Constitution regulates how judges charge juries, and the California Constitution establishes guidelines for the publication of judicial opinions.[52] Not surprisingly, the detailed prescriptions of state judicial articles have periodically required amendment to accommodate population shifts and changes in the demand for legal services.[53] Often, however, constitutional amendments have merely exacerbated existing problems and have themselves been subject to amendment. Since World War II, many states have reformed their judiciaries by unifying courts and centralizing administrative control in the state supreme court.[54] Others have instituted intermediate courts of appeal, thereby increasing the discretion of the

[50] Illustrative of the implications for executive-branch reorganization of a nonunified executive is Wyoming Constitution, art. 4, sec. 14, which had to be amended to eliminate the position of state examiner as part of a governmental reorganization effort. On the relationship between constitutionalized agencies and the state legislature, see *Florida Department of Natural Resources* v. *Florida Game and Fresh Water Commission*, 342 So.2d 495 (Fla. 1977), and *Whitehead* v. *Rogers*, 223 So.2d 330 (Fla. 1969).

[51] For the creation of the administrative office of the courts, see New Jersey Constitution, art. 6, sec. 7; for judicial disciplinary commissions, see New York Constitution, art. 6, sec. 22; for clerks of court, see Wyoming Constitution, art. 5, secs. 9 and 13; and for coroner and sheriff, see Louisiana Constitution, art. 5, secs. 29 and 27.

[52] On the quorum in New York appellate courts, see the New York Constitution, art. 6, sec. 2; on the charging of juries, see the Nevada Constitution, art. 6, sec. 12; and on the publication of opinions, see the California Constitution, art. 6, sec. 14.

[53] This paragraph follows the analysis in G. Alan Tarr, *Judicial Process and Judicial Policymaking* (St. Paul: West, 1994), 49–53.

[54] See Larry Charles Berkson and Susan B. Carbon, *Court Unification: History, Politics, and Implementation* (Washington, D.C.: Government Printing Office, 1978); and G. Alan Tarr, "Court Unification and Court Performance: A Preliminary Assessment," *Judicature* 64 (March 1981): 358.

states' supreme courts and lessening their workload.[55] Although these changes have contributed to sleeker, less detailed state judicial articles in some states, these articles remain among the least successful—and most heavily revised—provisions in state constitutions.

Local Government.   The federal Constitution altogether ignores local government, but it was also largely ignored by early state constitutions. These constitutions accepted the authority of existing local governments and the legitimacy of their prerogatives, in some instances even establishing representation for these governments in state legislatures. However, the state constitutional silence about local power ended during the mid–nineteenth century, when New York adopted the first constitutional provisions expressly regulating cities. Other states soon followed New York's lead. The shift in constitutional design resulted from a reconceptualization of the legal status of local governments. Local governments came to be understood as entities "whose powers are derived from and subject to the sovereign state legislature" rather than as component units of a quasi-federal state government.[56] This understanding of the state as a unitary sovereign and local governments as subordinate units was formalized in legal doctrine as "Dillon's rule," under which municipalities could exercise only those powers that were expressly granted by the state or that were indispensable to accomplish the declared purposes of the municipal corporation.[57] The effects on state constitutional design resulting from this changed understanding were dramatic. If units of local

[55] See Roger D. Groot, "The Effects of an Intermediate Appellate Court on the Supreme Court Work Product: The North Carolina Experience," *Wake Forest Law Review* 7 (October 1971): 548–72; Victor Eugene Flango and Nora F. Blair, "Creating an Intermediate Appellate Court: Does It Reduce the Caseload of a State's Highest Court?" *Judicature* 64 (August 1980): 74–84; and John M. Scheb and John M. Scheb II, "Making Intermediate Appellate Courts Final: Assessing Jurisdictional Changes in Florida's Appellate Courts," *Judicature* 67 (May 1984): 474–85.

[56] See Daniel J. Elazar, "State-Local Relations: Reviving Old Theory for New Practice," in Stephanie Cole, ed., *Partnership within the States: Local Self-Government in the Federal System* (Urbana, Ill.: Institute of Government and Public Affairs, 1975); James E. Herget, "The Missing Power of Local Government: A Discrepancy between Text and Practice in Our Early State Constitutions," *Virginia Law Review* 62 (June 1976): 1001–5; Michael E. Libonati, "Home Rule: An Essay on Pluralism," *Washington Law Review* 64 (January 1989): 51–71; and Michael E. Libonati, "Intergovernmental Relations in State Constitutional Law: A Historical Overview," *Annals of the American Academy of Political and Social Science* 496 (March 1988): 107–16.

[57] *Clinton v. Cedar Rapids and Missouri River Railroad,* 24 Iowa 455, 476 (1868); see also generally John Forest Dillon, *A Treatise on the Law of Municipal Corporations,* 5th ed., 5 vols. (Boston: Little, Brown, 1911). A useful overview of the transformation is Gerald E. Frug, "The City as a Legal Concept," *Harvard Law Review* 93 (April 1980): 1059–1154.

government owed their powers and their very existence to the state, then the state had to establish procedures for creating units of local government and determine the structure and powers of those units in considerable detail. Enshrined in the local government articles of state constitutions, these provisions often came to resemble municipal codes. Moreover, these codes grew and grew, as new eventualities required adjustments in the powers granted to particular localities or the redistribution of power among the various units of local government. Complaints about legislative interference, together with the drain on state legislative energies that detailed supervision of localities required, soon prompted efforts to replace micromanagement by the state government with local self-government. Missouri in 1875 pioneered one solution with the adoption of a "home rule" provision, which granted greater autonomy to local governments, and most state constitutions eventually followed Missouri's lead.[58] Indeed, a few recent constitutions have altogether reversed "Dillon's rule," authorizing local governments to tax, regulate, and otherwise deal with matters of local concern, unless specifically prohibited by statute.[59] These home-rule provisions have had a significant effect on state constitutions, because the broader the grant of local self-rule, the shorter and less detailed the constitutional provisions on local government need to be. In addition, fifteen states have adopted amendments requiring the state government to fund programs that they require local governments to undertake.[60] In 1995 Congress followed the states' lead in curbing unfunded mandates, although it pursued by statute a goal for which the states, with their greater ease of amendment, had sought a constitutional solution.[61]

PUBLIC POLICY

Relatively few provisions of the federal Constitution directly address public-policy issues, although the Constitution's grants of power can be interpreted as suggesting the purposes for which national power is to be exercised. State constitutions, in contrast, deal directly with matters of public policy, sometimes in considerable detail. State governments share

[58] Missouri Constitution, art. 9, secs. 20–25 (1875). The circumstances surrounding the adoption of these provisions are discussed in Joseph D. McGoldrick, *Law and Practice of Municipal Home Rule, 1916–1930* (New York: AMS Press, 1967).

[59] See, e.g., Illinois Constitution, art. 7; and Alaska Constitution, art. 10.

[60] See, for example, Michigan Constitution, art. 9, sec. 29. The judicial interpretation of this provision is discussed in Susan P. Fino, *The Michigan State Constitution: A Reference Guide* (Westport, Conn.: Greenwood Press, 1996), 207–9. For an overview of constitutional provisions requiring the funding of mandates, see Joseph F. Zimmerman, "State Mandate Relief: A Quick Look," *Intergovernmental Perspective* 28 (spring 1994): 28–32.

[61] Unfunded Mandates Reform Act of 1995, 2 U.S.C. secs. 621–56.

common policy responsibilities, and these are reflected in state constitutions. Thus, many state charters contain separate articles on finance, on taxation, on corporations, and on education. Other policy provisions reflect problems that are peculiar to a region—for example, eight western states adopted constitutional prohibitions on the employment of children in mines during the late nineteenth and early twentieth centuries.[62] Still other policy provisions are distinctive to particular states. A few deal with salient aspects of a state's economy: for example, Idaho's Constitution has articles on water rights and on livestock, and California on water resources development.[63] Others, such as New Mexico's article dealing with bilingual education, reflect the social composition of the state.[64] Some policy provisions are a product of the particular political movements regnant during the era in which they were adopted. For instance, the tax revolt of the late 1970s added to the California Constitution articles dealing with tax limitations and government spending limits, while the environmental movement of the late 1960s prompted Illinois to include an article on the environment in its 1970 constitution.[65] Finally, some state policy provisions are simply constitutionalized statutes. Article 10B of the California Constitution, which is entitled the Marine Resources Protection Act of 1990, is a case in point.[66]

Policy provisions in state constitutions may contain direct prohibitions on legislative action, such as the constitutional bans on the use of public funds in support of any religious institution or for any sectarian purpose.[67] Prohibitions in finance and taxation articles, which may range from limitations on the imposition of ad valorem taxes by local governments to bans on state assumption of local government debt, tend to be particularly detailed and specific.[68] Policy provisions in state constitutions may also take the form of policy directives. They may directly enact policy—the California Constitution's establishment of an eight-hour workday on public works is an example. Or they may establish policy guidelines for legislative enactments. In some instances legislative enactment may still be discretionary, as when the Illinois Constitution listed

[62] See Arizona Constitution, art. 18, sec. 2; Colorado Constitution, art. 16, sec. 3; Idaho Constitution, art. 13, sec. 4; Montana Constitution, art. 18, sec. 3; New Mexico Constitution, art. 17, sec. 2; North Dakota Constitution, art. 17, sec. 209; Oklahoma Constitution, art. 23, sec. 3; and Wyoming Constitution, art. 9.

[63] Idaho Constitution, arts. 15–16, and California Constitution, art. 10A.

[64] New Mexico Constitution, art. 12, sec. 8.

[65] California Constitution, arts. 13B–13C, and Illinois Constitution, art. 11.

[66] California Constitution, art. 10B.

[67] See, for example,, Connecticut Constitution, art. 7, sec. 1 and art. 8, sec. 2; Florida Constitution, art. 9, sec. 6; and Missouri Constitution, art. 9, sec. 8.

[68] See, for example, Florida Constitution, art. 7, sec. 9(b), and Nevada Constitution, art. 9, sec. 4.

the types of property that the General Assembly could exempt from property taxes, restricting the range of possible exemptions but leaving the legislature free to decide whether to grant those exemptions.[69] More often, however, constitutional directives for legislative enactments are mandatory, requiring legislative action and presumably permitting judicial enforcement if the legislature fails to act.[70]

Finally, the policy provisions in state constitutions may be statements of principle, committing the state to achieve particular ends.[71] The contrast between the language of these articles and the text of the federal Constitution is crucial. Although the federal Constitution grants Congress various powers, it never requires that these powers be exercised—for example, Congress did not regulate commerce among the several states in any substantial way for almost a century after the ratification of the Constitution, and it failed to enact appropriate legislation to enforce the equal protection clause of the Fourteenth Amendment despite obvious violations by southern states. In contrast, state constitutions impose specific duties on state governments. Thus, New Jersey is required to ensure a "thorough and efficient system of free public schools" for all children in the state; Illinois must "provide and maintain a healthful environment for the benefit of this and future generations"; Alaska must "provide for the promotion and protection of public health"; and Idaho is obliged "to pass all necessary laws to provide for the protection of livestock against the introduction or spread" of various diseases.[72] Although these provisions are not framed as rights protections and are not contained in state declarations of rights, they serve as the functional equivalent of positive rights. Even if these provisions do not specifically direct legislative action, they may be self-executing, providing a cause of action when government fails to meet its affirmative responsibilities.[73] If

[69] California Constitution, art. 14, sec. 2; and Illinois Constitution, art. 9, sec. 6.

[70] A useful discussion of mandatory and directory provisions is found in Williams, *State Constitutional Law: Cases and Materials*, 2d ed. (Charlottesville, Va.: Michie, 1993), 412–21. State legal standards governing litigants' standing to sue tend to be far more liberal than federal standards, thereby facilitating constitutional challenges to failures by state legislatures to meet their constitutional responsibilities. See Tarr and Porter, *State Supreme Courts in State and Nation* (New Haven: Yale University Press, 1988), 42–45.

[71] James Willard Hurst, *The Growth of American Law: The Lawmakers* (Boston: Little, Brown, 1950), 246.

[72] New Jersey Constitution, art. 8, sec. 4; Illinois Constitution, art. 11, sec. 1; Alaska Constitution, art. 7, sec. 4; and Idaho Constitution, art. 15, sec. 1.

[73] For a useful discussion, see Richard A. Goldberg and Robert F. Williams, "Farmworkers' Organizational and Collective Bargaining Rights in New Jersey: Implementing Self-Executing State Constitutional Rights," *Rutgers Law Journal* 18 (summer 1987): 729–63.

Not all constitutional language is self-executing and thus subject to judicial enforcement.

they are, they prompt litigants to recast what would be rights claims under the federal Constitution in terms of obligations that the state government owes its citizens.[74] If the provisions are not self-executing, they still impose requirements on conscientious legislators and governors who wish to remain faithful to their constitutional obligations.

STATE CONSTITUTIONAL PRACTICE

Perhaps the most striking contrast with federal constitutional practice is the states' reliance on the formal mechanisms of revision (replacement of one constitution by another) and amendment (the alteration of an existing constitution by the addition or subtraction of material) to promote constitutional change.[75] Since 1791, when the adoption of the Bill of Rights completed the task of founding the federal government, the federal Constitution has been amended less than once per decade. Moreover, the most dramatic constitutional developments, such as the growth of national power and the expansion of presidential prerogatives, have occurred largely without formal constitutional amendment.[76] In contrast, the American states have regularly revised and amended their constitutions. Only nineteen states still retain their original constitutions, and a majority of states have established three or more.[77] Louisiana's current constitution is the state's eleventh, and Georgia's its tenth. The level of

---

For example, in the Louisiana constitutional convention of 1973, educators persuaded delegates to insert in the constitution hortatory language regarding the importance of education (Louisiana Constitution, art. 8, preamble). However, this language was interpreted in *Simmons v. Sowela Technical Institute*, 470 So.2d 913 (La. 1985), as establishing moral duties rather than creating the basis for legal claims.

[74] See, for example, New Jersey's school finance cases—*Robinson v. Cahill*, 303 A.2d 273 (N.J. 1973), and *Abbott v. Burke*, 575 A.2d 359 (N.J. 1990)—in which the educational-equality claim was based on the New Jersey Constitution's requirement that the state provide a "thorough and efficient education" for all children. More generally, see Jonathan Feldman, "Separation of Powers and Judicial Review of Positive Rights Claims: The Role of State Courts in an Era of Positive Government," *Rutgers Law Journal* 24 (summer 1993): 1057–1100.

[75] This usage differs somewhat from the state judicial interpretation of the distinction between revision and amendment, which is employed primarily in determining whether or not a constitutional change can be adopted by constitutional initiative. On this latter distinction, see Williams, *State Constitutional Law*, 938–58.

[76] This has led some authors—most recently, Bruce Ackerman—to conclude that the federal Constitution can be amended outside the mechanisms suggested in Article 5. See Ackerman, *We the People*; and more generally, Sanford Levinson, ed., *Responding to Imperfection: The Theory and Practice of Constitutional Amendment* (Princeton: Princeton University Press, 1995).

[77] Unless otherwise indicated, data in this paragraph on the number of state constitutions and on state constitutional amendment are drawn from "State Constitutions," *Book of States, 1996–97*.

constitutional amendment likewise underscores the states' willingness to initiate formal constitutional change. As of 1996, over 9,500 amendments had been proposed to the states' current constitutions and over 5,900 adopted—an average of almost 120 amendments per state.[78] The Alabama Constitution of 1901 has been amended over 580 times, and the California Constitution of 1879 almost 500 times. Even these figures, impressive as they are, substantially underestimate the states' propensity for constitutional tinkering, because they omit amendments and proposed amendments to the states' earlier constitutions. For example, in 1980, three years before adopting a new constitution, Georgia submitted to its voters 137 proposed amendments—16 general amendments and 121 local amendments; and Louisiana's constitution of 1921 was amended 536 times before its replacement in 1974.[79]

While certain aspects of the federal Constitution—for example, the Bill of Rights and the tripartite governmental structure—have been viewed as too fundamental for amendment, no similar reticence has marked state constitutional change. The states have not only regularly replaced their constitutions but have also submitted sets of amendments to the voters that, taken together, have substantially altered the basic character of the state government.[80] Moreover, the issues addressed by state constitutional amendments are as diverse as the subjects treated in state constitutions. For example, a survey of amendments from 1986 to 1993 found that 13 percent concerned bills of rights and suffrage, 42 percent dealt with the structure of state government, 35 percent involved policy matters, and 10 percent concerned miscellaneous other matters.[81]

[78] The data are derived from Janice C. May, "Constitutional Amendment and Revision Revisited," *Publius* 17 (winter 1987): 162, updated on the basis of "State Constitutions," 3, table 1.1.

[79] See George D. Busbee, "An Overview of the New Georgia Constitution," *Mercer Law Review* 35 (fall 1983): 3; and Mark T. Carleton, "Elitism Sustained: The Louisiana Constitution of 1974," *Tulane Law Review* 54 (April 1980): 560.

[80] For example, the Massachusetts Constitution, the nation's oldest written constitution, was dramatically changed by waves of amendments in 1821 (nine amendments) and 1917–18 (nineteen amendments). The New Jersey Constitution of 1844 was altered by the adoption of twenty-eight amendments in 1875. And the Hawaii Constitution was fundamentally changed with the ratification of twenty-two amendments in 1968, only eighteen years after its adoption, and thirty-three more in 1978. For discussion of the changes in Hawaii, see Anne Feder Lee, *The Hawaii State Constitution: A Reference Guide* (Westport, Conn.: Greenwood Press, 1993), 11–20.

[81] These percentages were computed from data reported by May in "State Constitutions, 1992–93," 7, table B. For earlier analyses that produced comparable figures, see May, "Constitutional Amendment and Revision," 165 n. 52; and Elmer E. Cornwell Jr., "The American Constitutional Tradition: Its Impact and Development," in Kermit L. Hall, Harold M. Hyman, and Leon V. Sigal, eds., *The Constitutional Convention as an Amending Device* (Washington, D.C.: American Historical Association and American Political Science Association, 1981), 26–28, table 2.

Whereas Congress has originated all the amendments to the federal Constitution, the states have devised and utilized a variety of mechanisms to propose constitutional change.[82] Most state constitutional amendments have been proposed by state legislatures. In recent years, the proposed amendments have often originated in constitutional commissions, groups of experts and notables appointed by the legislature or executive to develop proposals either for consideration by the legislature or—in the case of Florida—for direct submission to the people for ratification.[83] In addition, forty-one state constitutions expressly authorize the legislature to convene constitutional conventions—indeed, fourteen require that the legislature periodically poll the populace on whether to call a convention— and state legislatures have assumed the power to call conventions even in the absence of express constitutional authorization. Altogether, over 230 state constitutional conventions have been held to create, revise, or amend state constitutions. Finally, eighteen states have adopted the constitutional initiative, which empowers citizens to propose amendments by petition directly to the voters (sixteen states) or to the legislature before submission to the voters (Massachusetts and Mississippi).

The use of the constitutional initiative illustrates another key difference between federal and state constitutional practice regarding constitutional change. Whereas the federal amendment process provides no mechanism for direct popular participation, the states have structured the process of constitutional change to maximize such participation.[84] Popular participation in the initiation of constitutional change occurs not only through the constitutional initiative but through popular votes on legislative proposals to call constitutional conventions and on the selection of delegates to those conventions.[85] Twelve states require that

---

[82] This paragraph relies on May, "Constitutional Amendment and Revision," 153–179; May, "State Constitutions"; Walter F. Dodd, *The Revision and Amendment of State Constitutions* (Baltimore: Johns Hopkins University Press, 1910; rpt. New York: Da Capo, 1970); and Roger Sherman Hoar, *Constitutional Conventions: Their Nature, Powers, and Limitations* (Boston: Little, Brown, 1919).

[83] Florida Constitution, art. 11, sec. 2. For discussion of the commission mode of amendment, see Robert F. Williams, "Are State Constitutional Conventions Things of the Past? The Increasing Role of the Constitutional Commission in State Constitutional Change," *Hofstra Journal of Public Policy* 1 (1996): 1–26.

[84] For a useful discussion of the popular role in state constitutional change, see Harry L. Witte, "Rights, Revolution, and the Paradox of Constitutionalism: The Processes of Constitutional Change in Pennsylvania," *Widener Journal of Public Law* 3 (1993): 383–476. American state practice is far more typical of the practice of constitutional change worldwide—see David Butler and Austin Ranney, eds., *Referendums around the World: The Growing Use of Direct Democracy* (Washington, D.C.: American Enterprise Institute Press, 1994).

[85] Two points should be noted about the extent of popular control over state constitutional conventions. First, in electing delegates, voters may be choosing among candidates put forward by the state's political parties. In Arizona, the selection of delegate candidates

amendments be proposed by majorities in two successive legislatures, giving citizens an opportunity to express their views on proposed constitutional changes in the intervening election.[86] Furthermore, in every state except Delaware, the people ratify all constitutional changes, however proposed, by referendum.[87]

A final distinctive feature of state constitutional practice regarding constitutional change is the involvement of state courts in overseeing the process of change. The reliance on formal constitutional change in the states has prompted opponents of proposed changes to challenge their legality in the courts. Whereas the United States Supreme Court has dismissed procedural challenges to the federal amendment process as "political questions," state courts have proved quite willing to address a wide range of issues associated with state constitutional change.[88] Several state courts have ruled on whether the state legislature can call a convention despite the absence of express authorization in the state constitution.[89] Others have considered the validity of mechanisms designed to facilitate ratification of amendments in states that required extraordinary majorities for approval or the validity of popular consent to an amend-

---

by party conventions ensured that they were "pledged to particular constitutional goals," and this facilitated party control. Whether it ensured popular control is open to question. See John D. Leshy, *The Arizona State Constitution: A Reference Guide* (Westport, Conn.: Greenwood Press, 1993), 4. Second, some states do not require that convention calls be submitted for popular approval. Also, on occasion—most recently in Louisiana in 1992— state legislatures have called themselves into session as constitutional conventions. The legitimacy of such a step is open to question, however, and generally such conventions have had little success in gaining popular support for their proposals. See Hoar, *Constitutional Conventions*, 79–80.

[86] See "State Constitutions," 5, table 1.2. Three other states—Connecticut, Hawaii, and New Jersey—permit submission of amendments either by an extraordinary legislative majority or by a majority vote in a second session following an intervening election.

[87] Although it has been the standard practice since the early nineteenth century to submit constitutional changes to the people, there have been exceptions. For example, the late-nineteenth-century conventions in Virginia, Mississippi, and Louisiana did not submit their proposed constitutions to the voters because their aim was to deprive African-Americans and poor whites of the vote, and they feared voters would fight their disenfranchisement. See Dodd, *Revision and Amendment*, 67–68.

[88] The leading federal case is *Coleman* v. *Miller*, 307 U.S. 433 (1939). For an overview of state activity, see Michael G. Colatuono, "The Revision of American State Constitutions: Legislative Power, Popular Sovereignty, and Constitutional Change," *California Law Review* 75 (July 1987): 1473–1512. On the relative unimportance of the "political questions" doctrine in state constitutional law, see Tarr and Porter, *State Supreme Courts in State and Nation*, 44–45.

[89] See, e.g., *Collier* v. *Frierson*, 24 Ala. 100 (1854); *State* v. *American Sugar Co.*, 137 La. 407 (1915); *State* v. *Dahl*, 6 N.D. 81 (1896); and *In Re Opinion to the Governor*, 178 A. 433 (R.I. 1935).

ment when publicity about its content and effects had been misleading.[90] The Indiana Supreme Court invalidated the legislature's attempt to convene itself as a constitutional convention, and the Iowa Supreme Court struck down popularly approved constitutional amendments because the proposed amendments were not entered into the legislative journals as required by the state constitution.[91] Some state constitutions restrict amendments to a "single subject," and in those states courts have heard challenges claiming that wide-ranging amendments encompassed more than a single subject.[92] State constitutions also restrict the use of the constitutional initiative to amendment, not revision, and so state courts have had to consider whether the far-reaching changes introduced by some amendments constituted revisions of the state constitution.[93] Some state constitutions impose additional restrictions on the constitutional initiative that have likewise promoted litigation.[94] Taken altogether, these cases reveal that state judges are active participants in the process of formal constitutional change.

CONCLUSION

This chapter's description of state constitutions and state constitutional change has highlighted what is distinctive in state constitutional design and state constitutional practice. Some of the distinctive features, such as the plenary character of state legislative power, reflect the fundamental premises of the nation's constitutional system. For when legislative power is divided in a federal system, one government must receive grants of power and the other retain residual power. Most of the distinctive features of state constitutionalism, however, arise from political choices by the states. Although state legislatures' possession of plenary legislative power may reflect the character of the nation's constitutional system, the states remain free to choose what sorts of constitutional limits to impose

[90] On mechanisms for facilitating ratification, see *State ex rel. Thompson* v. *Winnett,* 78 Neb. 379 (1907); *State* v. *Laylin,* 69 Ohio St. 1 (1903); and *May and Thomas Hardward Co.* v. *Birmingham,* 123 Ala. 306 (1898). On misleading publicity and popular consent, see *Bedner* v. *King,* 272 A.2d 616 (N.H. 1970).

[91] *Ellingham* v. *Dye,* 178 Ind. 336 (1912); and *Koehler* v. *Hill,* 60 Iowa 543 (1883), and *State* v. *Brookhart,* 113 Iowa 250 (1901).

[92] See, e.g., *Raven* v. *Deukmejian,* 801 P.2d 1077 (Cal. 1990); *Amador Valley School District* v. *State Board of Equalization,* 583 P.2d 1281 (Cal. 1978); and *Evans* v. *Firestone,* 457 So.2d 1351 (Fla. 1984).

[93] See, e.g., *Raven* v. *Deukmejian,* 801 P.2d 1077 (Cal. 1990); *Adams* v. *Gunter,* 238 So.2d 824 (Fla. 1970); and *McFadden* v. *Jordan,* 196 P.2d 787 (Cal. 1948).

[94] For example, the Alaska Constitution, art. 11, sec. 7, forbids the use of the initiative to enact local or special legislation, leading to constitutional challenges in *Walters* v. *Cease,* 388 P.2d 263 (Alas. 1964), and *Boucher* v. *Engstrom,* 528 P.2d 456 (Alas. 1974).

on that power. And the states over time have swung from few limitations in the late eighteenth century, to extensive and detailed restrictions in the late nineteenth century, to somewhat fewer restrictions by the late twentieth century. Although the incompleteness of the federal Constitution in a sense requires that state constitutions deal with local government, it does not determine how state constitutions will do so. Thus, the states have chosen over time to deal with local government in various ways, ranging from implicit recognition of local communities' right to self-government, to detailed regulation of the structure and powers of local governments, to broad grants of home rule. Although the nation's constitutional system assigns to the states the power to structure their state governments, it does not determine whether the states will follow the federal model or will depart from it. Nor does it determine whether states will revise and amend their constitutions frequently or constitutionalize policy matters or establish mechanisms for direct popular rule.

This chapter has for the most part treated state constitutions as a unit, ignoring variations among state charters. Obviously, these differences can be substantial. As chapters 3–5 will show, comparison of state constitutions adopted in different eras reveals significant variations in structure, substance, and underlying political theory. Yet even though the states' political choices have varied over time, the extent and character of the differences among state constitutions are less substantial than those between state and federal charters. Succeeding chapters elaborate the distinctive features of state constitutionalism, trace how they have developed, and assess the various explanations proposed to account for them. It is to these explanations that we now turn.

CHAPTER 2

Explaining State Constitutional Development

IF STATE CONSTITUTIONS differ from the federal Constitution and from each other as well, the obvious question is why. Perhaps the most salient difference between state constitutionalism and national constitutionalism, as well as the one with the broadest implications, is the frequency of state constitutional change through constitutional amendment and constitutional revision. Several explanations have been advanced to account for the states' propensity for formal constitutional change. The frequency of constitutional change might be attributable to public opinion favorable to such change within the states. Alternatively, the relative ease of constitutional revision and constitutional amendment in the states might explain the states' greater reliance on formal constitutional change, with interstate variations in the frequency of amendment and revision reflecting interstate differences in the legal requirements governing amendment and revision. Or the frequency of formal constitutional change might indicate that the states have failed to solve the basic political problems confronting them, necessitating recurring efforts to deal with those problems. The initial section of this chapter surveys the arguments and the evidence supporting these alternative explanations of state constitutional change.

The second section of this chapter is premised on the recognition that state constitutions do not exist in isolation, that they may be influenced in their structure, in the substance of their provisions, and in the changes they have undergone by constitutions and constitutional developments beyond the borders of their states. It therefore seeks to identify the various mechanisms of interstate and nation-to-state influence and assesses their impact on state constitutional development. In addition to its intrinsic interest, this account of the influence of constitutional developments in state and nation serves to clarify the differences between national and state constitutional traditions.

The concluding section of the chapter makes explicit the various perspectives on state constitutional development that underlie much of the scholarly literature on the topic and assesses the usefulness of those perspectives. One view is that state constitutions are best analyzed through the lens of political theory, with each document understood as reflecting the state's political culture, the dominant orientation toward politics and government in the state. Another view is that state constitutions are best understood through the lens of history, with each document reflecting the set of issues and constitutional prescriptions prevalent during the era in which it was created. A final view is that state constitutions are best seen through the lens of "ordinary politics," with the constitution reflecting neither an overarching political vision nor an historical moment but rather the continuation in another arena of the conflicts among political groups that generally dominate state politics. As shall be seen, although none of these accounts fully explains state constitutional development, each does contribute to an understanding of state constitutions.

ACCOUNTING FOR STATE CONSTITUTIONAL CHANGE

Attitudinal Explanations

Some scholars have attributed the frequency of formal constitutional change in the states to political attitudes within the states. On initial inspection, this claim may seem trivial: state constitutional amendments and proposed state constitutions are ratified by referendum, so it would seem that constitutional changes could hardly occur without popular support.[1] (As shall be seen, that may not be as clear as it initially appears.) However, the attitudinal explanation for constitutional change becomes more interesting if the claim is that state constitutional change is connected not only to public opinion about specific measures but also to established public perspectives on the desirability of frequent constitutional change. This in fact is the claim advanced by historian Morton Keller, who has suggested that the frequent revision and amendment of state constitutions reflect the conjunction of two popular attitudes: a dissatisfaction with the performance of state government and an optimism that tinkering with its institutional machinery can correct its deficiencies.[2] Such constitutional changes as the imposition of checks on state power to contract debt in mid-nineteenth-century constitutions, after imprudent promotional efforts had brought several states to the brink (or over the brink) of bankruptcy, appear to buttress Keller's thesis.[3] So too

---

[1] Since the 1820s, it has been standard practice to submit proposed state constitutions to the state electorate for ratification. Currently, only Delaware does not require that constitutional amendments be ratified by popular referendum. The main departures from the practice of popular ratification occurred in the late nineteenth and early twentieth centuries, when some Southern constitutions designed to disenfranchise African-Americans and poor whites were promulgated without popular ratification in order to forestall organized opposition to them. See Dodd, *Revision and Amendment*, 62–71.

[2] Morton Keller, "The Politics of State Constitutional Revision, 1820–1930," in Hall, Hyman, and Sigal, *Constitutional Convention*, 67–68.

[3] On the movement in New York, which led to the creation of the 1846 constitution, see L. Roy Gunn, *The Decline of Authority: Public Economic Policy and Political Develop-*

does the absence of a "cult of the constitution," which might impede constitutional change, in the states.[4] Also consistent with Keller's thesis are the twentieth-century constitutional reforms in several states designed to ease legal requirements for amending their constitutions and the states' increased reliance on constitutional amendment since the 1950s, both of which suggest a positive orientation toward constitutional change.[5] Many studies of constitutional change in specific states likewise posit a connection between public attitudes and the general orientation toward constitutional change in the state. For example, the continuation of Georgia's extraordinary propensity for constitutional amendment even after the adoption of a new constitution in 1982 suggests that the state citizenry has concluded that this is how politics should be conducted.[6] In contrast, according to Lawrence Schlam, the infrequency of formal constitutional change in Illinois both before and after the adoption of the 1970 constitution reflected a "disunified, individualistic, and factious" political culture that discouraged fundamental change on the basis of simple majorities.[7]

Nevertheless, the connection between public attitudes and state consti-

---

ment in New York, 1800–1860 (Ithaca, N.Y.: Cornell University Press, 1988), especially 183–91. More generally, see A. James Heins, *Constitutional Restrictions against State Debt* (Madison: University of Wisconsin Press, 1963).

[4] On the persistence of this cult at the federal level, see Levinson, *Constitutional Faith,* chap. 1.

My own experience confirms that there is no cult of the state constitution. I applied for a grant from the New Jersey Historical Commission to convene a conference in 1987, marking the fortieth anniversary of the highly successful New Jersey Constitution. This coincided with the bicentennial of United States Constitution, which directed attention to constitutional matters. Although I eventually received the grant, at the time of the application, the Historical Commission, whose responsibility it was to foster an interest in the history of the state, was altogether unaware that an important anniversary of the state constitution was approaching.

[5] For a general discussion of the movement to facilitate state constitutional change, see Colatuono, "Revision of State Constitutions."

[6] At the general election of 1980, 16 general amendments and 121 local amendments were submitted to Georgia's voters. This was not atypical. From 1945 until the effective date of the state's 1982 constitution, 1,530 amendments were proposed to the constitution of Georgia, and 1,174 were ratified. Of the adopted amendments 974 were local amendments, affecting only a single jurisdiction within the state. The adoption of the state's 1982 constitution eliminated the need for local amendments but scarcely slowed the pace of general amendments. From 1984 to 1992, Georgia voters considered 52 proposed amendments and ratified 39 of them. See Hill, *The Georgia State Constitution,* 20–23, and Busbee, "Overview of Georgia Constitution," 3.

[7] Lawrence Schlam, "State Constitutional Amending, Independent Interpretation, and Political Culture: A Case Study in Constitutional Stagnation," *DePaul Law Review* 43 (winter 1994): 269–378. See also Daniel J. Elazar, *Cities of the Prairie: The Metropolitan Frontier and American Politics* (New York: Basic Books, 1970), chap. 7.

tutional change is both more complex and more problematic than it initially appears. Although one might assume that popular ratification of a constitutional amendment indicates public agreement with the change, this may be a rash conclusion. Voter knowledge about, and interest in, most state constitutional amendments is quite limited, as indicated both by turnout figures and, when other elections are occurring simultaneously, by ballot fatigue.[8] Amendments have been ratified in Louisiana by as few as 6 percent of registered voters, and figures from other states are not much better.[9] In such circumstances one cannot infer much about popular sentiment from voter endorsement or disapproval of proposed amendments. Furthermore, even when voters do cast ballots for or against an amendment, the context in which an amendment is proposed may be just as important as public attitudes in determining its fate. In Florida, for example, a proposed right-to-privacy amendment was defeated in 1978, largely because it was on the ballot with other unpopular proposals, but was adopted handily only two years later when those proposals were not on the ballot.[10] Voters in other states have likewise voted for or against unrelated proposed amendments as a package.[11] This means that the popular verdict on an amendment may reflect something other than strong agreement or disagreement with it.

Another problem with attitudinal explanations of state constitutional change is that they rarely specify who constitutes the "public" whose attitudes are alleged to be decisive. Yet both the history of constitutional change and the process by which it occurs underscore the need for clarity on this point. Over the course of the nation's history, the impetus for formal constitutional change in the states has shifted dramatically. During the first half of the nineteenth century, campaigns for constitutional revision were typically popular movements, opposed at times by officials

[8] The problem of meaningful consent is also raised by the politics surrounding proposed amendments. Particularly interesting is *Bedner* v. *King*, 272 A.2d 616 (N.H. 1970), in which the New Hampshire Supreme Court ruled that voters' consent to an amendment was not invalid merely because publicity about its content and effects was misleading.

[9] Carleton, "Elitism Sustained," 564; and Janice C. May, *The Texas Constitutional Revision Experience in the '70s* (Austin, Tex.: Sterling Swift Publishing, 1975), 24.

[10] Rebecca Mae Salokar, "Creating a State Constitutional Right to Privacy: Unlikely Alliances, Uncertain Results," in G. Alan Tarr, ed., *Constitutional Politics in the States: Contemporary Controversies and Historical Patterns* (Westport, Conn.: Greenwood Press, 1996), 73–97.

[11] See, for example, Hawaii's adoption of all thirty-four proposed amendments in 1978 and Louisiana's rejection of all fifty-three amendments in 1970. Lee, *The Hawaii State Constitution,* 18; and Carleton, "Elitism Sustained," 561–63. It should also be noted, in light of the Florida turnaround, that in recent years in Mississippi twelve of the thirty constitutional amendments that initially failed succeeded when reintroduced. See John W. Winkle III, *The Mississippi State Constitution: A Reference Guide* (Westport, Conn.: Greenwood Press, 1993), 14–15.

who feared (often quite rightly) that a new constitution would diminish their powers.[12] Yet by the latter half of the twentieth century, campaigns for constitutional reform were generally initiated and managed by political elites and "good government" groups, often in the face of public apathy or hostility.[13] During the 1970s, for example, voters in eight states rejected proposals for constitutional conventions, and from 1965 to 1980 state electorates ratified only three of the eight new constitutions proposed by conventions.[14] Even popular campaigns for constitutional change, such as the term limitations movement, have quickly come under the control of professional political operatives.[15] In light of this shift, Keller's claim of a prevailing "public" attitude in favor of constitutional change appears problematic at best. Moreover, as the reference to con-

[12] In Virginia, for example, when population growth in the interior prompted demands for reapportionment, the state legislature for several years refused to call a convention. See Merrill D. Peterson, ed., *Democracy, Liberty, and Property: The State Constitutional Conventions of the 1820's* (Indianapolis: Bobbs-Merrill, 1966), 271–75. In Maryland, when the legislature refused to call a convention, reformers responded by taking steps to convene an extralegal convention, and the legislature eventually capitulated. See John Alexander Jameson, *A Treatise on Constitutional Conventions: Their History, Powers, and Modes of Proceeding,* 4th ed. (Chicago: Callaghan and Company, 1887; rpt. New York: Da Capo, 1972), 216. In Rhode Island the legislature's refusal to sanction a convention did lead to the convening of an extralegal convention and the Dorr Rebellion. See Marvin E. Gettleman, *The Dorr Rebellion: A Study in American Radicalism, 1823–1849* (New York: Random House, 1973). In New York, the Council of Revision vetoed legislation that made direct provision for a convention. See Hurst, *Growth of American Law,* 207. And in North Carolina the legislature sought to control constitutional change by strictly limiting the sorts of amendments that could be proposed by the constitutional convention rather than risking an unlimited convention. See John V. Orth, *The North Carolina State Constitution: A Reference Guide* (Westport, Conn.: Greenwood Press, 1993), 8. For an overview, see G. Alan Tarr, "State Constitutional Politics: An Historical Perspective," in Tarr, *Constitutional Politics in States,* 3–23.

[13] The centrality of elite reformers in state constitutional reform during the twentieth century is exemplified by the efforts of the National Municipal League to spur constitutional change. See its Model State Constitution and its many publications—e.g., John P. Wheeler Jr., *Salient Issues of Constitutional Reform* (New York: National Municipal League, 1961)—extolling constitutional change. The League's efforts are discussed in chapter 5. The popular suspicion of constitutional reform can be seen in the frequency with which voters have rejected either proposals to call conventions or the constitutions submitted to them by conventions. See Elmer E. Cornwell Jr., Jay S. Goodman, and Wayne R. Swanson, *State Constitutional Conventions* (New York: Praeger, 1975), 187 and passim; Tip H. Allen Jr., and Coleman B. Ransome Jr., *Constitutional Revision in Theory and Practice* (University: Bureau of Public Administration, University of Alabama, 1962), 152–54; and—for an illuminating case study—John P. Wheeler, *Magnificent Failure: The Maryland Constitutional Convention of 1967–1968* (New York: National Municipal League, 1972).

[14] Albert L. Sturm, "The Development of American State Constitutions," *Publius* 12 (winter 1982): 81–84.

[15] See John David Rausch Jr., "The Politics of Term Limitations," in Tarr, *Constitutional Politics in States,* 98–127.

flicts between advocates and opponents of constitutional change suggests, state constitutional change is a multistage process, and the groups that control the initiation of change often differ from those that formulate the changes or ratify them. The complexity of the process, with different groups dominant at its various stages, further complicates efforts to draw a connection between public attitudes and state constitutional change.

Finally, there is a risk that attitudinal explanations of state constitutional change may become tautological. Formal constitutional changes are alleged to occur, or fail to occur, because of popular attitudes toward constitutional change. However, often the primary evidence of these attitudes is the presence or absence of constitutional change. At a minimum, these problems suggest that one should be cautious about attributing constitutional amendments or revisions to popular support for such change and should recognize the complexities in the relationship between public attitudes and constitutional reform.

Legal Requirements

Some commentators have maintained that the frequency of formal constitutional change in the states reflects state legal requirements, which in most states make it relatively easy to amend or revise the state constitution. Eighteen states currently permit constitutional amendments to be proposed by a simple majority in each house of the legislature, five more by simple majorities in two sessions with an intervening election, and nine by a three-fifths vote in each house.[16] In forty-four states, only a simple majority vote in a referendum is required to ratify proposed amendments, and in Delaware popular ratification is not even required. In addition, in eighteen states voters can propose constitutional amendments directly, with thirteen permitting ratification of those proposals by a simple majority of those voting on the measures.[17] Finally, fourteen states require a periodic popular vote on calling a constitutional convention, with only a simple majority necessary to convene one.

Yet even if states can today alter their constitutions rather easily, this does not mean that prior state constitutions contained similarly permissive provisions for constitutional change. In fact, five pre-1800 constitutions—those of New York, Virginia, North Carolina, Pennsylva-

[16] Data on the methods of constitutional change in the various states are found in May, "State Constitutions, 1992–93," 21–25, tables 1.2, 1.3, and 1.4.

[17] See "Comment: California's Constitutional Amendomania," *Stanford Law Review* 1 (January 1949): 279–88; and James M. Fischer, "Ballot Propositions: The Challenge of Direct Democracy to State Constitutional Jurisprudence," *Hastings Constitutional Law Quarterly* 11 (fall 1983): 43–90.

nia (1790), and New Jersey—failed to specify any mechanism at all for their amendment or revision.[18] During the nineteenth century, many state constitutions imposed burdensome amendment requirements. Alabama's constitution of 1819, for example, provided for legislative proposal and popular approval but left it to the succeeding legislature to determine if the approved amendment should take effect.[19] New York's constitution of 1821 prescribed that amendments had to pass two successive legislatures, first by a majority of elected members, second by two-thirds of the elected members of each house, before they could be ratified at a general election.[20] Several other states retained similar requirements until the 1850s, when they began to dispense with the requirement of a second legislative approval.[21] Pennsylvania, New Jersey, and Tennessee allowed amendments to be proposed only at certain intervals, and New Hampshire only by means of a convention.[22] Finally, Alabama, Nebraska, Ohio, and Tennessee discouraged constitutional amendment by requiring that amendments be ratified by extraordinary electoral majorities.[23] If legal requirements are decisive in determining the rate of constitutional change, one would expect that the rate of amendment in the

---

[18] Dealey, *Growth of State Constitutions,* 32–33. The Pennsylvania Constitution of 1776 and the Vermont Constitution of 1793 each provided for constitutional amendment only through the operation of a Council of Revision. The problem of missing mechanisms for constitutional change persisted into the nineteenth century: for example, the Virginia constitutions of 1830 and 1851 likewise made no provision for amendment.

[19] Alabama Constitution (1819), art. 6. For a discussion of constitutional amendment through state legislatures, see Dodd, *Revision and Amendment,* 120–21.

[20] New York Constitution (1821), art. 8, sec. 1. This cumbersome mode of amendment limited amendments to eight in twenty-five years. New York's 1846 constitution substantially liberalized the process of amendment. See Gunn, *The Decline of Authority,* 171 and 195–96; and Peter J. Galie, *The New York State Constitution: A Reference Guide* (Westport, Conn.: Greenwood Press, 1991), 13–14.

[21] The provisions for amendment in the Tennessee Constitution of 1834 and the Connecticut Constitution of 1818, to cite but two examples, resembled New York's: proposal by two sessions of the state legislature. Tennessee retained this mode of amendment in its 1870 constitution. See Lewis L. Laska, *The Tennessee State Constitution: A Reference Guide* (Westport, Conn.: Greenwood Press, 1990), 10 and 18. More generally, see Dodd, *Revision and Amendment,* 131.

[22] Dodd, *Revision and Amendment,* 266–67.

[23] Dodd, *Revision and Amendment,* 196–97; Robert D. Miewald and Peter J. Longo, *The Nebraska State Constitution: A Reference Guide* (Westport, Conn.: Greenwood Press, 1993), 15; Laska, *The Tennessee State Constitution,* 10 and 18; and Allen and Ransome, *Constitutional Revision,* chap. 2. The Alabama Constitution of 1875 required ratification by a majority of the qualified electors in the state. The Ohio Constitution of 1851 and the Nebraska Constitution of 1875 demanded ratification by a majority of all those casting ballots at the election at which the amendment was submitted for approval. The Tennessee Constitution required approval by a majority of as many citizens of the state as last voted for representatives.

various states would correspond to the ease or difficulty of instituting such amendments.[24] Some anecdotal evidence supports this conclusion. The effectiveness of legal barriers to amendment is best shown by the Tennessee Constitution, which—burdened with cumbersome procedures for proposing and ratifying amendments—remained unaltered from 1870 to 1953.[25] Yet legal barriers to constitutional change have not always proved insuperable, as some states have found ingenious ways to circumvent burdensome constitutional requirements. Faced with ratification requirements similar to those in Tennessee, enterprising officials in Alabama, Nebraska, and Ohio redesigned the ballot to place the onus on voters to voice their disapproval of amendments.[26] In other instances, state constitutional requirements were frankly ignored. The North Carolina Constitution of 1776, for example, which governed the state until 1860, had no provision for amendment; but the state legislature called a convention in 1835, which proposed several amendments that were then submitted to the voters for ratification.[27] According to one authority, twenty-seven state conventions met during the nineteenth century without any authority in their constitutions for assembling.[28]

In the first systematic examination of the issue, Donald Lutz confirmed the influence of state legal requirements on the frequency of formal constitutional change or, more specifically, on the rate of constitutional

[24] The rate of amendment—that is, the average number of amendments per year since the state's constitution came into effect—is a better measure than the total number of amendments, given the differing duration of state constitutions.

[25] Laska, *The Tennessee State Constitution,* 18–19, and Allen and Ransome, *Constitutional Revision,* chap. 2. Illinois faced similar difficulties until it adopted a "gateway amendment"—see Schlam, "State Constitutional Amending," 353–76.

[26] Dodd, *Revision and Amendment,* 196–97. In Alabama, voters were required to signify their rejection of an amendment by removing a statement of approval from the ballot. In Nebraska and Ohio, political parties were permitted to endorse amendments, and voters who voted a straight party ticket would thus automatically endorse proposed amendments.

[27] Don E. Fehrenbacher, *Constitutions and Constitutionalism in the Slaveholding South* (Athens: University of Georgia Press, 1989), 5–6.

[28] Jameson, *Treatise on Constitutional Conventions,* chap. 4. During the twentieth century, the Rhode Island Supreme Court overruled precedent and held that the legislature could summon a convention, even though the state constitution did not expressly authorize it. *In Re Opinion to the Governor,* 178 A. 433 (R.I. 1935).

When constitutional requirements for amendment could not be circumvented, state officials sometimes ignored constitutional mandates. In Illinois, Governor Adlai Stevenson acknowledged that such action was a practical necessity in order to avoid "anachronisms." See Peter Suber, *The Paradox of Self-Amendment: A Study of Logic, Law, Omnipotence, and Change* (New York: Peter Lang, 1990), 17. In New York, judges have approved various devices developed to circumvent constitutional debt restrictions and "contort[ed] and strain[ed]" provisions on housing to keep them "abreast of changing housing needs." See Galie, *New York State Constitution,* 165–66 and 266–68.

amendment in the states.[29] Analyzing the effects of the mode of amendment on the rate of amendment for all fifty current state constitutions, Lutz discovered that the difficulty of the amendment process, together with the length of the state constitution, "largely explained" the variance in amendment rates among the states.[30] Lutz's study represents a significant advance in understanding state constitutional amendment. Nevertheless, it leaves several questions unanswered. First, because Lutz focuses exclusively on the amendment of current state constitutions, his study does not determine whether legal requirements were equally important during earlier periods in American history. Second, Lutz does not examine the effect of changes in constitutional requirements for amendment on amendment rates within individual states. If Lutz's theory is correct, one would expect that the rate of amendment would vary in response to changes in legal requirements. But if states develop a settled public opinion with regard to constitutional amendment, as other scholars have suggested, then one might expect changes in constitutional requirements to have very limited effects (although perhaps the change in amendment requirements could itself indicate a shift in state public opinion). Finally, even if the ease of constitutional change substantially influences the rate of such change, it is not altogether clear what conclusion should be drawn from this. The question remains as to why some states have instituted stringent requirements and others more lenient ones. The establishment of legal requirements that either encourage or discourage formal constitutional change is itself an important political choice, so Lutz's findings ultimately direct inquiry back to the political forces promoting or retarding state constitutional change.[31]

Political Failures

Some commentators have concluded that the frequency of state constitutional change reflects the inability of the states to deal adequately with the problems besetting them. Political scientist Clement Vose, for example, has argued that frequent state constitutional amendment and revision indicate that the states' "leadership and institutions are simply inferior in quality."[32] Many twentieth-century constitutional reformers have

[29] Donald S. Lutz, "Toward a Theory of Constitutional Amendment," *American Political Science Review* 88 (June 1994): 355–70.

[30] Lutz, "Theory of Constitutional Amendment," 365.

[31] For a recent attempt to address this question, see Schlam, "State Constitutional Amending."

[32] Vose's quotation is found in "Discussion of 'The American Constitutional Tradition: Its Impact and Development,'" in Hall, Hyman, and Sigal, *Constitutional Convention*, 50.

agreed, attributing the states' frequent recourse to revision and amendment to a recurring need to update their overly detailed constitutions in order to keep them abreast of the needs of contemporary society.[33] From this perspective, then, revision and amendment are best understood as alternative means—comprehensive versus piecemeal—for modernizing outdated state constitutions.

Although the failure of state governments to confront problems, in part because of outdated constitutions, was a familiar refrain of mid-twentieth-century reformers, this refrain may itself be outdated as a result of recent changes in state governments and state constitutions.[34] In any event, the available evidence only partially supports the reformers' claims about the relationship between state constitutional obsolescence and constitutional change. Donald Lutz's findings do confirm a connection between the length of state constitutions and the frequency with which they are amended, although correlation alone cannot prove the reformers' claim that constitutional length produces a "need" for constitutional change. Yet if the reformers were correct, one might expect that older constitutions would be amended more frequently because they would be less up-to-date than more recent charters. This is not the case: Lutz found that the older the constitution, the lower its annual rate of amendment.[35] In fact, in recent years the newest state charters have been amended more frequently than have the oldest ones.[36]

Finally, contrary to the reformers' assumptions, revision and amend-

---

In making this claim, he is, of course, echoing a sentiment that has existed at least since the Constitutional Convention of 1787.

[33] See, for example, W. Brooke Graves, ed., *Major Problems in State Constitutional Revision* (Chicago: Public Administration Service, 1960); and Wheeler, *Salient Issues.*

[34] See, for example, Alan Rosenthal and Maureen Moakley, eds., *The Political Life of the American States* (New York: Praeger, 1984); Ann O'M. Bowman and Richard C. Kearney, *The Resurgence of the States* (Englewood Cliffs, N.J.: Prentice-Hall, 1986); and Ann O'M. Bowman, "The Resurgence of the States: Laboratories under Pressure," in Franz Gress, Detlef Fechtner, and Matthias Hannes, eds., *The American Federal System: Federal Balance in Comparative Perspective* (Frankfurt am Main: Peter Lang, 1994), 111–39. The change in state government effectiveness has prompted calls even from liberals for devolution of functions to the states. See Alice M. Rivlin, *Reviving the American Dream* (Washington, D.C.: Brookings, 1992).

[35] Lutz, "Theory of Constitutional Amendment," 360, table 1. Lutz hypothesizes that a low rate of amendment, combined with a low replacement rate, indicates that the process of revision is dominated by a judicial body. However, he offers no evidence on this point.

[36] The average rate of amendment since ratification for the six constitutions adopted since 1970 is 1.60 amendments per annum, whereas the rate of amendment since 1970 for constitutions adopted prior to 1850 is 1.37 amendments per annum. These figures are computed from data supplied by Sturm, *Thirty Years of State Constitution-Making: 1938–1968* (New York: National Municipal League, 1970), 29–31, table 5; and by May, "State Constitutions, 1992–93," 19, table 1.1.

ment have not served as alternative mechanisms for dealing with constitutional obsolescence. If they had, one would expect that frequent revision of a state's organic law would preclude frequent amendment, and vice versa. Yet often states that have adopted multiple constitutions have also amended them frequently. For example, Louisiana's tenth constitution, adopted in 1921, was amended over 530 times before being replaced in 1972, and its replacement has itself been amended over fifty times. In contrast, Rhode Island's only constitution has been amended just thirty-six times.[37] This suggests that more is involved in state constitutional change than merely failures of political leadership or the demands of modernization. In some states, constitutional change may be a standard aspect of its politics, and constitutional revision and amendment thus represent the continuation of ordinary state politics by other means, invested with no more solemnity than other forms of lawmaking.[38] In other states, constitutional revision and amendment may reflect the emergence of new political forces, which have sought constitutional recognition of their numbers and their interests. In still others, they may provide opportunities to pose basic choices about the principles and policies that will guide the state. The multiplicity of purposes served by formal constitutional change in the states contrasts with amendment of the federal Constitution and underscores the distinctive character of state constitutional politics.

This is not to deny, of course, that a state constitution may be influenced by the federal Constitution or by other state constitutions. It is to the character and extent of such influences that this chapter now turns.

Constitutional Commonalities and Influences from beyond State Borders

Imposition of Federal Requirements on State Constitutions

ADMISSION OF NEW STATES

The potential for direct federal influence on state constitutions is greatest when states are applying for admission to the Union, because the Constitution, by empowering Congress to admit new states to the Union, in effect gives it the power to establish the conditions under which they

[37] Data are drawn from May, "State Constitutions, 1992–93," 19, table 1.1; and Hargrave, *The Louisiana State Constitution,* 16–17. For an overview that confirms the anecdotal evidence, see Lutz, "Theory of Constitutional Amendment," 360, table 2.

[38] Thus, James Dealey observed that the frequency of amendment in some states "so confuses the distinction between fundamental and statutory law, that in such states the constitutions represent a kind of statutory law altered by a somewhat more difficult procedure than that used in the case of ordinary statutes." See Dealey, *Growth of State Constitutions,* 120.

will be admitted.[39] In the enabling acts by which it authorizes prospective states to devise constitutions and apply for statehood, Congress can impose conditions as to the substance of state constitutions, and state constitution-makers must meet those conditions in order to secure a favorable vote on admission.[40] Moreover, if a proposed constitution contains provisions of which Congress or the president disapproves, either can refuse to approve legislation admitting the state until the offending provisions are altered or removed. Finally, recognition of this congressional and executive power, together with the states' eagerness to attain statehood, may deter constitution-makers from including anything in their charters that is likely to excite opposition in Congress.

Some of the conditions for admission that Congress has imposed on prospective states have been general and noncontroversial. Enabling acts of the late nineteenth century, for example, required that state governments be "republican in form" and "not be repugnant to the Constitution of the United States or the principles of the Declaration of Independence."[41] Other requirements, likewise standard in enabling acts of the late nineteenth century, involved more substantive matters. Thus, constitutional conventions were instructed to secure a "perfect toleration of religious sentiment" and to provide for "the establishment and maintenance of systems of public schools . . . free from sectarian control."[42] This latter requirement, a product of conflicts between Protestants and Catholics over public education, ensured that most state constitutions

[39] The main provision dealing with the admission of new states is Article 4, section 3 of the United States Constitution. Further constitutional support for congressional conditions on admission is provided by section 4, which directs the federal government to "guarantee to each State in the Union a Republican Form of Government."

In addition to imposing conditions on prospective states, Congress also supervised the constitutions that Southern states adopted in the aftermath of the Civil War, requiring an acceptable constitution as a condition for "readmission." However, the effects of these congressional efforts were short-lived as most Southern states repudiated their Reconstruction constitutions as soon as they could, typically replacing them with documents that by the late nineteenth century entrenched white political control. These developments are discussed in chapter 4.

[40] Some states—for example, Wyoming in 1889—called conventions and drafted constitutions even without congressional authorization. In such circumstances, however, Congress still had to approve the proposed constitution and confer statehood. On the Wyoming example, see Robert B. Keiter and Tim Newcomb, *The Wyoming State Constitution: A Reference Guide* (Westport, Conn.: Greenwood Press, 1993), 4–5.

[41] See, for example,, the Enabling Act of 1864 (13 Stat. 30), which authorized the people of Nevada to form a constitution and apply for admission; and the Enabling Act of 1889 (25 Stat. 676), which authorized the Dakotas, Montana, and Washington to form constitutions and apply for admission. These enabling acts are reprinted in William F. Swindler, *Sources and Documents of United States Constitutions,* 10 vols. (Dobbs Ferry, N.Y.: Oceana, 1976), 6:261 and 64.

[42] Swindler, *Sources and Documents,* 6:261 and 64.

incorporated more stringent and specific checks on governmental support for religion than were found in the federal Constitution.[43] Finally, some states have been obliged to adopt or eliminate particular provisions as the price for statehood. As a condition for admission, Congress in 1906 required Oklahoma to locate its capital in Guthrie until 1913. And after Arizona proposed a constitution that included the recall of judges, President Taft vetoed the statehood bill, forcing Arizona to delete the provision.[44]

The impact of these congressional mandates should not be overestimated. Many of the congressional requirements were probably superfluous: presumably no prospective state would have adopted a non-republican constitution, or one blatantly inconsistent with the federal Constitution, even in the absence of congressional directives. Even some more specific congressional requirements may have been unnecessary. For example, even without congressional urging, the constitutions of most existing states in the late nineteenth century provided for a system of public schools and banned sectarian influences in those schools. Moreover, as the United States Supreme Court's decision in *Coyle* v. *Smith* (1911) indicated, states—once admitted—possessed "all of the powers of sovereignty and jurisdiction which pertain to the original States."[45] They were therefore free to repudiate any inconvenient restrictions placed on them under Congress's power to admit states to the Union. Thus, Oklahoma moved its capital three years prior to the date specified by Congress, and Arizona reinstituted the recall of judges immediately upon admission to the Union.[46]

FEDERAL CONSTITUTIONAL REQUIREMENTS

Federal constitutional mandates affecting the structure and operation of state governments may also influence state constitutions, either restricting the range of choice for state constitution-makers or inducing states to alter their constitutions to bring them into conformity with federal requirements. The original Constitution directed the federal govern-

[43] For discussion of these conflicts, see Tarr, "Church and State"; and Robert F. Utter and Edward J. Larson, "Church and State on the Frontier: The History of the Establishment Clauses in the Washington State Constitution," *Hastings Constitutional Law Quarterly* 15 (spring 1988): 451–78.

[44] Leshy, *The Arizona State Constitution*, 17–18; and Stephen Botein, "'What We Shall Meet Afterwards in Heaven': Judgeship as a Symbol for Modern American Lawyers," in Gerald L. Geison, ed., *Professions and Professional Ideologies in America* (Chapel Hill: University of North Carolina Press, 1983), 55.

[45] *Coyle* v. *Smith*, 221 U.S. 559 (1911).

[46] Requirements imposed by Congress that are not based on its power to admit states, even if contained in the enabling act, do continue in force and cannot be ignored by the states. See *Fain Land & Cattle Co.* v. *Hassell*, 790 P.2d 242 (Ariz. 1990).

ment to "guarantee to every State in this Union a Republican Form of Government" and upheld the supremacy of federal law within its sphere over "any Thing in the Constitution or Laws of any State."[47] Subsequent amendments have added to the federal constitutional restrictions on the states. Yet these federal requirements have had only selective and episodic effects on state constitutionalism.

The Guarantee Clause. The guarantee clause, which obliges the federal government to guarantee to every state a republican form of government, appears to offer a basis for close federal supervision of state constitutional arrangements.[48] Yet this "sleeping giant," as Charles Sumner once described it, seems to have had little effect on state constitutionalism.[49] In part, this reflects the United States Supreme Court's refusal to use the clause as a basis for reviewing the structure and operation of state governments. In *Luther* v. *Borden* (1849), the Court ruled that the determination as to whether a state had a republican government was a political question, assigned by the Constitution to Congress, and that congressional determinations on the matter were binding on all other branches.[50] It reaffirmed this position in *Pacific States Telephone & Telegraph Co.* v. *Oregon* (1912), in which it rejected a challenge under the guarantee clause to Oregon's use of the initiative for lawmaking, and in *Baker* v. *Carr* (1962), even as it indicated its willingness to address the issue of legislative apportionment under the equal protection clause of the Fourteenth Amendment.[51]

[47] United States Constitution, Article 4, section 4, and Article 6, section 2. These provisions are generally known as the guarantee clause and the supremacy clause. There is little evidence that other restrictions on the states—such as those found in Article 1, section 10 of the federal Constitution—have affected state constitutions.

[48] However, one commentator, Deborah Jones Merritt, has read the guarantee clause as restricting federal power to interfere with state autonomy, based on the assumption that the clause promises the states a "republican form of government," i.e., the right to structure their own political processes, provided that they structure them in a republican manner. See her "The Guarantee Clause and State Autonomy," *Columbia Law Review* 88 (January 1988): 1–78; and "Republican Governments and Autonomous States: A New Role for the Guarantee Clause," *University of Colorado Law Review* 65 (1994): 815–33.

[49] *Congressional Globe,* 40 Cong., 1 sess., 614 (12 July 1867), quoted in William M. Wiecek, *The Guarantee Clause of the U.S. Constitution* (Ithaca, N.Y.: Cornell University Press, 1972), 2. Wiecek's volume provides the most thorough consideration of the clause and its place in American constitutional law.

[50] *Luther* v. *Borden,* 7 Howard 1 (1849). For critiques of the Supreme Court's interpretation of the guarantee clause, see Philippa Strumm, *The Supreme Court and "Political Questions": A Study in Judicial Evasion* (University: University of Alabama Press, 1974); and Wiecek, *Guarantee Clause.*

[51] *Pacific States Telephone & Telegraph Co.* v. *Oregon,* 223 U.S. 118 (1912); and *Baker* v. *Carr,* 369 U.S. 186 (1962).

In part, too, the desuetude of the guarantee clause reflects a more general federal reluctance to oversee the internal politics of the states. During the first half of the nineteenth century, opponents of slavery argued that the clause prohibited Congress from recognizing any new states that permitted slavery; but perhaps because of the presence of slave states already in the Union, this argument did not succeed. Prior to the Civil War, the clause had effect only in the unique circumstances of the Dorr Rebellion, when the federal government had to determine which of two competing governments was in fact the government of Rhode Island.[52] During the Civil War, congressional Republicans considered using the clause as the basis for reconstruction policy; but the clause served this function only briefly.[53] By 1867, "[t]he effective impact of the guarantee clause began to dissipate," as the Radical Republican consensus behind it dissolved, and Congress sought other constitutional bases for its Reconstruction efforts.[54] Although state constitutions were adopted in the South under congressional supervision, they were abandoned when Reconstruction ended, as the Southern states quickly adopted new constitutions or fundamentally revised their Reconstruction charters.[55] In the early twentieth century, opponents of the initiative and referendum invoked the clause, but the courts consistently rejected their claims.[56] Since then, the clause has had no effect on state constitutional development.[57]

The Supremacy Clause. The supremacy clause of the federal Constitution confirms that within its sphere federal law is superior to state law,

[52] On antislavery interpretations of the guarantee clause, see Wiecek, *Guarantee Clause,* chap. 5. On the controversy in Rhode Island, see Gettleman, *The Dorr Rebellion.*

[53] See Herman Belz, *Reconstructing the Union: Theory and Policy during the Civil War* (Ithaca, N.Y.: Cornell University Press, 1969), chaps. 6–8; Harold M. Hyman, *A More Perfect Union: The Impact of the Civil War and Reconstruction on the Constitution* (New York: Alfred A. Knopf, 1973), chaps. 26–28; and Eric Foner, *Reconstruction: America's Unfinished Revolution, 1863–1877* (New York: Harper and Row, 1988).

[54] Wiecek, *Guarantee Clause,* 210.

[55] See Michael Perman, *The Road to Redemption: Southern Politics, 1869–1879* (Chapel Hill: University of North Carolina Press, 1984), chap. 9. These developments are discussed in chapter 4.

[56] *Pacific Telephone and Telegraph Co.* v. *Oregon,* 223 U.S. 118 (1912); *Kiernan* v. *City of Portland,* 223 U.S. 151 (1912); *State ex rel. Topping* v. *Houston,* 94 Neb. 445 (1913); *Marshall* v. *Dye,* 231 U.S. 250 (1913); *State ex rel. Foote* v. *Board of Commissioners,* 93 Kans. 405 (1914); and *Ohio ex rel. Davis* v. *Hildebrant,* 245 U.S. 565 (1916).

[57] In recent years, however, some state judges and legal scholars have argued that the guarantee clause should be resuscitated as a check on the use of the initiative and referendum in the states. See the dissent of Justice Hans A. Linde in *State* v. *Wagner,* 752 P.2d 1136, 1197; Hans A. Linde, "When Is Initiative Lawmaking Not 'Republican Government'?" *Hastings Constitutional Law Quarterly* 17 (fall 1989): 159–73; and, more generally, the symposium on the guarantee clause in *University of Colorado Law Review* 65 (1994): 709–946.

that federal enactments—be they constitutional provisions, statutes, or administrative regulations—take precedence over state constitutional provisions in cases of conflict. During the nation's first century, collisions between federal law and state constitutions were rare—not until 1867, when the Supreme Court in *Cummings* v. *Missouri* overturned a Missouri loyalty-oath requirement, was a state constitutional provision invalidated as inconsistent with the federal Constitution.[58] Even so, the fear of conflicts with inchoate federal constitutional requirements, such as those pertaining to water rights, at times constrained state constitution-makers.[59] During the twentieth century, federal policy initiatives increased the opportunities for conflict between federal policies and state policies, including policies enshrined in state constitutions.[60] Even more important have been the adoption of the Fourteenth Amendment, the incorporation under it of most provisions of the federal Bill of Rights, and the more aggressive review of state constitutions by the federal judiciary. Thus, the U.S. Supreme Court has struck down a Colorado constitutional amendment affecting the rights of homosexuals as a denial of equal protection of the laws, a Maryland religious test for state officials as a violation of the First Amendment, and an Arkansas limitation on the consecutive terms that a member of Congress could serve under the qualifications clause of Article 1.[61] Often the effects of such rulings on state constitutions have extended beyond the provisions that have been invalidated. They have also rendered unenforceable analogous provisions in other state constitutions and encouraged states to amend their constitutions to eliminate provisions inconsistent with federal constitutional law.[62]

[58] *Cummings* v. *Missouri*, 4 Wall. 277 (1867); Foner, *Reconstruction*, 272.

[59] Donald J. Pisani, *From Family Farm to Agribusiness: The Irrigation Crusade in California and the West, 1850–1931* (Berkeley and Los Angeles: University of California Press, 1984), 159.

[60] For examples of federal legislation preempting state constitutions, see *North Carolina ex rel. Morrow* v. *Califano*, 445 F.Supp. 532 (E.D.N.C. 1977), and *Utility Workers of America* v. *Southern California Edison Co.*, 852 F.2d 1083 (9th Cir. 1988, *cert. denied*, 489 U.S. 1078 [1989]). For an example of federal common law preempting a state constitution, see *Hinderlider* v. *La Plata River & Cherry Creek Ditch Co.*, 304 U.S. 92 (1938). Even federal regulations override state provisions—see *Fidelity Federal Savings & Loan Association* v. *De La Cuesta*, 458 U.S. 141, 153–54 (1982). For an excellent overview, see Williams, *State Constitutional Law*, 117–44.

[61] *Romer* v. *Evans*, 517 U.S. 620 (1996); *Torasco* v. *Watkins*, 367 U.S. 488 (1961); and *U.S. Term Limits, Inc.* v. *Thornton*, 514 U.S. 779 (1995).

[62] For example, in response to the U.S. Supreme Court's ruling in *Gideon* v. *Wainwright*, 372 U.S. 335 (1963), Hawaii in 1968 constitutionalized the right of indigent defendants to have counsel provided by the state (Hawaii Constitution, art. 1, sec. 14). See Lee, *The Hawaii State Constitution*, 61–62; and Norman Meller, *With an Understanding Heart: Constitution-Making in Hawaii* (New York: National Municipal League, 1971), 97–98.

Federal constitutional amendments affecting voting and apportionment have had the most pronounced effect on state constitutions. The federal Constitution originally left voting qualifications and apportionment to the states, and disputes over those issues became a recurring source of political conflict in the states.[63] The federalization of voting law began with the adoption of the Fifteenth Amendment, requiring that states not discriminate in their voting qualifications on the basis of race, and continued with the adoption of the Nineteenth Amendment (women's suffrage), the Twenty-Fourth Amendment (poll tax), and the Twenty-Sixth Amendment (eighteen-year-old vote).[64] These amendments imposed uniform national standards for voting, removing a major source of constitutional controversy from state control.[65] Many states subsequently brought their constitutions into conformity with the federal requirements, either excising inconsistent provisions or adopting amendments analogous to the federal amendments.[66] Beginning in the 1960s, the Fourteenth Amendment spawned successful challenges to state systems of legislative apportionment and to state regulations of voting, such as poll taxes and residency requirements.[67] Congress also enacted the Voting Rights Act of 1965, and this act—together with its 1982 amendments—dramatically expanded and intensified federal supervision

[63] See, inter alia, James A. Henretta, "The Rise and Decline of 'Democratic-Republicanism': Political Rights in New York and the Several States, 1800–1915," in Paul Finkelman and Stephen E. Gottleib, eds., *Toward a Usable Past: Liberty under State Constitutions* (Athens: University of Georgia Press, 1991), 50–90; Chilton Williamson, *American Suffrage: From Property to Democracy* (Princeton: Princeton University Press, 1960); and Morgan Kousser, *The Shaping of Southern Politics: Suffrage Restrictions and the Establishment of the One-Party South, 1880–1910* (New Haven: Yale University Press, 1974). These disputes are discussed in greater detail in chaps. 3–5.

[64] Although it had little effect at the time and has since become an historical artifact, section 2 of the Fourteenth Amendment penalized states that denied the right to vote to "any of the male inhabitants of such State, being twenty-one years of age, and citizens of the United States . . . except for participation in rebellion, or other crime."

[65] Even after the adoption of the Twenty-Sixth Amendment, states theoretically could enfranchise those under the age of eighteen; however, this has not become a serious constitutional issue in any state.

[66] When the states failed to change their constitutions in line with federal constitutional requirements, federal courts invalidated the state constitutional requirements. See, for example, *Hunter v. Underwood,* 471 U.S. 222 (1985).

[67] The leading state legislative-apportionment case is *Reynolds v. Sims,* 377 U.S. 533 (1964). Key later cases include *Lucas v. Colorado General Assembly,* 377 U.S. 713 (1964); *Brown v. Thomson,* 462 U.S. 835 (1983); and *Davis v. Bandemer,* 478 U.S. 109 (1986). Decisions of the United States Supreme Court invalidating state constitutional or legislative regulations of voting include *Harper v. Virginia State Board of Elections,* 383 U.S. 663 (1966) (poll tax); *Kramer v. Union Free School District No. 15,* 395 U.S. 621 (1969) (property-ownership requirements); and *Dunn v. Blumstein,* 405 U.S. 330 (1972) (residency requirements).

over state electoral laws and practices. Yet these federal interventions have not altogether precluded an independent state role. For example, many state constitutions require that local boundaries be respected in districting decisions, and state apportionment commissions and state courts have continued to enforce that requirement, insofar as it can be reconciled with the federal "one person, one vote" standard.[68] Nonetheless, the federal actions have transformed a field that had once been central to state constitutional politics into a considerably less important aspect of state constitutionalism.

The Force of Federal Example

Direct federal imposition of uniform standards, as occurred with the transformation of voting qualifications and apportionment from matters of state to federal law, is quite rare. The federal Constitution has exerted its greatest influence on state constitutions by providing a model for emulation. Yet it is difficult to measure this influence with any precision.[69] Many features of the federal Constitution—such as protections of rights, popular rule, a separation of powers, and an independent judiciary—are likewise found in state constitutions; so when a new state constitution incorporates these features, it is difficult to determine whether the federal Constitution or its state counterparts provided the model. Even the presence of textual similarities between the federal Constitution and subsequent state constitutions is not determinative. In some instances federal constitution-makers derived their formulations from earlier state charters, and these rather than the federal document may have guided later state constitution-makers as well.[70]

Despite these caveats, there are instances in which it is clear that states modeled their provisions on those in the federal Constitution. At times, immediate emulation of the federal model reveals the direct federal influence. For example, Pennsylvania, Delaware, New Hampshire, and Kentucky all adopted the federal mode of judicial selection within a decade

---

[68] See *Fonfara v. Reapportionment Commission,* 610 A.2d 153 (Conn. 1992); and, more generally, Robert M. Sukol, "Developments in State Constitutional Law, 1992: Legislative Branch Reapportionment: Decennial State Constitutional Controversies," *Rutgers Law Journal* 24 (summer 1993): 1106–32.

[69] It may be, of course, that the difficulty in documenting patterns of causation is less important than establishing those instances in which the state and federal constitutions share common principles.

[70] See, for example, Lutz, "State Constitutional Pedigree"; and, more generally, Thurston Greene, *The Language of the Constitution* (Westport, Conn.: Greenwood Press, 1991).

after the Constitution was ratified.[71] At times too, distinctive federal language reappears in state charters. For example, twenty-three states have adopted language patterned after the freedom of speech and press provisions of the First Amendment; twelve have equal protection clauses similar to the Fourteenth Amendment's; and eleven prohibit religious establishments in terms comparable to the First Amendment's establishment clause.[72] In fact, in at least one instance, state constitution-makers modeled their provisions on a federal provision that failed of adoption. From 1968 to 1976, at the same time that the equal-rights amendment to the federal Constitution was under consideration, fourteen states adopted their own "little ERAs." The language of these provisions tracks the federal amendment, and their legislative histories reveal a desire to provide comparable protections in the state and federal documents.[73]

Nevertheless, assertions that the federal Constitution is central to state constitutional design are simply wrong.[74] They ignore the fact that many state constitutional provisions have no federal analogue and that even those that do often differ substantially from federal provisions. Such assertions also ignore the fact that state constitution-makers confront distinctive problems for which the experience of federal constitution-makers offers no guidance. Most importantly, they ignore the testimony of state constitution-makers themselves, who have indicated that they looked to state constitutions rather than to the federal Constitution for direction and for constitutional models. As Christian Fritz has demonstrated, delegates to nineteenth-century state constitutional conventions viewed constitution making as a progressive enterprise, in which succeeding generations built upon the experience of their predecessors and readjusted past practices to present requirements.[75] Implicit in this view was an under-

[71] James Schouler, *Constitutional Studies: State and Federal* (New York: Dodd, Mead, 1897), 286.

[72] Ronald K. L. Collins, "Bills and Declarations Digest," 2503, 2492, and 2498–99. In none of these instances was the federal constitutional language derivative from the language of prior state constitutions.

One should recognize the divergent conclusions that can be drawn from these figures. The figures also indicate that twenty-seven states have speech and press guarantees quite different from the First Amendment's, thirty-eight have equality guarantees dissimilar to the equal protection clause, and thirty-nine have guarantees of a separation of church and state that differ from the federal establishment clause.

[73] Tarr and Porter, "Gender Equality"; and Barbara A. Brown, Ann Freedman, Harriet Katz, and Ann Price, *Women's Rights and the Law* (New York: Praeger, 1977).

[74] This is only true in the sense that the incompleteness of the federal Constitution provides the agenda for state constitution-makers, requiring them to fill in the gaps in the federal Constitution. See Lutz, "Constitution as Incomplete Text"; and Kermit L. Hall, "Mostly Anchor and Little Sail: The Evolution of American State Constitutions," in Finkelman and Gottlieb, *Toward a Usable Past*, 393–95.

[75] See Christian G. Fritz, "The American Constitutional Tradition Revisited: Prelimi-

standing that "constitution-making in the past—even in the glorious Revolutionary period of American history—was less perfect and possibly even crude when compared with 'modern' ideas of drafting fundamental law."[76] Given this judgment about federal constitution-makers and given the quite different problems confronting their state successors, it is hardly surprising that the influence of the federal Constitution on state charters has been limited.

Thus it is in constitutional interpretation rather than in constitutional design that one would expect the federal Constitution to exert its greatest influence, and this is in fact the case. In civil-liberties cases, state constitutional interpretation has long been influenced by federal interpretations, even when the texts of the state and federal guarantees are quite dissimilar. Prior to the emergence of the "new judicial federalism" in the 1970s, attorneys and state judges oftentimes assumed that state and federal rights guarantees should be interpreted as affording equivalent protections.[77] In fact, when state constitutional issues arose, state courts were particularly likely to look to federal precedent for direction.[78] Even after the emergence of the new judicial federalism, state judges typically confronted state constitutional claims framed in terms of federal doctrines and precedents with which they were already familiar and comfortable. So it is hardly surprising that the categories and conceptions of federal constitutional law have decisively influenced the interpretation of state rights guarantees.[79] Indeed, in some instances states have incorporated the concepts and rulings of federal decisional law directly into their constitutions. California has outlawed the use of busing beyond that re-

---

nary Observations on State Constitution-Making in the Nineteenth-Century West," *Rutgers Law Journal* 25 (summer 1994): 945–98, for a particularly trenchant treatment of this issue. The discussion in this section to a considerable extent follows Fritz's.

[76] Fritz, "American Constitutional Tradition Revisited," 973.

[77] See Robert Force, "State 'Bills of Rights': A Case of Neglect and the Need for a Renaissance," *Valparaiso University Law Review* 3 (1969): 125–82; Shirley S. Abrahamson, "Criminal Law and State Constitutions: The Emergence of State Constitutional Law," *Texas Law Review* 63 (March–April 1985): 1141–93; Shirley S. Abrahamson and Diane S. Gutmann, "The New Federalism: State Constitutions and State Courts," *Judicature* 71 (August–September 1987): 88–99; Shirley S. Abrahamson, "Divided We Stand: State Constitutions in a More Perfect Union," *Hastings Constitutional Law Quarterly* 18 (summer 1991): 723–44; and G. Alan Tarr, "The Past and Future of the New Judicial Federalism," *Publius* 24 (spring 1994): 63–79.

[78] Peter K. Harris, "The Communication of Precedent among State Supreme Courts," Ph.D. diss., Yale University, 1980, 145.

[79] Tarr and Porter, *State Supreme Courts in State and Nation,* 21–22. Indeed, the influence of federal constitutional law extends beyond the civil-liberties realm. See, for example, *Brown v. Heymann,* 297 A.2d 572 (N.J. 1972), and—more generally—William F. Swindler, "State Constitutions for the Twentieth Century," *Nebraska Law Review* 50 (1971): 593–96.

quired to remedy violations of the equal protection clause of the federal Constitution.[80] Florida has required that its search-and-seizure provision "be construed in conformity with the Fourth Amendment to the United States Constitution, as interpreted by the United States Supreme Court."[81] And Hawaii by amendment constitutionalized the U.S. Supreme Court's ruling in *Gideon* v. *Wainwright*.[82]

The influence of federal doctrinal developments on state civil-liberties law is, however, only part of the story. Many state constitutional cases do not involve civil liberties, and outside that realm, federal judicial doctrine has exerted considerably less influence on state constitutional law.[83] Nor is this surprising. State constitutions encompass a wider range of subjects than does the federal Constitution, and thus state courts are regularly called upon to address constitutional issues involving taxation, the powers of local government, and state or local indebtedness (to name but a few) never addressed by federal courts.[84] The inclusion of "statutory" material in state constitutions also requires state courts to devise consti-

---

[80] California Constitution, art. 1, sec. 7.

[81] Florida Constitution, art. 1, sec. 12.

[82] Hawaii Constitution, art. 1, sec. 14, constitutionalizing *Gideon* v. *Wainwright*, 372 U.S. 335 (1963). See Lee, *The Hawaii State Constitution*, 62–63.

[83] A study of state supreme court caseloads from 1870 to 1970 found that cases based "on provisions peculiar to state constitutions" made up the majority of the constitutional cases in those courts from 1870 to 1900. In later periods, the percentage of constitutional cases devoted to these provisions declined, as the number involving "the procedural due process rights of criminal defendants" increased. These latter cases, however, typically involved issues of federal rather than state constitutional law. See Robert A. Kagan, Bliss Cartwright, Lawrence M. Friedman, and Stanton Wheeler, "The Business of State Supreme Courts, 1870–1970," *Stanford Law Review* 30 (November 1977): 150.

A more recent study of the caseloads of six state supreme courts, including the activist California and New Jersey Supreme Courts, found that in 1975 roughly 60 percent of their state constitutional cases involved rights claims. See Susan P. Fino, *The Role of State Supreme Courts in the New Judicial Federalism* (Westport, Conn.: Greenwood Press, 1987), 69, fig. 4.1. Even cases associated with civil liberties in federal courts may be quite different in state courts. Fino discovered that almost 20 percent of state equal-protection cases involved challenges to various forms of commercial regulation, and almost 39 percent concerned general rules of civil and criminal procedure. See Susan P. Fino, "Judicial Federalism and Equality Guarantees in State Supreme Courts," *Publius* 17 (winter 1987): 51–67.

[84] The distinctive features of state constitutions are discussed in chapter 1. Representative cases concerning the listed topics include, for tax policy, *McBurney* v. *Ruth*, 527 So.2d 1265 (Ala. 1988), and *City of Phoenix* v. *Popkin*, 378 P.2d 242 (Ariz. 1963); for local government powers, *California Federal Savings & Loan Association* v. *City of Los Angeles*, 812 P.2d 916 (Cal. 1991), and *City of Lewiston* v. *Knieriem*, 865 P.2d 821 (Id. 1984); and for state indebtedness, *New York Public Interest Research Group, Inc.* v. *Carey*, 369 N.E.2d 558 (N.Y. 1976), and *State Bond Commission* v. *All Taxpayers*, 525 So.2d 521 (La. 1988). Both the distinctive topics of state constitutional law and the cases arising under them could be multiplied almost indefinitely.

tutional doctrine independently of federal constitutional law.[85] Even when state courts confront state constitutional issues also addressed by federal courts—for example, separation-of-powers issues—the influence of federal constitutional doctrine is limited.'[86] In part, this reflects judges' recognition of differences in institutional design between the federal nd state governments—state legislatures' possession of inherent (non-enumerated powers), limited legislative sessions, a nonunitary executive, and so forth.[87] In part too, it may reflect the timing of litigation. In contrast with civil-liberties cases, state courts have often confronted separation-of-powers issues and developed their own analyses prior to litigation in federal courts. For example, four state supreme courts had already invalidated the legislative veto before the United States Supreme Court decided *Immigration and Naturalization Service* v. *Chadha* (1983), and *Chadha* affected neither the direction of subsequent state decisions nor the grounds on which the courts ruled.[88] But whatever the reasons, the fact remains that federal influence on state civil-liberties law is not indicative of the overall influence of federal rulings on state constitutional interpretation.

Interstate Influences

There is no requirement that state constitution-makers adopt provisions similar to those in other states or that state judges adhere to constitutional rulings or doctrines developed by other states' courts. Yet as the literature on the diffusion of innovations suggests, states regularly look to other states for solutions to the common problems they face.[89] This horizontal federalism has certainly affected state constitutional develop-

[85] See, for example, *Davis* v. *City of Berkeley,* 794 P.2d 46 (Cal. 1989) on the siting of public housing; *Centennial Associates* v. *Clark,* 384 So.2d 616 (Ala. 1980) on banks' interest rates; and *Rubio* v. *Carlsbad Municipal School District,* 744 P.2d 919 (N.M. 1987) on compulsory school attendance.

[87] The U.S. Supreme Court has long recognized that state governments need not conform to the same strictures on the separation of powers that bind the federal government. See, for example, *Prentiss* v. *Atlantic Coast Line R.R.,* 211 U.S. 210, 255 (1908); *Sweezy* v. *New Hampshire,* 354 U.S. 234, 255 (1957); and *Highland Farms Dairy* v. *Agnew,* 300 U.S. 608, 612 (1937).

[88] *Immigration and Naturalization Service* v. *Chadha,* 462 U.S. 919 (1983). Intercourt influence in legislative-veto cases is discussed in Levinson, "Decline of Legislative Veto."

[89] Major contributions to this literature include Jack L. Walker, "The Diffusion of Innovations among American States," *American Political Science Review* 63 (September 1969): 880–89; Virginia Gray, "Innovation in the States: A Diffusion Study," *American Political Science Review* 67 (December 1973): 1174–85; and "Symposium: Policy Diffusion in a Federal System," *Publius* 15 (fall 1985): 1–132.

ment.[90] However, the mechanisms by which it has occurred and the extent to which it has imposed a constitutional uniformity on the American states deserve consideration.

Interstate borrowing affected state constitutional design from the very outset. For those drafting the initial state constitutions, the unfamiliarity of the task, time constraints, and the pressing demands of war and governance encouraged reliance on constitutional models developed in other states. The Continental Congress facilitated this process by providing a venue for the exchange of constitutional ideas. Thus, when representatives of Vermont came to lobby for recognition of their statehood, the drafters of the Pennsylvania constitution passed copies of it to the Vermonters.[91] And when North Carolina was ready to draft a constitution, one of its delegates to the Continental Congress collected and sent to the state legislature the plans of government from several states.[92] Also facilitating constitutional borrowing was the circulation after 1780 of compilations of existing state constitutions.[93] Not surprisingly, then, similar provisions appeared in a number of early state constitutions.

If anything, the passage of time has increased interstate borrowing. During the nineteenth century, some states seeking congressional approval for their admission to the Union sought to avoid controversy by modeling their constitutions on those of existing states. In addition, settlers carried constitutional ideas west with them—indeed, some delegates to western conventions had previously served as delegates in the states from which they emigrated—and reproduced in their new homes the constitutional arrangements with which they were familiar.[94] Common problems also led to common solutions. Thus, John Hicks has noted that

[90] For general discussions of the operation of horizontal federalism, see Mary Cornelia Porter and G. Alan Tarr, introduction to Porter and Tarr, eds., *State Supreme Courts: Policymakers in the Federal System* (Westport, Conn.: Greenwood Press, 1982), xxi–xxii (hereafter cited as *Policymakers*); and Tarr and Porter, *State Supreme Courts in State and Nation*, 27–40. This section draws upon those earlier treatments.

[91] Robert F. Williams, "The Influence of Pennsylvania's 1776 Constitution on American Constitutionalism during the Founding Era," *Pennsylvania Magazine of History and Biography* 112 (January 1988): 35. Choosing between the Pennsylvania and New York constitutions in designing their own charter, Vermonters modeled their constitution on Pennsylvania's. See William C. Hill, *The Vermont State Constitution: A Reference Guide* (Westport, Conn.: Greenwood Press, 1992), 4–6.

[92] Fletcher M. Green, *Constitutional Development in the South Atlantic States, 1776–1860: A Study in the Evolution of Democracy* (Chapel Hill: University of North Carolina Press, 1930), 67; and Orth, *North Carolina State Constitution*, 2.

[93] Fritz, "American Constitutional Tradition Revisited," 976.

[94] See Christian G. Fritz, "Rethinking the American Constitutional Tradition: National Dimensions in the Formation of State Constitutions," *Rutgers Law Journal* 26 (summer 1995): 983.

during the late nineteenth century several western states, seeking to promote mining and irrigation, adopted similarly expansive provisions on eminent domain to encourage those activities.[95] And Morgan Kousser has described how in the South during the same period the interstate exchange of constitutional ideas and legal materials furthered a "public conspiracy" to restrict suffrage.[96] Finally, on several occasions constitutional innovations in one or a few states unleashed a contagion of emulative change. The transition to an elective judiciary illustrates the process: after Iowa and New York in 1846 made all judges elective, eleven other states also did so (in whole or in part) over the next four years, and nine more did so in the succeeding decade.[97]

Whether in new states or old, convention delegates during the nineteenth century relied heavily on compilations of existing state constitutions, which clarified the progress of constitutional thinking and provided models for emulation.[98] Delegates frequently referred to other states' constitutions in convention debates. During the New York convention of 1821, for example, various delegates cited the experience of other states on subjects as diverse as the Council of Revision, the appointive power, and suffrage qualifications.[99] As a delegate to the Wyoming convention of 1889 put it, "[S]o far as nine-tenths of our labor is concerned, we have only to exercise an intelligent and discriminating judgment in our study of the work of the constitutional builders who have preceded us."[100] Interstate appropriation of whole provisions was common. For example, the California Constitution of 1849 incorporated Iowa's stringent regulation of corporations and its prohibition of banks of issue, as well as New York's prohibition of special legislative charters.[101] And the Missouri Constitution of 1875 contained over thirty sections of detailed restrictions on the state legislature, almost all of which were copied from the Illinois constitution of 1870 and the Pennsylvania Constitution of 1873.[102] The extent of this borrowing led one dele-

[95] John D. Hicks, *The Constitutions of the Northwest States* (Lincoln: University of Nebraska University Studies, 1923), 146–47.

[96] Kousser, *Shaping of Southern Politics*, 39–40.

[97] Henry Hitchcock, *American State Constitutions: A Study of Their Growth* (New York: G. P. Putnam's Sons, 1887), 50–54.

[98] The analysis in this paragraph follows that of Fritz, "American Constitutional Tradition Revisited," 975–84.

[99] Merrill D. Peterson, *Democracy, Liberty, and Property,* 145, 177–78, 188–90, 197–99, and 217–18.

[100] Quoted in Hicks, *Constitutions of Northwest States,* 34.

[101] David Alan Johnson, *Founding the Far West: California, Oregon, and Nevada, 1940–1890* (Berkeley and Los Angeles: University of California Press, 1992), 102 and 124.

[102] Hitchcock, *American State Constitutions,* 35. For further examples, see Robert B.

gate toward the end of the California convention of 1849 to lament his colleagues' lack of originality, insisting that the preamble at least should contain "a few lines of our own manufacture."[103]

Developments during the twentieth century have facilitated the process of interstate borrowing. Among the most important of these is the increased use of constitutional commissions, which have the resources of staff, time, and expertise necessary to study the constitutions of other states before they suggest constitutional amendments.[104] From 1939 to 1969 alone, fifty such commissions were established in thirty-two states.[105] Likewise important has been the practice of establishing preparatory commissions to assemble pertinent information, including analyses of the constitutions of other states, for delegates to state constitutional conventions. Illustrative of this was the work of the Legislative Reference Bureau of the University of Hawaii, which prepared seventeen background studies reviewing the experience of other states and relating that experience to the situation in Hawaii.[106] Finally, the nationalization of state constitutional politics has also contributed to interstate borrowing. Interest groups have become increasingly involved in promoting constitutional changes nationwide, which has prompted a transfer of information, including the substance of proposed constitutional reforms, from state to state. The adoption of victims' rights amendments and term-limits amendments illustrates this process. In sum, the professionalization of constitutional reform has increased the availability of information on the constitutions and constitutional experiences of other states.

The multiplicity of models provided by other states' constitutions, however, has prevented interstate borrowing from degenerating into a passive copying process. Rather, state constitution-makers have been obliged, in the words of the Wyoming delegate quoted earlier, to "exercise an intelligent and discriminating judgment" in choosing which provisions to adopt. Sometimes these choices have been influenced by the familiarity of constitutional arrangements. Western pioneers, for example,

---

Dishman, *State Constitutions: The Shape of the Document,* rev. ed. (New York: National Municipal League, 1968), 8–10.

[103] Quoted in Fritz, "American Constitutional Tradition Revisited," 981.

[104] Useful descriptions of state constitutional commissions and their operation, which also detail the increased reliance on such commissions since the 1930s, include Sturm, *Thirty Years,* chap. 3; and Williams, "Things of the Past?" Updated figures on the use of constitutional commissions are found in Sturm, "Development of State Constitutions," 86, table 7, and the annual chapters on state constitutions in the *Book of the States* (Lexington, Ky.: Council of State Governments, various years).

[105] Sturm, *Thirty Years,* 35–36, table 6.

[106] Sturm, *Thirty Years,* 68–69.

brought with them certain constitutional ideas and sought to reproduce the institutions of their home states (though often the ideas were modified as a result of interaction with settlers from other states, changed circumstances, and the influence of prevailing ideas of a constitutional era).[107] At other times the choices reflected the delegates' desire to avail themselves of the most up-to-date thinking on constitutional matters by consulting the most recent constitutions.[108] At still other times convention delegates drew upon the constitutions of neighboring states that shared similar circumstances and political orientations. But frequently the constitution-makers' choices were eclectic. Delegates borrowed constitutional ideas from a variety of states and created a new synthesis. In addition, they frequently adapted the provisions they borrowed to the circumstances or political perspectives of their state. Pennsylvania's Declaration of Rights of 1776 offers a prime example. Although it largely followed the Virginia Declaration of Rights, the Pennsylvania declaration acknowledged the presence of Quakers in the state by expressly recognizing the rights of conscientious objectors.[109] It also gave a more democratic thrust to the state government by adding the right to instruct representatives and petition for redress of grievances.[110]

A variety of factors have affected the extent and character of interstate borrowing. One factor, of course, is the nature of the constitutional problem being addressed. Some problems are so state-specific that no other state's experience is helpful, whereas others are common to several or to all states. In the former case, no borrowing occurs, whereas in the latter borrowing is likely. A second factor is the stage in a state's constitutional development. When states adopt their initial constitutions, they are particularly likely to look beyond their borders, either to profit from the experience of other states or to import standard formulations. When states revise their constitutions, however, they usually do so not to effect a total change but rather to address specific problems. They therefore tend to retain noncontroversial provisions from their previous charter without consulting alternatives from other states. A third factor is the salience of the constitutional issue being addressed. If the issue is not salient or controversial, then the tendency is to borrow with little exam-

---

[107] Elazar, "Principles and Traditions," 18.

[108] Fritz, "American Constitutional Tradition Revisited," 973–74.

[109] Pennsylvania Constitution of 1776, Declaration of Rights, sec. 8; retained in the constitution of 1790, art. 6, sec. 2.

[110] Pennsylvania Constitution of 1776, Declaration of Rights, sec. 16. For discussion of other differences, see J. Paul Selsam, *The Pennsylvania Constitution of 1776: A Study in Revolutionary Democracy* (Philadelphia: University of Pennsylvania Press, 1936), 178–79. The Pennsylvania Constitution of 1790 eliminated the power of instructing representatives—see Pennsylvania Constitution of 1790, art. 9, sec. 20.

ination readily available constitutional language. This explains the similarities among the preambles of state constitutions and among some provisions of state declarations of rights. If the issue is a salient and controversial one, however, delegates tend to debate at length the appropriate resolution and the constitutional language in which it will be framed. Although the constitutions of other states are likely to be consulted, often they will offer conflicting models; so delegates will have to craft a solution adapted to the circumstances and political divisions in the state that, while perhaps drawing on the formulations of other states, reflects a considered judgment rather than mere appropriation of convenient text.

BROADER PERSPECTIVES ON STATE CONSTITUTIONALISM

Political Culture

Implicit in most prior research on state constitutions, including much of the work surveyed in this chapter, are certain broader perspectives on, or comprehensive understandings of, state constitutions and state constitutional development.[111] One such perspective, identified most closely with Daniel Elazar and his students, emphasizes the importance of political culture for understanding state constitutionalism. A state's political culture reflects the "persistent patterns of underlying political attitudes and values—and characteristic responses to political concerns"—found in the state.[112] This is crucial to understanding a state's constitution, Elazar argues, because the predominant political forces in the state tend to enshrine their basic political values in the state charter.[113] Thus, state constitutions embody "practical public expressions of political theory and the purposes of government," reflecting "public conceptions of the proper roles of government and politics."[114] Elazar acknowledges that this aspect of state constitutions may not be immediately apparent; some effort may be required to extract the underlying political theory from a

[111] The analysis in this section elaborates an earlier treatment of these themes in Tarr, "State Constitutional Politics," 4–5.

[112] Elazar, *Cities of the Prairie*, 256; see also Daniel J. Elazar, *American Federalism: A View from the States*, 3d ed. (New York: Harper and Row, 1984). For treatments of political culture that differ from Elazar's, see Michael Thompson, Richard Ellis, and Aaron Wildavsky, *Cultural Theory* (Boulder, Colo.: Westview, 1990); Gabriel A. Almond and Sidney Verba, *The Civic Culture: Political Attitudes and Democracy in Five Nations* (Princeton: Princeton University Press, 1963); and Stephen Welch, *The Concept of Political Culture* (New York: St. Martin's, 1993). For a political-culture approach to state constitutions distinct from Elazar's, see Johnson, *Founding the Far West*.

[113] In states with competing political cultures, such as Illinois, the state constitution may reflect a compromise between political forces. See Elazar, *Cities of the Prairie*, 288–89.

[114] Elazar, "Principles and Traditions," 11.

constitution's resolutely practical provisions. Moreover, states with different political cultures may adopt similar provisions for quite different reasons.[115] Nevertheless, the implications of Elazar's position are clear: if states have different political cultures, the contrast should be reflected in the form and substance of their constitutions, and if the political culture of a state changes, so too should the state's constitution. Elazar views the national political culture as a synthesis of three major political subcultures—the individualistic, moralistic, and traditionalistic—found in the American states.[116] He identifies three constitutional traditions (Whig, federalist, and managerial) associated with these political subcultures and six constitutional patterns reflecting the interplay of constitutional traditions and historical developments.[117] Some commentators have criticized Elazar's categories, arguing (for instance) that the match between political subcultures and constitutional traditions is not exact.[118] Others have modified Elazar's inventory of constitutional patterns.[119] Our current concern is less with the adequacy of Elazar's categories than with his approach, which suggests that state constitutions can be analyzed as coherent statements of political principle.

National Political Forces

A second perspective, best exemplified in the research of Albert Sturm, emphasizes the influence of national political movements and historical forces, rather than distinctive state political cultures, on state constitutional development.[120] According to Sturm, factors such as the movement westward of the early nineteenth century, the concern for political reform of the early twentieth century, and the reapportionment revolution of the 1960s have provided the impetus for constitutional change.[121] They have also determined the issues that most concerned constitution-makers and the sorts of solutions that were devised for dealing with them. Thus, state constitutional politics can be viewed as national politics writ small. Accordingly, one would expect a constitution adopted during the middle third of the nineteenth century to reflect the values of

[115] Daniel J. Elazar, *Cities of the Prairie Revisited: The Closing of the Metropolitan Frontier* (Lincoln: University of Nebraska Press, 1986), 104–5.

[116] Elazar, *American Federalism*, 93–120.

[117] Elazar, "Principles and Traditions," 12–22.

[118] See Thompson, Ellis, and Wildavsky, *Cultural Theory*, 241.

[119] See, for example, Hall, "Mostly Anchor."

[120] Sturm, "Development of State Constitutions." Other studies that emphasize the periodicity of state constitutions include Hall, "Mostly Anchor"; and Hurst, *Growth of American Law*.

[121] Sturm, "Development of State Constitutions," 63 and 72–73.

Jacksonian democracy and one adopted during the early twentieth century to embody the prescriptions of the Progressive movement.

"Ordinary Politics"

A third perspective, seldom made explicit, views state constitutional development as merely a continuation in a new arena of the ordinary politics of the state.[122] According to this view, because the process of constitutional change is a political one, change can only occur if it reflects the prevailing distribution of political forces in the state. This is most obvious in the case of constitutional amendments, which in most instances are proposed by the state legislature.[123] (The adoption of amendments by constitutional initiative changes, but does not eliminate, the political aspects of the process.) However, it is also true of the creation or revision of state constitutions. People who are active in state politics usually serve as delegates to the conventions that draft state constitutions, and their deliberations are affected by the same interest groups that exert influence in the legislative and executive arenas. A successful ratification campaign requires support from government officials, both political parties, and established political groups, none of whom are likely to support a document that threatens their power or takes unpopular stands on divisive issues.[124] In sum, the same groups and opinions that dominate ordinary politics in the state can be expected to dominate constitutional politics as well.

Although this view of state constitutionalism bears some resemblance to Elazar's, what distinguishes it is its understanding of state politics. The ordinary-politics perspective conceives of politics as a competition among groups seeking to advance their interests or to secure short-term advantage. In constitutional politics this often takes the form of a conflict

[122] Illustrative of this perspective are Cornwell, Goodman, and Swanson, *State Constitutional Conventions: The Politics of the Revision Process in Seven States* (New York: Praeger, 1975); and Charles Press, "Assesssing the Policy and Operational Implications of State Constitutional Change," *Publius* 12 (winter 1982): 99–111.

[123] This is reflected in William Havard's analysis of the process of constitutional change in Florida, which concluded that "the legislature was extremely careful to avoid losing control of the revision process at any point." See William C. Havard, "Notes on a Theory of State Constitutional Change: The Florida Experience," *Journal of Politics* 21 (February 1959): 103.

[124] Studies of the membership of constitutional conventions confirm the political background of most delegates. See, for example, Cornwell, Goodman, and Swanson, *State Constitutional Conventions*, chap. 3. When the normal participants in the political process do not serve as delegates to a constitutional convention, the document produced by the convention is likely to lack the political support needed for ratification. See, for example, Wheeler, *Magnificent Failure*.

between the forces of reform and those defending the status quo. This perspective depreciates the role of ideas or conceptions of the public good as factors in politics, disparaging the "statesman model" of constitutional development as unrealistic.[125] Given this understanding of state constitution-making, one would not expect the products of this process to embody a coherent design or an overarching perspective on politics any more than one would expect it of a collection of state statutes. Rather, state constitutions register the result of group conflict within the state at the point at which their various provisions were adopted.

Building upon the Perspectives

Each of these perspectives affords valuable insights into state constitutional development—or, more negatively, none of them by itself provides a fully adequate understanding of state constitutionalism.[126] Most likely, any comprehensive account of state constitutionalism must incorporate elements of all three perspectives. Such a synthesis is possible in part because, although the preceding description highlighted the distinctiveness of each perspective, there are also common elements and overlaps among them. The indigenous political forces emphasized by the ordinary-politics perspective, for example, may well reflect the political culture of the state or mirror political cleavages found throughout the nation. Moreover, national political developments can influence the political culture of a state or affect the fortunes of political forces within it. The political-culture and ordinary-politics perspectives both emphasize the importance of intrastate factors, whereas the national-forces perspective obviously views national factors as decisive. Yet because adjacent states often share a common political culture, both the political-culture and national-forces perspectives, in contrast with the ordinary-politics perspective, look for interstate similarities in constitutional politics and constitutional design. Finally, the political-culture perspective suggests that a state constitution typically manifests a coherent view of politics, whereas the national-forces perspective expects coherence only among provisions adopted within a particular era, and the ordinary-politics perspective expects none at all.

The next three chapters examine the constitutional experience of the American states with these perspectives in mind. Chapter 3 considers

---

[125] See, for example, Cornwell, Goodman, and Swanson, *State Constitutional Conventions*, 33–34; and Press, "Assessing the Policy," 111.

[126] This should not be taken as criticism of the authors identified with the three perspectives. In order to clarify the various perspectives, this analysis has treated them as ideal types, ignoring various nuances and qualifications offered by the authors.

state constitutionalism during the American Founding, the most intensively studied period of state constitutional development. Chapter 4 examines state constitutional development during the nineteenth century, the era of greatest constitutional revision. Chapter 5 surveys state constitutionalism during the twentieth century, an era marked by a decline in constitutional revision, a rise in constitutional amendment, and a new reliance on judicial interpretation as a mechanism of constitutional development.

CHAPTER 3

Eighteenth-Century State Constitutionalism

THE LAST QUARTER of the eighteenth century was a period of intense constitution-making activity in the American states. By 1800, the sixteen states that comprised the Union had adopted twenty-four constitutions, and four other state constitutions were proposed but rejected (see table 3.1). (In contrast, only eighteen amendments to state constitutions were adopted during the period, and ten states did not amend their constitutions at all.[1]) Prior to independence, some colonies viewed the framing of constitutions as a mechanism for promoting a dissolution of ties with Great Britain. Thus, when Massachusetts applied to the Continental Congress in May 1775 for the "most explicit advice, respecting the taking up and exercising the powers of civil government," it did so largely to prod Congress toward decisive action.[2] Similar petitions from New Hampshire and South Carolina in the fall of 1775 exerted further pressure on Congress, which equivocated, recommending that each state devise whatever form of government it deemed necessary "during the Continuance of the present dispute between Great Britain and the colonies."[3] Following this advice, New Hampshire in January 1776 drafted a constitution; and three other states—South Carolina, Virginia, and New Jersey—also did so prior to the Declaration of Independence. The Declaration accelerated the process of constitution making, so that by mid-1777 ten of the original states had adopted constitutions. Two states, Connecticut and Rhode Island, retained their colonial charters with only minor modifications as their fundamental law into the nineteenth century. Massachusetts took longer to devise its constitution, rejecting an initial version in 1778 before adopting in 1780 the constitution that it has retained to the present day.

Some early state constitutions were admittedly provisional: New Jersey's, for instance, included a section under which the constitution be-

---

[1] The amendments to the early state constitutions are collected in Swindler, *Sources and Documents*.

[2] Gordon S. Wood, *The Creation of the American Republic, 1776–1787* (New York: Norton, 1969), 129–31.

[3] Quoted in Wood, *Creation of American Republic*, 130. The Continental Congress may have refrained from imposing a single framework of government out of a fear that some states would not abide this imposition.

TABLE 3.1
State Constitutions, 1776–1800

State	Year(s) of Adoption
Connecticut	Retained colonial charter (1818)
Delaware	1776 1792
Georgia	1777 1789 1798
Kentucky	1792 1799
Maryland	1776
Massachusetts	1780
New Hampshire	1776 1784
New Jersey	1776
New York	1777
North Carolina	1776
Pennsylvania	1776 1790
Rhode Island	Retained colonial charter (1842)
South Carolina	1776 1778 1790
Tennessee	1796
Vermont	1777 1786 1793
Virginia	1776

came inoperative in the event of a reconciliation with Britain.[4] Other early constitutions, although not designed as temporary, proved to be so. Within two decades after adopting their initial constitutions, six states had replaced them; and by 1800 Georgia, South Carolina, and Vermont were on their third constitutions. Yet nine constitutions framed before 1800 survived more than fifty years.[5] Six states revised their charters from 1788 to 1800, and Kentucky and Tennessee devised their initial constitutions during the 1790s, giving these states the opportunity to draw upon the model provided by the federal Constitution.

These eighteenth-century documents differed from later state constitutions in both their length and their contents. If one excludes the often-lengthy preambles to these constitutions, several of the initial documents

[4] The New Jersey Constitution of 1776, article 23, stated: "Provided always, and it is the true Intent Meaning of this Congress, that if Reconciliation between Great Britain and these Colonies should take place, and the latter be again taken under the Protection and Government of the Crown of Great Britain, this Charter shall be null and void, otherwise to remain firm and inviolable." Similar provisions are found in the preambles of the New Hampshire and South Carolina constitutions framed prior to independence.

[5] Some of the earliest state constitutions proved the most durable. Four constitutions framed in 1776—those of New Jersey, Virginia, Maryland, and North Carolina—all lasted over half a century. Their durability challenges the assumption that over time the states' experience in constitution making led to greater expertise and produced better results.

were even shorter than the federal Constitution.[6] For the most part these constitutions confined themselves to creating the state's governmental institutions, defining the processes by which these institutions would operate, outlining how and by whom state offices would be filled, and delineating rights. Many features characteristic of later state constitutions were severely circumscribed or altogether absent. The early constitutions rarely attempted to set public policy or to prescribe matters of public finance.[7] They did not define either the structure or powers of local governments, although most used counties or towns as basic units in apportioning one or both houses of the state legislature.[8] They imposed few restrictions on those legislatures beyond those contained in their declarations of rights, and four state constitutions did not even include declarations of rights.[9] Finally, six state constitutions failed to prescribe any procedures for their amendment or revision.[10]

[6] Although these early constitutions—like their successors—were heavily criticized, their critics seldom complained that the constitutions included excessive detail or constitutionalized matters that did not warrant inclusion in a constitution. The only such criticism involved the state declarations of rights, which, according to Alexander Hamilton in *Federalist* no. 84, consisted largely of "aphorisms . . . which would sound much better in a treatise of ethics than in a constitution of government." See Clinton Rossiter, ed., *The Federalist Papers* (New York: New American Library, 1961), 513.

[7] There were inevitably some instances of constitutional legislation. Some states dealt with naturalization in their constitutions: see Pennsylvania Constitution of 1776, sec. 42; North Carolina Constitution of 1776, art. 40; New York Constitution of 1777, art. 42; and Vermont Constitution of 1777, sec. 38. Vermont outlawed slavery, and two other New England states included provisions that set them on the path to abolition: Vermont Constitution of 1777, Declaration of Rights, art. 1; Massachusetts Constitution of 1780, Declaration of Rights, art. 1; and New Hampshire Constitution of 1784, Bill of Rights, arts. 1 and 2. Several states also dealt, albeit briefly, with public education: see, for example, Pennsylvania Constitution of 1776, sec. 44; North Carolina Constitution of 1776, art. 41; Vermont Constitution of 1777, sec. 40; and Massachusetts Constitution of 1780, chap. 5, sec. 2 (which was copied in the New Hampshire Constitution of 1784). The most extensive constitutional policymaking involved state policy toward religion. Pertinent state constitutional provisions are discussed in Chester J. Antieau, Phillip M. Carroll, and Thomas C. Burke, *Religion under the State Constitutions* (Brooklyn: Central Book Company, 1965); Thomas J. Curry, *The First Freedoms: Church and State in America to the Passage of the First Amendment* (New York: Oxford University Press, 1986); Leonard W. Levy, *The Establishment Clause: Religion and the First Amendment* (New York: Macmillan, 1986), chaps. 1–2; and William Lee Miller, *The First Liberty: Religion and the American Republic* (New York: Alfred A. Knopf, 1986).

[8] For competing explanations of this omission, see Herget, "Missing Power"; and Libonati, "Home Rule."

[9] Those states without formal declarations of rights in their initial constitutions include New Hampshire, South Carolina, New Jersey, and New York. Several of these constitutions did include some rights guarantees in the body of the document. Connecticut and Rhode Island, which were governed under their charters, also had no declarations of rights.

[10] Those states without formal procedures for amendment or revision in their initial

The pressure of events explains some of these omissions. The New York legislature, for example, was almost constantly on the run from the British forces—two members wryly suggested that it might be better "first to endeavour to secure a State to govern, before we established a form to govern it by"—and fear of invasion prompted the New Jersey legislature to frame and adopt a constitution in less than two weeks.[11] Inexperience in constitution making may also have been a factor. Three of the first four states to draft constitutions omitted declarations of rights and mechanisms for constitutional change, whereas most later constitutions included them.[12] However, some omissions reflected deliberate choices. None of the states that adopted their constitutions in the 1780s or 1790s or that revised their constitutions during that period included provisions on local government or on public finance.[13] And no state imposed detailed constitutional limitations on state legislative power until well into the nineteenth century.[14] Thus, the understanding of constitutional design clearly differed from that of later eras.

Some scholars have argued that the political theory of the early state constitutions differs fundamentally from that of the federal Constitu-

---

constitutions included New Hampshire, South Carolina, Virginia, New Jersey, North Carolina, and New York. In addition, Connecticut and Rhode Island had no established procedures in the charters they initially relied upon as fundamental law. See Hoar, *Constitutional Conventions,* 8.

[11] The two delegates are quoted in Willi Paul Adams, *The First American Constitutions: Republican Ideology and the Making of the State Constitutions in the Revolutionary Era* (Chapel Hill: University of North Carolina Press, 1980), 85–86. Allan Nevins speculated that the haste of New Jersey's constitution-makers was due in part to the news that "Howe had landed at Sandy Point." See Nevins, *The American States during and after the Revolution* (New York: Macmillan, 1924), 139. For a more detailed analysis of constitution making in New Jersey, see Charles Erdman Jr., *The New Jersey Constitution of 1776* (Princeton: Princeton University Press, 1929).

[12] Virginia, the third state to adopt a constitution, did develop a declaration of rights, but it was framed and adopted separately from the "Constitution or Form of Government."

[13] The Kentucky constitutional convention of 1792, for example, rejected a major effort to constitutionalize tax policy. See Joan Wells Coward, *Kentucky in the New Republic: The Process of Constitution Making* (Lexington: University Press of Kentucky, 1979), 35–36. Article 1, section 27 of the Tennessee Constitution of 1796 contained the first hint of state constitutional regulation of public finance, forbidding taxation on goods manufactured in the state.

[14] The Georgia Constitution of 1789 was amended in 1795 to limit the state legislature to those powers expressly enumerated in the constitution. However, article 1, section 22 of the Georgia Constitution of 1798 reversed this, indicating that "[t]he general assembly shall have power to make all laws and ordinances which they shall deem necessary and proper for the good of the State, which shall not be repugnant to this constitution." For discussion of these developments, see Donald S. Lutz, *Popular Consent and Popular Control: Whig Political Theory in the Early State Constitutions* (Baton Rouge: Louisiana State University Press, 1980), 164 n. 23.

tion.[15] State constitutions, they insist, embodied civic-republican political theory, which emphasized a participatory politics and the sacrifice of private interests and rights in the service of the common good. In contrast, the federal Constitution embodied Federalist political theory, which recognized that most people were motivated by self-interest and success in the private sphere and created a politics that would guarantee the protection of rights of individuals. However, other scholars have denied that a major shift occurred in American political thought during the late eighteenth century.[16] What is clear is that those attending the Philadelphia convention of 1787 viewed most state constitutions as seriously defective, models for avoidance rather than emulation.[17] This was hardly

[15] Wood, *Creation of American Republic*. Wood's account of state constitutions is at the heart of the scholarly controversy over civic republicanism. Other scholars of the American Founding who have insisted that there was a fundamental ideological divide during the Founding, with civic republicanism and Lockean liberalism as the competing alternatives, include Bernard Bailyn and J. G. A. Pocock. See Bailyn, *Ideological Origins of the American Revolution* (Cambridge, Mass.: Belknap Press, 1967); and Pocock, *The Machiavellian Moment: Florentine Political Thought and the Atlantic Republican Tradition* (Princeton: Princeton University Press, 1975). For analyses of early state constitutions informed by Wood's account, see Elazar, "Principles and Traditions"; and Lutz, *Popular Consent*.

[16] Some scholars have denied that there is a fundamental disjunction between Lockean liberalism and civic republicanism. Works elaborating this position include Thomas L. Pangle, *The Spirit of Modern Republicanism: The Moral Vision of the American Founders and the Philosophy of Locke* (Chicago: University of Chicago Press, 1988); Michael Zuckert, *Natural Rights and the New Republicanism* (Princeton: Princeton University Press, 1994); and Paul A. Rahe, *Republics Ancient and Modern: Classical Republicanism and the American Revolution* (Chapel Hill: University of North Carolina Press, 1992). Akhil Reed Amar has taken a different tack, arguing that civic-republican themes are found in the federal Constitution, particularly the Bill of Rights. See Akhil Reed Amar, "The Bill of Rights as a Constitution," *Yale Law Journal* 100 (March 1991): 1131–1210. Finally, Marc Kruman has insisted that the political theory of the federal Constitution is likewise evident in the earliest state constitutions. See Marc W. Kruman, *Between Authority and Liberty: State Constitution Making in Revolutionary America* (Chapel Hill: University of North Carolina Press, 1997).

[17] In a July 4 address attended by the delegates to the convention, Benjamin Rush suggested that the authors of the early state constitutions "understood perfectly the principles of liberty" but most "were ignorant of the forms and combinations of power in republics." Quoted in Edward S. Corwin, "The Progress of Constitutional Theory between the Declaration of Independence and the Meeting of the Philadelphia Convention," in Richard Loss, ed., *Corwin on the Constitution*, vol. 1 (Ithaca, N.Y.: Cornell University Press, 1981), 58. James Madison in *Federalist* no. 47 echoed these sentiments, observing that the state constitutions "carry strong marks of the haste, and still stronger of the inexperience, under which they were framed." See *The Federalist Papers*, 307. For negative assessments of state constitutions at the Philadelphia convention, see Max Farrand, ed., *The Records of the Federal Convention of 1787*, 4 vols. (New Haven: Yale University Press, 1966), 1:26–27, 48, 133–36, 360, 424, 511–13, 525, 533, 571; 2:35, 74, 112–13, 285, 288. It is thus no surprise that the Founders' task has been described as "saving the revolution." See Charles R. Kesler, *Saving the Revolution: The Federalist Papers and the American Founding* (New York: Free Press, 1987).

surprising, for several state constitutions instituted annual elections, eschewed checks and balances, stripped the executive of meaningful powers, and/or concentrated almost all power in the legislature. However, not all state constitutions shared these objectionable features. Some anticipated the strengthened executive, the checks and balances, the extended legislative terms, and other features of the federal Constitution; in fact they may have served as models for federal constitution-makers.[18] Although it is conceivable that the state and federal constitutions adopted the same provisions for different reasons, the diversity among state constitutions and the resemblance between some of them and the federal Constitution caution against blanket statements about differences in political perspective between state and federal charters.

EIGHTEENTH-CENTURY CONSTITUTIONAL DEVELOPMENT: AN OVERVIEW

The initial years of American constitution-making were unique in American constitutional development. All the states faced a common agenda of constitutional problems inherent in the formation of new governments: justifying the change of regime, establishing the authority of their new constitutions, determining what elements in the population would participate in governing, creating political institutions, and safeguarding rights. As noted in chapter 1, historically three issues—the intrastate distribution of political power, the scope of state governmental power, and the relation of the state to economic activity—have dominated state constitutional politics. However, only the first of these emerged as a major concern during the eighteenth century. This was not for lack of controversy over the exercise of state power or over state economic policies (although the exigencies of waging war tempered constitutional conflicts in most states during the Revolution).[19] Rather, it was simply that these political issues did not become *state constitutional* issues. The victors in state politics rarely wrote their economic prescriptions into the state constitution.[20] State policies were transformed into constitutional issues, but

[18] Both the text and design of the federal Constitution reveal the extent to which the Philadelphia convention borrowed from state constitutions. For a detailed survey, see Bryce, *The American Commonwealth,* 1:609–13.

[19] A notable exception was Pennsylvania, which experienced fierce conflict over the state constitution from 1776 to 1790. For an account of this conflict, see Selsam, *Pennsylvania Constitution of 1776.* Yet even in Pennsylvania the conflict centered—at least overtly—more on structural features of the constitution, such as unicameralism and the separation of powers, than on qualifications for political participation, regional rivalries, or economic policy.

[20] On the economic conflicts in the states during the late eighteenth century, see Nevins, *American States;* Jackson Turner Main, *The Sovereign States, 1775–1783* (New York: New Viewpoints, 1973); and Ronald Hoffman and Peter J. Albert, eds., *Sovereign States in an Age of Uncertainty* (Charlottesville: University Press of Virginia, 1981).

this occurred at the national level. Abuses of power by state legislatures and unjust state economic policies were among the primary complaints of the delegates to the Philadelphia convention, and they ensured that the federal Constitution addressed itself to these issues.[21]

Some of the similarities found among state constitutions of the era can be traced to the states' common experience of British tyranny, which they understood in terms of a shared republican political theory. The recognition that they confronted common problems also prompted states to consult the constitutions of all the other states, and their inexperience in constitutional design encouraged extensive borrowing. Vermont, for example, copied major portions of Pennsylvania's 1776 constitution, and states as diverse as North Carolina, Massachusetts, and Pennsylvania all incorporated most protections of the Virginia Declaration of Rights into their constitutions. What variation did exist among state governments of the period could be attributed primarily to two factors. One was the states' retention of distinctive institutional arrangements and practices from their colonial governments. These might include, depending on the state, the structure of the court system, the organization of local government, suffrage requirements, and the system of apportionment. Even distinctive features, such as the unicameral legislature in Pennsylvania, had their origins prior to independence.[22] The other factor was the development of constitutional theory in the states in response to political experience. According to Donald Lutz, this evolution was reflected in three "waves" of state constitution-making.[23] During the first wave (immediately prior to and following independence), a reaction to abuses by the Crown led constitution-makers to concentrate power in state legislatures. The states' greater experience in constitutional design, together with their admittedly brief experience with unchecked legislative power, prompted a second wave of constitution making, beginning with the New York Constitution of 1777, in which executive power was augmented. Following 1787, the new model for constitutional design offered by the federal Constitution inaugurated a third wave of constitutional reform. Thus, according to this view, the diversity among state constitutions reflects the differing views of appropriate constitutional design at their dates of origin. Although our analysis will qualify somewhat the sharp distinctions that Lutz draws, there is no denying the evolution of constitutional thought during the late eighteenth century.

---

[21] Article 1, section 8 of the United States Constitution grants certain commercial and monetary powers to Congress that had previously been exercised by state governments; Article 1, section 10 prohibits state governments from exercising various powers.

[22] See Selsam, *Pennsylvania Constitution of 1776*, 183–84.

[23] Lutz, *Popular Consent*, 44–52.

THE PROBLEM OF AUTHORITY

A pressing issue confronting those who framed the initial state constitutions was justifying the states' assumption of governmental authority. To some extent, they could point to the authorization from the Continental Congress as justification for the states' actions. Yet for the most part their justification was based on the doctrine of popular sovereignty and on consent theory. State constitution-makers thus also had to explain how they could claim the authority to speak and act for the people of the state. Their resolution of these issues in turn influenced their approach to formal constitutional change.

The Assumption of Governmental Authority

The four constitutions adopted prior to independence justified the assumption of governmental authority as a temporary expedient necessitated by the breakdown of government in the colonies. The New Hampshire Constitution adopted in January 1776 established a government "for the preservation of peace and good order, and for the security of the lives and properties of the inhabitants of this colony" that was "to continue during the present unhappy and unnatural contest with Great Britain."[24] The South Carolina Constitution of 1776 insisted that reconciliation with Britain was "an event which . . . we still earnestly desire," and—as noted previously—the New Jersey Constitution included an escape clause rendering the constitution inoperative in the event of such a reconciliation.[25]

After the Declaration of Independence, the constitutions framed in late 1776 included lengthy preambles justifying independence and the formation of new governments on the basis of social-compact theory.[26] They asserted that "all political power is vested in and derived from the people only" and that the people consequently have "an incontestable, unalienable, and indefeasible right" to "reform, alter, or totally change [government] when their protection, safety, prosperity, and happiness require it."[27] Indeed, several insisted that even British rule over the colonies had

[24] New Hampshire Constitution of 1776, par. 2.

[25] South Carolina Constitution of 1776, Preamble.

[26] This is made most explicit in the preamble of the Massachusetts Constitution of 1780, which states: "The body-politic is formed by a voluntary association of individuals; it is a social compact by which the whole people covenants with each citizen and each citizen with the whole people that all shall be governed by certain laws for the common good." See also Vermont Constitution, Preamble; Virginia Constitution, Declaration of Rights, sec. 1; and Delaware, Declaration of Rights, art. 1.

[27] On political power as rooted in consent, see, for example, North Carolina Constitu-

its basis in consent. Connecticut, which retained its Charter government, maintained that the "form of Civil Government" was "contained" in the Charter received from Charles II but "adopted by the People of the State."[28] With this theoretical underpinning in place, the preambles reviewed the tyrannical actions and violations of rights by the king and Parliament that had led the American people to withdraw their consent. The New York Constitution of 1777 even incorporated verbatim extended excerpts from the Declaration of Independence in its preamble. This catalog of offenses made sense from a social-compact perspective, because the creation of a new compact required explanation of why the old one was no longer binding. The dissolution of government produced by the withdrawal of popular consent required the formation of a new government that would "promote their safety and happiness." Some preambles defined this safety and happiness in terms of the exercise of individual rights. The Pennsylvania Constitution of 1776, for example, saw the formation of a new government as necessary "for the security and protection of the community as such, and to enable the individuals who compose it to enjoy their natural rights, and the other blessings which the Author of existence has bestowed on man."[29] And the Massachusetts Constitution declared that the end of government was "to secure the existence of the body-politic, to protect it, and to furnish the individuals who compose it with the power of enjoying, in safety and tranquillity, their natural rights and the blessings of life."[30] Other states' preambles spoke in more general terms, seeking a constitution "most conducive to [the people's] happiness and prosperity" or one that would "best conduce to the safety and happiness of their constituents."[31] By the time the states revised their original constitutions, they no longer needed to justify

---

tion of 1776, Declaration of Rights, art. 1; Massachusetts Constitution of 1780, Preamble; and New Hampshire Constitution of 1784, Bill of Rights, art. 1. The most detailed declaration of the right of the people to alter their governments is found in the Massachusetts Constitution of 1780, art. 7. For discussion of these provisions, see Lutz, *Popular Consent*, chaps. 2–3; and Akhil Reed Amar, "The Consent of the Governed," *Columbia Law Review* 94 (March 1994): 457–508. A more general overview is provided by Christian G. Fritz, "Alternative Visions of American Constitutionalism: Popular Sovereignty and the Early American Constitutional Debate," *Hastings Constitutional Law Quarterly* 24 (winter 1997): 287–357.

[28] Connecticut Constitutional Ordinance of 1776, Preamble.

[29] Pennsylvania Constitution of 1776, Preamble. See also Vermont Constitution of 1777, Preamble; and Massachusetts Constitution of 1780, Preamble.

[30] Massachusetts Constitution of 1780, Preamble.

[31] Maryland Constitution of 1776, Preamble; and Georgia Constitution of 1777, Preamble.

the creation of governments, so most deleted these justifications from their constitutions.[32]

The Authority to Frame a Constitution

If all political power was "vested in and derived from the people," then the question became how the people could exercise that power. Although legislative assemblies adopted the earliest state constitutions, almost immediately questions arose about their authority to act for the people.[33] The notion that a legislature, even if "a full and free representation of the people," might lack sufficient authority reflected a recognition, present from the outset, that constitutions differed from ordinary statutes and that greater popular input and control were required for their adoption.[34] In the absence of an established mechanism for ensuring this popular input and control, the states experimented with various alternatives. Among those states that drafted constitutions, every state except Virginia and South Carolina called for special elections for the bodies that would draft the documents, in order to secure authorization and canvass public sentiment.[35] South Carolina scheduled a year of public discussion before drafting its 1778 constitution. Delaware pioneered the idea of a distinct body for framing a constitution. Georgia and Massachusetts abandoned the taxpaying qualification for voting in order that the entire people could participate in the creation of their constitutions. After the adoption of its constitution, New Jersey ordered that one thousand copies be printed and "dispers[ed]" among the citizenry for their consideration.[36] Maryland, North Carolina, and Pennsylvania took a step further, distributing copies of their constitutions to the people for their response before

[32] For example, the preamble to the South Carolina Constitution of 1778 is about one-sixth the length of the preamble to the state's 1776 constitution.

[33] Illustrative of the contemporary recognition of the problem is "The Alarm: or, an Address to the People of Pennsylvania on the Late Resolve of Congress," reprinted in Charles S. Hyneman and Donald S. Lutz, eds., *American Political Writing during the Founding Era*, 2 vols. (Indianapolis: Liberty Press, 1983), 1:321–27. The present account draws primarily on Adams, *The First American Constitutions*, chap. 3; Green, *Constitutional Development*, 61–62; Wood, *Creation of American Republic*, chap. 8; Lutz, *Popular Consent*, chap. 3; and Kruman, *Between Authority and Liberty*, chap. 2. Kruman emphasizes that the legislative assemblies were typically not state legislatures but revolutionary bodies and thus more likely to involve something approximating a direct representation of the people.

[34] South Carolina Constitution of 1776, art. 1. Several other early constitutions also emphasized the representative character of the body that adopted them. See Fritz, "Alternative Visions," 322–34.

[35] Kruman, *Between Authority and Liberty*, 20.

[36] Erdman, *New Jersey Constitution*, 38.

final passage. Eventually, of course, popular input into and control over constitution making were institutionalized through popular election of conventions specially empowered to draft constitutions, with ratification by referendum. However, not until 1780 with the adoption of the Massachusetts Constitution were these two elements coupled in the process of constitutional creation, and prior to 1800 only one other state constitution (the New Hampshire Constitution of 1784) was framed using this procedure.[37]

These various efforts to institutionalize a popular role in constitution making underscore the states' recognition that a constitution's authority rested on consent. The eventual adoption of the constitutional convention and referendum as the mechanisms to ensure such consent also typifies the process of interstate borrowing of constitutional innovations. Such innovations usually gain acceptance only gradually, as states experiment with alternative solutions to a common problem before eventually adopting a particular approach, and this is what occurred in this case.

Implications for Constitutional Change

The shared understanding that the people are the source of constitutional authority alerted the states to a further problem: if a legislature could not create a constitution, then neither could it re-create the constitution by altering it. In particular, a legislature could not enhance the powers that the constitution granted to it nor exercise those withheld from it.[38] But for this stricture to be effective, there had to be some means of ensuring that the legislature—and other branches as well—abided by the constitution.[39] In addition, in order to discourage circumvention of

---

[37] It may not be coincidental that popular ratification developed in two New England states, where the institution of town meetings provided a mechanism for assessing the will of the people. For an examination of how this worked in practice, see Oscar Handlin and Mary Handlin, eds., *The Popular Sources of Political Authority: Documents on the Massachusetts Constitution of 1780* (Cambridge, Mass.: Belknap Press, 1966). Submission of constitutions to the people for approval did not become an established practice until 1829. See Dodd, *Revision and Amendment*, 64–65. The delay in adopting the Massachusetts model may have reflected a general satisfaction with the adequacy of other means of securing popular consent.

[38] This is not to deny that state legislatures sometimes acted as if they had authority to change state constitutions unilaterally. For examples, see Wood, *Creation of the American Republic*, 274–75. Yet Wood's examples involve either unimportant transgressions—for example, the New Jersey legislature substituting "state" for "colony" in the constitution following independence—or actions taken in wartime emergencies. No legislature proclaimed a general power to alter the state constitution. Indeed, the New Jersey legislature refused to undertake revision of the state constitution three times during the 1790s because it viewed that as beyond its power. See Erdman, *New Jersey Constitution*, 76–77.

[39] This analysis emphasizes legislative overstepping of constitutional bounds because the

constitutional limitations, there also had to be avenues for legitimate constitutional change, when such change was needed.

Ensuring Constitutional Fidelity

Several early state constitutions sought to encourage constitutional fidelity by exhortation, declaring that the legislature "shall have no power to add to, alter, abolish, or infringe any part of this Constitution."[40] Some demanded oaths of state officials that they would not violate their constitutional trust. Yet typically these oaths asked too little or too much. An example of the former was the requirement found in the New Jersey Constitution that legislators swear not to enact laws that would "annul or repeal" the constitutional requirements of annual legislative sessions, religious freedom, and jury trial.[41] This left one to wonder whether other constitutional requirements could be violated with impunity. An example of the latter was the oath demanded of officeholders by the Pennsylvania Constitution, pledging them not to "directly or indirectly do any act or thing prejudicial or injurious to the constitution or government thereof." Opponents of the constitution attacked the provision, arguing that it infringed on their right to seek constitutional change, and the validity of their complaint was recognized by allowing them to annex a reservation to the oath.[42]

Some early state constitutions did propose institutional devices for enforcing constitutional limitations. The most famous of these was the Council of Censors, established under the Pennsylvania and Vermont constitutions.[43] The council, which met every seven years, was charged with reviewing whether violations of the constitution had occurred or whether experience had exposed deficiencies in the state's constitution. However, because it was for the most part limited to recommending action by the legislature, the effectiveness of its recommendations depended

---

early state constitutions tended to concentrate powers in the legislature. In the words of James Wilson, "[T]he executive and the judicial as well as the legislative authority was now the child of the people; but, to the two former, the people behaved like step-mothers. The legislature was still discriminated by excessive partiality; and into its lap, every good and precious gift was profusely thrown." Quoted in Charles C. Thach, *The Creation of the Presidency, 1775–1789: A Study in Constitutional History* (Baltimore: John Hopkins Press, 1922), 27. See also *Federalist* nos. 47–48.

[40] North Carolina Constitution of 1776, art. 44; Maryland Constitution of 1776, Declaration of Rights, art. 59; Delaware Constitution of 1776, art. 30; Pennsylvania Constitution of 1776, sec. 9; Georgia Constitution of 1777, art. 7; and Vermont Constitution of 1777, sec. 8.

[41] New Jersey Constitution of 1776, art. 23.

[42] Pennsylvania Constitution of 1776, sec. 40; Nevins, *American States,* 257.

[43] The best recent discussion of this institution is found in Lutz, *Popular Consent,* chap. 6. James Madison discusses the Council of Censors in *Federalist* nos. 48 and 50.

on popular pressure for appropriate action. Similarly ineffective were constitutional provisions mandating a separation of powers. Although these provisions decreed that no branch should exercise the powers properly belonging to another, the experience of the states showed that "a mere demarcation on parchment of the constitutional limits of the several departments [was] not a sufficient guard against encroachments."[44] Those state constitutions that made governors dependent on legislatures and stripped them of weapons to counter legislative encroachments actually facilitated legislative violations of the separation of powers. Only those constitutions that granted governors independent authority and adequate powers produced a durable separation of powers.[45]

Intentionally omitted from this list of enforcement mechanisms is judicial enforcement of constitutional requirements. The notion that judges could invalidate all governmental actions inconsistent with their interpretation of the constitution was simply unknown in the 1770s and early 1780s and would have been considered far beyond the scope of legitimate judicial power.[46] Only three states expressly granted the judiciary a role in reviewing legislation: New York through judicial participation with the executive on the Council of Revision, and New Hampshire and Massachusetts through advisory opinions on constitutionality. However, the decisions of the Council of Revision could be overridden by two-thirds of the legislature, and the advisory opinions of judges in New Hampshire and Massachusetts were not binding.[47] Moreover, state judiciaries were typically too subservient to state legislatures to provide a consistently effective check. Most judges were elected by the legislatures, some for quite limited terms, and in several states they could be removed on address by a majority of the legislature.[48] Indeed, when a Rhode Is-

---

[44] *Federalist* no. 48, 313.

[45] On early state governors, see Thach, *Creation of the Presidency,* chap. 2; and Wood, *Creation of American Republic,* chaps. 4 and 10. The powers of state executives were considerably enhanced during the 1780s and 1790s.

[46] Even scholars with quite different understandings of the development of judicial power concur in this assessment, viewing the alleged state "precedents" for judicial review during the 1780s as involving practices quite distinct from modern judicial review. See, for example, Sylvia Snowiss, *Judicial Review and the Law of the Constitution* (New Haven: Yale University Press, 1990), chap. 2; and Robert L. Clinton, *Marbury v. Madison and Judicial Review* (Lawrence: University Press of Kansas, 1989), chap. 3.

[47] New York Constitution of 1777, art. 3; Massachusetts Constitution of 1780, chap. 3, art. 2; and New Hampshire Constitution of 1784, part 2, "Judiciary Power." Judicial advisory opinions seem to serve the same purpose as the findings of the Council of Censors, an example of somewhat different institutions serving a common function.

[48] See Wood, *Creation of American Republic,* 152–61. State constitutions were slow to mark off the judiciary as a distinct branch of government. New Jersey, for example, did not even vest ultimate judicial authority in the courts; rather, the governor and Legislative Council served as the state's "Court of Appeals in the Last Resort." See the New Jersey Constitution of 1776, art. 9; and, more generally, Friedman, *History of American Law,*

land court refused to enforce a statute, the judges were called before the legislature to explain their ruling and threatened with removal, and at the next judicial election all but one lost their seats.[49]

State constitutions therefore relied primarily on the state's citizenry for enforcement of constitutional limitations, with annual election of legislators the key element of this process.[50] Several constitutions encouraged a "frequent recurrence to fundamental principles," and some admonished voters to "pay particular attention to these principles" in choosing representatives.[51] This reliance on popular enforcement of constitutional guidelines comported with the strongly popular character of early state governments, which will be discussed shortly. It also reflected an assumption that constitutional violations resulted primarily from officials' deviations from the popular will rather than from unconstitutional aims among the populace. This in turn was based on the notion that the major political conflict was between governors and governed rather than among competing groups within the population.

FORMAL CONSTITUTIONAL CHANGE

The emphasis on popular authority in early state constitutions is also apparent in how they dealt with formal constitutional change. Seventeen constitutions prior to 1800 specified mechanisms for their amendment or revision, most favoring popularly elected constitutional conventions for both. Provisions for conventions ranged from authorization of a single convention fifteen years after ratification (Massachusetts), to authoriza tion of a convention by two-thirds of the Council of Censors (Pennsylvania and Vermont), to legislative convening of a convention at its discretion (Tennessee and Kentucky, among others).[52] Three states—Maryland,

---

139–40. Although there was some effort to increase the independence of the judiciary in the 1780s and 1790s, one commentator has concluded that "[s]tate constitutions after 1789 would pay lip service to the Federalist principle, but four of the seven constitutions written in the third wave would still make the judiciary a complete creature of the legislature." Lutz, *Popular Consent,* 97.

[49] Snowiss, *Judicial Review,* 22, recounting *Trevett v. Weeden* (1786), an unpublished decision described in James M. Varnum, *The Case of Trevett v. Weeden* (Providence: John Carter, 1787). For a study of the uneven development of judicial independence in one state, see G. S. Rowe, *Embattled Bench: The Pennsylvania Supreme Court and the Forging of a Democratic Society* (Newark: University of Delaware Press, 1994).

[50] For a listing of the terms of office of legislators under eighteenth-century state constitutions, see Lutz, *Popular Consent,* 88, table 4.

[51] See, for example, Massachusetts Constitution of 1780, Declaration of Rights, art. 18; Vermont Constitution of 1777, Declaration of Rights, sec. 16; and Virginia Constitution, Declaration of Rights, sec. 15.

[52] The authority of the Council of Censors to call a convention appeared to include the power to set the agenda for the convention, although there is some question as to whether this was intended. See Cecilia M. Kenyon, "Constitutionalism in Revolutionary America,"

Delaware, and South Carolina (1778)—permitted constitutional amendment by the state legislature but required extraordinary majorities to adopt the amendments. Seven states at one time or another had a constitution that did not specify a procedure for constitutional change, and five of those constitutions remained in effect in 1800. But their failure to specify a mechanism for constitutional change was not meant to preclude such change. Rather, it reflected either inadvertence or, more interestingly, the view that such provisions were unnecessary.

What eighteenth-century state constitutions did include was an explicit recognition that political power came from the people, from which they concluded, in the words of the Virginia Declaration of Rights, that "the community hath an indubitable, unalienable, and indefeasible right to reform, alter, or abolish government in such manner as shall be by that community judged most conducive to the public weal."[53] This confirmed that the people did not require amendment or revision provisions to change the constitution; such provisions did not grant a power but merely specified a procedure by which it could be exercised. Certainly the establishment of the states' initial constitutions, undertaken in the absence of legal authorization, illustrated that very point. Perhaps less obviously, it also implied that the people's authority to institute constitutional change was undiminished even in states that did specify amendment procedures; those procedures were simply one means by which constitutional change could be undertaken.[54] State constitutional practice during the late eighteenth century (and beyond) coincided with this understanding: Georgia in 1788 and Pennsylvania in 1790 ignored constitutionally specified procedures in revising their constitutions, justifying their actions as based on the inherent authority of the people to change their form of government.[55]

In a sense, these declarations of popular authority to alter the constitution might be said to have domesticated the Lockean right to revolution. By recognizing the right of the people to change the constitution peace-

---

in J. Roland Pennock and John W. Chapman, eds., *Constitutionalism* (New York: New York University Press, 1979), 105–6.

[53] Virginia Declaration of Rights, art. 3. Most other state constitutions included comparable language: see, for example, Pennsylvania Constitution of 1776, Declaration of Rights, sec. 5; Massachusetts Constitution of 1780, Preamble, and Declaration of Rights, art. 7; New Hampshire Constitution of 1784, Bill of Rights, art. 10; and Georgia Constitution of 1776, Preamble.

[54] Amar, "Consent of the Governed," and Fritz, "Alternative Visions."

[55] Dodd, *Revision and Amendment*, chap. 2; and—more generally—J. Franklin Jameson, *Treatise on Constitutional Conventions*. In "The Consent of the Governed," Akhil Amar argues that *Federalist* no. 40 also supports the idea of popular authority to revise constitutions without following constitutionally prescribed forms.

ably, they reduced the necessity of recourse to violent revolution to secure good government. Yet in another sense, the declarations went considerably beyond Locke. Serious violations of rights or a plan to tyrannize were not necessary to trigger constitutional revision; changing popular views of what would produce effective government were a sufficient justification for constitutional change.[56]

RIGHTS

The Virginia Declaration of Rights inaugurated the practice of including separate protections for rights in state constitutions, and after its adoption, only four states failed to include a declaration of rights in their constitutions.[57] Subsequent declarations added to Virginia's inventory of rights—Pennsylvania, for example, included the right to instruct representatives and to petition for redress of grievances, and Tennessee a right to navigate the Mississippi River—or dealt in greater detail with topics such as church and state.[58] Nevertheless, the similarities among the states' declarations of rights are striking. All proclaim the same political principles and protect the same set of basic rights. Moreover, because

[56] A similar argument is made by Fritz, "Alternative Visions," 294–96.

[57] On the derivation of the Virginia Declaration of Rights (and other state declarations of rights), see A. E. Dick Howard, *The Road from Runnymede: Magna Carta and Constitutionalism in America* (Charlottesville: University Press of Virginia, 1968); and Donald S. Lutz, *The Origins of American Constitutionalism* (Baton Rouge: Louisiana State University Press, 1988), 62. New Jersey's constitution-makers, who completed work on the state's constitution only twenty days after the Virginia Declaration of Rights was adopted, did not have the Virginia declaration available to them. The New Jersey Constitution omitted a declaration of rights, although some rights—for example, the right to counsel in criminal cases, religious liberty, and the right to trial by jury—were protected in the body of the document, and the common law continued in operation. See New Jersey Constitution, arts. 16–19, 22. Other states without a declaration of rights in their constitutions are Georgia (1777, 1789), South Carolina (1776, 1778, and 1790), and New York (1777). Georgia embedded a few rights in its first two constitutions and added a declaration of rights to its 1798 charter. See Georgia Constitution of 1777, arts. 56 and 58–61, and Georgia Constitution of 1789, art. 4, secs. 3–6. South Carolina's earliest constitution antedated the Virginia declaration, and its later constitutions protected some rights in the body of the document but failed to create a full-fledged declaration of rights. See South Carolina Constitution of 1778, secs. 40–43, and South Carolina Constitution of 1790, arts. 8–9. The New York Constitution recognized the importance of protecting rights—according to the preamble, its aim was formation of a government "best calculated to secure the rights and liberties of the good people of this State"—but included only guarantees of religious liberty and trial by jury, together with a ban on bills of attainder. It did, however, guarantee the continued operation of the common law, which presumably afforded further protections. See New York Constitution of 1777, arts. 35, 38, 41.

[58] See Pennsylvania Constitution of 1776, Declaration of Rights, art. 16; and Tennessee Constitution of 1796, art. 11, sec. 31.

they all draw upon the Virginia declaration, their protections often match each other word for word.

The Distinctiveness of State Declarations of Rights

Early state declarations of rights differ from the federal Bill of Rights in several respects.[59] One difference is the frequent (though not consistent) use of the hortatory *ought,* rather than the more mandatory *shall,* in the state declarations. The Virginia Declaration of Rights, for example, declares that "excessive bail *ought* not to be required"; the Pennsylvania Declaration that "freedom of the press *ought* not to be restrained"; the New Hampshire Declaration that "[a]ll penalties *ought* to be proportioned to the nature of the offense"; and the Massachusetts Declaration that "[a]ll elections *ought* to be free."[60] Although this usage declined in the 1790s, perhaps reflecting the influence of the federal Bill of Rights, some constitutions framed during that decade retained the earlier hortatory language.[61] A second difference is the state declarations' inclusion of general statements of political principle not susceptible to judicial enforcement. The Pennsylvania Declaration of Rights, for instance, declared that "government is, or ought to be, instituted for the common benefit, protection and security of the people, nation or community; and not for the particular emolument or advantage of any single man, family or set of men, who are a part only of that community."[62] Similarly, the Delaware Declaration of Rights asserted that "a well regulated Militia is the proper, natural and safe Defense of a free Government"; and the Virginia Declaration of Rights that "all men are by nature equally free and independent, and have certain inherent rights, of which, when they enter into a state of society, they cannot, by any compact, deprive or divest their posterity."[63] Even provisions that might be enforceable sometimes included explanatory or justificatory verbiage—Delaware's guarantee of suffrage rights, for example, began by noting that "the Right in

[59] Despite these differences, the influence of the state declarations of rights was substantial: of the twenty-seven guarantees in the federal Bill of Rights, all but one (the Ninth Amendment) appeared in pre-1787 state declarations of rights. See Lutz, *Origins of American Constitutionalism,* 62.

[60] Virginia Constitution of 1776, Declaration of Rights, sec. 9; Pennsylvania Constitution of 1776, Declaration of Rights, art. 12; New Hampshire Constitution of 1784, Bill of Rights, art. 18; and Massachusetts Constitution, part 1, art. 9. Emphasis added in all instances.

[61] See Lutz, *Popular Consent,* 67, table 3. The constitutions of Kentucky and Tennessee, newly framed in the 1790s, also consistently employed *shall* rather than *ought.*

[62] Pennsylvania Constitution of 1776, Declaration of Rights, art. 5.

[63] Delaware Constitution of 1776, Declaration of Rights, art. 18; and Virginia Constitution of 1776, Declaration of Rights, sec. 1.

the People to participate in the Legislature, is the Foundation of Liberty and of all free Government."[64]

A third difference is the inclusion of community, as well as individual, concerns within state declarations of rights. One such provision is the Massachusetts article recognizing the relation between religion and civil government and permitting the people to authorize their legislature to support religion.[65] Others include the limitations found in several state constitutions on abuses of the freedom of the press and on religious practices contrary to the good order of the society.[66] Several early constitutions even include the police power within their declarations of rights.[67] A fourth difference is the tendency to frame what are today understood as individual rights in terms of protections for the political community. Thus, the Virginia Declaration of Rights asserts that "the freedom of the press is one of the great bulwarks of liberty, and can never be restrained but by despotic governments," and the Delaware Declaration of Rights that "Trial by Jury of Facts where they arise is one of the greatest Securities of the Lives, Liberties and Estates of the People."[68] A final difference is the apparent mixture of structural and rights provisions. Some matters of governmental structure and procedure are found in state declarations of rights, while what today would be understood as rights guarantees occasionally appear in the body of state constitutions. Examples of the former include provisions for judicial tenure during good behavior, for executive rotation in office, and for a separation of powers in state declarations of rights.[69] Examples of the latter include the bans on excessive bail, on sanguinary laws, and on imprisonment for bankruptcy in the body of Pennsylvania's constitution.[70]

What accounts for these unfamiliar features in early state declarations of rights? Some scholars have suggested that the early state guarantees reveal an inexperience and ineptitude in constitution making, which was overcome by the time of the federal Constitution. Leonard Levy, for ex-

[64] Delaware Constitution of 1776, Declaration of Rights, art. 6.

[65] Massachusetts Constitution of 1780, part 1, art. 3.

[66] See, for example, Pennsylvania Constitution of 1790, art. 9, sec. 7; and New Hampshire Constitution of 1784, art. 1, secs. 4–5.

[67] See, for example, the Pennsylvania Constitution of 1776, Bill of Rights, art. 3; and the Delaware Constitution of 1776, Declaration of Rights, art. 4.

[68] Virginia Constitution of 1776, Declaration of Rights, sec. 12; and Delaware Constitution of 1776, Declaration of Rights, art. 13.

[69] On judicial tenure during good behavior, see Maryland Constitution of 1776, Declaration of Rights, art. 30; and New Hampshire Constitution of 1784, Declaration of Rights, art. 35. On executive rotation, see Maryland Constitution of 1776, Declaration of Rights, art. 31. On the separation of powers, see Virginia Constitution of 1776, Declaration of Rights, sec. 5; and Massachusetts Constitution of 1780, Declaration of Rights, art. 30.

[70] Pennsylvania Constitution of 1776, secs. 28, 29, and 38.

ample, looking to the frequent substitution of *ought* for *shall,* derided state guarantees as "flabby" and "namby-pamby."[71] From this point of view, the federal Bill of Rights's elimination of the admonitory and hortatory language characteristic of state declarations of rights, as well as its separation of structural and rights provisions, marked an unqualified advance in constitutional design. However, if one views state declarations of rights in the light of republican political theory, they appear neither primitive nor unusual.[72] Rather, the declarations of rights literally served to declare the fundamental political principles that were to guide the government and to ensure that these principles were made effectual. That was why they typically preceded the "frame of government" that created political institutions and distributed powers among them. To accomplish these purposes, the state declarations necessarily included a mixture of structural concerns, political maxims, and rights guarantees. Moreover, the insusceptibility of various provisions to judicial enforcement was not a flaw, because the declarations were addressed not to the state judiciary primarily but to the people's representatives, who were to be guided by them in legislating, and even more to the liberty-loving and vigilant citizenry that was to oversee the exercise of governmental power.

For those who drafted the state declarations of rights, this reliance on popular majorities to secure rights posed no problem because they believed that the main threats to rights, both collective and individual, were despotic officials and those seeking special privileges, rather than the people as a whole. Minority faction, not majority faction, posed the greatest danger. Thus, even when declarations of rights admonished the people to "a firm adherence to justice, moderation, temperance, frugality, and virtue," this was done to secure "free government" and "the blessings of liberty" for the "people," not to restrain majority tyranny.[73] To protect

---

[71] Leonard Levy, *Emergence of a Free Press* (New York: Oxford University Press, 1985), 184. See also Selsam, *Pennsylvania Constitution of 1776,* 204; and Bernard Schwartz, *The Great Rights of Mankind: A History of the American Bill of Rights* (New York: Oxford University Press, 1977), 90–91. This sentiment is not limited to contemporary observers. In his *Commentaries on the Constitution of the United States,* book 3, chap. 44, sec. 979, Justice Joseph Story remarked, "That a bill of rights may contain too many enumerations, and especially such as, more correctly belong to the ordinary legislation of a government, cannot be doubted. Some of our state bills of rights contain clauses of this description, being either in their character and phraseology too loose, and general, and ambiguous."

[72] See Lutz, *Popular Consent,* chap. 3; and Robert C. Palmer, "Liberties as Constitutional Provisions: 1776–1791," in William E. Nelson and Robert C. Palmer, *Liberty and Community: Constitution and Rights in the Early American Republic* (New York: Oceana, 1987), 61–86. The succeeding analysis draws heavily on both these sources.

[73] Virginia Constitution of 1776, Declaration of Rights, sec. 15. The contrast with *Federalist* no. 10, as well as with modern rights theory—for example, Dworkin, *Taking Rights Seriously*—could hardly be more striking.

against official threats to liberty, the declarations emphasized popular control of government, which was understood as the basis for all other rights. To some extent this control was achieved through direct popular involvement in governing: the right to a jury trial was the only right protected in every state constitution.[74] However, popular rule also demanded—and the declarations of rights championed—frequent and "equal" elections, with participation by "all men, having sufficient evidence of permanent common interest with, and attachment to, the community."[75] Officials were to be strictly "accountable" and "amenable" to the people, who could instruct them, petition them for redress of grievances, and ultimately "reduce [them] to a private station."[76] Dangerous powers, like the power to suspend laws, were assigned to the "representatives of the people," who presumably could be controlled by the populace.[77] Moreover, these representatives were to be closely watched, a process facilitated by constitutional requirements that the legislature regularly publish votes and proceedings.[78] Limits on reeligibility for office and other structural provisions found in state declarations of rights served to promote an identity of interests between the people and their representatives. So too did the requirements in all but two states that representatives be residents of the districts they represented.[79] If all else failed, the declarations recognized that "a well-regulated militia, composed of the body of the people, trained to arms, is the proper, natural, and safe defense of a free state."[80]

[74] William E. Nelson, *Americanization of the Common Law: The Impact of Legal Change on Massachusetts Society, 1760–1830* (Cambridge: Harvard University Press, 1975), 96. The Massachusetts Constitution of 1780, Declaration of Rights, art. 15, provided that "this method of procedure shall be held sacred."

[75] Virginia Constitution of 1776, Declaration of Rights, sec. 6; see also Delaware Constitution of 1776, Declaration of Rights, art. 6, and Vermont Constitution of 1777, Declaration of Rights, arts. 7–8. Having established the principle that those with sufficient stake in the community should participate in governing, the declaration of rights left specification of that principle to statute or to the body of the constitution, and the states differed considerably in their determination as to what constituted a sufficient stake.

[76] Virginia Constitution of 1776, Declaration of Rights, secs. 2 (accountability of magistrates) and 5 (removal of officials by election). Four states—Massachusetts, North Carolina, Pennsylvania, and Vermont—included a right to instruct representatives in their constitutions; see Thomas E. Cronin, *Direct Democracy: The Politics of Initiative, Referendum, and Recall* (Cambridge: Harvard University Press, 1989), 24.

[77] Virginia Constitution of 1776, Declaration of Rights, sec. 7.

[78] As Marc Kruman has noted, this requirement represented a change in practice from colonial times, when assemblies in the name of legislative independence generally deliberated in private. See his *Between Authority and Liberty*, 81.

[79] Edmund S. Morgan has emphasized the importance of this deviation from British practice. See his *Inventing the People: The Rise of Popular Sovereignty in England and America* (New York: Norton, 1988), 247.

[80] Virginia Constitution of 1776, Declaration of Rights, sec. 13.

Popular government and rotation in office likewise guarded against special privileges, against government conducted for the benefit of the few instead for the public good.[81] Thus several state constitutions emphasized that government was instituted for the common good rather than for the good of a segment of the society. The Pennsylvania Constitution of 1776 made explicit the connection between commitment to the common good and suspicion of special privilege, requiring rotation in office so that "the danger of establishing an inconvenient aristocracy will be effectually prevented."[82] State declarations of rights supplemented these safeguards with mandatory language forbidding hereditary offices and limiting "exclusive or separate emoluments or privileges from the community" to those who had earned them through "public services."[83] Some states also included, either in their declarations of rights or in the bodies of their constitutions, provisions designed to prevent the formation of an aristocracy—what Robert Palmer has called the "structural necessities for the basic liberty of republicanism."[84] Among these were bans on sanguinary laws, protections for the liberty to fowl and hunt, and prohibitions of entails.[85] Finally, state declarations of rights acknowledged the right of the people to "reform, alter, or abolish" governments that failed to serve the public good.

The declarations' emphasis on majority rule, together with their use of the less emphatic *ought* in delineating rights, might seem to indicate a lack of commitment to individual rights. Indeed, some scholars have concluded that eighteenth-century state constitutions "subordinate the individual to society."[86] But this conclusion fails to distinguish between violations of rights and legitimate restrictions on them. It also assumes a fundamental incompatibility between majority rule and the protection of rights, as well as between individual rights and the common good. These distinctly modern assumptions were not shared by those who framed the early declarations of rights.[87] As Robert Palmer has observed, "The rights in the Declaration of Rights were not guarantees at all, but were serious principles of government by which government was expected to

---

[81] On the importance of antipathy toward aristocracy and privilege in the political thought of the era, see Gordon S. Wood, *The Radicalism of the American Revolution* (New York: Alfred A. Knopf, 1992), parts 1 and 3.

[82] Pennsylvania Constitution of 1776, Declaration of Rights, sec. 19.

[83] Virginia Constitution of 1776, Declaration of Rights, sec. 4.

[84] Palmer, "Liberties as Constitutional Provisions," 67.

[85] See, for example, Pennsylvania Constitution of 1776, secs. 38, 43, and 37. For discussion of these, see Palmer, "Liberties as Constitutional Provisions," 66–67; and Wood, *Creation of American Republic*, 410.

[86] See, for example, Ronald M. Peters Jr., *The Massachusetts Constitution of 1780: A Social Compact* (Amherst: University of Massachusetts Press, 1980), 193–94.

[87] See Novak, *The People's Welfare*, chap. 1, for further elaboration of this point.

abide. Precisely because they were principles, however, they were subject to qualification for the communal well-being."[88] The key question then became whether government was abiding by those principles, whether rights were being qualified only for the common good. For state constitution-makers, the answer was not to make rights absolute but to create a government with a propensity to respect rights and then to make that government answerable to those with an interest in safeguarding rights. In short, the ultimate solution for protecting rights was republican government itself.

State Declarations of Rights in the 1790s

The federal Bill of Rights, of course, largely dispensed with the political maxims, structural guidelines, and hortatory and explanatory language characteristic of early state declarations of rights.[89] But state constitution-makers for the most part did not follow the federal lead. All state declarations of rights adopted during the 1790s guaranteed some specific rights not found in the federal Bill of Rights. Although the language of some state protections was identical to that of federal guarantees, it is as likely that both borrowed from earlier state guarantees as that there was a borrowing from the federal Bill of Rights. Indeed, what is striking is that no state declaration of rights spoke of "respecting an establishment of religion" or "abridging the freedom of speech or of the press" or employed other formulations that appeared for the first time in the federal document. Moreover, no state sought to conform to the federal model by deleting statements of political principle from their declarations of rights when they revised them in the 1790s; and Kentucky and Tennessee, the two new states, without controversy incorporated some of these statements into their declarations, copying directly from the Virginia Declaration of Rights. The federal model may have prompted Delaware and Pennsylvania to substitute *shall* for *ought* throughout their revised declarations, and Kentucky and Tennessee also copied the federal Constitution's mandatory phraseology, possibly to facilitate admission to the Union. But New Hampshire and Vermont retained the earlier hortatory language.[90] Although it is difficult to know whether the states' retention of elements from pre-1790 declarations of rights represented conscious choice or inertia, it is clear that the federal model had only a limited effect on state declarations of rights adopted in the 1790s. As shall be seen, the

---

[88] Palmer, "Liberties as Constitutional Provisions," 66.

[89] For an account that stresses the continuities between state and federal bills of rights, uncovering majoritarian and structural features in the federal guarantees, see Amar, "Bill of Rights."

[90] See Lutz, *Popular Consent,* 67, table 3.

influence of the federal Constitution on other aspects of state constitutions was likewise limited.

GOVERNMENTAL DESIGN

Republican Government

All state constitution-makers endorsed republican government, though they differed somewhat in their understanding of what that entailed. The Pennsylvania Constitution of 1776—"the most widely publicized, praised, and condemned of all the constitutions of the Revolution"— illustrates how far some state constitution-makers went in attempting to eliminate the gap between popular will and governmental action.[91] The Pennsylvania charter concentrated virtually all governmental power in a unicameral legislature, granting it—in addition to specific grants of power—"all other powers necessary for the legislature of a free state or commonwealth."[92] This assembly was to be apportioned on the basis of the number of taxable inhabitants—"the only principle which can at all times secure liberty, and make the voice of a majority of the people the law of the land"—and its members were elected annually in order to ensure accountability to the people.[93] In order to prevent a gulf between rulers and ruled, the Pennsylvania Constitution prescribed the same qualifications for holding office as for voting, abolishing property qualifications but retaining a tax-paying requirement. It also prescribed a rotation in office for the assembly and the executive council, both to avoid "the danger of establishing an inconvenient aristocracy" and to ensure that "more men will be trained to public business."[94] Finally, it wove various plebiscitary elements into the government. Popular control over lawmak-

[91] Williamson, *American Suffrage*, 92.

[92] Pennsylvania Constitution of 1776, sec. 9. The contrast with the other branches of Pennsylvania government was striking. The plural executive, popularly elected in districts for staggered three-year terms (sec. 20), could appoint some officers and had a limited pardoning power, but its main responsibility was carrying out the legislative will. The "judges of the supreme court of judicature" were appointed by the executive council for seven-year terms (sec. 23) but remained dependent on the legislature, since they were "removable for misbehaviour at any time by the general assembly" (sec. 23).

[93] Pennsylvania Constitution of 1776, sec. 17. The apportionment provision actually went into effect only seven years after the framing of the constitution, but the distribution of seats in the state legislature even during the interim period reflected the distribution of population far better than the apportionment of Pennsylvania's colonial legislature. See Kruman, *Between Authority and Liberty*, 73–74.

[94] The franchise extended not only to taxpayers but to the adult sons of freeholders, even if they did not pay taxes. Qualifications for office were the same as for the vote—see Pennsylvania Constitution of 1776, sec. 6; on rotation in office, see secs. 8 and 19.

ing was to be enforced by requiring a period for popular consideration of proposed legislation, with "the reasons and motives for making such laws . . . fully and clearly expressed in the preambles." Except "on occasions of sudden necessity," laws would not take effect prior to the election of a new assembly, thereby creating an opportunity to install legislators committed to revoking unpopular legislation.[95] This, combined with the right of the people to "instruct their representatives," served to reinforce the point that "the people of this State have the sole, exclusive, and inherent right of governing" and that "all officers of government . . . are their trustees and servants."[96]

Other eighteenth-century state constitutions were, like Pennsylvania's, eloquent on the power of the people to institute and control government. They also embraced annual elections as a key element of republican government: all the original states except South Carolina established annual elections for their lower houses, and South Carolina bowed to this consensus in 1778. Even the "constitutional counterrevolution" of 1790 in Pennsylvania did not touch annual election for the lower house. Although the Massachusetts Constitution of 1780 is often viewed as the antithesis of the Pennsylvania Constitution of 1776, it established annual elections not only for the lower house of the legislature but for the upper house and the executive as well.[97] In fact, of the twelve states with bicameral legislatures prior to 1789, seven instituted annual elections for members of the upper house; and by 1789 eleven of the fourteen states, including three of the four with popular election of executives, had one-year terms for their governors.

Most states also followed Pennsylvania's lead in seeking to link representation to population, at least for the lower houses of their legislatures.

[95] Pennsylvania Constitution of 1776, sec. 15. Staughton Lynd described the requirement that legislation be published for popular consideration before taking effect as "bicameralism from below." See Staughton Lynd, *Intellectual Origins of American Radicalism* (New York: Pantheon, 1968), 171.

[96] Pennsylvania Constitution of 1776, Declaration of Rights, arts. 16, 3, and 4.

[97] This accords with the view of Donald Lutz, who wrote: "The 1780 Massachusetts Constitution was the most important one written between 1776 and 1789 because it embodied the Whig theory of republican government, which came to dominate state level politics; the 1776 Pennsylvania Constitution was the second most important because it embodied the strongest alternative" (Lutz, *Popular Consent,* 129). For similar assessments, see Kenyon, "Constitutionalism in Revolutionary America"; J. R. Pole, *Political Representation in England and the Origins of the American Republic* (New York: St. Martin's, 1966), part 3; Williamson, *American Suffrage,* 104; and Wood, *Creation of American Republic,* 217–31. Both the Pennsylvania and Massachusetts constitutions have received book-length discussions and have been featured in discussions of constitution making during the period. See Selsam, *Pennsylvania Constitution of 1776;* and Peters, *Massachusetts Constitution of 1780.* For a detailed discussion of the influence of the Pennsylvania Constitution, see Williams, "Influence of Pennsylvania's Constitution."

To some extent, the early state constitutions did compromise full equality by continuing the colonial practice of tying representation to units of local government—towns in New England, counties or a combination of towns and counties elsewhere. However, this likely reflected tradition and convenience, given the initial unavailability of census data, more than a view of the states as confederations of towns or counties.[98] For whereas a true confederation would involve equal representation for each component unit, most states superimposed representation by numbers on that system. The New York Constitution of 1777 provided both for districts with equal numbers of people and for periodic redistricting to adjust for population shifts, and by 1790 several states had adopted similar provisions.[99] In some states, however, sectional rivalries and the search for political advantage prevented a principled resolution of the issue of representation. The constitutions in these states typically are marked by a detailed delineation of how representatives were to be apportioned among existing local governmental units.

Finally, although no other state copied the array of plebiscitary devices pioneered by Pennsylvania, many early state constitutions did adopt some of the measures it instituted to forestall a gap from developing between governors and governed. Thus five state constitutions followed Pennsylvania's in expressly authorizing the instruction of representatives, and the practice was widespread even in states that did not expressly recognize it in their constitutions.[100] Several state constitutions also followed Pennsylvania in requiring rotation in office. Six states in their initial constitutions set term limits for governors, three for senators, and seven for various local officials.

Yet their shared commitment to republican government did not prevent important differences between the Pennsylvania Constitution and those in other states, as well as among those other constitutions. While the states all accepted the standard that citizens should have a sufficient stake in the community to participate in governing, they differed considerably as to what constituted a sufficient stake, with most southern constitutions defining electorates less than half the size of those in New

---

[98] The confederation argument is most persuasively advanced by Elazar, "State-Local Relations."

[99] Lutz, *Popular Consent,* 109.

[100] Massachusetts Constitution of 1780, Declaration of Rights, art. 19. See John Phillip Reid, *The Concept of Representation in the Age of the American Revolution* (Chicago: University of Chicago Press, 1989), chap. 8; Kenneth Bresler, "Rediscovering the Right to Instruct Legislators," *New England Law Review* 26 (winter 1991): 355–94; and Margaret E. Monsell, "'Stars in the Constellation of the Commonwealth': Massachusetts Towns and the Constitutional Right of Instruction," *New England Law Review* 29 (winter 1995): 285–309.

England.[101] Most states assumed their preindependence property qualifications for voting were an adequate measure of stake in the community:
only three in their initial constitutions followed Pennsylvania's lead in
reducing property qualifications for voting, although none joined Massachusetts in "rounding upward" the property requirement that existed
prior to independence.[102]

In marked contrast to Pennsylvania's suspicion of "an inconvenient
aristocracy," several states sought to create what Gordon Wood has termed
"repositories of classical republican honor and wisdom, where superior
talent and devotion to the common good would be recognized and re-
warded by the people."[103] However, identifying and giving institutional
form to this natural aristocracy proved difficult. Lacking alternative measures, states fastened on wealth as an indicator of wisdom and virtue. Thus,
most state constitutions (unlike Pennsylvania's) established higher property qualifications for holding office than for voting, installing a graduated
system of property requirements that increased from lower house to upper
house to governor.[104] North Carolina and New York even imposed more
stringent property qualifications for voting for their upper houses.[105] All
but three state constitutions created bicameral legislatures, expecting that
the higher property requirement for senators would produce a body with a
distinctive institutional ethos and a broader understanding of the public
good. Yet this rarely occurred.[106] Instead, quite quickly the justification for
giving an institutional voice to wealth shifted: whereas originally wealth
had been understood as an indicator of wisdom and virtue, it came to be
seen as a separate interest in society that deserved representation. This is
best reflected in Massachusetts' establishment of an upper house specifi-

[101] Lutz, *Origins of American Constitutionalism,* 58; and Williamson, *American Suffrage,* chap. 6.

[102] For a survey of legal qualifications for voting, see Adams, *The First American Constitutions,* 293–307. The retention of preindependence voting qualifications must be seen in
context; some states that retained property requirements had liberalized them in the decade
prior to independence. Moreover, inflation had the effect over time of reducing voting qualifications expressed in terms of local currency—see Williamson, *American Suffrage,* 121.
Finally, scholars have concluded that even Massachusetts' new property qualification disenfranchised relatively few adult males. See Pole, *Political Representation,* 208–9; Handlin
and Handlin, *Popular Sources,* 34–39; and Robert E. Brown, *Middle-Class Democracy and
the Revolution in Massachusetts* (Ithaca, N.Y.: Cornell University Press, 1955).

[103] Wood, *Creation of American Republic,* 209.

[104] Typically, the property qualification for a seat in the upper house was roughly twice
as high as for one in the lower house. Virginia and Delaware, however, did not establish
different qualifications for their upper and lower houses. See Lutz, *Popular Consent,* 90,
table 5.

[105] Lutz, *Popular Consent,* 91, table 6.

[106] The best discussion of this failure is Jackson Turner Main, *The Upper House in
Revolutionary America* (Madison: University of Wisconsin Press, 1967).

cally to represent property, with senators apportioned among counties on the basis of the amount of taxes paid.[107]

These differences among state constitutions reflect different understandings of the operation of republican government and of the potential threats to liberty. John Adams, the main architect of the Massachusetts Constitution, took social stratification as a given and recognized that one stratum in society might seek to tyrannize over another. He therefore drew on the tradition of mixed government, with different institutions representing different strata of the society, seeking to construct a government that would not only minimize the likelihood of tyranny but also pursue the common good. Over time, most states agreed, seeking to reflect the diversity of their societies in their institutions. The main holdout, at least until 1790, was Pennsylvania. The framers of the Pennsylvania Constitution of 1776 were not so naive as to assume that there were no divisions within the state; indeed, the fourteen years that the constitution was in effect were marked by extraordinary turmoil between proponents and opponents of the constitution. However, they believed that popular differences were to be overcome, subsumed rather than represented, and that political conflict was a problem to be solved rather than an endemic feature of political life. Or they may have believed that, given the social homogeneity in America, the fundamental differences dividing the society were not among the people but between the people and aristocratic elements seeking to defeat the popular will. Whatever the explanation, the Pennsylvania Constitution embodied the notion that simple democracy, the direct translation of the popular will into government policy, conduced to the public good.[108]

Governmental Structure

1776–1777

The state constitutions framed during 1776 and early 1777 concentrated virtually all governing power in state legislatures. Instead of providing for an executive branch that could safely be entrusted with executive powers, the constitutions simply transferred many traditionally

---

[107] Wood, *Creation of American Republic,* chap. 6. New Hampshire copied Massachusetts' apportionment scheme in devising its own senate.

[108] The understanding of popular government underlying the Massachusetts Constitution is elaborated in Peters, *Massachusetts Constitution of 1780,* chap. 4; and in Wood, *Creation of American Republic,* 197–222. The first view of the understanding underlying the Pennsylvania Constitution is found in Selsam, *Pennsylvania Constitution of 1776,* 207–15, and the second in Wood, *Creation of American Republic,* 230–44.

executive powers to the legislatures.[109] Most, for instance, lodged the appointment power in the legislature. Only South Carolina gave the governor a veto, and it withdrew the power two years later. Even those powers granted to the executive often were subject to regulation and control by the legislature. The Maryland Constitution of 1776, for example, granted the governor the power of pardon and reprieve "except in such cases where the law shall otherwise direct," and the North Carolina Constitution of 1776 authorized the governor to exercise executive powers only "according to the laws of the state."[110] In every state the weakened executive was also hemmed in by an executive council, which in most instances were chosen by state legislatures. Yet the most fundamental check on executive power came from the executive's dependence on the legislature for selection and continuation in office. In eight of the nine states that adopted constitutions during this period, governors were elected by the legislature, and in seven they served only a one-year term. In such circumstances, it was almost superfluous for the Virginia and Maryland constitutions to insist that the executive should not "under any pretense" exercise "any power or prerogative by virtue of any law, statute, or custom of England."[111]

1777–1787

The New York Constitution inaugurated the second wave of state constitution-making by providing a model for republican government with a substantially enhanced executive. The constitution secured the independence of the governor by providing for election by the people for a three-year term and making the governor eligible for reelection. It also granted the governor executive powers, such as the power to grant pardons and to convene and prorogue the legislature.[112] The governor could directly participate in the legislative process by reporting on the state of the state and recommending measures conducive to its well-being.[113] Finally, the governor exercised substantial powers in concert with other officials, serving with members of the judiciary on a Council of Revision

---

[109] Thach, *Creation of the Presidency,* 27; Kelly, Harbison, and Belz, *The American Constitution,* 73; and M. J. C. Vile, *Constitutionalism and the Separation of Powers* (Oxford: Clarendon Press, 1967), 133–46.

[110] Maryland Constitution of 1776, art. 33; and North Carolina Constitution of 1776, art. 19.

[111] Virginia Constitution of 1776 (no section specified); and Maryland Constitution of 1776, art. 33.

[112] New York Constitution of 1777, art. 18.

[113] New York Constitution of 1777, art. 19.

that had the power to veto legislation and with members of the senate on a Council on Appointment that appointed executive officers.[114]

The five other state constitutions adopted during this period are marked by a struggle to decide whether it was possible to reconcile a strong, independent executive with republican government.[115] Four states did follow New York in providing for popular election of the executive, but three of these gave the executive a one-year term, and none gave him a term of office longer than that of the lower house of the legislature. The executives established by the constitutions of South Carolina (1778) and New Hampshire (1784) both resembled those of the preceding era, exercising limited powers and constrained by legislatively elected councils. Vermont attempted to solve the problem of executive power, in both its 1777 and 1786 constitutions, with a plural executive, consisting of a governor and a twelve-member council that were popularly elected state-wide for the same (single-year) term. This executive was given the powers of appointment and pardon, the responsibility of faithful execution of the laws, and—under the 1786 constitution—a suspensory veto over legislation.[116] Finally, Massachusetts in 1780 created a strong governor, the first state executive to possess a veto unencumbered by a council of revision or executive council.

1788–1800

During the decade following the adoption of the federal Constitution, the states had the opportunity to revise their constitutions and model them on the federal charter. Yet although six states adopted seven new state constitutions and other states amended their constitutions, what is striking is how limited an impact the federal Constitution had on the structure of state governments during this period. The state legislatures offer a prime example. After the federal Constitution established a two-year term for representatives, only one state (South Carolina) abandoned annual election of the lower house, and it merely returned to a position it had first adopted in 1776. The federal influence on senatorial terms was

[114] New York Constitution of 1777, arts. 3 and 23. John Jay, who proposed the Council of Appointment, intended for the governor to make all appointments and the senators to confirm or reject them, but the provision did not explicitly state this. A convention called in 1801 to resolve the division of responsibility on the council concluded that the power to nominate was a concurrent right of both the governor and the council, thus weakening gubernatorial power. See Galie, *New York State Constitution,* 4–6.

[115] M. J. C. Vile has observed that "[t]he history of constitutional doctrine in the decade between the Constitution of Georgia and the Federal Constitution is, in part at least, the history of a search for a rationale for dealing with the former prerogatives of the Crown." See his *Constitutionalism and Separation,* 143.

[116] Vermont Constitution of 1777, chap. 2, secs. 17–18; and Vermont Constitution of 1786, chap. 2, secs. 10, 11, and 16.

somewhat greater. While eleven of the seventeen constitutions adopted prior to 1787 had one-year terms for senators, two of the first four constitutions adopted after 1787—the Georgia Constitution of 1789 and the Pennsylvania Constitution of 1790—established senates for the first time, with longer terms of office; and the other two, the South Carolina and Delaware constitutions, continued multiyear senatorial terms. Two new states, Kentucky and Tennessee, also introduced multiyear terms in the 1790s. However, the New Hampshire Constitution of 1792 and the Vermont Constitution of 1793 continued to provide for the annual election of senators, and the Georgia Constitution of 1798 reversed the decision of nine years previous and provided for annual election of senators.[117] Finally, no state emulated the U.S. Constitution's system of indirect selection of senators. Prior to 1787, only one state, Maryland, employed indirect election; and it ultimately abandoned the system in the face of unrelenting criticism that it was undemocratic.[118] Although Kentucky in 1792 opted for a system of indirect election, it looked to the Maryland Constitution rather than the federal Constitution for direction, copying the exact language of the Maryland provision.[119] Seven years later it too abandoned that system in favor of direct election.

The story is much the same for state executives. Kentucky in 1792 did adopt the federal model: the governor was indirectly elected, served a four-year term, was indefinitely reeligible, and possessed extensive powers. However, seven years later it eliminated indirect election and gubernatorial reeligibility and reduced the vote necessary to override the governor's veto. Elsewhere, the federal model played little role in the development of the state executive. Although some state constitution-makers, like their federal counterparts, sought to establish an independent executive, they relied on direct popular election for that purpose, continuing the movement away from legislative selection that had preceded the federal convention by a decade. From the federal convention to 1800, only two existing states—Georgia and Pennsylvania—followed the federal example and lengthened the governor's term of office. Also, as noted previously, by the time of the federal convention, gubernatorial powers had already been strengthened in some states, with the introduction of the veto power and gubernatorial control over appointments. The most striking enhancement of gubernatorial power was found in the

---

[117] Lutz, *Popular Consent*, 88, table 4. More generally, see Main, *Upper House*.

[118] The initial attacks on the Maryland Senate are discussed in Wood, *Creation of American Republic*, 251–54. Later attacks prompted a compromise in 1801, by which the indirect election of senators was temporarily salvaged in return for extension of the suffrage to all white males. See Williamson, *American Suffrage*, 149. The transition to a directly elected senate in 1837 is described in Green, *Constitutional Development*, 240–48.

[119] Coward, *Kentucky in New Republic*, 28.

Massachusetts Constitution, and during the last decade of the eighteenth century, it was this constitution—and not the federal Constitution—that served as the primary model for state constitution-makers.[120]

The limited influence of the federal Constitution suggests that a distinctive state constitutionalism continued even after 1787. States found that their sister states shared similar problems and were therefore a better source of instruction than the federal Constitution. In addition, state constitution-makers apparently did not share the dissatisfaction with existing state constitutions voiced by various Federalists. Indeed, many Americans appeared quite satisfied with the state governments they had, as the comments of leading Anti-Federalists illustrate.[121] Finally, it should be noted that state constitutions did change considerably in the decade following independence, so many of the problems with the initial state constitutions had already been addressed by 1787.

CONCLUSIONS

Some scholars have argued that state constitutions reflect the compromises and short-term solutions of day-to-day state politics rather than overarching political principles. For eighteenth-century state constitutions, however, this is simply not accurate. One can certainly detect in them the push and pull of ordinary politics, particularly as they deal with apportionment and other aspects of the intrastate division of political power. Yet what is most striking is the way they embody political principles—coherent understandings of the nature of republican government, the sources of political conflict, and the threats to liberty—and the efforts of their framers to craft processes and institutions to effectuate those principles.[122] This concern for political principle might be attributed in part to factors peculiar to the founding of political societies, such as the theoretical self-consciousness characteristic of those involved in the act of founding. In addition, standards of constitutional design during the late eighteenth century encouraged the inclusion of justificatory and explanatory material in preambles and state declarations of

[120] This paragraph draws on Lutz, *Popular Consent*, 93–95; Thach, *Creation of the Presidency*; Adams, *The First American Constitutions*, 266–74; and Wood, *Creation of American Republic*, 435–53.

[121] See Herbert F. Storing, ed., *The Complete Anti-Federalist*, 7 vols. (Chicago: University of Chicago Press, 1977), 2:138–39, 179–80, 263; 4:72–73, 77, 109; 5:149.

[122] These comments are not intended to deny the usefulness of the ordinary-politics perspective. Even if one accepts the notion that state constitutions reflect a coherent political perspective, the ordinary-politics view is a valuable reminder of the political character of constitution making and alerts one to the possibility that anomalous provisions may reflect a need to accommodate competing interests.

rights. This may have promoted among state constitution-makers an awareness of the theoretical underpinnings of their work, although the inclusion of explanatory and justificatory material could as likely have reflected that awareness as created it. Finally, the states' reliance on revision rather than amendment for constitutional change fostered a comprehensive perspective on state constitutions and reduced the likelihood that theoretically inconsistent elements would be incorporated in them.

Whatever the explanation, a concern for and consensus on basic issues of political principle did exist, and this contributed to the similarities among early state constitutions. So too did the sense of common purpose among the constitution-makers in various states as they sought to give shape and authority to new governments that were consistent with republican principles, protective of rights, and committed to the public good. Indeed, the recognition that their counterparts in other states had addressed many of the same problems encouraged inexperienced constitution-makers to look beyond their borders for solutions. This interstate borrowing led to the transfer not only of particular provisions but also of conceptions of constitutional design. This reveals itself both in what is said and in what is left unsaid in eighteenth-century state constitutions. By and large, the states constitutionalized the same political concerns and refrained from constitutionalizing others. In no state was there significant debate about what should or should not be included in a constitution.

Within the consensus in favor of republican government, there was of course room for differences among state constitutions. These differences generally did not follow regional lines, and thus distinctive state political cultures, typically associated with region, were not crucial in constitution making during the eighteenth century.[123] Instead, given the evolution of constitutional thought during the period, the date of a constitution's adoption is usually a better indicator of its content than the region in which it originated. Nevertheless, attempts to identify various "waves" of state constitution-making run the risk of distortion, because constitutional development in the states did not proceed in linear fashion. Constitutional innovations introduced in a single state often found acceptance only gradually, as states experimented with alternative solutions to a problem or clung for a while to past practices. This pattern can be seen in the responses to New York's creation of a strong executive and to Massachusetts' adoption of a convention and popular ratification for constitution making. Other initiatives attracted support in only a few states and

---

[123] This is not to say that political culture played no role. There are clear differences in constitutional style between Massachusetts, say, and Georgia, even when the constitutions created similar institutions.

ultimately were abandoned. Cases in point are Pennsylvania's establishment of a unicameral legislature and its Council of Censors. Finally, some innovations attracted no support at all but continued within a single state. Maryland's indirect election of its state senate is a prime example. Thus, the patterns of constitutional change among the states were more complex—and the dynamics more interesting—than periodization might suggest.

This chapter's survey of eighteenth-century state constitutions has documented changes in constitutional thought and constitutional design, best understood as revealing an evolution in political thought rather than as reflecting a disjunction between Whig theory at the state level and Federalist theory at the national.[124] The growing appreciation of the separation of powers, of checks and balances, and of the need for a more vigorous executive found in various state constitutions of the late 1770s and early 1780s represented a shift in republican constitutional theory. Many of the changes introduced in state constitutions anticipated features of the federal Constitution. Nevertheless, it would be a mistake to view early state constitutions as nothing more than precursors of the federal Constitution. Even after its adoption, the states for the most part went their own way, looking to sister states and to their own political traditions in designing or revising their constitutions rather than emulating the federal charter.

This tendency to look to state constitutions rather than to the federal Constitution for guidance reflected a belief that there was something distinctive about state constitutions, a theme introduced in chapter 1. But the grounds for this distinctiveness are quite different from those typically used to distinguish contemporary state constitutions from the federal Constitution. Contemporary state constitutions are distinguished primarily by their length, their detail, and the frequency with which they have been revised and amended. Yet several eighteenth-century state constitutions were shorter and less detailed than the federal Constitution; only three states adopted more constitutions than the national government did during the late eighteenth century, and none was more frequently amended. Rather, the perception that state constitutions were distinctive rested on a sense that the problems and responsibilities of the states were different from those of the federal government. Scholars such as Donald Lutz with this difference in mind have spoken of the United States Constitution as an "incomplete constitution." Although this characterization of the federal charter is accurate, the formulation implies

---

[124] The idea of a disjunction between state and federal constitutional theory, between civic-republican (Whig) theory and Federalist theory, underlies the influential analysis in Wood, *Creation of American Republic*.

that state constitutions fill in the gaps in the federal document. This chapter suggests, however, that the character and focus of the early state constitutions were established prior to 1787, and the existence of earlier state provisions to some extent—for example, with regard to voting qualifications and apportionment—precluded federal involvement.

The revision of the Georgia Constitution in 1798 concluded an era of extraordinary constitutional creativity. The success of these efforts can be seen in the fact that over the next two decades no state revised its constitution. Yet this served merely as a respite in state constitution-making. During the nineteenth century, thirty-one states framed their first constitutions, and the states revised their constitutions sixty-four times—on average, a new state constitution was adopted almost every year. This century of extraordinarily active constitution-making is the subject of the next chapter.

CHAPTER 4

Nineteenth-Century State Constitutionalism

IN NO PERIOD is the divergence between the state and federal constitutional experiences clearer than in the nineteenth century. The federal Constitution was amended only four times during the entire century—once to correct a defect revealed by the presidential election of 1800 and three times in the aftermath of the Civil War. In contrast, campaigns for political change that the federal Constitution accommodated without amendment—such as Jacksonian democracy, the Granger movement, and Populism—produced fundamental shifts in state constitutions. The antebellum period has been described, quite accurately, as "an era of permanent constitutional revision" in the states (see fig. 4.1).[1] From 1800 to 1860, thirty-seven new state constitutions were adopted. Fifteen of the twenty-four states in the Union by 1830 revised their constitutions by 1860, two of them twice (see table 4.1).[2] In fact, during one decade, from 1844 to 1853, more than half the existing states held constitutional conventions.[3] During the last half of the nineteenth century, when a concern for continuity dominated national constitutional theory, state constitution-making was epidemic, particularly in the South.[4] From 1861 to 1900, twenty states revised their constitutions, some several times, adopting forty-five new constitutions in all. Even this figure underestimates the level of state constitution-making; for voters also rejected several proposed constitutions, including six from 1877 to 1887.[5] Of those states that joined the Union from 1800 to 1850, only two had not revised their constitutions by century's end; altogether, ninety-four state constitutions were adopted during the nineteenth century.

More than the frequency of formal constitutional change distinguished federal and state constitutionalism in the nineteenth century. Different

---

[1] Daniel T. Rodgers, *Contested Truths: Keywords in American Politics since Independence* (New York: Basic Books, 1987), 93.

[2] Altogether, fifty constitutional conventions were held during the period, and those states that did not revise their constitutions amended them, some extensively. Massachusetts adopted sixteen amendments, Maine nine, and Connecticut eight. See Dealey, *Growth of State Constitutions*, 48–51.

[3] Rodgers, *Contested Truths*, 94.

[4] Kahn, *Legitimacy and History*, chap. 4.

[5] Morton Keller, *Affairs of State: Public Life in Late Nineteenth Century America* (Cambridge, Mass.: Belknap Press, 1977), 320.

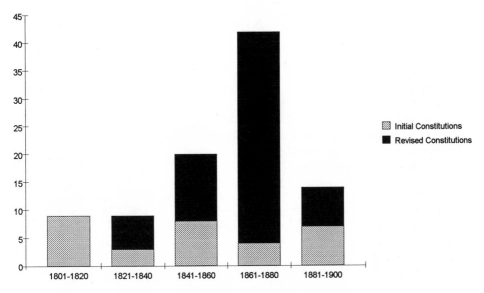

Figure 4.1. Nineteenth-century constitution-making

issues dominated the constitutional agendas of state and nation. Issues salient in many states included the extension of the franchise, the curtailment of legislative power, state governmental participation in promoting economic development and allocating natural resources, and the relations between state and local governments. None of these issues figured prominently in federal constitutional politics. Even when both state and federal constitutions addressed an issue, often the state approach was distinctive. The constitutional treatment of the rights of African-Americans illustrates this. During the antebellum era, regional differences precluded an effective federal constitutional response to the problem of slavery, but state constitutions both north and south dealt with slavery and with the rights of free blacks.[6] After the Civil War, the Thirteenth, Fourteenth, and Fifteenth Amendments were added to the federal Constitution to secure the rights of African-Americans. Yet while these amendments left much to subsequent legislation, state constitutions defined in detail the rights of African-Americans to vote, to hold office, to attend integrated schools, to contract interracial marriages, and so on.

[6] The primary attempt by the federal government to craft a solution to the problem of slavery was the United States Supreme Court's ruling in *Scott* v. *Sandford*, 19 Howard 393 (1857). The treatment of slavery in antebellum Southern constitutions and the voting rights of free blacks are discussed later in this chapter.

TABLE 4.1
Nineteenth Century State Constitution-Making

1801–1820	1821–1840	1841–1860	1861–1880	1881–1900
Alabama	Arkansas	California	Alabama (4)	Delaware
Connecticut	Delaware	Illinois	Arkansas (4)	Florida
Illinois	Florida	Indiana	California	Idaho
Indiana	Michigan	Iowa (2)	Colorado	Kentucky
Louisiana	Mississippi	Kansas	Florida (3)	Louisiana
Maine	New York	Kentucky	Georgia (4)	Mississippi
Mississippi	Pennsylvania	Louisiana (2)	Illinois	Montana
Missouri	Tennessee	Maryland	Louisiana (4)	New York
Ohio	Virginia	Michigan	Maryland (2)	North Dakota
Total: 9	Total: 9	Minnesota	Mississippi	South Carolina
Original: 9	Original: 3	New Jersey	Missouri (2)	South Dakota
		New York	Nebraska (2)	Utah
		Ohio	Nevada	Washington
		Oregon	North Carolina	Wyoming
		Rhode Island	Pennsylvania	Total: 14
		Texas	South Carolina (3)	Original: 7
		Virginia	Tennessee	Confederacy: 4
		Wisconsin	Texas (3)	
		Total: 20	Virginia	
		Original: 8	West Virginia (2)	
			Total: 42	
			Original: 4	
			Confederacy: 29	

And whereas the federal Constitution was, at least in the decades follow-ing the Civil War, committed to guaranteeing the rights of African-Americans, state constitutions differed widely in their attitude toward the protection of those rights, sometimes even within individual states. Thus, Louisiana's constitution of 1868 forbade discrimination in public educa-tion, whereas the constitution it adopted in 1879 was silent on the sub-ject and its 1898 constitution mandated racially segregated schools.[7]

A further difference involved the prevailing attitudes toward the fun-damental law of state and of nation. During the nineteenth century the federal Constitution achieved an almost sacred status as the crowning work of an extraordinary political generation.[8] In the states, reverence for the founders of state constitutions and their handiwork was notably lacking, as the orgy of nineteenth-century constitution-making attests. The veneration of the U.S. Constitution rested upon the belief that it embodied a political wisdom that future generations were bound to pre-serve. State constitution-makers, in contrast, came to view constitution making as a progressive enterprise, requiring the constant readjustment of past practices and institutional arrangements in light of changes in circumstance and political thought. The social and demographic trans-formations that many states underwent within decades of their admission to the Union made the argument of changed circumstances particularly persuasive.[9] In addition, state constitution-makers believed that the ex-perience of self-government had expanded the fund of knowledge about constitutional design, so that later generations were better situated to frame constitutions than were their less experienced, and hence less ex-pert, predecessors.[10] Given this attitude, it is hardly surprising that state

[7] Louisiana Constitution of 1868, title 7, art. 135; and Louisiana Constitution of 1898, art. 248. For discussion of these changes, see Hargrave, *The Louisiana State Constitution*, 9–12.

[8] Numerous commentators have remarked on the extraordinary veneration accorded to the Constitution. See, inter alia, Kahn, *Legitimacy and History,* chap. 2; Michael Kammen, *A Machine That Would Go of Itself: The Constitution in American Culture* (New York: Alfred A. Knopf, 1986), chap. 5; Levinson, *Constitutional Faith,* chap. 1; and Lerner, "Con-stitution and Court."

[9] The population of California, for example, increased seventeenfold during the thirty years between the adoption of its first and second constitutions, and the population of Tennessee more than sixfold in the three decades immediately preceding the revision of its 1796 constitution. See Carl Brent Swisher, *Motivation and Political Technique in the Cali-fornia Constitutional Convention, 1878–79* (New York: Da Capo, 1969), 6; and Laska, *The Tennessee State Constitution,* 7. For thoughtful consideration of the social, economic, and demographic changes in a set of western states and their constitutional consequences, see Johnson, *Founding the Far West,* chaps. 7–9.

[10] Rodgers, *Contested Truths,* 91; Fritz, "American Constitutional Tradition Revisited," 971–75; and Christian G. Fritz, "Constitution Making in the Nineteenth-Century Ameri-can West," in John McLaren, Hamar Foster, and Chet Orloff, eds., *Law for the Elephant,*

constitutions during the nineteenth century reflected, as James Bryce has suggested, "the natural history of [the] democratic communities" they governed.[11]

Constitutional Commonalities and Their Causes

Horizontal Federalism

The same factors that produced distinctive constitutional experiences in state and nation have tended to promote similarities in the constitutions and the constitutional experiences of the states. The belief in the progress of constitutional knowledge is a case in point. This belief not only led states to revise their fundamental law in order to benefit from advances in knowledge but also influenced where they looked for guidance. The interest in "modern" constitutional design discouraged borrowing from older constitutions, including the federal Constitution, and encouraged appropriating provisions and ideas from the most recently revised state constitutions. Convention delegates in Maine in 1820, for example, largely ignored the Massachusetts Constitution under which they had lived and looked instead to Connecticut, Delaware, Indiana, Kentucky, and New Hampshire for current constitutional wisdom.[12] A delegate to the convention that framed the California Constitution of 1849 explained the delegates' reliance on the Iowa Constitution as a model by noting that "it was one of the latest and shortest."[13] The ready availability of compilations of constitutions by the middle of the nineteenth century enabled delegates to search nationwide for pertinent provisions, reducing the influence of region and political culture on state charters. Thus, those who drafted the Texas Constitution of 1876 looked for inspiration to the Missouri Constitution of 1875 and the Pennsylvania Constitution of 1873, and the drafters of the Wyoming Constitution of 1889 to the Colorado, Pennsylvania, Illinois, and Montana constitutions.[14] Over time, this borrowing produced a degree of uniformity among state constitutions, because constitutions drafted during the same era tended to draw upon the same models. Still, Thomas Cooley's description of state constitutions at the close of the nineteenth century as "little better than proof impressions

---

Law for the Beaver: Essays in the Legal History of the North American West (Regina, Sask.: Canadian Plains Research Center, 1992), 302–4.

[11] Bryce, *The American Commonwealth*, 1:434.

[12] Marshall J. Tinkle, *The Maine State Constitution: A Reference Guide* (Westport, Conn.: Greenwood Press, 1992), 4.

[13] Quoted in Christian G. Fritz, "More Than 'Shreds and Patches': California's First Bill of Rights," *Hastings Constitutional Law Quarterly* 17 (fall 1989): 18–19.

[14] Janice C. May, *The Texas State Constitution: A Reference Guide* (Westport, Conn.: Greenwood Press, 1996), 14; and Keiter and Newcomb, *The Wyoming State Constitution*, 4.

of a single original" exaggerates their similarities.[15] Given changes over time in the prevailing models for state constitutions, substantial differences remained between constitutions framed early in the century and those framed later. Carryover provisions from earlier charters, as well as provisions reflecting state-specific problems or politics, further differentiated even those constitutions drafted during the same era.

The State Constitutional Agenda

The common agenda of state constitutional issues also promoted similarities among nineteenth-century state constitutions. In part, this shared constitutional agenda resulted from the division of constitutional responsibility between state and nation.[16] Because the federal Constitution did not establish national qualifications for voting, these qualifications became a hotly contested issue in most states. The federal Constitution also left to state constitutions the task of defining the scope of state legislative power, and this too emerged as a major concern. Finally, the national government's reluctance for over a century to become involved in the regulation of economic enterprise obliged the states to deal with fundamental questions of political economy.

In part too, the states' shared constitutional agenda reflected the influence of political movements active in the various states. These movements—such as Jacksonian democracy and Populism—identified problems requiring constitutional resolution and defined the range of acceptable solutions to them. The campaigns for extension of the franchise and for restrictions on the power of railroads and other corporations exemplify this phenomenon. Although their effects were national in scope, these movements for constitutional reform involved parallel state-based campaigns rather than national organizations. The gradual elimination of impediments to white manhood suffrage in almost all the states during the first half of the nineteenth century, for example, occurred without national strategy or direction.[17] Thus, rather than state constitutional politics being national politics writ small, the exact opposite was true.

Yet underlying the constitutional conflicts over the intrastate distribution of political power, the state's role in the economy, and other matters

[15] *North Dakota Convention Debates,* 66, quoted in Hicks, *Constitutions of Northwest States,* 33.

[16] Donald S. Lutz has referred to the (intentional) failure of the federal Constitution to address certain matters and their consignment to the states as the "incompleteness" of the federal Constitution. See the discussion in chapter 1 of his "Constitution as Incomplete Text," 23–32. Of course, the matters consigned to the states had typically been addressed by the state constitutions that preceded the drafting of the 1787 federal Constitution.

[17] Green, *Constitutional Development,* 199–200.

was a more fundamental question, namely, how to secure republican government.[18] Although state constitution-makers seldom articulated their understanding of republican government, one can infer it from the concerns and disputes that dominated nineteenth-century constitutional politics in the states. First of all, republican government required popular rule, which nineteenth-century constitution-makers understood as entailing more democratic arrangements than their predecessors had contemplated. Minimally, popular rule required that all politically relevant people have the opportunity to participate in governing, so over time state constitutions extended the franchise and removed eligibility requirements for office. Popular rule also implied a responsiveness to the popular will throughout the government, which state constitutions sought to achieve through popular election of most officeholders and through equitable systems of representation (though at times a concern for safeguarding existing advantages tempered the enthusiasm for equitable representation). However, nineteenth-century constitution-makers understood republican government to entail not only government by the people but also government for the people. State constitutions recognized—some explicitly, others implicitly—that there was a good common to the society as a whole, which government was obliged to pursue.[19] This common good was defined less by what it was than by what it was not, namely, rule by or on behalf of a segment of society.[20] Nineteenth-century constitution-makers believed that powerful minorities, rather than tyrannical majorities, posed the most serious threat to liberty, and so they included numerous provisions designed to protect the many against the special privileges and advantages of the wealthy or well-connected few.[21]

[18] This point was nicely summarized by Ernst Freund early in the twentieth century: "For over a hundred years the American people have experimented upon the problem of how to give correct and adequate expression to that elusive political factor, the popular will. An abiding faith in popular government has been accompanied by an ever-renewed dissatisfaction with the forms and organs through which it was sought to be realized." Freund, *Standards of American Legislation* (Chicago: University of Chicago Press, 1917), 148.

[19] See, for example, North Carolina Constitution of 1868, art. 1, sec. 2; North Dakota Constitution of 1889, art. 1, sec. 2; Ohio Constitution, art. 8, sec. 1; and Oregon Constitution of 1857, art. 1, sec. 1. For a revealing discussion, see Novak, *The People's Welfare*, especially chap. 1.

[20] See Rush Welter, *The Mind of America: 1820–1860* (Chicago: University of Chicago Press, 1975), 77–78: "The whole thrust of Jacksonian thought was in the first instance negative, an effort to eliminate institutions and practices. . . . The 'aristocracy' that Jacksonians complained of consisted of selective access to power, prosperity, or influence. At bottom it was a political rather than a social or economic concept: in Jacksonian eyes, an 'aristocrat' was someone who was empowered by law to affect the economic and social welfare of his contemporaries, or who enjoyed legal privileges that he could turn to his own account in an otherwise competitive economy." See also Hurst, *Growth of American Law,* 241. This Jacksonian thrust carried over into the latter half of the nineteenth century.

[21] See, for example, Ohio Constitution of 1851, art. 1, secs. 2 and 1, and art. 8, secs. 4–

To investigate more closely how a commitment to republican government affected state constitutional development, it is useful to turn to those recurring issues—the intrastate distribution of power, the relation between the state and the economy, and the scope of state legislative power—that dominated state constitutional politics during the nineteenth century. However, three observations should preface this discussion. First, the constitution-makers' commitment to republican government was hardly new. The concern for impartial government, for government seeking the good of all rather than of a select few, echoed a theme prominent in eighteenth-century state constitutionalism, thus underscoring the continuities in state constitutional thought.[22] Nonetheless, this concern emerged with particular force in the nineteenth century, as the size and power of economic entities increased and as the expansion of the states' role in encouraging and directing economic development increased the opportunities for favoritism to these entities and the benefits deriving from such favoritism. Second, although state constitution-makers' commitment to republican government was genuine, at times political principle conflicted with political advantage, and in such instances constitution-makers not infrequently ignored the demands of principle or attempted to redefine them to meet the political needs of the moment. Finally, state constitution-makers' endorsement of republican principles raised as many questions as it resolved. To take but one example, their endorsement of popular rule obliged them to define who constituted the politically relevant "people," and—as conflicts over the political rights of blacks and women revealed—this remained a politically charged issue throughout the century.[23]

THE INTRASTATE DISTRIBUTION OF POLITICAL POWER

Conflict over the intrastate distribution of political power during the nineteenth century focused on the apportionment of state legislatures and on voting qualifications. Reformers appealed to the right of "the people" to govern in order to justify reapportionment and expansion of the fran-

---

5; Pennsylvania Constitution of 1873, art. 3; and South Carolina Constitution of 1868, art. 1, secs. 36 and 39. Other such provisions will be identified in the succeeding discussion.

22 See, for example, Pennsylvania Constitution of 1776, Declaration of Rights, sec. 5; and, more generally, the examples discussed in chapter 3.

23 Over the course of the antebellum period, most state constitutions effectively defined African-Americans as not part of the politically relevant portion of the American people, denying even free blacks the right to vote. In most states women were also excluded from suffrage for most of the century. In the aftermath of Reconstruction, African-Americans were again denied equal membership in the political community, particularly in the South. Only late in the nineteenth century were women admitted to political equality in a few states. This topic is addressed in detail later in the chapter.

chise, while their opponents stressed the need to protect diverse interests and to limit the franchise to those who had a sufficient stake in the society or to the members of a particular race.[24] These arguments were not only "a matter of principle but also an instrument of politics."[25] As a delegate to the Virginia convention of 1829 acknowledged, "all our metaphysical reasoning and our practical rules, all our scholastic learning and political wisdom, are but the arms employed . . . in a contest for power," pitting previously excluded or underrepresented groups against those advantaged by the prevailing distribution of power.[26]

Apportionment

At the beginning of the nineteenth century, seven state constitutions provided for equal representation of political subdivisions in one house of the legislature; and all state constitutions guaranteed some representation to counties or towns, regardless of population, in at least one house.[27] In New England, where towns formed the geographical basis for representation, population shifts aggravated the initial inequalities, even when constitutions provided for some adjustments for population disparities among towns. By 1840 in Rhode Island, for example, a majority of seats in the lower house were controlled by rural districts with only one-third of the state's population.[28] In several southern and Mid-Atlantic states, constitutionally prescribed apportionment schemes ensured the dominance of coastal regions despite population growth in the interior. Delaware, Maryland, Virginia, and North Carolina all prescribed the apportionment of their legislatures in their initial constitutions, with no provision for reapportionment in response to demographic changes.[29] Even when population was the basis for apportionment, conflict arose as to the population base to be used in determining representation. In southern states, residents of slave-owning areas wanted to count the number of total inhabitants or at least to use the "federal ratio" of white inhabitants plus three-fifths of enslaved inhabitants; whereas residents of non-slave-owning areas sought to base representation solely on the number of

[24] See Rodgers, *Contested Truths*, chap. 3.

[25] Pole, *Political Representation*, 254.

[26] Chapman Johnson, quoted in Peterson, *Democracy, Liberty, and Property*, 285.

[27] See Robert G. Dixon, *Democratic Representation: Reapportionment in Law and Politics* (New York: Oxford University Press, 1968), 62–63, chart 1.

[28] Williamson, *American Suffrage*, 246.

[29] Delaware Constitution of 1792, arts. 3–4; Maryland Constitution of 1776, arts. 2, 4, 5, and 14–16; Virginia Constitution of 1776, arts. 12–13; and North Carolina Constitution of 1776, arts. 2–3. For discussion of these provisions and attempts to change them, see Green, *Constitutional Development*; Fehrenbacher, *Constitutions and Constitutionalism*; and Orth, *North Carolina State Constitution*, 2–12.

white inhabitants, which would have substantially increased their seats in the state legislature.[30]

Because state constitutions controlled the apportionment of state legislatures, only constitutional reform could redress the grievances of those dissatisfied with the system of representation. Campaigns for constitutional conventions developed independently in several of the early states. In some, legislators eventually bowed to the intense pressures for change and called conventions. Yet because the representation at these conventions typically reflected the prevailing distribution of power in the state, the demands of underrepresented areas seldom were fully met. Thus, the Connecticut convention of 1818 altogether ignored existing disparities, which continued to increase over time, and conventions in Virginia in 1829 and 1850 so disappointed the western parts of the state that they eventually resolved the representation issue by withdrawing and forming West Virginia.[31] In a few states, such as North Carolina, state legislatures proposed constitutional amendments to address complaints about malapportionment rather than risk a convention.[32] Finally, in still other states legislative intransigence led dissatisfied groups to threaten or convene extralegal constitutional conventions to address their concerns. For example, when the Rhode Island legislature adamantly refused even to sanction a convention, insurgent elements under the leadership of Thomas Dorr called one anyway, devised a constitution, and held elections under the new constitution, so that the state temporarily had two competing governments.[33]

The early states' failure to deal successfully with legislative apportionment during the first half of the nineteenth century meant that the issue continued to fester, provoking periodic efforts to remedy inequities. Yet most states admitted to the Union during the nineteenth century also based representation in one or both houses at least in part on political subdivisions.[34] Louisiana and Montana required equal representation for geographic units in their senates.[35] Other states, such as Missouri,

[30] Fehrenbacher, *Constitutions and Constitutionalism,* 12–14.

[31] See Wesley W. Horton, *The Connecticut State Constitution: A Reference Guide* (Westport, Conn.: Greenwood Press, 1993), 11–14; A. E. Dick Howard, *Commentaries on the Constitution of Virginia* (Charlottesville: University Press of Virginia, 1974); and Robert M. Bastress, *The West Virginia State Constitution: A Reference Guide* (Westport, Conn.: Greenwood Press, 1995), 3–9.

[32] Orth, *North Carolina State Constitution,* 8–11.

[33] On the events in Rhode Island, see Gettleman, *The Dorr Rebellion.* On extralegal conventions in other states, see Henretta, "Rise and Decline," 62–63; and, more generally, Jameson, *Treatise on Constitutional Conventions.*

[34] For a summary of apportionment formulas in the original state constitutions, see Dixon, *Democratic Representation,* 72–75, chart 3.

[35] Louisiana Constitution of 1812, art. 2, sec. 10; and Montana Constitution of 1889, art. 6, sec. 4.

employed population as the primary criterion but capped the representation of urban counties.[36] Many state constitutions assigned representatives on the basis of population but mandated that each county should have at least one representative.[37] This use of counties for representation let states avoid the difficulty and expense of drawing equipopulous districts. In most midwestern and western states, the use of counties may also have seemed politically neutral, because those states did not inherit the severe conflicts between settled areas and frontier regions or between urban and rural interests found in the eastern states. These factors made reliance on political subdivisions relatively noncontroversial, at least initially, a matter of convenience rather than of principle.[38]

Nevertheless, by the end of the nineteenth century, both older states and newer states were experiencing constitutional conflicts rooted in the representation of political subdivisions. Some of these conflicts reflected the unanticipated impact of political changes. For example, the Kansas Constitution guaranteed one seat in the lower house for each county, with the remaining seats distributed according to population. This initially produced relatively minor population disparities, because the state had only 34 counties. But when the number of counties rose to 105, without a corresponding expansion in the size of the legislature, the number of seats apportioned on the basis of population fell drastically, even with the same apportionment formula, and the resulting population disparities prompted calls for reform.[39] More frequently, however, conflicts resulted from population shifts that accentuated urban-rural divisions. As the disparities in population among legislative districts increased, so too did the resistance of rural legislators, who recognized that remedying the disparities would entail a major loss of political power.[40] In the late nineteenth century, rural legislators in the East found allies among Republican reformers, who insisted that republican government required that rural

[36] Missouri Constitution of 1865, art. 4, sec. 2. This formula originated in an 1848 amendment to the Missouri Constitution of 1820, art. 3, secs. 2 and 4, and was retained in the Missouri Constitution of 1875, art. 4, sec. 2.

[37] See, for example, Arkansas Constitution of 1874, art. 8, sec. 1; Idaho Constitution of 1889, art. 19, sec. 2; and Michigan Constitution of 1835, art. 4, secs. 3–4.

[38] This was not true across the board. Politics in a few of these states—California and Illinois, among others—was dominated by north-south cleavages, which aggravated conflicts over apportionment. For an insightful analysis, see Hurst, *Growth of American Law*, 238–40.

[39] See Gordon E. Baker, *State Constitutions: Reapportionment* (New York: National Municipal League, 1960), 4.

[40] Delaware, for example, constitutionalized its system of malapportionment. Article 2, section 2 of its 1897 constitution specified legislative districts in detail, on an undemocratic basis, and made no provision for reapportionment. See Dealey, *Growth of State Constitutions*, 97.

communities not be overwhelmed by the legislative power of urban areas dominated by (Democratic) party machines.[41] These coalitions—more marriages of convenience than principled partnerships—not only blocked remedial action but in some instances adopted new apportionment formulas designed to limit further the power of urban areas. The New York Constitution of 1894, for example, increased the number of representatives assigned to each county, decreased those assigned on the basis of population, and capped representation for urban areas in both houses of the legislature.[42]

Political Participation

Constitutional disputes continued throughout the century over the composition of state electorates. The original thirteen states restricted the franchise to either freeholders or taxpayers. Some states admitted to the Union from 1800 to 1820, such as Ohio, continued that practice; while others, such as Alabama, instituted white manhood suffrage.[43] From the 1820s to Reconstruction, property and taxpaying requirements came under sustained attack in state constitutional conventions. A delegate to the Pennsylvania convention of 1838 summarized the basic argument: "does property, merely, elevate the character of an individual?—does it brighten the intellectual vision or fit the possessor in any degree, for the better discharge of the duties of a citizen?"[44] Animated by this Jacksonian faith in the common man (and in some southern conventions by appeals to racial unity as well), delegates demolished the last barriers to white manhood suffrage.[45] Even conservative delegates, fearful of being branded opponents of popular rule, joined the assault.[46] In some sparsely populated states eager to attract settlers, white aliens were also enfranchised as soon as they expressed their intention to become citizens, and

[41] Henretta, "Rise and Decline," 66–67; and Richard L. McCormick, *From Realignment to Reform: Political Change in New York State, 1893–1910* (Ithaca, N.Y.: Cornell University Press, 1981).

[42] New York Constitution of 1894, art. 5, secs. 3–4. For discussion of these changes, see McCormick, *From Realignment to Reform.*

[43] Ohio Constitution of 1802, art. 4, sec. 1; and Alabama Constitution of 1819, art. 3, sec. 5.

[44] Quoted in Rosalind L. Branning, *Pennsylvania Constitutional Development* (Pittsburgh: University of Pittsburgh Press, 1960), 25.

[45] On the connection between racial unity and suffrage expansion, see Williamson, *American Suffrage,* 233, 262. Some constitutions of the period even prohibited property requirements for voting. For examples of such prohibitions, see Mississippi Constitution of 1832, Bill of Rights, sec. 20; Minnesota Constitution of 1857, art. 1, sec. 17; and Kansas Constitution of 1859, Bill of Rights, sec. 20.

[46] These battles are discussed in Rodgers, *Contested Truths,* chap. 3, and in Williamson, *American Suffrage,* chaps. 10–14.

Minnesota also extended the vote to Indians "who have adopted the language, customs, and habits of civilization."[47] Only New England opposed the trend toward franchise expansion: Rhode Island imposed a property requirement for voting in its 1842 constitution, and amendments in the 1850s to the Connecticut and Massachusetts constitutions established literacy tests for voting.[48]

Ironically, the campaign to extend the franchise to white males was paralleled by an effort to disenfranchise African-Americans and other people of color. Most eighteenth-century state constitutions did not list race as a voting qualification; but in the early nineteenth century, states entering the Union began to restrict the vote to whites.[49] In some states, the decision to exclude African-Americans was made by popular referendum, as states submitted black suffrage as a separate referendum item accompanying a proposed constitution.[50] In others, convention delegates followed the developing practice of disenfranchisement in revising their constitutions. Even northern states such as Michigan and Minnesota insisted on white manhood suffrage in their initial constitutions, and Oregon specifically excluded Chinese residents from voting as well.[51] Delegates to the New York convention of 1821 imposed more stringent voting requirements on blacks than whites after narrowly defeating a disenfranchisement proposal, and those requirements were retained in

[47] See, for example, Minnesota Constitution of 1857, art. 7, sec. 1; Nebraska Constitution of 1866, art. 2, sec. 2; and Oregon Constitution of 1857, art. 2, sec. 2. See Don E. Fehrenbacher, "Constitutional History, 1848–1861," in Levy, *American Constitutional History*, 96; and Dealey, *Growth of State Constitutions*, 150.

[48] See Patrick T. Conley, *Democracy in Decline: Rhode Island's Constitutional Development, 1776–1841* (Providence: Rhode Island Historical Society, 1977); and Schouler, *Constitutional Studies*, 234–41.

[49] The only constitution as of 1800 with racial qualifications for voting was the South Carolina Constitution of 1790, art. 1, sec. 4. In some other states, such as Kentucky, which extended the franchise to "free male citizens," free blacks were not considered citizens and were excluded from voting. See Kentucky Constitution of 1792, art. 3, sec. 1; and Lowell B. Harrison, *Kentucky's Road to Statehood* (Lexington: University Press of Kentucky, 1992), 122. For an early example of the shift to racial qualification in northern constitutions, see Ohio Constitution of 1802, art. 4, sec. 1. For general discussions of the phenomenon of racial exclusion from the franchise, see Rodgers, *Contested Truths*, chap. 3; Henretta, "Rise and Decline," 52–54; and Eric Foner, "From Slavery to Citizenship: Blacks and the Right to Vote," in Donald W. Rogers, ed., *Voting and the Spirit of American Democracy* (Urbana: University of Illinois Press, 1990).

[50] For an example of a referendum provision, see Iowa Constitution of 1846, art. 11, sec. 14. More generally, see Ellis Paxon Oberholtzer, *The Referendum in America* (New York: Da Capo, 1971), 119–20.

[51] Michigan Constitution of 1835, art. 2, sec. 1; Michigan Constitution of 1850, art. 7, sec. 1; Minnesota Constitution of 1857, art. 7, sec. 1; and Oregon Constitution of 1857, art. 2, sec. 2. For discussion of the debate over exclusion of Chinese from the franchise, see Johnson, *Founding the Far West*, 180–81.

the constitution of 1846.[52] Only the New England states (with the exception of Connecticut) refused to impose racially discriminatory qualifications for voting, so that by 1860 only five states permitted free blacks to vote.[53]

The decade following the Civil War marked the high point of suffrage expansion. The ratification of the Fifteenth Amendment in 1870 led Northern states to eliminate express legal restrictions on black suffrage, although some border states continued efforts to contain the black vote. An 1870 amendment to the Maryland Constitution, for example, added a property qualification for voting, which was expected to fall more heavily on African-Americans.[54] Reconstruction constitutions in the South endorsed universal manhood suffrage even before the adoption of the Fifteenth Amendment.[55] Some of these constitutions disenfranchised unregenerate rebels, though the breadth of the exclusions varied from state to state and typically lasted less than a decade. Other Reconstruction constitutions excluded few or no Confederates, despite concerns about their reclaiming political power, because denying the vote to a class of citizens seemed to convention delegates inconsistent with their principled commitment to manhood suffrage.[56]

The last decades of the nineteenth century witnessed a major shift in perspective and in constitutional provisions. With the end of Reconstruction, Southern states embraced the position of a delegate to the Georgia convention of 1877, who boasted: "I will fix it so that the people shall rule and the Negro shall never be heard from."[57] Nine former members of the Confederacy held constitutional conventions from 1874 to 1902, seeking through literacy tests, poll taxes, and other devices to achieve what had been pursued earlier through violence and intimidation.[58] Horizontal federalism facilitated this "public conspiracy," with Southern

[52] See Henretta, "Rise and Decline," 52–55.

[53] Leon F. Litwack, North of Slavery: The Negro in the Free States, 1790–1860 (Chicago: University of Chicago Press, 1961), 91–94.

[54] For discussion of these and other attempts to limit the extent or effect of black suffrage, see Foner, Reconstruction, 319–23, 422.

[55] For a useful study of the process of franchise extension in one state, see Phyllis F. Field, The Politics of Race in New York: The Struggle for Black Suffrage in the Civil War Era (Ithaca, N.Y.: Cornell University Press, 1982).

[56] Foner, Reconstruction, 324.

[57] Quoted in Kousser, Shaping of Southern Politics, 209. Note the implicit definition of the white population as "the people."

[58] The best account of the transformation of voting requirements is Kousser, Shaping of Southern Politics. Other helpful works include Perman, The Road to Redemption; Joel Williamson, The Crucible of Race: Black-White Relations in the American South since Emancipation (New York: Oxford University Press, 1984); and Malcolm Cook McMillan, Constitutional Development in Alabama, 1798–1901: A Study in Politics, the Negro, and Sectionalism (Chapel Hill: University of North Carolina Press, 1955).

states freely borrowing suffrage-reduction mechanisms and constitutional language from sister states. As J. Morgan Kousser has noted,

> There was a slight pause after the first enactment of any particular mechanism, perhaps to test the reaction of Northerners and the state's own electors. When Congress did not intervene, and when voters did not rise up against the disenfranchisers, legislators in other states felt free to write similar laws.[59]

The late-century movement to restrict the franchise was not limited to the South. Disfavored groups were also singled out for disenfranchisement in some western states: the California Constitution of 1879 disenfranchised Chinese residents, and the Idaho Constitution of 1889 both Chinese and Mormons.[60] In the East, the main concern was immigrant voters and the political machines that they supported, although suffrage reformers typically portrayed their goals as raising the quality of the voting public and eliminating corruption and fraud in elections. Some of the qualifications for voting inserted in northern constitutions to limit the immigrant vote paralleled those employed in the South. Thus, in the last two decades of the nineteenth century, several states adopted educational requirements for voting—usually requiring an ability to read and write English—and Rhode Island imposed a poll tax. Northern constitutions experimented with other suffrage restrictions as well. The New York Constitution of 1894, for example, introduced secret voting and the use of voting machines in place of paper ballots, both of which required voters to be able to read the names of candidates, and imposed burdensome registration requirements and a ninety-day waiting period for naturalized citizens before voting.[61] Several states also withdrew the franchise from aliens seeking citizenship.[62]

The sole exception to the movement for suffrage contraction was the campaign for woman suffrage.[63] Women seeking the vote early on appropriated the arguments for popular sovereignty used to enfranchise

---

[59] Kousser, *Shaping of Southern Politics,* 40.

[60] California Constitution of 1879, art. 2, sec. 1; and Idaho Constitution of 1889, art. 6, sec. 3. On the role of race in the California convention of 1879, see Swisher, *Motivation and Political Technique,* chap. 6; and Johnson, *Founding the Far West,* 252–56. On anti-Chinese and anti-Mormon sentiment in Idaho, see Donald Crowley and Florence Heffron, *The Idaho State Constitution: A Reference Guide* (Westport, Conn.: Greenwood Press, 1994), 6–7; and Dennis Colson, *Idaho's Constitution: The Tie That Binds* (Moscow: University of Idaho Press, 1991), chap. 8.

[61] See McCormick, *From Realignment to Reform,* 53–54; and Keller, *Affairs of State,* 527.

[62] These states included Florida, Michigan, Minnesota, Alabama, Colorado, and North Dakota. See Keller, *Affairs of State,* 527.

[63] This chapter's account of the campaign for women's suffrage relies on Alan P. Grimes, *The Puritan Ethic and Woman Suffrage* (New York: Oxford University Press, 1967); Beverly Beeton, *Women Vote in the West: The Woman Suffrage Movement, 1869–1896* (New York: Garland, 1986); and Eleanor Flexner, *Century of Struggle: The Women's Rights Movement in the United States* (Cambridge, Mass.: Belknap Press, 1975).

white males, an ironic twist on the insistence by conservatives that manhood suffrage was unreasonable because it would logically lead to woman suffrage. After the mid–nineteenth century, few constitutional conventions escaped consideration of the issue. Initially, as the New York convention of 1867 and the California convention of 1879 illustrate, overwhelming majorities rejected the vote for women, although a few states did permit them to vote on school issues or other matters.[64] By the late nineteenth century, however, the suffrage movement began to achieve some notable successes, beginning in the western states. Colorado, Idaho, Utah, and Wyoming all adopted women's suffrage in the last decade of the nineteenth century, the latter two by including woman suffrage in their original constitutions.[65]

STATE AND ECONOMY

The reluctance of Congress to fashion national economic policy during the nineteenth century, together with prevailing economic theories about the need for promotional efforts and regulation, virtually ensured state intervention in the economy and constitutional conflicts arising out of the scope and character of that involvement. The character of this intervention revealed the states' ambivalence about economic development and its prerequisites. States eagerly sought economic prosperity for their citizens; yet they remained suspicious of groups and organizations whose economic success seemed to undermine the social order, to threaten the economic prospects of others, or to rest on advantages not available to the general citizenry. They therefore sought, with some trepidation, to rein in those whose success appeared to rest on unfair advantage, all the while fearful of the consequences of impeding economic development. Nineteenth-century state constitutions reflect this ambivalence.

Economic Promotion and the Dual Perspective on Economic Activity

ECONOMIC PROMOTION IN ANTEBELLUM AMERICA

During the early nineteenth century, it was widely assumed that many important economic functions, particularly the development of transportation and infrastructure, would not occur without the encouragement

---

[64] See Galie, New York State Constitution, 15; Joseph P. Grodin, Calvin R. Massey, and Richard B. Cunningham, The California State Constitution: A Reference Guide (Westport, Conn.: Greenwood Press, 1993), 14; and Dealey, Growth of State Constitutions, 152–53.

[65] These developments are discussed in Gordon Morris Bakken, Rocky Mountain Constitution Making, 1850–1912 (Westport, Conn.: Greenwood Press, 1987), chap. 8.

and support of government.[66] State governments therefore offered a wide array of inducements to encourage economic development. Southern states borrowed funds to enlarge banking facilities and support railroad development, issuing state bonds to supply working capital.[67] Many northern and midwestern states constructed canals and other public works, often in partnership with private concerns, in order to facilitate the transportation of goods to major markets. The states also granted special charters to private corporations—such as turnpike corporations, bridge corporations, and railroad corporations—and enlisted them in developing transportation and communication links by dispensing benefits ranging from subsidies to outright grants of monopoly rights. The Jacksonian opposition to *federal* support for internal improvements as beyond the powers granted to Congress by the Constitution, helps explain why the states took the lead in these promotional efforts. So too does the prevailing mercantilist assumption that development depended on special protections for enterprises potentially unprofitable without them.[68] Corruption of state legislatures by potential recipients of state largesse undoubtedly played a role as well.[69] But particularly influential in promoting the states' often-reckless promotional efforts were the hope of economic windfalls—what Marvin Meyers has called "the gaudy mid-thirties dream of sudden fortune"—encouraged by the spectacular success of the Erie Canal, and the fear of being left behind, as other states courted prosperity with speculative ventures.[70] As J. Willard Hurst has

[66] Our account of state economic boosterism relies on Herbert Hovenkamp, *Enterprise and American Law, 1836–1937* (Cambridge: Harvard University Press, 1991); Louis Hartz, *Economic Policy and Democratic Thought: Pennsylvania, 1776–1860* (Cambridge: Harvard University Press, 1948); Oscar Handlin and Mary Flug Handlin, *Commonwealth: A Study of the Role of Government in the American Economy: Massachusetts, 1774–1861* (Cambridge, Mass.: Belknap Press, 1969); Heins, *Constitutional Restrictions against Debt*; and Gunn, *The Decline of Authority*.

[67] For a thorough examination of policy in one state, see Milton Sydney Heath, *Constructive Liberalism: The Role of the State in Economic Development in Georgia to 1860* (Cambridge: Harvard University Press, 1954).

[68] Hovenkamp, *Enterprise and American Law*, 37–38; and Hartz, *Economic Policy*, chap. 3.

[69] The mechanisms of corruption took various forms. In Pennsylvania, "[a]nticipating demand for particular types of [corporate] charters, lobbyists not uncommonly put through the charters, then offered them for sale to the interested parties. . . . The legislature at times helped these hucksters of 'floating' charters by refusing to enact charters for persons wishing to incorporate so that they would have to purchase at enhanced prices charters already authorized" (Branning, *Pennsylvania Constitutional Development*, 42).

[70] For data on the economic consequences of the completion of the Erie Canal, see Reginald McGrane, *Foreign Bondholders and American State Debts* (New York: Macmillan, 1935), 5. The quotation is drawn from Marvin Meyers, *The Jacksonian Persuasion: Politics and Belief* (Stanford, Calif.: Stanford University Press, 1957), 114.

noted, "All had in common a deep faith in the social benefits to flow from a rapid increase in productivity; all shared an impatience to get on with the job by whatever means functionally adapted to it, including the law."[71]

Coexisting in some tension with this enthusiasm for the release of productive forces, however, was a suspicion of special privilege. This suspicion was reflected in eighteenth-century constitutional demands for impartial government, for a "government . . . instituted for the common benefit, protection and security of the people, nation or community; and not for the particular emolument or advantage of any single man, family, or set of men."[72] Such provisions were not an expression of class antagonisms. Rather, they reflected a judgment about the forms and sources of wealth. Nineteenth-century Americans framed the distinction implicit in this judgment in various ways. Jacksonians typically contrasted the "real people," whose stable income resulted from honest, sober work, with the "money power," whose wealth arose from financial manipulation and special privilege.[73] Antebellum economists distinguished "producers," who created true wealth and therefore deserved economic rewards, both from laborers and, more importantly, from "capitalists," who used their privileged market and legal position to create false paper-money wealth.[74] Yet whatever the formulation, the prevailing belief was that one's economic success should reflect one's contribution to the real wealth of the society.

Constitutional efforts to reconcile the release of economic energies with the avoidance of special privilege began early in the nineteenth century. New York, concerned that the process of incorporation had become too politicized, in 1821 required a two-thirds vote of each house to create or renew a corporate charter.[75] Delaware in 1831 pioneered the use of reservation clauses, under which states retained the right to amend imprudent or corrupt grants to private entities and regulate grantees in the public interest. A number of states followed Delaware's lead. Several states also adopted antimonopoly provisions or equality guarantees designed to safeguard the majority from minority privilege.[76] The main impetus for constitutional change came from the economic collapse of

[71] James Willard Hurst, *Law and the Conditions of Freedom in the Nineteenth-Century United States* (Madison: University of Wisconsin Press, 1956), 7.

[72] Pennsylvania Constitution of 1776, Declaration of Rights, art. 5.

[73] Meyers, *The Jacksonian Persuasion*, chaps. 2 and 5.

[74] Tony A. Freyer, *Producers versus Capitalists: Constitutional Conflict in Antebellum America* (Charlottesville: University Press of Virginia, 1994).

[75] New York Constitution of 1821, art. 7, sec. 9.

[76] Robert F. Williams, "Equality Guarantees in State Constitutional Law," *Texas Law Review* 63 (March–April 1985): 1195–1224.

1837, when nine states defaulted on their debts. In its aftermath, state constitutions were revised or amended to curtail legislative promotion of economic development and remove public authority from allocation decisions. As a delegate to the Ohio convention of 1850–51 plaintively put it, "I wish to see the State Government brought back to its simple and appropriate functions, [leaving] railroad, canal, turnpike and other corporate associations, to get along on their own credit, without any connection or partnership with the State whatever."[77] The New York Constitution of 1846, for example, forbade lending of the state's credit and required direct popular approval for new debt.[78] Most existing states adopted similar provisions, and all states entering the Union after 1845 wrote some sort of debt restriction into their constitutions. Many states also mandated general incorporation laws, either forbidding special incorporation laws (with their privileges and incentives) or permitting them only, as in New York, when "the objects of the corporation cannot be attained under general laws."[79] The Virginia Constitution of 1851 sought to prevent legislative corruption by prohibiting employees of banks from serving in the legislature.[80] The Illinois Constitution of 1848, which directed the general assembly to "encourage internal improvement, by passing liberal laws of incorporation for that purpose," exemplified the effort to secure economic development without special privilege.[81]

Two aspects of these constitutional changes are particularly noteworthy. First, the constitutional reforms were not confined to those states that had suffered from overzealous efforts to promote economic development. Rather, the experience in those states served a cautionary function, inducing other states to construct constitutional barriers to prevent such abuses from occurring within their borders. Second, while twentieth-century reformers have attacked state constitutions as excessively long and detailed, the history recounted here suggests that some of the length and detail of state constitutions represented a considered response to real problems. State legislatures had proved unworthy of trust, and it was therefore deemed necessary to restrict their powers. Because state legis-

---

[77] Quoted in Kermit L. Hall, *The Magic Mirror: Law in American History* (New York: Oxford University Press, 1989), 103–4.

[78] New York Constitution of 1846, art. 7, sec. 9.

[79] New York Constitution of 1846, art. 3, sec. 18. For a thorough analysis of this constitution's economic provisions, see Gunn, *The Decline of Authority,* 183–89.

[80] Virginia Constitution of 1851, art. 4, sec. 7.

[81] Illinois Constitution of 1848, art. 10, sec. 6. Yet the constitution prefaced this extension of the opportunity to obtain corporate status in sections 1–5 with severe restrictions on corporations with banking powers or privileges. Among these was a requirement that any statute authorizing such corporations not go into effect unless approved by popular referendum, thus underscoring the notion that the citizenry could be trusted to veto unwarranted privilege.

latures possessed plenary legislative power, successful restriction required prohibitions and limitations that were specific and detailed. Much of the constitutional legislation that swelled state constitutions during the antebellum period thus reflected not a lack of skill in constitution making or a misunderstanding of constitutionalism but rather a determined attempt to restrict state legislative forays into economic boosterism and favoritism.

ECONOMIC PROMOTION IN THE POSTWAR ERA

The same cycle of promotional enthusiasm followed by retrenchment that had characterized the antebellum era repeated itself in the decade or so after the Civil War. In the South, delegates to constitutional conventions hoped to resurrect and redirect their ravaged economies by a constitutional policy of subsidy and promotion.[82] Indeed, even before adjourning, delegates to the North Carolina convention of 1868 voted over $2 million in financial assistance to railroads. Every Reconstruction constitution permitted direct subsidies to railroads and other private entities, most authorized the loan of state credit as well, and some for the first time established limited liability for corporate stockholders. At the same time, these constitutions did attempt to forestall anticipated abuses. Thus, Arkansas banned all special acts of aid and incorporation (while permitting general aid and general incorporation laws); Alabama required a two-thirds vote in both houses to lend the state's credit to any company; and North Carolina required that new debts be covered by taxes or state bonds.[83] The promotional thrust of these documents affected other constitutional provisions as well. For instance, delegates in several conventions rejected arguments to repudiate state debts incurred after secession out of a concern to maintain business confidence in their states.[84]

The economic crisis of 1873 sharpened criticism of government expenditures among white southerners and swelled demands for tax relief, leading to a shift of constitutional direction in the South. If the economic keynote of Reconstruction constitutions was economic revival, the aim of post-Reconstruction constitutions was, in the words of a delegate to the Alabama convention of 1875, "to govern as little as possible."[85] Even

[82] Our account of postwar economic policy in the South primarily relies on Mark W. Summers, *Railroads, Reconstruction, and the Gospel of Prosperity: Aid under the Radical Republicans, 1865–1877* (Princeton: Princeton University Press, 1984); Perman, *The Road to Redemption*; and Foner, *Reconstruction*.

[83] Arkansas Constitution of 1868, art. 5, sec. 48; Alabama Constitution of 1868, art. 4, secs. 32 and 33; and North Carolina Constitution of 1868, art. 5, sec. 5.

[84] Summers, *Railroads, Reconstruction*, 23–24. For an illustrative provision, see North Carolina Constitution of 1868, art. 1, sec. 6.

[85] Quoted in Perman, *The Road to Redemption*, 201.

before the adoption of new constitutions, amendments curtailed state promotional efforts. Thus, a Florida amendment forbade the use of public credit for the benefit of any individual or corporation, and a South Carolina amendment made loans of credit conditional on referendum support by two-thirds of all voters.[86] Delegates to the constitutional conventions of the mid-1870s also attempted to preclude future efforts to subsidize economic growth. The Alabama Constitution of 1875, for example, eliminated the post of commissioner of industrial resources and imposed an absolute ban on state, county, or local aid to corporations for internal improvements.[87] Delegates in Georgia and Louisiana repudiated railroad bonds and tightened legislative strictures against their repayment.[88] Those who championed these constitutional changes assumed either that frugal government would attract investment to their states or that agriculture, rather than industry, was basic to the states' economic revival.

In the North, the renewed promotional zeal was constrained somewhat by the constitutional restrictions adopted in the 1840s. Nonetheless, according to Harry Scheiber the postwar era was "the high-water mark of munificent . . . public aid to railroad corporations."[89] State governments skirted constitutional restraints on state aid by approving local aid to railroad companies. From 1866 to 1873, state legislatures approved over eight hundred proposals to grant local aid to railroad companies. New York, Illinois, and Missouri together authorized over $70 million worth of aid.[90] The Ohio Constitution barred both state and local aid; but voters in Cincinnati, eager for a rail link to the upper South, voted bonds for the public construction and operation of the rail line, and other municipalities followed suit.[91] Not surprisingly, when the economic crisis of 1873 struck, local governments found themselves overcommitted. As Morton Keller has observed, "nothing so clearly illustrates the changing relationship of railroads to the polity as does [the] shift from eager competition for railroad development to desperate efforts to avoid the ensuing legacy of debt."[92] In the wake of this change of attitude, further restrictions were added to northern constitutions to prevent a repetition of reckless promotional efforts.

---

[86] Summers, *Railroads, Reconstruction,* 285.

[87] Alabama Constitution of 1875, art. 4, sec. 54. For discussion of these developments, see McMillan, *Constitutional Development in Alabama,* 196–200.

[88] Perman, *The Road to Redemption,* 206–9.

[89] Harry N. Scheiber, "Federalism and the American Economic Order, 1789–1910," *Law and Society Review* 10 (fall 1975): 110.

[90] Keller, *Affairs of State,* 165.

[91] Keller, *Affairs of State,* 167.

[92] Keller, *Affairs of State,* 423.

REGULATION AND CORPORATE POWER

Throughout the antebellum era, state governments had by statute and the common law pervasively regulated economic activity to ensure fair competition and safeguard public safety, health, and morals.[93] In the aftermath of the Civil War, however, the states faced a new regulatory challenge, because the nation had entered a new economic era, one in which large corporations, such as railroads, wielded significant economic and political power.[94] The threat posed by these corporate giants prompted farmers and laborers, particularly in the Midwest, to organize to combat their influence. Because farmer and labor groups distrusted state governments, which they believed (often correctly) were dominated or corrupted by corporate wealth, they looked to constitutional reform for relief, hoping to achieve their goals through constitutional revision. Illinois's "Granger constitution" of 1870, with its detailed provisions on grain elevators and its regulation of railroads, exemplifies their efforts.[95] Late in the nineteenth century, several western states also drafted their initial constitutions or revised their early constitutions as a response to the rise of large corporations and their economic and political power.

State constitution-makers during the late nineteenth and early twentieth centuries reaffirmed the inalienable power of the legislature to regulate corporations for the public good and devised a wide variety of mechanisms to curtail the abuse of corporate power.[96] First, they incorporated into their constitutions detailed legislation regulating railroads and other corporations and protecting consumers and labor.[97] Idaho's 1889 charter declared railroads to be public highways and subjected their rates to legislative regulation.[98] The Montana and Wyoming constitutions abro-

[93] The best overview of state regulation during the first three-quarters of the nineteenth century is Novak, *The People's Welfare*.

[94] Indications of this concern about corporate power surfaced even prior to the Civil War. See Johnson, *Founding the Far West*, 122–25, for an account of the debate over corporate power in the California convention of 1849.

[95] Illinois Constitution of 1870, art. 13, secs. 1–4. Some Granger provisions were challenged as violations of the federal Constitution, but the U.S. Supreme Court rejected the challenge in *Munn* v. *Illinois,* 94 U.S. 113 (1877). For a discussion of the Illinois Constitution and its provisions protecting farmers, see Friedman, *History of American Law,* 349–50.

[96] See, for example, Montana Constitution of 1889, art. 15, sec. 3.

[97] In fact, the constitutionalization of detailed economic legislation can be traced as far back as the Florida Constitution of 1839, whose banking article was patterned after a New York statute of the previous year. The provision was sufficiently detailed and complete that the Florida legislature did not need to enact a state banking law. See Freund, *Standards of American Legislation,* 163.

[98] Idaho Constitution, art. 11, sec. 5. For discussion of the development of the corporations article of the Idaho Constitution, see Colson, *Idaho's Constitution,* chap. 7.

gated the "fellow-servant" rule, a common-law doctrine that prevented workers from collecting in court litigation for work-related injuries; the Wyoming charter also forbade labor contracts that released employers from liability for injuries suffered by workers; and the North Dakota Constitution forbade the exchange of worker "blacklists" between corporations.[99] Second, constitution-makers created institutions designed to monitor and, where necessary, curb illicit practices and abuses. Thus, the Idaho Constitution established a labor commissions, and the Wyoming Constitution an inspector of mines.[100] Third, constitution-makers specifically withdrew legislative authority to enact statutes that might advantage corporate interests. The Idaho and Montana constitutions, for instance, both specifically forbade enactment of retroactive laws favorable to railroads.[101] Finally, state constitution-makers attempted to prevent corruption of state officials by corporate interests by establishing constitutional limitations on the gifts and other benefits that those officials could accept from them.[102]

Yet convention records reveal that many delegates opposed stringent restrictions on corporations. This opposition to regulation was not confined to apologists "owned" by the corporations. For if corporations were feared as a source of corruption and oppression, their importance as a source of capital for economic development was also recognized. Constitution-makers acknowledged, albeit reluctantly, that the prosperity of their states was inextricably linked to the success of large "foreign" corporations and feared that excessive restrictions might drive those corporations from the state. Western delegates in particular perceived this connection and, while imposing some restrictions, rejected more stringent ones and offered important concessions designed to attract corporations. One such concession, incorporated into the Colorado and Idaho constitutions, permitted the taking of private property for private as well

[99] Montana Constitution of 1889, art. 15, sec. 16; Wyoming Constitution of 1889, art. 9, sec. 4, and art. 10, sec. 4; and North Dakota Constitution of 1889, art. 17, sec. 212. For discussion of these provisions, see Hicks, *Constitutions of Northwest States*, 92–95; Bakken, *Rocky Mountain Constitution Making*, 80 and 85; and Keiter and Newcomb, *The Wyoming State Constitution*, 188–89 and 193–96.

[100] Idaho Constitution of 1889, art. 13, secs. 1 and 8; and Wyoming Constitution of 1889, art. 9, sec. 1. For discussion of these provisions, see Bakken, *Rocky Mountain Constitution Making*, chap. 7; Colson, *Idaho's Constitution*, 127–29; and Hicks, *Constitutions of Northwest States*, 92–95.

[101] Idaho Constitution, art. 11, sec. 12; and Montana Constitution of 1889, art. 15, sec. 13. The Idaho provision is discussed in Colson, *Idaho's Constitution*, 125; and Crowley and Heffron, *The Idaho State Constitution*, 206.

[102] For surveys of pertinent provisions, see Hicks, *Constitutions of Northwest States*, 56–63; and Friedman, *History of American Law*, 349–50.

as public use, provided that just compensation was paid.[103] Such provisions supported the development of mining interests in those states, particularly large-scale, capital-intensive quartz mining.[104] Another significant concession was Nevada's elimination of taxation on mines. Opponents of the exemption charged that its beneficiaries would be "foreigners—aliens, who wish us no good."[105] Proponents conceded the point but successfully maintained that taxation of mines would drive away the "foreign" capital that was essential to developing the only resource the state possessed. These same arguments were reiterated as other conventions considered what constitutional restrictions to place on corporations. In Montana, for example, a proposal to make corporation directors and stockholders jointly liable for corporate debts was defeated after a delegate argued that it would "not only drive all foreign capital invested in the state away but would prevent all future inquiries."[106] In Colorado, another limitation was defeated after a delegate charged that if adopted, "not another mile of railroad [would] be built" in the state.[107]

The Scope and Distribution of State Power

The power of state legislatures is circumscribed only by the grants of power to the federal government and by limitations found in the federal Constitution or in state constitutions. Eighteenth-century state constitutions imposed few restrictions on state legislatures beyond those included in their declarations of rights, and even these were typically framed as admonitory principles rather than as specific legal restraints. This absence of detailed limitations may have reflected a belief that there was little to fear from a body that represented the people; alternatively, it may have indicated a confidence that broad suffrage, frequent elections, and the power to instruct representatives afforded sufficient checks on legislative abuses. Whatever the explanation, experience with an almost unfettered legislative power during the nineteenth century soon dispelled those notions. Loss of faith in the judgment and probity of legislators led state constitution-makers to impose increasingly stringent procedural and substantive restrictions on state legislatures and to transfer powers from state legislatures to other officials or to the people directly. During the nineteenth century also, most state constitutions abandoned annual election and extended the term of office for state legislators, perhaps indicat-

---

[103] Colorado Constitution, art. 2, sec. 14; and Idaho Constitution, art. 1, sec. 14.
[104] Colson, *Idaho's Constitution*, 64–65.
[105] Quoted in Johnson, *Founding the Far West*, 224.
[106] Quoted in Bakken, *Rocky Mountain Constitution Making*, 78.
[107] Bakken, *Rocky Mountain Constitution Making*, 77.

ing less confidence in the electoral connection as a check on legislative abuses.

CONSTITUTIONAL RESTRICTIONS ON STATE LEGISLATURES

In 1835 Alexis de Tocqueville observed that "the legislature of each state is faced by no power capable of resisting it."[108] But beginning in the 1830s, state constitution-makers sought to impose limits on these supreme legislatures. Initially, their restrictions focused on the process of legislation. Some state constitutions required extraordinary majorities to

---

[108] Alexis de Tocqueville, *Democracy in America,* ed. J. P. Mayer (Garden City, N.Y.: Doubleday, 1969), 89. Tocqueville's more general criticisms of nineteenth-century state constitutions and his insistence on the superiority of the federal Constitution are worth detailed consideration.

First, Tocqueville notes that "the federal constitution differs essentially from that of the states in its intended aims, but it is very similar in the means of attaining those aims" (151). This observation underscores the different responsibilities of nation and state, which might account for constitutional differences. Although Tocqueville suggests the means for achieving the aims are "very similar," he is referring to the "form of government." He detects substantial differences in the powers of the various branches, nation and state, as well as in the constitutions' views of popular rule.

Second, Tocqueville suggests that the superiority of the federal Constitution derives in part from the fact that the federal constitution-makers benefited from the (negative) experience of state constitution-makers. He notes that this, of course, does not explain the federal Constitution's superiority to state constitutions of newly admitted states nor to new constitutions adopted by the original states. In both these instances, state constitution-makers could presumably have benefited from the federal constitutional experience. Tocqueville argues, however, that these state constitution-makers did not look to the federal model for direction. Instead, they "have almost always exaggerated rather than diminished the defects in the earlier constitutions" (152).

Third, Tocqueville sees as the major defect of state constitutions their excessively popular character. In contrast with the federal Constitution, which makes the people merely the source of governmental powers, state constitutions tie legislators to "the slightest wishes of their constituents" by short terms of office. In addition, bicameral state legislatures offer no check to popular whims, since the "two parts of the legislature were composed of the same elements elected in the same manner" (153). Related to this is the tendency to concentrate power in these legislatures, with the executive "just a blind and passive tool of its will" and the judiciary less independent because of limited tenure and insecure emoluments.

Tocqueville's comments thus confirm that a different constitutional perspective animates state constitutions. State constitutions are different in their aims. They are also different in their institutional features. Although state institutions appear similar to those of the federal government, their character is quite distinct. These dissimilarities did not diminish with the creation of post-1787 constitutions; rather, they continued both in states that had begun their constitutional experience with independence and in states newly admitted to the Union. Finally, state constitutions are different in their understanding of the role of the citizenry in government. Whereas the federal Constitution sees the populace as the source of power but views representation as a necessary corrective for popular passions, state constitutions are much more willing to allow the citizenry to direct the policy of the state government.

adopt certain types of legislation, under the assumption that it would be more difficult to marshal such majorities for dubious endeavors.[109] Others imposed procedural restrictions designed to prevent duplicity and promote greater openness and deliberation, assuming that greater transparency in the legislative process would deter legislative abuses or at least increase accountability for them. Thus, state constitutions mandated that all bills be referred to committee, that they be read three times prior to enactment, that their titles accurately describe their contents, that they embrace a single subject, that they not be altered during their passage so as to change their original purpose, and so on. Other provisions required that the amendment or revision of laws not proceed by mere reference to their titles, that statutes be phrased in plain language, that taxing and spending measures be enacted only by recorded vote, and—most importantly—that no special laws be enacted where a general law was possible.[110] By the end of the nineteenth century, most state constitutions included several of these procedural requirements.

Even more important were the substantive restrictions imposed on state legislatures. These constitutional restrictions, likewise designed to prevent legislative partiality, seemed to reflect—in the words of a late-nineteenth-century observer—a "belief that legislatures are by nature utterly careless of the public welfare, if not hopelessly corrupt."[111] Constitutional prohibitions on loaning the credit of the state to private entities and the bans on special corporation acts, discussed earlier, exemplify these concerns. So too does the imposition in most states from 1840 to 1870 of a constitutional requirement of equal and uniform taxation, restricting the unfettered legislative discretion that had previously prevailed.[112] In the wake of the Civil War, constitutional prohibitions on

[109] See, for example, New York Constitution of 1821, art. 7, sec. 9; and Mississippi Constitution of 1832, art. 7, sec. 8.

[110] For illustrative provisions, see reference of bills to committee—Pennsylvania Constitution of 1873, art. 3, sec. 2; three readings of bills before enactment—North Carolina Constitution of 1876, art. 2, sec. 23; title of bills to accurately reflect contents—Ohio Constitution of 1851, art. 2, sec. 16; bills to embrace only a single subject—South Carolina Constitution of 1868, art. 3, sec. 17; no change in the purpose of a bill during passage—Pennsylvania Constitution of 1873, art. 3, sec. 1; no revision or amendment of bills by reference—Oregon Constitution of 1857, art. 4, sec. 22; bills to be phrased in plain language—Oregon Constitution of 1857, art. 4, sec. 21; enactment by recorded vote—Virginia Constitution of 1851, art. 4, sec. 27; and general laws rather than special laws—Missouri Constitution of 1875, art. 4, sec. 53. For discussion of these restrictions, see Williams, "State Constitutional Limits"; Ruud, "No Law Shall Embrace"; and Charles C. Binney, *Restrictions upon Local and Special Legislation in State Constitutions* (Philadelphia: Kay and Brother, 1894).

[111] Binney, *Restrictions upon Legislation*, 9.

[112] See, for example, Ohio Constitution of 1851, art. 12, sec. 2; and Oregon Constitution of 1857, art. 9, sec. 1. For discussion of this change and its implications, see Morton J.

legislative action proliferated. For example, as late as 1860, Missouri's constitution imposed only three subject-matter restrictions on the legislature, but its 1875 constitution contained fifty-six.[113] Most restrictions were designed to combat special privilege and the threat of corruption by forbidding legislators from enacting special or local laws in specific areas of public policy.[114] Thus, state legislatures were forbidden to grant divorces, change names, remit fines or forfeitures, refund money paid into the state treasury, change the rules of evidence in any judicial proceeding, change county seats, and on and on.[115] The Illinois Constitution of 1870 prohibited the state legislature from addressing twenty fields of local or private concern, the Pennsylvania Constitution of 1873 forty, and the California Constitution of 1879 thirty-three.[116] Moreover, once a limitation was enshrined in a few constitutions, the interstate borrowing of provisions virtually guaranteed its appearance in others as well, as constitution-makers sought to avoid granting "too lax a discretion to transient representatives of the people."[117] A delegate to South Dakota's constitutional convention summarized the prevailing view: "The object of constitutions is to limit the legislature."[118]

Finally, nineteenth-century state constitutions limited the frequency and length of legislative sessions. At the outset of the century, state con-

---

Horowitz, *The Transformation of American Law, 1870–1960* (New York: Oxford University Press, 1992), 21–23; and, more generally, Wade J. Newhouse, *Constitutional Uniformity and Equality in State Taxation*, 2d ed. (Buffalo: William S. Hein, 1984).

[113] Henry Hitchcock, *American State Constitutions* (New York: G. P. Putnam's Sons, 1887), 35.

[114] Local and private laws dominated legislative business in the late nineteenth century. In Kentucky in 1883–84, for example, 94 percent of statutes concerned local or private matters. See Sheryl G. Snyder and Robert M. Ireland, "The Separation of Governmental Powers under the Constitution of Kentucky: A Legal and Historical Analysis of *L.R.C. v. Brown*," *Kentucky Law Journal* 73 (1984–85): 168. For data on Pennsylvania, see Keller, *Affairs of State*, 111; for New York, see Gunn, *The Decline of Authority*, 187–88. These local laws, especially those awarding trolley, water, gas, or other franchises, were widely recognized as a "perennial fountain of corruption" (Bryce, *The American Commonwealth*, 1:542). For a discussion of the political understanding underlying the restrictions on state legislatures, see Williams, "Equality Guarantees"; and Donald Marritz, "Making Equality Matter (Again): The Prohibition against Special Laws in the Pennsylvania Constitution," *Widener Journal of Public Law* 3 (1993): 161–215.

[115] These examples are all drawn from Binney, *Restrictions upon Legislation*, 131–80.

[116] Keller, *Affairs of State*, 112. For a comprehensive catalog of the constitutional restrictions on state legislatures, see Binney, *Restrictions upon Legislation*, 131–80.

[117] Schouler, *Constitutional Studies*, 210 n. 2. Some state-specific limitations were also imposed in response to abuses within particular states. For example, after the Kentucky legislature raided the common school fund during a recession, the state's 1851 constitution mandated that the fund be used only for education. See Kentucky Constitution of 1851, art. 11, sec. 1.

[118] Quoted in Hicks, *Constitutions of Northwest States*, 52.

stitutions imposed no limits on legislative sessions, and annual sessions were the norm. As early as 1835, however, the North Carolina Constitution limited the legislature to biennial regular sessions, and the Virginia Constitution of 1851 mandated that the legislature meet biennially "and not oftener," with sessions limited to ninety days.[119] After the Civil War, there was a nationwide movement to curb legislative sessions. A delegate to the California convention of 1879 even proposed that "[t]here shall be no legislature convened from and after the adoption of this Constitution, . . . and any person who shall be guilty of suggesting that a Legislature be held, shall be punished as a felon without benefit of clergy."[120] Although limiting legislative sessions served the reformers' goal of economy in government, equally important was their assumption that shorter sessions gave legislators less opportunity to do harm. By 1900, thirty-three state constitutions limited the length of legislative sessions, and only six state legislatures met annually.[121]

POPULAR RULE

Although nineteenth-century state constitution-makers believed that the main threat to effectual popular rule came from those seeking to obtain or retain special advantages, they also recognized the need to remove legal barriers to popular rule. This involved more than simply the extension of the vote to previously disenfranchised groups. During the first half of the nineteenth century, almost all states, acknowledging that political virtue was not confined to the wealthy or the orthodox, also abolished property and religious qualifications for officeholding.[122] Even more important, they dramatically expanded the range of offices subject to popular election and control. All states entering the Union during the nineteenth century opted for popular election of their governors, as did most existing states when they revised their constitutions. By 1860 only South Carolina retained legislative selection.[123] Nineteenth-century state constitutions made other executive offices elective as well—by 1880, over two-thirds of the states elected their secretary of state, their state

[119] On the North Carolina debate, see Green, *Constitutional Development*, 230–31; for Virginia, see the Virginia Constitution of 1851, art. 4, sec. 8. More generally, see Dealey, *Growth of State Constitutions*, 52–53.

[120] Quoted in Keller, *Affairs of State*, 114.

[121] Dealey, *Growth of State Constitutions*, 186–87.

[122] Some states did retain belief in God as a requirement for holding office. See, for example, Maryland Constitution of 1867, Declaration of Rights, art. 57. For an overview of religious qualifications for office and their elimination, see Antieau, Carroll, and Burke, *Religion under State Constitutions*, chap. 5.

[123] See, for example, New Jersey Constitution of 1844, art. 5, sec. 2; and Virginia Constitution of 1851, art. 5, sec. 2. It is noteworthy that Virginia retained legislative selection of the governor in its 1829 constitution.

treasurer, their auditor, and their attorney general.[124] Even technical offices such as state surveyor, canal commissioner, and prison inspector were made subject to popular election.[125] As a delegate to the Kentucky convention of 1850 complained, "[W]e have provided for the popular election of every public officer, save the dog catcher, and if the dogs could vote, we should have that as well."[126] Most state constitutions also shifted from appointment to election of sheriffs and other key local officials. Finally, every state entering the Union from 1846 to 1900 instituted popular election of judges, and many existing states abandoned legislative or executive appointment. Indeed, in the fourteen years after the influential Iowa and New York constitutions of 1846 instituted popular election of judges, twenty states moved from appointment to election for some or all of their judges; so that by 1861, twenty-four of the thirty-four states selected judges by election rather than by appointment.[127]

Popular election of state and local officials did more than empower the populace. It also reduced the power of state legislators, who in most states had controlled the appointment of executive officers, local officials, and judges. In addition, popular election of state officials signaled a shift in the understanding of popular government, as popular authority was vested not only in the legislature but in all branches of state government. As a result of popular election, executive officials could claim that they had just as strong a connection to the people, the source of all political authority, as did the legislature. This popular political base was essential for judges as well, because they were expected to make public policy. A delegate to the New York convention of 1846 noted that restrictions on the legislature invited an expansion of judicial power: "In reorganizing the legislative department we have made it less powerful for general legislation . . . [thus] a large share of judicial legislation will be inevitable, and we must endeavor to supply it."[128]

INSTITUTIONAL CHECKS ON STATE LEGISLATURES

Paralleling this movement toward popular election of executive officials and judges was an effort to enhance the autonomy and powers of governors, so that they could better check legislative abuses. By 1860, New York had eliminated its Council of Revision and Council of Appointment; Maryland, Rhode Island, Vermont, and Virginia had jet-

[124] McCarthy, *Widening Scope*, 52–55.

[125] New York Constitution of 1846, art. 5, secs. 2 and 3.

[126] Quoted in Kermit L. Hall, "The Judiciary on Trial: State Constitutional Reform and the Rise of an Elected Judiciary, 1846–1860," *Historian* 44 (May 1983): 340–41.

[127] On the election of judges, see Philip L. Dubois, *From Ballot to Bench: Judicial Elections and the Quest for Accountability* (Austin: University of Texas Press, 1980), chap. 1; and Hall, "The Judiciary on Trial."

[128] Quoted in Hall, "The Judiciary on Trial," 350–51.

tisoned their cumbersome governor's councils; and no state entering the Union after 1820 established any body with whom the governor exercised executive power.[129] All states entering the Union after 1800 except Ohio and West Virginia gave their governor a veto over legislation in their original constitutions, and by 1860 most of the original states had likewise done so when they revised their constitutions.[130] In the aftermath of the Civil War, efforts to enhance gubernatorial power continued in most states. Reconstruction constitutions in South Carolina, Tennessee, and Virginia all established gubernatorial vetoes.[131] New York and Pennsylvania approved constitutional amendments that increased to two-thirds of the total membership (as opposed to two-thirds of those voting) the legislative majority needed to override a gubernatorial veto.[132] By 1900, a number of states had given their governors the item veto, extended the governor's term of office, and/or had made governors eligible for reelection.[133] Yet at the same time that state constitution-makers were strengthening the governor's role vis-à-vis the legislature, they were undercutting the governor's administrative authority by dispersing executive power through popular election of executive officers and the proliferation of independent state agencies.[134]

After the Civil War, elected state judges also were increasingly willing to check state legislatures. The New York Court of Appeals, which had ruled only sixty-five laws unconstitutional prior to the Civil War, struck down almost two hundred from 1870 to 1900; and the Supreme Judicial Court of Massachusetts, which had invalidated only ten laws prior to 1860, struck down thirty-one from 1860 to 1893.[135] The Ohio Supreme

---

[129] On the changes in New York, see Galie, *New York State Constitution*, 6–10; on the changes in Maryland and Vermont, see Dealey, *Growth of State Constitutions*, 53, and Hill, *The Vermont State Constitution*, 14–15. Illinois adopted a Council of Revision modeled after New York's in its 1818 constitution (art. 3, sec. 19) but abandoned it in favor of a gubernatorial veto in its 1848 constitution (art. 4, sec. 21). As of 1860, the only states that retained gubernatorial councils were in New England (Maine, New Hampshire, and Massachusetts). See Schouler, *Constitutional Studies*, 272–73.

[130] John A. Fairlie, "The Veto Power of the State Governor," *American Political Science Review* 11 (August 1917): 473–93.

[131] South Carolina Constitution of 1868, art. 4, sec. 23; Tennessee Constitution of 1870, art. 3, sec. 18; and Virginia Constitution of 1870, art. 4, sec. 8.

[132] James A. Henretta, "Rethinking the State Constitutional Tradition," *Rutgers Law Journal* 22 (summer 1991): 824.

[133] For an incisive overview of the development of state executive branches during the nineteenth century, see Henretta, "Rethinking State Constitutional Tradition," 821–26.

[134] In New York, for example, there were only ten state agencies in 1800 but eighty-one in 1900. See Larry Sabato, *Goodbye to Good-Time Charlie: The American Governorship Transformed*, 2d ed. (Washington, D.C.: CQ Press, 1983), 6.

[135] Edward S. Corwin, "The Extension of Judicial Review in New York: 1783–1905," *Michigan Law Review* 15 (February 1917): 283–85; and Keller, *Affairs of State*, 362.

Court struck down fifty-seven statutes from 1880 to 1900, and the Virginia Supreme Court invalidated roughly one-third of all state statutes brought before it in the late nineteenth century.[136] In part, this new judicial activism stemmed from the more detailed constitutional limitations imposed on state legislatures; for when states imposed procedural and substantive limitations, state courts became the obvious forum for enforcing them.[137] Indeed, the Missouri Constitution of 1870 specifically authorized state judges to resolve conflicts over whether the legislature had passed a special law when a general law was possible, and an amendment to the Kansas Constitution did likewise.[138] In part, however, the unprecedented judicial intervention reflected a new judicial willingness to rule on the validity of the state economic regulations that proliferated in the late nineteenth century. Many scholars have dismissed the courts' rulings as merely reflecting a judicial aversion to legislation that interfered with laissez-faire capitalism.[139] This explanation, however, fails to explain why courts upheld some statutes while invalidating others. More recent scholars have recognized that state courts distinguished between valid economic regulations and invalid class legislation, based on whether they believed the challenged statutes served the public welfare or merely promoted the narrow interests of a particular group or class.[140] In drawing this distinction, the courts were attempting to reinforce a basic theme of nineteenth-century state constitutionalism, namely, that government must govern in the interest of all. Thus, the sameconcern for effectual republican government that motivated state constitution-makers appears to have motivated the judges enforcing state constitutional guidelines.

[136] Keller, *Affairs of State,* 362.

[137] Friedman, *History of American Law,* 355–62.

[138] Missouri Constitution of 1875, art. 4, sec. 53, clause 32; and Kansas Constitution, 1906 amendment to art. 2, sec. 17. For a discussion of the background of the amendment and the judiciary's responsibilities under it, see *Anderson v. Board of Commissioners of Cloud County,* 95 P. 583 (Kan. 1908).

[139] See, for example, Carl Brent Swisher, *American Constitutional Development* (Boston: Houghton Mifflin, 1943); Loren P. Beth, *The Development of the American Constitution, 1877–1917* (New York: Harper and Row, 1971); and William F. Swindler, *Court and Constitution in the Twentieth Century: The Old Legality, 1889–1932* (Indianapolis: Bobbs-Merrill, 1969).

[140] A recent excellent presentation of this position is Howard Gillman, *The Constitution Besieged* (Durham, N.C.: Duke University Press, 1993). Other revisionist accounts include Alan Jones, "Thomas M. Cooley and 'Laissez-Faire' Constitutionalism: A Reconsideration," *Journal of American History* 53 (March 1967): 751–71; Michael Les Benedict, "Laissez-Faire and Liberty: A Re-evaluation of the Meaning and Origins of Laissez-Faire Constitutionalism," *Law and History Review* 3 (fall 1985): 293–331; and David M. Gold, *The Shaping of Nineteenth-Century Law: John Appleton and Responsible Individualism* (Westport, Conn.: Greenwood Press, 1990).

DIRECT POPULAR GOVERNMENT

As a general rule, the states have not been nearly as sanguine as has the federal government about the advantages of representative government over direct democracy. Thus, a number of states have periodically sought to ensure that the popular will would prevail by outflanking the state legislature, by substituting direct popular rule for rule by permanent governmental institutions. During the heyday of constitutional conventions in the nineteenth century, some delegates claimed that the conventions displaced normal government and restored political power directly to the people. As an Illinois delegate enthused in 1847, "We are what the people of the State would be, if they were congregated here in one mass meeting."[141] Based on this theory of popular sovereignty through convention sovereignty, delegates on occasion assumed the responsibilities of legislators, imposing taxes and enacting laws.[142] Indeed, the South Carolina convention of 1860 did not relinquish its authority to the state legislature until a year and a half into the Civil War.

More generally, distrust of state legislatures led conventions to seek to supplant state legislatures by inserting detailed policy prescriptions into state constitutions themselves. This eagerness for popular legislation prompted not only a proliferation of constitutional conventions but also an easing of procedures for constitutional amendment during the latter half of the nineteenth century.[143] One impetus for constitutional legislation was a concern about official corruption. Thus, the Illinois Constitution of 1848 mandated that public contracts for fuel and stationery be given to the lowest bidder, and the Alabama Constitution of 1875 forbade railroads from awarding free passes to state or municipal officials.[144] But as Governor Arthur Mellette recognized in presenting the case for constitutional legislation at the South Dakota convention of 1889, a broader understanding of popular government underlay these efforts:

> If it is right, if you know what is the proper thing to embrace in your legislation, the more there is in the constitution the better for the people. One of the greatest evils is excessive legislation—the constant change every two years of the laws, and the squabbles and debates over the different questions that con-

[141] Quoted in Rodgers, *Contested Truths*, 98.

[142] For surveys of these forays into legislation by constitutional conventions, see Rodgers, *Contested Truths*, 92–101; and Dodd, *Revision and Amendment*, chap. 3. For a major challenge to the legal authority of conventions to supersede state legislatures, see Jameson, *Treatise on Constitutional Conventions*.

[143] See Dodd, *Amendment and Revision*, chap. 4.

[144] Illinois Constitution of 1848, art. 4, sec. 25; and Alabama Constitution of 1875, art. 13, sec. 23.

stantly arises. It is wise, in my judgment, after the people have decided in which direction their interests lie, to embody them in the fundamental law of the land and make it permanent.[145]

Because convention delegates typically viewed themselves as peculiarly representative of the people, they assumed that their deliberations were untainted by the narrow parochialism and partisan "squabbles" that plagued state legislatures. They therefore believed it their duty to include extensive legislation in the constitution, where it would not be easily subject to change by political factions. This constitutional legislation included both broad policy directives and detailed prescriptions. The level of detail is illustrated by the Missouri Constitution of 1875, which rank-ordered the state's priorities for the expenditure of public funds (first, interest on debt; next, the sinking fund; next, education; next, costs of assessing and collecting revenue, etc.), and the Illinois Constitution of 1870, which even dealt with the covert mixing of two grades of grain in the same elevator.[146] One may well question whether such provisions banished factional politics from policy formulation or merely invited it into the constitutional realm. Nevertheless, the longer, more prescriptive and proscriptive state constitutions characteristic of the late nineteenth century reflected a desire to assert a public interest against ordinary politics.

DIFFERENCES AMONG STATE CONSTITUTIONS

Although this narrative has highlighted the commonalities in nineteenth-century state constitutions and constitutional development, there are differences among them as well. Some of these differences reflect distinctive orientations toward constitutional design. Louisiana is a prime example, adopting a series of constitutions that resembled "the basic civil codes of European countries—long, detailed, and not particularly revered"— rather than the constitutions of its sister states.[147] In other instances, issues distinctive to a state or salient only within its borders have at times dominated its constitutional politics. Examples include the distribution of Indian lands at the Mississippi convention of 1832, the state lottery at the Louisiana convention of 1879, and Mormonism at the Idaho conven-

---

[145] Quoted in Hicks, *Constitutions of Northwest States*, 54.

[146] Missouri Constitution of 1875, art. 4, sec. 43; and Illinois Constitution of 1870, art. 13, sec. 2. The Illinois Constitution, in fact, contained an entire article on warehouses. Needless to say, the examples of constitutional legislation could easily be multiplied.

[147] Elazar, "Principles and Traditions," 21. William Swindler, in his ten-volume collection of all state constitutions, was obliged to devote an entire volume to Louisiana constitutions.

tion of 1889.[148] Yet the most striking differences among state constitutions during the nineteenth century were regional.[149] State constitutional development in New England and in the South illustrates both the range and character of these regional variations.

New England

What was distinctive about constitutional development in New England was the region's relative isolation from several of the century's major movements for constitutional change. Most states regularly altered their constitutions during the nineteenth century, but no New England state revised its constitution during the period, thus minimizing opportunities to borrow from constitutions in other regions. The New England states were also less affected than other states by Jacksonian democracy.[150] As a result, whereas most states embraced white manhood suffrage prior to the Civil War, Massachusetts, New Hampshire, and Rhode Island restricted the vote in state elections to taxpayers, Maine and Vermont did so for town meetings or local elections, and—as noted previously—only Connecticut established a racial qualification for voting.[151] And whereas most states provided for the popular election of judges and executive officials, the New England states largely bucked these trends. Maine, Massachusetts, New Hampshire, and Rhode Island all retained judicial selection by the governor or the legislature, and Connecticut did so for appellate judges.[152] The New England states also continued to allow their legislatures to appoint most executive officials.[153] Perhaps most im-

[148] Winkle, *The Mississippi State Constitution,* 5–6; Hargrave, *The Louisiana State Constitution,* 9–10; and Crowley and Heffron, *The Idaho State Constitution,* 5–7.

[149] For penetrating accounts that emphasize regional differentiation in constitutional development, see Elazar, "Principles and Traditions"; and Hall, "Mostly Anchor." For accounts organized around particular regions, see Bakken, *Rocky Mountain Constitution Making;* Hicks, *Constitutions of Northwest States;* and Johnson, *Founding the Far West.*

[150] For a general overview, see Richard P. McCormick, *The Second American Party System: Party Formation in the Jacksonian Era* (Chapel Hill: University of North Carolina Press, 1966). A useful single-state study is Donald B. Cole, *Jacksonian Democracy in New Hampshire, 1800–1851* (Cambridge: Harvard University Press, 1970).

[151] Massachusetts rejected an amendment to establish manhood suffrage in 1853, New Hampshire did so in 1851, and Rhode Island's 1842 constitution restricted the suffrage to native-born taxpayers and foreign-born freeholders. Maine and Vermont limited local suffrage to taxpayers. See Williamson, *American Suffrage,* 198, 265, 268, 271, 277.

[152] Hall, "The Judiciary on Trial," 337 n. 2. In fact, constitutional conventions in Massachusetts and New Hampshire during the 1850s specifically rejected popular election of judges. By constitutional amendments in 1850 and in 1870, Vermont adopted popular election of inferior court judges and then appellate judges.

[153] See, for example, Connecticut Constitution of 1818, art. 4, secs. 19–20; Maine Constitution of 1819, art. 5, sec. 3, par. 1, and sec. 4, par. 1; and Rhode Island Constitution, art. 8, sec. 1.

portantly, the New England states did not join the movement to long constitutions replete with constitutional legislation and restrictions on state legislatures. Instead, throughout the century they continued to demonstrate considerable faith in the use of public power for the public good, imposing few restrictions on their legislatures and adopting little constitutional legislation.[154]

Nevertheless, one should not exaggerate the distinctiveness of constitutional development in New England—or in any other region. Although no New England state revised its constitution, three—Connecticut, Maine, and Rhode Island—did draft their initial constitutions during the nineteenth century. Massachusetts proposed a new constitution in 1853 and Rhode Island one in 1898, although neither was ratified by the voters. Moreover, the New England states did adopt a significant number of constitutional amendments.[155] The narrow focus of these amendments rarely provided an occasion for drawing upon models from beyond the region or for borrowing provisions from other states. However, when Rhode Island adopted its constitution in 1842, the charter responded, just like others adopted during the era, to the collapse of overambitious public attempts to promote economic development. It contained a debt limitation, the requirement of an extraordinary majority to appropriate funds for local or private purposes, and the requirement of an intervening election before the legislature acted on a bill of incorporation.[156] These features underscore how the era in which a constitution is adopted crucially affects its contents.

The South

During the antebellum era, constitutional development in the South largely resembled that in other regions.[157] The frequency of constitu-

---

[154] This faith in the exercise of public power is reflected in the New England states' involvement in the direction and management of productive enterprise in the late eighteenth century and the first half of the nineteenth century. See Handlin and Handlin, *Commonwealth*. It is reflected more generally in the moralistic political culture that reigns in the region. See Elazar, *American Federalism;* and Elazar, "Principles and Traditions," 18–19.

[155] During the nineteenth century, Connecticut adopted twenty-nine amendments, Massachusetts thirty-six, Maine twenty-nine, Rhode Island sixteen, and Vermont twenty-six. See, in addition to the texts of the constitutions, Tinkle, *The Maine State Constitution*, 13; and McCarthy, *Widening Scope*, 15.

[156] Rhode Island Constitution of 1842, art. 4, secs. 13, 14, and 17.

[157] The leading student of antebellum Southern constitutionalism has concluded, "Perhaps the outstanding feature of state constitutional development in the slave-holding South was its similarity to such development elsewhere." See Don E. Fehrenbacher, *Sectional Crisis and Southern Constitutionalism* (Baton Rouge: Louisiana State University Press, 1995), xvii.

tional change in the South was no greater than in the North. From 1800 to 1860, the seven existing slaveholding states adopted nine constitutions, while the ten existing free states adopted twelve; and only two of the slaveholding states admitted during the period revised their constitutions, while five of the ten free states that were admitted did so.[158] Moreover, southern and northern states generally confronted the same constitutional agenda—suffrage expansion, apportionment, economic development, etc.—and adopted more or less the same constitutional solutions to those problems.

What most distinguished antebellum southern constitutions was, of course, their treatment of slavery; yet this issue was less salient than might have been expected. The antebellum constitutions of six southern states— Florida, Louisiana, North Carolina, South Carolina, and Tennessee— never mentioned slavery. Most of those that did so simply borrowed or adapted provisions from the Mississippi Constitution of 1817, which banned the uncompensated emancipation of slaves, required that slaves be treated with humanity, and authorized the legislature to ban the importation of slaves as merchandise into the state.[159] It may be that the limited attention to slavery in most southern constitutions reflected a lack of controversy about the institution. Indeed, it was precisely in those states in which slavery was controversial that convention delegates provided the strongest constitutional protections for it. Thus, Virginia, whose antislavery western counties were increasing in political power, and Kentucky, which had elected antislavery delegates to its 1792 constitutional convention, included safeguards for slavery in their constitutions.[160]

Another oft-remarked feature of antebellum southern constitutions was their tendency to circumscribe the autonomy and authority of state

[158] Fehrenbacher, *Constitutions and Constitutionalism*, 5.

[159] Mississippi Constitution of 1817, sec. 6, "Slaves," pars. 1–3. Similar provisions are found in Alabama Constitution of 1819, art. 6, "Slaves," sec. 1; and Arkansas Constitution of 1836, art. 7, "Emancipation of Slaves," sec. 1. The Mississippi Constitution of 1832 banned the interstate slave trade (art. 6, "Slaves," sec. 2).

[160] On the controversy in Kentucky, see Coward, *Kentucky in New Republic*, 36–45. The pertinent constitutional provisions are the Kentucky Constitution of 1792, art. 9, and the Kentucky Constitution of 1799, art. 8, sec. 1. The Virginia Constitution of 1851 (art. 3, secs. 19–21) forbade free blacks from remaining in the states for more than a year after obtaining their freedom, under penalty of reenslavement; forbade the legislature from emancipating slaves; and authorized it to restrict or impose conditions on private emancipations. It is noteworthy that the constitutional defense of slavery in Virginia coincided with changes in apportionment that increased the political influence of non-slave-owning areas and raised concern about the imposition of taxes on slaves. See Fehrenbacher, *Constitutions and Constitutionalism*, 28.

governors.[161] Certainly there is evidence of this. North Carolina retained legislative selection of its governor until 1835, Virginia until 1852, and South Carolina until 1860.[162] North Carolina, South Carolina, Tennessee, and Virginia did not grant their governors a veto; while in Alabama, Arkansas, and Florida, vetoes could be overridden by simple majorities in each house.[163] Yet not all southern constitutions encouraged gubernatorial impotence. The initial constitutions of Louisiana, Mississippi, and Texas all provided for popular election of the governor and required a two-thirds majority to override gubernatorial vetoes.[164] In addition, the Louisiana and Texas charters granted the governor the power to appoint key officials, while the Mississippi charter placed no limit on gubernatorial reelection.[165] Thus, the differences among southern state constitutions were as great as those between southern and nonsouthern charters.

Constitutional development in the South in the decades following the Civil War, however, was dramatically different from that in other regions. Eschewing reliance on their previous charters, the ten southern states that devised new constitutions during Reconstruction repudiated their constitutional past in favor of a new perspective and frame of reference.[166] This was hardly surprising; for the enfranchisement of African-Americans, the disqualification of unregenerate Confederates, and boycotts by conservative Democrats ensured that insurgent elements dominated the conventions that framed the Reconstruction constitutions.[167] These charters guaranteed the rights of African-Americans. However, they did much

[161] See, for example, Fehrenbacher, *Constitutions and Constitutionalism,* 16.

[162] North Carolina Constitution of 1776, art. 15, amended in 1835; Virginia Constitution of 1830, art. 4, sec. 1, and Virginia Constitution of 1851, art. 5, sec. 2; and South Carolina Constitution of 1790, art. 2, sec. 1. More generally, see Fehrenbacher, *Constitutions and Constitutionalism,* 16.

[163] Alabama Constitution of 1819, art. 4, sec. 16; Arkansas Constitution of 1836, art. 5, sec. 16; and Florida Constitution of 1838, art. 3, sec. 16.

[164] Louisiana Constitution of 1812, art. 3, secs. 1 and 20; Mississippi Constitution of 1817, art. 4, secs. 1 and 15; and Texas Constitution of 1845, art. 5, secs. 2 and 17.

[165] Louisiana Constitution of 1812, art. 3, sec. 9; and Texas Constitution of 1845, art. 5, secs. 16 and 23.

[166] This is not to say that Reconstruction constitution-makers did not retain noncontroversial constitutional provisions from preceding constitutions. See Michael Les Benedict, "The Problem of Constitutionalism and Constitutional Liberty in the Reconstruction South," in Kermit L. Hall and James W. Ely Jr., eds., *An Uncertain Tradition: Constitutionalism and the History of the South* (Athens: University of Georgia Press, 1989), 241–42. The analysis in this paragraph, unless otherwise noted, relies on Benedict's article and on Foner, *Reconstruction,* 316–33.

[167] Only in Virginia and North Carolina, among states for which the votes were published by race, did over 40 percent of registered white voters even cast a ballot in the elections to hold conventions. Benedict, "Problem of Constitutionalism," 232.

more. They encouraged government support for economic enterprise and substantially expanded the scope of government responsibility with provisions for state-funded public education, poor relief, and the establishment of penitentiaries and asylums.[168] Several conventions looked outside the region for direction, reconstituting tax policy on the basis of a general property tax as in the North, reconstructing local government to dislodge local oligarchies along New England lines, and so on.[169]

A Democratic newspaper predicted that the radical changes introduced by these Reconstruction constitutions would "last just as long as the bayonets which ushered them into being, shall keep them in existence, and not one day longer."[170] The prediction proved accurate, as nine southern states adopted new constitutions from 1875 to 1902.[171] Even after the compromise of 1876 led to the withdrawal of federal troops, fears of federal intervention and the presence of a sizable black electorate delayed direct efforts to reintroduce white supremacy.[172] Not until 1890–1902 did southern states hold conventions whose main purpose was to disenfranchise African-Americans. Southern conventions of the 1870s instead focused on reorienting the politics of their states by rejecting the activist role for state government espoused in Reconstruction constitutions.[173] Some of the stringent restrictions on government imposed by these new constitutions, such as bans on state or local aid to private enterprises, paralleled those adopted in the North during the late nineteenth century. However, southern constitutions went considerably further in attempting to shrink and redirect government. They reduced government budgets by mandating extremely low tax rates, curtailing government borrowing, and capping expenditures.[174] They also attempted to lower the cost of

[168] Illustrative provisions include Alabama Constitution of 1867, art. 4, sec. 34 (poor relief); Louisiana Constitution of 1868, title 7, art. 135 (public education); and Florida Constitution of 1868, art. 11, secs. 1–2 (asylums and penitentiaries).

[169] Foner, *Reconstruction*, 328.

[170] Quoted in Foner, *Reconstruction*, 333. Even prior to their replacement, many white southerners did not accord legitimacy to the Reconstruction constitutions.

[171] Although North Carolina did not adopt a new constitution, it likewise undertook major constitutional changes, adopting eight amendments in 1873 and thirty more, affecting thirty-six separate sections of its constitution, in 1876. See Orth, *North Carolina State Constitution*, 15–17.

[172] Some states did seek to circumscribe black political power, albeit indirectly. Faced with black electoral majorities, Democrats in coastal regions of North Carolina pressed for a constitutional amendment to enable them to regain control of their local governments. The amendment, adopted in 1876, ensured white control by eliminating popular election of county officials, authorizing the state legislature to appoint justices of the peace, who in turn would appoint county commissioners. See Perman, *The Road to Redemption*, 198–99.

[173] The analysis in this paragraph draws particularly upon Perman, *The Road to Redemption*, chap. 9; and McMillan, *Constitutional Development in Alabama*, chaps. 11–13.

[174] Arkansas, for example, set a tax rate of 1 percent for state government and 0.5

government by reducing the length and frequency of legislative sessions and by abolishing offices they deemed unnecessary. Sometimes the elimination of offices served a dual purpose: the Alabama Constitution of 1875 eliminated the state board of education and commissioner of industrial resources, posts created in 1868 to further the key Reconstruction goals of education and economic development.[175] Southern constitutions of the 1870s also slashed salaries for state offices. Georgia, for example, cut the governor's salary by a quarter; Louisiana reduced executive salaries by over 50 percent; and when a delegate to the Texas convention of 1876 attempted to ridicule the campaign for economy in government by proposing that legislators receive a salary of two dollars per day, his proposal was adopted.[176]

Aside from race, perhaps the most controversial issue confronting southern constitution-makers was state debt, which had grown enormously during Reconstruction. Some state constitutions forthrightly repudiated the debt incurred during Reconstruction. Other states, while not directly endorsing repudiation, adopted provisions exempting the state from civil suit, thereby immunizing themselves in the event of a future repudiation of state debt.[177] Repudiation was attractive to state constitution-makers for several reasons. It relieved their states from crushing financial burdens, symbolically renounced the policies that had produced those burdens, and ensured that investment capital would not be available in the future to underwrite industrial expansion, thus by default reorienting state economic development in an agrarian direction.

CONCLUSIONS

During the nineteenth century, state constitutions became more polished and professional, as their framers built upon the constitutional experience of their own states and developments in sister states. The shape of the documents and their contents also changed. Over the course of the century, state constitutions increasingly became instruments of government rather than merely frameworks for government. Whereas early state constitutions—and the federal Constitution—engaged in little de-

---

percent for county governments. See Arkansas Constitution of 1874, art. 16, secs. 8–9. Alabama capped the state appropriation for education at one hundred thousand dollars, and constitutional limits on local taxation made it difficult for local governments to supplement it. Alabama Constitution of 1875, art. 10, sec. 7, and art. 12, sec. 5.

[175] McMillan, *Constitutional Development in Alabama*, 180. The Alabama Constitution also eliminated the office of lieutenant governor, likewise created by the Alabama Constitution of 1868.

[176] Perman, *The Road to Redemption*, 205–10.

[177] See, for example, Arkansas Constitution of 1874, art. 5, sec. 20.

tailed policymaking, most state constitutions by midcentury had begun to specify what state legislatures could not do and how they would conduct their business. By the end of the nineteenth century, restrictions on state legislatures had proliferated and had been supplemented by similarly detailed provisions regarding local government, plus a healthy—or, according to twentieth-century constitutional reformers—unhealthy dose of constitutional legislation. As a result, more major issues were resolved by constitution-makers and by constitutional interpreters.

This constitutionalization of state politics occurred in part because political parties and interest groups recognized that if they were blocked in the legislature, they could advance their aims in the constitutional arena.[178] Thus, underrepresented regions in Rhode Island, Virginia, and other states sought constitutional conventions, as did Granger forces in Illinois and other states after the Civil War. The attraction was not merely an alternative forum but also a promise of permanency. By enshrining their policies in state constitutions, groups hoped to forestall political change. Thus, even after statutes had effectively curtailed black suffrage in the South, its opponents still sought to constitutionalize black disenfranchisement so that, in the words of Congressman Thomas Hardwick, "the Negro shall not be left around the corner, awaiting the awakening hand of the corruptionist whenever division shall again break the white ranks."[179]

However, the constitutionalization of state politics involved more than a search for group advantage. For constitutional regulations of legislative procedures and limitations on special legislation, which accounted for much of state constitutional growth, seldom served the agendas of either political party or of interest groups. Rather, these provisions were designed precisely to limit the influence of such groups, to combat politics as usual, to change the way in which politics was conducted and the policies that it produced. Kermit Hall has suggested that the restrictions in nineteenth-century constitutions reflected an "antigovernment bias," but it may be more accurate to characterize this bias as an opposition to a particular way of conducting government rather than to government per se.[180]

The constitutional convention served as the key institution for the constitutionalization of state politics. In the eyes of the delegates and their supporters, these conventions provided the opportunity to escape politics as usual and pursue the public good. Consequently, as James Bryce has noted, the delegates "neither wished nor cared to draw a line of distinc-

[178] Hall, "Mostly Anchor."
[179] Quoted in Kousser, *Shaping of Southern Politics,* 221.
[180] Hall, "Mostly Anchor," 405.

tion between what is proper for a constitution and what ought to be left to be dealt with by the state legislature."[181] For in replacing legislative policymaking with constitutional policymaking, they believed, they were replacing a politics of corruption and parochial advantage with a politics of the public interest. Instead of ordinary politics penetrating into constitution making, they sought a penetration of the more pristine politics of constitution making into the realm of legislation.

It is a mistake to dismiss these views as simply self-serving or naive. The problems of legislative corruption and ill-considered legislation that state constitution-makers confronted were quite real problems, problems that the ordinary political process had not solved and may in fact have created. Thus the constitutionalization of state politics was appealing because it offered the hope of circumventing the normal political process and restricting its operation. To a large extent, this hope of countering and containing state legislative excesses was not realized. Although the overall level of state legislation did fall in the late nineteenth century following adoption of the substantive restrictions on state legislatures, Morton Keller, a leading historian of the era, has concluded that the legislatures nonetheless enacted "an increasing number of laws that touched on important areas of American social and economic life."[182] And according to Willard Hurst, although constitutional restrictions gave "strong-minded judges" a weapon for calling legislators to account, state legislatures easily circumvented most procedural requirements and transformed at least some substantive limits, such as bans on local legislation, into "matters of draftsman's form."[183] Thus despite the efforts to rein in legislative power, James Bryce's conclusion at the end of the nineteenth century echoed Tocqueville's earlier assessment that "the legislature . . . is so much the strongest force in the several states that we may almost call it the Government and ignore all the other authorities."[184]

The verdict of twentieth-century constitutional reformers was even more harsh. According to these reformers, the detailed restrictions and constitutional legislation of late-nineteenth-century state constitutions not only failed to solve the problems of state government; they aggravated those problems by reducing legislative discretion and preventing

[181] Bryce, *The American Commonwealth,* 1:394.

[182] Keller, *Affairs of State,* 110–15 and 321.

[183] Hurst, *Growth of American Law,* 234; and James Willard Hurst, *Law and Social Order in the United States* (Ithaca, N.Y.: Cornell University Press, 1977), 88–97. In contrast, Ernst Freund has suggested that the prohibitions on special legislation and on public aid to private corporate enterprise were "undoubtedly beneficial and probably constitute the most important achievements of American public policy in dealing with private enterprise." See Freund, *Standards of American Legislation,* 174.

[184] Bryce, *The American Commonwealth,* vol. 1, chaps. 40, 41, and 44.

state governments from responding to changing conditions and emerging problems. Indeed, by hamstringing state government, these constitutions encouraged a transfer of power to the federal government, whose very different Constitution posed little obstacle to policy innovation. As the next chapter reveals, these attacks, in conjunction with other factors, would lead to dramatic changes in the character of state constitutions.

CHAPTER 5

Twentieth-Century State Constitutionalism

IF the nineteenth century was the acme of wholesale state constitution-making, the twentieth century is its nadir. Only twelve states revised their constitutions from 1901 to 1997, although five others did adopt their first—and only—constitutions during the period (see table 5.1).[1] The United States Supreme Court's decisions requiring the apportionment of both houses of state legislatures on a "one person, one vote" basis sparked a burst of activity—from 1965 to 1974 seven states adopted new constitutions—but long stretches of inactivity were far more common.[2] From 1922 to 1944, no state revised its fundamental law, and from 1977 to 1997, only one did so. Even in the decade following the Supreme Court's reapportionment rulings, constitutional reformers enjoyed only mixed success. From 1965 to 1974, voters rejected six constitutions proposed by conventions and three others submitted by state legislatures.[3] State electorates have been reluctant even to contemplate constitutional revision. Whereas in the nineteenth century states held 144 constitutional conventions, during the twentieth century they have held only sixty-four. Of these, more than a quarter were prompted by the Court's reapportionment rulings, five others were necessary to draft the initial constitutions for new states, and a significant proportion of the rest were limited conventions called to propose amendments rather than to revise state constitutions.[4] Voters in recent years have regularly defeated proposals to hold

---

[1] Altogether, twenty-three state constitutions were adopted in the twentieth century, with Georgia and Louisiana each adopting three and Michigan and Virginia each adopting two. Unless otherwise indicated, data on constitution making and constitutional amendment used in this and succeeding paragraphs are drawn from May, "State Constitutions, 1992–93," 19, table 1.1.

[2] The most important Supreme Court ruling compelling reapportionment of state legislatures was *Reynolds v. Sims,* 377 U.S. 533 (1964).

[3] The states in which constitutions proposed by conventions were rejected include Arkansas (1970), Maryland (1968), New Mexico (1969), New York (1967), North Dakota (1972), and Rhode Island (1968). States in which constitutions submitted by legislatures were rejected include Idaho (1970), Kentucky (1966), and Oregon (1970). See Sturm, "Development of State Constitutions," 73. For a study of several constitutional conventions of the period, see Cornwell, Goodman, and Swanson, *State Constitutional Conventions.*

[4] For example, New Hampshire has held eight conventions since 1900, but none was concerned with constitutional revision; until 1964, a constitutional convention was the only authorized means for amending the state constitution. Tennessee has convened five conven-

TABLE 5.1
State Constitution-Making in the Twentieth Century

1901–1920		1961–1980	
Alabama	1901	Michigan	1963
Virginia	1902	Connectticut	1965
Oklahoma	1907*	Florida	1968
Michigan	1908	Illinois	1970
Arizona	1911*	North Carolina	1970
New Mexico	1911*	Virginia	1970
Louisiana	1913	Montana	1972
		Louisiana	1974
1921–1940		Georgia	1976
Louisiana	1921		
		1980–1996	
1941–1960		Georgia	1982
Georgia	1945		
Missouri	1945		
New Jersey	1947		
Hawaii	1950*		
Alaska	1956*		

ªThe state's initial constitution.

constitutional conventions.[5] In fact, the only state constitutional convention of the last decade was called without voter approval. In 1992 the Louisiana legislature designated itself as a convention, but voters disapproved of the ploy, overwhelmingly defeating all its proposals at the polls.[6]

The relative infrequency of state constitutional revision is somewhat surprising, given the extraordinary changes in American government and politics during the twentieth century, even if many of those changes have involved a "bumping up" of issues to the national level. It is likewise surprising in view of the sustained efforts of political elites to promote state constitutional reform. The leading reform group, the National Mu-

---

tions, but these likewise proposed only amendments. Altogether, from 1938 to 1968, twelve of twenty-six conventions were limited conventions. See Sturm, *Thirty Years,* 56–60, table 11.

[5] From 1950 to 1968 state legislatures proposed twenty-two conventions, but in only eleven instances were the convention calls approved. See Sturm, "Development of State Constitutions," 81; Sturm, *Thirty Years,* 56–60, table 11; and May, "State Constitutions, 1992–93."

[6] The constitutional revision was defeated by a margin of 62 percent to 38 percent. See May, "State Constitutions, 1992–93," 4.

nicipal League, inaugurated a campaign for constitutional change in 1921, published its Model State Constitution three years later, and continued to champion constitutional reform for over half a century.[7] As the expansion of federal authority altered the relationship between nation and state, the league was joined by other "good government" groups, which insisted that the states could not meet the demands of modern government without fundamental constitutional change, and by state legislatures, which established constitutional commissions to recommend reforms.[8] Some groups also proposed major structural reforms in state governments that might have led to constitutional revision.[9] But despite these efforts, few states initiated comprehensive changes. Instead, other mechanisms for state constitutional development assumed greater importance. States expanded their use of piecemeal amendment to address constitutional problems. In addition, during the latter decades of the twentieth century, political activists rediscovered the constitutional initiative, employing it to restructure and constrain state government, as well as to pursue specific policy objectives. Finally, beginning in the 1970s, state courts assumed a more prominent role in state constitutional development, relying on state declarations of rights to provide more expansive protections for rights than were available under the federal Constitution, a phenomenon commonly known as the new judicial federalism.[10]

---

[7] Altogether, the National Municipal League published six versions of its Model State Constitution, with the initial version appearing in 1924 and its revised sixth version in 1968. See *A Model State Constitution* (New York: National Municipal League, 1924), and *Model State Constitution,* 6th ed. (New York: National Municipal League, 1968). These model constitutions are discussed later in the chapter.

[8] During the 1950s, the key document advocating state constitutional reform was the report of the Kestenbaum Commission: Commission on Intergovernmental Relations, *A Report to the President for Transmittal to the Congress* (Washington, D.C., June 1955), 37–38. During the 1960s, state constitutional reform was championed by the Committee for Economic Development in several of its publications: *Modernizing Local Government* (1966), *Modernizing State Government* (1967), and *A Fiscal Program for a Balanced Federalism* (1967). For discussion of the establishment of constitutional commissions and their contributions to reform, see Sturm, *Thirty Years,* chap. 3.

[9] These include the campaigns for reorganization of state executive branches and for the unification of state courts. On the former, see Arthur E. Buck, *The Reorganization of State Governments in the United States* (New York: Columbia University Press, 1938); James L. Garnett, *Reorganizing State Government: The Executive Branch* (Boulder, Colo.: Westview, 1980); and Thomas E. Kynerd, *Administrative Reorganization in Mississippi Government: A Study in Politics* (Jackson: University Press of Mississippi, 1978), chap. 1. On the latter, see Berkson and Carbon, *Court Unification;* and G. Alan Tarr, "The Effect of Court Unification on Court Performance: A Preliminary Assessment," *Judicature* 64 (March 1981): 356–68.

[10] The literature on the new judicial federalism is vast. Overviews are provided by Mary Cornelia Porter, "State Supreme Courts and the Warren Court: Some Old Inquiries for a New Situation," in Porter and Tarr, *Policymakers;* "Developments in the Law—The Inter-

This chapter surveys these developments and assesses their implications for state constitutionalism. It focuses initially on the piecemeal transformation of state constitutions by amendments and in particular on the evolution during the twentieth century of two enduring issues in state constitutional politics, the intrastate distribution of power and the relation between the state and the economy. Next, it traces the development of the national movement for state constitutional reform, analyzes the constitutional vision underlying the reformers' prescriptions, and assesses the effects of that movement on state constitutions. It then describes a competing vision of state constitutions and state government that emerged in the late twentieth century and its proponents' use of the constitutional initiative to give effect to that view. Finally, it traces the emergence of the new judicial federalism in the 1970s and analyzes what this development suggests about the character of state constitutionalism in the twentieth century.

CONSTITUTIONAL AMENDMENT AND CONSTITUTIONAL REVISION

During the twentieth century, formal constitutional change in the states has occurred primarily through constitutional amendment. Most states have amended their constitutions far more frequently during the twentieth century than in previous eras.[11] Although some amendments have been proposed by conventions and others by initiative, the vast majority have originated in state legislatures, and the ratification rate of amendments proposed by state legislatures has far surpassed that of constitu-

---

pretation of State Constitutional Rights," *Harvard Law Review* 95 (April 1982): 1324–1502; Ronald K. L. Collins, Peter J. Galie, and John Kincaid, "State High Courts, State Constitutions, and Individual Rights Litigation since 1980: A Judicial Survey," *Publius* 16 (summer 1986): 141–62; and Tarr, "Past and Future."

[11] Comprehensive data on the amendment of state constitutions during the nineteenth century has yet to be compiled, but the comments of observers and studies of individual states confirm the increase in amendment during the twentieth century. Writing in 1910, Walter F. Dodd observed that "[t]he proposal of numerous constitutional amendments has been to a large extent a development of the past twenty years, but the amending process has been used most frequently during the last decade" (see his *Revision and Amendment*, 269 and—for supporting data—268–70). Studies of individual states also document the increasing reliance on constitutional amendment. In North Carolina, for example, there were only four proposed amendments to the state's constitution during the last quarter of the nineteenth century, and one of those failed of adoption (Orth, *North Carolina State Constitution,* 17). In Connecticut from 1818 to 1913, there were thirty-five amendments; in Maine from 1849 to 1912, twenty-eight; and in Rhode Island from 1854 to 1911, sixteen (McCarthy, *Widening Scope,* 15). Of course, given the diversity of the states, there are a few exceptions. For example, Vermont ratified twenty-six amendments prior to 1900 but only twenty-four during the twentieth century (Hill, *The Vermont State Constitution,* 22–23).

tional initiatives.[12] From 1970 to 1993, for example, voters overall approved 68 percent of 4,284 proposed amendments, but only 39 percent of the eighty-six constitutional initiatives put forth in twelve states during the period.[13] As the century has progressed, the pace of state constitutional amendment has quickened.[14] As of 1945, only ten states had averaged at least one amendment per year since adopting their current constitutions. But by 1960, fifteen states had done so; by 1975, despite a spate of constitutional revision, twenty had; and by 1990, twenty-eight.[15] Data from individual states confirm the trend. From 1900 to 1950, Nebraska ratified only fifty-nine amendments; but from 1950 to 1990, it ratified 134.[16] From 1912 to 1969, New Mexico adopted seventy-three amendments, but from 1969 to 1995, ninety-eight.[17] From 1877 to 1945, amendment-prone Georgia adopted 301 amendments, but from 1946 to 1982, 1,174.[18] Also increasing over time has been the ratification rate for proposed amendments. For example, New Mexico ratified only 35 percent of proposed amendments from 1912 to 1945 but 65 percent thereafter.[19] And in Mississippi voters approved 65 percent of amendments from 1890 to 1960 but 91 percent thereafter.[20]

[12] Two states developed other mechanisms for the proposal of constitutional amendments. For most of the nineteenth century in Vermont, amendments were proposed by the Council of Censors (Hill, *The Vermont State Constitution,* 12–18). The Florida Constitution of 1969 authorized the constitutional commission it created to submit proposals directly to the people for ratification (see Florida Constitution of 1969, art. 9, sec. 2). For discussion of this feature, see Talbot D'Alemberte, *The Florida State Constitution: A Reference Guide* (Westport, Conn.: Greenwood Press, 1991), 146–47.

[13] *Book of the States 1980–81* (Chicago: Council of State Governments, 1980), 3, table B; and David B. Magleby, "Direct Legislation in the American States," in Butler and Ranney, *Referendums around the World,* 251, table 7-5. The 39 percent adoption rate for constitutional initiatives from 1970 to 1993 is actually unusually high; the overall rate from 1898 to 1992 is 36 percent. See David B. Magleby, "Let the Voters Decide? An Assessment of the Initiative and Referendum Process," *University of Colorado Law Review* 66 (1995): 26, table 2.

[14] One scholar has estimated that from 1900 to 1935, about twenty-five hundred amendments were submitted and about fifteen hundred ratified. See Charles C. Rohlfing, "Amendment and Revision of State Constitutions," *Annals of the American Academy of Political and Social Science* 181 (September 1935): 180–87. In comparison, data from 1970 to 1993 reveal that 4,284 amendments were proposed and 2,900 approved. See May, "State Constitutions, 1992–93," 2, table A.

[15] These figures were computed from data in the *Book of the States* (Chicago: Council of State Governments, various years). These volumes also provide data on the number of amendments proposed and adopted in each biennium.

[16] Miewald and Longo, *The Nebraska State Constitution,* 22, table 1.

[17] Chuck Smith, *The New Mexico Constitution: A Reference Guide* (Westport, Conn.: Greenwood Press, 1996), 15–24.

[18] Hill, *The Georgia State Constitution,* 11 and 21, table 1.

[19] Smith, *New Mexico State Constitution,* 16–23.

[20] See Winkle, *The Mississippi State Constitution,* 14, table 1.

The New State Constitutional Politics

As reported in chapter 2, the frequency with which state constitutions are amended is correlated with their length and with their ease of amendment. This finding is consistent with the expectations of constitutional reformers, who have attributed the increased reliance on constitutional amendment to the deficiencies of state constitutions.[21] According to these reformers, the decision of state constitution-makers in the late nineteenth century to burden their state charters with detailed prescriptions and proscriptions not only lengthened the constitutions but also, by building rigidities into the documents, limited the states' capacity to adapt to changing situations or address emerging problems. The states have therefore been obliged to alter their constitutions continually merely in order to govern.[22] Oftentimes, constitutional rigidities in a few key areas have required repeated attention, because amendments solved immediate problems without addressing the underlying deficiencies.[23] For example, New York adopted eight amendments to its judicial article from 1967 to 1990, while thirteen of the sixty-six amendments to the West Virginia Constitution have been adopted simply to authorize the state to sell bonds.[24] Certainly, the most heavily amended sections of state constitutions are those whose restrictions are the most severe. From 1970 to 1993, for example, state provisions dealing with finance and taxation— notorious for their detail and restrictiveness—were the most heavily amended provisions in every biennium but one.[25]

[21] For a representative presentation of the reform critique, see Wheeler, *Salient Issues.*

[22] The connection between ease of amendment and frequency of amendment also figures in here. Throughout the twentieth century states have undertaken to ease requirements for constitutional amendment, either by adopting amendment by initiative or simplifying the process of legislative proposal. As one commentator noted in 1935: "It is highly significant that of the seven constitutions adopted since 1907, all have abandoned the time-consuming requirement that amendments must be approved by two successive legislatures, and five of the seven permit amendments to be initiated by petition." See Rohlfing, "Amendment and Revision," 183.

[23] As Frank Grad has observed, "Whenever a narrowly limiting provision is amended by adding an exception to the limitation, the general scope of the provision is likely to become even more narrowly limited in that the stated exception may be taken by implication to disallow other exceptions not expressly stated. Every detailed constitution thus develops certain sore points, which become the foci for veritable clusters of constitutional amendments" (Grad, "The State Constitution," 44–45).

[24] Galie, *New York State Constitution,* 29; and Bastress, *The West Virginia Constitution,* 21.

[25] *Book of the States,* various years. The sole exception was 1986–87, in which amendments to finance and taxation provisions ranked second behind amendments to legislative articles. See May, "State Constitutions, 1992–93," 7, table B. The connection between detail and frequency of amendment is particularly strong even when finance and taxation

Thus, most twentieth-century amendments have facilitated the operation of state governments, making adjustments in an existing body of law rather than introducing grand changes.[26] Seldom has this process of continuing constitutional adjustment excited much public interest—one observer described voters as "militantly indifferent" to such changes.[27] Yet legislators and governmental officials have been anything but indifferent, because these amendments could crucially affect their positions, powers, and prospects. As a result, amendment politics has typically been a "political insider" politics. State legislatures have usually proposed amendments not in response to a public outcry but because of problems identified in the course of governing.[28] Even in politically competitive states, proposed amendments have often enjoyed bipartisan support.[29] Voters have sometimes ignored the proposed amendments or on occasion have voted against a set of amendments because of opposition to a single controversial proposal. Nevertheless, given the infrequency of organized opposition to amendments proposed by state legislatures, about 70 percent of them are ratified, albeit often by a small percentage of the potential electorate.[30]

Some states have resorted to constitutional amendments for more than tuning up the machinery of government. California, Georgia, and Louisiana in particular have chosen to shift many ordinary political disputes to the constitutional realm, using constitutional amendment as legislation by other means. Indeed, according to one commentator, constitutional amendment in Louisiana is "sufficiently continuous to justify including it

---

are not the prime target of amendments. In New York, for example, where amendments have focused on the judiciary, the judicial article comprises about one-fourth of the New York Constitution. See Gerald Benjamin and Melissa Cusa, "Constitutional Amendment through the Legislature in New York," in Tarr, *Constitutional Politics in States,* 65.

[26] Another common form of legislative adjustment is the removal of deadwood from the state constitution. This can occur through constitutional amendment or through constitutional revision. For examples of the former, see Francis H. Heller, *The Kansas State Constitution: A Reference Guide* (Westport, Conn.: Greenwood Press, 1992), 35; Laska, *The Tennessee State Constitution,* 25; and May, *Texas Constitutional Revision Experience,* 4. For an example of the latter, see Hargrave, *The Louisiana State Constitution,* 17–18.

[27] May, *Texas Constitutional Revision Experience,* 183.

[28] Illustrative of the process is how states deal with amendments affecting a single jurisdiction, so-called local amendments. In Georgia, the legislature automatically adopted proposed local amendments if they were supported by legislators from the locality, a form of "legislative courtesy," a process that greatly facilitated constitutional adjustments. From 1946 to 1982, 974 of the 1,174 amendments to the Georgia Constitution were local amendments. See Hill, *The Georgia State Constitution,* 21–22.

[29] For an enlightening study of the way one legislature separates the proposed amendments it supports from those it does not, see Benjamin and Cusa, "Constitutional Amendment," 47–70.

[30] May, "State Constitutions, 1992–93," 2, table A.

with Mardi Gras, football, and corruption as one of the premier components of state culture."[31] In some instances states have opted to amend their constitutions because it was easier than legislating. In Georgia, the practice of legislative courtesy encouraged the adoption of local amendments, whereas legislation affecting a locality ran the risk of gubernatorial veto.[32] And in Idaho, creating exceptions by amendment to the constitution's debt limitations on local government proved easier than meeting the provision's supermajority requirement for incurring debt.[33] In other instances interest groups and factions within the legislature have championed constitutional amendments to enshrine policy decisions in the fundamental law, hoping thereby to make it more difficult for them to be overturned.[34] (Of course, if enshrining policy by amendment was not difficult—and high-amendment states seldom impose demanding requirements for amendment—then unenshrining it should be no more difficult.) Even state legislatures less prone to amendment have sometimes referred contentious issues to the electorate. Finally, in some states the proliferation of amendments has established constitutional amendment as an accepted political option, thereby promoting further amendments.

Whether constitutional amendments enable states to make the necessary adjustments for effective government depends on the willingness of voters to endorse the proposed adjustments. When such adjustments have been rejected, there has been a tendency to reintroduce them, in the hope that they would be adopted the second time around. This tactic has often succeeded. In Mississippi, for example, twelve of the thirty amendments rejected from 1890 to 1990 were resubmitted and ratified.[35] But resubmission has not always worked. For example, since 1920, Nebraska voters have rejected thirteen proposed amendments that would have

[31] Carleton, "Elitism Sustained," 560. Other commentators have described New York's use of amendment as "integrated into the overall political process more fully and explicitly than in other states." See Cornwell, Goodman, and Swanson, *State Constitutional Conventions*, 20.

[32] Hill, *The Georgia State Constitution*, 22. This situation changed with the adoption of the 1983 constitution.

[33] Michael C. Moore, "Constitutional Debt Limitations on Local Government in Idaho—Article 8, Section 3, Idaho Constitution," *Idaho Law Review* 17 (fall 1980): 55–85. See also Crowley and Heffron, *The Idaho State Constitution*, 169–74.

[34] Friedman, *History of American Law*, 118–19; and Carleton, "Elitism Sustained," 561. It is thus hardly coincidental that Lewis Froman found a correlation between interest group strength and the number of amendments proposed and adopted. Lewis A. Froman Jr., "Some Effects of Interest Group Strength in State Politics," *American Political Science Review* 60 (December 1966): 952–62.

[35] Winkle, *The Mississippi State Constitution*, 14. For a detailed listing of submissions and resubmissions in one state over three decades, see James K. Pollock, *The Initiative and Referendum in Michigan* (Ann Arbor: University of Michigan Press, 1940), 78–86, appendix 3.

raised the constitutionally prescribed salary for state legislators.[36] More importantly, voters periodically have rejected not merely a particular amendment but the entire pattern of adjustment-by-amendment on which the system rested. When that has occurred, it has obliged state legislators to summon conventions to undertake more systematic reform. Thus, in Louisiana, the legislature called the convention of 1972 after voters rejected all fifty-three proposed amendments in 1970 and thirty-six of forty-two proposed amendments in 1972.[37] In Georgia, constitutional revision resulted in part from the voters' defeat of 118 of 133 amendments in 1978.[38]

Issues in State Constitutional Politics

Prior chapters have documented that state constitutional politics involves not only issues specific to particular states and periods but also enduring concerns such as the intrastate distribution of political power, the relation of the state to the economy, and the scope of state government. This section examines state constitutional controversies over the intrastate distribution of political power and over the relation of the state to the economy, noting both the concern for political principle and the interplay of competing interests. A later section on twentieth-century constitutional reform describes the continuing debate over the scope of state government.

THE INTRASTATE DISTRIBUTION OF POLITICAL POWER

To some extent constitutional change during the early twentieth century continued and completed developments begun in the preceding century. For example, the Alabama Constitution of 1901 and the Virginia Constitution of 1902 represented the culmination of the constitutional phase of southern efforts to reestablish white supremacy in the aftermath of Reconstruction.[39] Other Southern states amended their constitutions in the early twentieth century to disenfranchise blacks and some poor whites—North Carolina, for example, adopted amendments instituting a literacy test (with a grandfather clause) and a poll tax.[40] On a happier note, the campaigns for women's suffrage begun in the western states spread eastward and enjoyed increasing success. Although twelve states

---

[36] Miewald and Longo, *The Nebraska State Constitution*, 22.

[37] Hargrave, *The Louisiana State Constitution*, 16.

[38] Hill, *The Georgia State Constitution*, 19.

[39] McMillan, *Constitutional Development in Alabama*; and Ralph Chipman McDaniel, *The Virginia Constitutional Convention of 1901–1902* (Baltimore: Johns Hopkins Press, 1928).

[40] Orth, *North Carolina State Constitution*, 18.

rejected suffrage amendments during the first two decades of the century, twelve adopted amendments establishing women's suffrage prior to 1920, including eight that had previously rejected it. Thirteen more enacted women's suffrage by statute, several in response to the failure of amendment efforts.[41] With the ratification of the Nineteenth Amendment in 1920, the franchise issue disappeared from state constitutional agendas and did not reemerge until the 1960s.

Both the absence of constitutional revision for much of the century and the flurry of activity following the Supreme Court's reapportionment rulings testify to continuing conflicts over the intrastate distribution of power.[42] For the most part, these conflicts involved a competition for advantage rather than a clash of principles. In the late nineteenth and early twentieth centuries, rural interests and antimachine forces combined to reduce the use of population as a basis for apportionment of state legislatures and to diffuse representation throughout the states.[43] One approach, pioneered by Delaware, was to specify legislative districts in detail in the state constitution, with no provision for reapportionment.[44] Another, employed in several other states, was to reconstruct the upper house along the lines of the U.S. Senate, introducing equal representation for geographic units, although occasionally with minor modifications for population disparities. Urbanization and shifts in population subsequently magnified the initial disparities created by these changes. Once the apportionment formulas were established, however, concern about losing power led legislators from rural areas to oppose convention calls, lest their disproportionate representation in state legislatures be threatened. For example, in 1936 in Rhode Island, though the Democratic Party had made a convention a "prime party objective," Democratic senators from several country towns strongly resisted a convention bill.[45] In New Jersey, efforts at constitutional reform stalled for three decades because of disagreement about the apportionment issue, and tabling the issue was the price exacted for constitutional revision in 1947.[46] In some states determined citizens were able to force reappor-

[41] Marjorie Spruill Wheeler, ed., *One Woman, One Vote: Rediscovering the Woman Suffrage Movement* (Troutdale, Ore.: NewSage Press, 1995), 375–77, appendix 1.

[42] For useful general discussions, see Dixon, *Democratic Representation*, 82–89; and Robert B. McKay, *Reapportionment: The Law and Politics of Equal Representation* (New York: Twentieth Century Fund, 1965), 460–75.

[43] For useful case studies of this phenomenon, see Henretta, "Rise and Decline"; and McCormick, *From Realignment to Reform*. This topic is also addressed in chapter 4.

[44] Dealey, *Growth of State Constitutions*, 97.

[45] Hurst, *Growth of American Law*, 239.

[46] See Richard J. Connors, *The Process of Constitutional Revision in New Jersey: 1940–1947* (New York: National Municipal League, 1970); and Richard N. Baisden, *Charter for*

tionment, but even then legislators usually limited redistricting to marginal shifts in seats, while blocking an overall reallocation.[47]

Even when state constitutions mandated representation on the basis of population, some states simply ignored requirements to reapportion. As of 1960, twelve state senates and twelve lower houses had not been reapportioned for over thirty years, with the Alabama and Tennessee legislatures unchanged since 1901.[48] Yet not all deviations from "one person, one vote" reflected legislative resistance or obsolescent apportionment formulas. Between 1952 and 1962, Michigan, California, Washington, and Colorado all rejected initiatives that would have increased the influence of population on the apportionment of their upper houses.[49] These outcomes suggest that sometimes more than the self-interest of well-placed minorities supported the states' decision to give disproportionate representation to rural areas. The U.S. Supreme Court's reapportionment rulings required forty-six states to redistrict, abandoning their constitutional requirements of geographic representation and other modifications of the population principle, in order to comply with the Court's standard.[50] During the 1960s and 1970s, Supreme Court rulings and congressional legislation invalidating other state constitutional regulations of the franchise, such as extended-residency requirements, poll taxes, and literacy tests, further diminished state control over the intrastate distribution of political power.[51] Federal intervention did not immediately end disputes over the distribution of political power, but it did transform them. Apportionment politics no longer involved constitutional provisions or conflicting political principles. Instead, freed from the need to respect geographic or political boundaries by the Court's insistence on interdistrict equality in population, it shifted to a subconstitutional search for partisan or group advantage through the artful creation of legislative districts. Yet the Supreme Court indicated that these districting decisions likewise were subject to federal constitutional scrutiny, intervening to invalidate partisan gerrymandering and race-conscious district-

---

New Jersey: The New Jersey Constitutional Convention of 1947 (Trenton: New Jersey Department of Education, 1952).

[47] On the limited character of most of reapportionments prior to the 1960s, see Baker, *State Constitutions*, 16–17.

[48] Dixon, *Democratic Representation*, 84.

[49] Dixon, *Democratic Representation*, 89–90.

[50] Leroy Hardy, Alan Heslop, and Stuart Anderson, "Introduction," in Hardy, Heslop, and Anderson, eds., *Reapportionment Politics: The History of Redistricting in the 50 States* (Beverly Hills, Calif.: Sage Publications, 1981), 19.

[51] On residency requirements, see *Dunn v. Blumstein*, 405 U.S. 330 (1972), which invalidated article 4, section 1 of the Tennessee Constitution; on poll taxes for voting in state elections, see *Harper v. Virginia Board of Elections*, 383 U.S. 663 (1966); and on literacy tests, see *Katzenbach v. Morgan*, 384 U.S. 641 (1966).

ing.[52] By century's end, the federalization of voting qualifications and judicial supervision of apportionment had in effect eclipsed the intrastate distribution of political power as an important issue in state constitutional politics.[53]

STATE AND ECONOMY

Some twentieth-century constitutional provisions dealing with economic concerns reflect the success of interest groups seeking benefits or advantages, while others reflect an attempt to serve the economic needs of all state residents and to orient the state toward a particular view of the public interest. The distributive policies built into state constitutions differ little in their substance or political origins from those found in state statutes; they reflect the state-enforced power of groups seeking economic advantage.[54] These constitutionalized statutes have taken many forms, ranging from Louisiana's guarantee of compensation for landowners on whose property levees were constructed to protect them, to Alabama's amendments promoting development of the cotton, grain, and catfish industries, to New Mexico's property tax exemptions for heads of families and for veterans.[55] The constitutionalization of group economic interests was designed to place them beyond the reach not only of inconstant legislators but also of state judges. This was an important consideration because state courts continued to invalidate state economic legislation on due-process and equal-protection grounds, even after federal courts abandoned their supervision of economic legislation.[56] However, groups' use of constitutional amendment to protect their interests could also be interpreted, at least in part, as a testament to the success of provisions prohibiting legislators from conferring special advantages. Constitutional bans on special legislation, on state investment in private concerns, and on granting the credit of the state to private entities may have obliged economic groups to pursue their interests via constitutional amendment.

[52] *Davis* v. *Bandemer,* 478 U.S. 109 (1986); *Shaw* v. *Reno,* 509 U.S. 630 (1993); and *Miller* v. *Johnson,* 513 U.S. 1071 (1995).

[53] But see *Fonfara* v. *Reapportionment Commission,* 610 A.2d 153 (Conn. 1992).

[54] John A. Hetherington, "State Economic Regulations and Substantive Due Process of Law," *Northwestern University Law Review* 53 (1979): 248–49.

[55] Louisiana Constitution, art. 14, sec. 32; Alabama Constitution, amendments 388, 453, and 492; and New Mexico Constitution, art. 8, sec. 5.

[56] Peter J. Galie, "State Courts and Economic Rights," *Annals of the American Academy of Political and Social Science* 496 (March 1988): 76–87; James C. Kirby Jr., "Expansive Judicial Review of Economic Regulations under State Constitutions," in Bradley McGraw, ed., *Developments in State Constitutional Law* (St. Paul: West, 1985); and Susan P. Fino, "Remnants of the Past: Economic Due Process in the States," in Friedelbaum, *Human Rights.*

Some state constitutional provisions reflect a broader concern for the proper operation of the economy and for the economic well-being of the state's inhabitants. As chapter 4 has shown, during the late nineteenth century, it was widely believed that the main threat to this well-being was the power of railroads and other large corporations. This concern carried over into state constitutions of the Progressive Era. The most striking illustration of this was the set of amendments adopted in California in 1911 that established a railroad commission to regulate all public utilities, revised the tax system to shift more of the burden to corporations and banks, and provided for employers' liability, a minimum wage, and enhanced powers of eminent domain.[57] Provisions adopted during the same period in other states also emphasized the protection of workers from exploitation. Thus, Idaho in 1902 amended its constitution to require the legislature to enact laws protecting the health and safety of workers in factories and mines; Montana in 1904 prohibited employment of children in mines and prescribed an eight-hour day for miners; and Wyoming in 1914 established a Workingmen's Compensation State Fund.[58] The concern for protecting workers surfaced again during the New Deal. In 1938, shortly after the passage of the Wagner Act, New York added to its declaration of rights a "bill of rights for labor," constitutionalizing preexisting statutory policies establishing a right to organize and bargain collectively and fixing maximum hours and guaranteeing prevailing wages for public employees.[59] By 1950 both New Jersey and Hawaii had followed New York's lead in constitutionalizing the right to bargain collectively.[60] However, other states during the postwar era

[57] See Dealey, *Growth of State Constitutions,* 107–8; Spencer C. Olin Jr., *California's Prodigal Sons: Hiram Johnson and the Progressives, 1911–1917* (Berkeley and Los Angeles: University of California Press, 1968), 12–17; and Grodin, Massey, and Cunningham, *The California State Constitution,* 16–18. The railroad commission replaced an earlier commission that had been co-opted by the Southern Pacific Railroad; see George E. Mowry, *The California Progressives* (Chicago: Quadrangle Books, 1951), 18. For discussion of parallel developments in other states, see Hurst, *Growth of American Law,* 240–46.

[58] For the Idaho amendment, see Idaho Constitution, art. 13, sec. 2; and for background on its development, see Crowley and Heffron, *The Idaho State Constitution,* 218–19. For the Montana amendments, see Montana Constitution, art. 18. For the Wyoming amendment, see Wyoming Constitution, art. 10, sec. 4; and for background on its development, see Keiter and Newcomb, *The Wyoming State Constitution,* 193–96. For a survey of state provisions affecting labor, see McCarthy, *Widening Scope,* 106.

[59] New York Constitution, art. 1, sec. 17. For elaboration of the origins and significance of these provisions, see Galie, *New York State Constitution,* 63–65. Earlier New York had safeguarded the right to damages for wrongful death and overrode a judicial ruling preventing the establishment of a system of workers compensation. See New York Constitution, art. 1, secs. 16 and 18, the latter overruling *Ives v. South Buffalo Railroad Co.,* 94 N.E. 431 (N.Y. 1911).

[60] New Jersey Constitution, art. 1, sec. 19; and Hawaii Constitution, art. 13, sec. 1.

viewed the appropriate balance between management and labor quite differently. Florida and Missouri balanced their recognition of the right to organize with a recognition of the "right to work," while Arizona, Arkansas, and South Dakota constitutionalized the right to work but did not mention collective bargaining.[61]

Although some early state provisions could be construed as recognizing a public responsibility for aspects of social welfare, New York pioneered in this field by committing itself explicitly to providing for the social welfare of its residents.[62] In 1938 it adopted a set of five amendments recognizing that "the aid, care and support of the needy," "the protection and promotion of the health of the inhabitants of the state," and "the care and treatment of persons suffering from mental disorder or defect," were all public concerns.[63] It also authorized the state to provide housing for low-income citizens.[64] These provisions did not empower the state to provide for social welfare, although they did remove any doubts that the state's plenary legislative power extended to those responsibilities. Rather, like earlier state constitutional provisions regarding education, these provisions articulated an understanding of the public interest and committed the state to a course of action in pursuit of it. However, until the 1960s and 1970s, only Hawaii followed New York in giving constitutional status to a broad array of positive rights.[65] Then, with a shift in the focus of political concern, several state constitutions obliged state governments to provide for the environmental well-being of their citizens. Indeed, every state constitutions written from 1959 to the present has committed the state to protection of the environment, and six states have also amended their constitutions to

---

Hawaii drafted its constitution in 1950, although it did not become a state until 1959. On the impact of the New Jersey provision, see Goldberg and Williams, "Farmworkers' Bargaining Rights." On the impact of the Hawaiian provision, see Lee, *The Hawaii State Constitution*, 181–82.

[61] Missouri Constitution, art. 1, sec. 29; Florida Constitution, art. 1, sec. 6; Arizona Constitution, art. 25; Arkansas Constitution, amendment 34; and South Dakota Constitution, art. 6, sec. 2. The "right to work" refers to the right not to be denied employment even if one does not belong to a labor union.

[62] For a survey of state constitutional provisions arguably concerned with positive rights, see Burt Neuborne, "State Constitutions and the Evolution of Positive Rights," *Rutgers Law Journal* 20 (summer 1989): 881–901.

[63] New York Constitution, art. 17, secs. 1, 3, 4. See Galie, *New York State Constitution*, 25 and 263–65.

[64] New York Constitution, art. 18, sec. 1.

[65] The Hawaii Constitution did not frame its provisions in terms of rights; rather, it expressly recognized the legislature's power to enact laws in various areas of public health and welfare. See Hawaii Constitution, art. 9. It should be noted that although most states did not constitutionalize their commitment to social welfare, they did of course enact legislation on the topic.

do so.[66] Taken together, these positive-rights provisions signaled a reorientation of state economic policy, from regulating the market to ensure that it worked well to intervening to achieve results not likely to be obtained through the operations of the market. However, the impact of these provisions should not be exaggerated. Despite the economic dislocations of the twentieth century, most states did not change their economic constitutions. Moreover, even in states that did, courts have often been reluctant to enforce the new constitutional provisions.[67] Finally, the flow of power over economic policy to the national government during the twentieth century has reduced the significance of state regulation of the economy.

STATE CONSTITUTIONAL REFORM

Many state constitutions continue to reflect the perspective on politics and government that underlay their creation, despite the proliferation of amendments. Twentieth-century state constitutions for the most part owe their vision of government and politics to the movement for state constitutional reform that arose during the Progressive Era but enjoyed its greatest success in the decades following World War II. Yet in the late twentieth century, the reformers' successes spawned a new movement for constitutional reform, pursuing a very different agenda.

The Progressive Era and Constitutional Reform

The Progressive movement arose in the late nineteenth century in response to the profound changes occurring in America's economy, society, and government. Many Progressives believed that institutional reforms were crucial to combating the problems of the emerging urban-industrial society and achieving their goals of enhanced democracy, institutional

[66] For examples of state environmental provisions, see Illinois Constitution, art. 11; and Pennsylvania Constitution, art. 1, sec. 27. For overviews of these provisions, see Barton H. Thompson Jr., "Environmental Policy and the State Constitution: The Role for Substantive Policy Guidance," in Bruce E. Cain and Roger G. Noll, *Constitutional Reform in California: Making State Government More Effective and Responsive* (Berkeley, Calif.: Institute of Governmental Studies Press, 1995); Margaret J. Fried and Monique J. Van Damme, "Environmental Protection in a Constitutional Setting," *Temple Law Review* 68 (fall 1995): 1369–1401; and A. E. Dick Howard, "State Constitutions and the Environment," *Virginia Law Review* 58 (February 1972): 193–229.

[67] See Feldman, "Separation of Powers"; and Jose L. Fernandez, "State Constitutions, Environmental Rights Provisions, and the Doctrine of Self-Execution: A Political Question?" *Harvard Environmental Law Review* 17 (1993): 333–87. For a somewhat less pessimistic conclusion, see Peter J. Galie, "Social Services and Egalitarian Activism," in Friedelbaum, *Human Rights*.

rationality, and social justice. They sought to free political decision-making from the dominance of special interests through direct democracy, championing the initiative, referendum, and recall. To ensure that direct democracy would promote good government, they emphasized elevating the quality of public opinion through education, through political leadership, and—for some Progressives—through literacy tests and other restrictions on the franchise. Having concluded that "party bosses" were responsible for much of the waste and corruption in government, the reformers attempted to limit their power through nonpartisan elections or in partisan elections through the selection of candidates in primaries. Finally, Progressive reformers attempted to revitalize government by restructuring political institutions to remove obstacles to effective leadership and concerted action. Chief among these obstacles, they believed, were the separation of powers and checks and balances found in American constitutions; accordingly, they attempted to reduce the influence of these constitutional mechanisms in order to facilitate more effectual governmental action. They also proposed the creation of a bureaucracy that, freed from politics, would have broad discretion to use its neutral expertise to administer policy in the public interest. And, perhaps most importantly, they favored a strong executive in whom political authority and responsibility could be concentrated.[68]

Initially, the Progressives focused on reforming municipal government. Thus it is not surprising that the organization that eventually spearheaded the campaign for state constitutional reform in the twentieth century, the National Municipal League, was formed in 1894 out of the National Conference for Good City Government.[69] However, during the early twentieth century the Progressives also pursued at the state level their three goals of enhanced democracy, institutional rationalization, and social justice. Between 1902 and 1918, thirteen states adopted the initiative, and more initiatives were proposed and adopted from 1910 to 1919 than in any subsequent decade.[70] In 1918, responding to reform

[68] This account of the Progressive agenda is drawn from Richard Hofstadter, *The Age of Reform: From Bryan to F.D.R.* (New York: Alfred A. Knopf, 1968); Robert H. Wiebe, *The Search for Order, 1877–1920* (New York: Hill and Wang, 1967); Arthur S. Link and Richard L. McCormick, *Progressivism* (Arlington Heights, Ill.: Harlan Davidson, 1983); Benjamin Parke DeWitt, *The Progressive Movement* (New York: Macmillan, 1915); Martin J. Schiesl, *The Politics of Efficiency: Municipal Administration and Reform in America, 1800–1920* (Berkeley and Los Angeles: University of California Press, 1977); and Vile, *Constitutionalism and Separation,* chap. 10.

[69] Frank Mann Stewart, *A Half Century of Municipal Reform: A History of the National Municipal League* (Berkeley and Los Angeles: University of California Press, 1950), chap. 2. The historical treatment of the league relies primarily on this volume.

[70] For a listing of the states that adopted the initiative and the years of adoption, see Janice C. May, "The Constitutional Initiative: A Threat to Rights?" in Friedelbaum, *Hu-*

efforts spurred by President Taft's Commission on Economy and Efficiency, Massachusetts amended its constitution to reorganize and consolidate state agencies, and New York and Virginia did the same in the 1920s. Twenty-three other states reorganized and consolidated their executive branches by 1937 without constitutional amendment.[71] Finally, as noted previously, several western states in which Progressivism was strong adopted constitutional provisions specifically designed to protect workers and rein in the power of large corporations.

Nevertheless, comprehensive reform of state constitutions emerged as an issue only in the waning years of the Progressive Era. Then, the recognition that municipal reform required broad home-rule powers led the National Municipal League to expand its agenda to state constitutional revision. In 1919 the league sponsored a mock state constitutional convention to address the problems of state government, and this led to the promulgation of a Model State Constitution in 1921 and to the publication of that document with explanatory articles three years later.[72] This model constitution incorporated standard Progressive reforms, such as the initiative and referendum, as well as provisions on municipal home rule, a merit-based civil service, and the reform of county government.[73] Drawing on parliamentary models, it also proposed a radical restructuring of state legislatures and executives to reduce interbranch and intrabranch conflicts and to promote vigorous governmental action.[74] Thus, the first Model State Constitution called for a unicameral legislature with

---

man Rights, 164. For data on the use of the initiative, see Magleby, "Direct Legislation, 232, fig. 7-2. Early initiatives were used for purposes as diverse as instituting the executive budget (California in 1922) to changing the basis for apportionment of the state legislature (Arizona in 1912). For an overview of the uses of the initiative, see David D. Schmidt, *Citizen Lawmakers: The Ballot Initiative Revolution* (Philadelphia: Temple University Press, 1989), 15–20. Basing his estimate on figures from 1990 to 1992, Magleby has projected that the use of the initiative from 1990 to 1999 will surpass that from 1910 to 1919.

[71] On state administrative reorganizations, see Buck, *Reorganization of State Governments;* Garnett, *Reorganizing State Government;* and Kynerd, *Administrative Reorganization in Mississippi.*

[72] *A Model State Constitution* (1924).

[73] Model State Constitution, secs. 33–40 (initiative and referendum); secs. 78–85 (home rule); sec. 90 (civil service); and secs. 86–89 (county government).

[74] Thus, in defending the proposals for the legislature, H. W. Dodds insisted that they only seemed radical within the American context, because they drew on "successful experience elsewhere" and "certain recognized advantages enjoyed by other English speaking people." H. W. Dodds, "The Legislature," in *A Model State Constitution* (1924), 20. John A. Fairlie also likened the proposals for the executive to the practice "in most European and other foreign countries" and suggested that the league refrained from suggesting parliamentary governments for the states largely because "for some time to come such a reversal of established American methods will not be approved." John A. Fairlie, "The Executive," in *A Model State Constitution* (1924), 25 and 26.

proportional representation, for the governor and major department heads to sit in the legislature, for the creation of a "legislative council" composed of the governor and legislative leaders to plan and manage the legislative agenda, and for removal of the governor upon a vote of no confidence by two-thirds of the legislature.[75] In addition, in order to prevent deadlocks over policy, voters were invited to decide by referendum the fate of measures passed by the state legislature but vetoed by the governor or proposed by the governor but rejected by less than two-thirds of the legislature.[76]

With the decline of Progressivism in the 1920s, such radical proposals had little appeal. Even Nebraska's adoption of a unicameral legislature in 1934 owed more to the support of Senator George Norris than to the proposals of the National Municipal League.[77] Perhaps the most pointed commentary on the indifference that greeted the initial Model State Constitution is the fact that for twenty-one years after its publication, no state revised its constitution.

Postwar Constitutional Reform

In the decades following World War II, the movement for state constitutional reform attracted new adherents. Political commentators joined the chorus of criticism of state constitutions, denouncing them as the states' "greatest shame" and arguing that they bore "no more resemblance to a constitution than a garbage dump does to a park."[78] So too did official bodies, such as the federal Kestenbaum Commission, and groups such as the Committee for Economic Development.[79] Buoyed by this support, state constitutional reformers enjoyed some notable successes. From 1945 to 1960, New Jersey, Hawaii, and Alaska all adopted constitutions that were extensively influenced by the Model State Constitution. In New Jersey the main groups supporting constitutional revision, as well as the commission preparing materials for delegates, drew extensively on the Model State Constitution and National Municipal League personnel in

[75] Model State Constitution, sec. 13 (unicameral legislature); sec. 47 (executive participating in legislative sessions, although not voting); secs. 29–32 (legislative council); and sec. 48 (legislative removal of executive). Although the governor and department heads could participate in legislative debate, they could not vote on bills.

[76] Model State Constitution, sec. 27.

[77] Miewald and Longo, *The Nebraska State Constitution,* 19.

[78] Robert S. Allen, ed., *Our Sovereign State* (New York: Vanguard, 1949), xv, xvi. Another influential popular critique of state constitutions was Terry Sanford, *Storm over the States* (New York: McGraw-Hill, 1967).

[79] Commission on Intergovernmental Relations, *Report to the President;* and Committee for Economic Development in several of its publications: *Modernizing Local Government, Modernizing State Government,* and *Fiscal Program.*

drafting their proposals; and the delegates relied on these in framing the 1947 constitution.[80] For Hawaii and Alaska, which were drafting their initial constitutions and thus were not shackled by past versions, the Model State Constitution encapsulated the best in constitutional thought, replacing the need to consult all other states' constitutions, as had been the practice in new states in the nineteenth century.[81] In the decade following *Reynolds* v. *Sims* (1964), when several states revised their constitutions, the Model State Constitution again served to frame the constitutional debate and provide a nonpartisan model for constitution-makers. State constitutional commissions, groups of experts formed to prepare materials for the delegates, played a crucial role in disseminating the reform perspective. In a study of seven constitutional conventions during this period, Elmer Cornwell and his associates found that all the revised state constitutions moved closer to the Model State Constitution, some dramatically so.[82]

The version of constitutional reform adopted by postwar constitution-makers, however, differed from earlier versions. Perhaps stung by the indifference that greeted the publication of its initial Model State Constitution, the National Municipal League jettisoned many of its most radical recommendations. Thus, the fourth edition, published in 1941, removed the governor from the legislative council, thereby enhancing the separation of powers; and the sixth edition, published in 1968, eliminated the legislative council, proportional representation, and the referendum on stalled legislation.[83] These changes reflected as well a shift in the reformers' frame of reference. The initial Model State Constitution had drawn heavily on foreign parliamentary models, presumably based on the assumption that only such systems could ensure effective government. Later versions, however, portrayed reform as choosing the best

[80] The main groups supporting constitutional revision were the New Jersey Committee for Constitutional Revision and the League of Women Voters. For analysis of the influence of the Model State Constitution on the New Jersey Constitution, see Connors, *Process of Constitutional Revision*, 136–38 and 202–4.

[81] Both Hawaii and Alaska relied on the Model State Constitution directly and, when they looked to the New Jersey Constitution for guidance, indirectly. On constitution making in Hawaii, see Meller, *With an Understanding Heart*; on constitution making in Alaska, see Gerald A. McBeath, *The Alaska State Constitution: A Reference Guide* (Westport, Conn.: Greenwood Press, 1997), and *Alaska's Constitution: A Citizen's Guide*, 3d ed. (Juneau: Alaska Legislative Research Agency, 1992).

[82] See Cornwell, Goodman, and Swanson, *State Constitutional Conventions*, 156–59. Parallels between the Model State Constitution and revised state constitutions do not, of course, prove that delegates consulted it in drafting their documents—correlation is not causation. It is more likely that delegates sought to avail themselves of the best understanding of state constitutional design, and this understanding had been decisively influenced over time by the Model State Constitution.

[83] *Model State Constitution*, 4th ed. (New York: National Municipal League, 1941); and *Model State Constitution*, 6th ed.

from existing American institutions and practices. Thus, beginning with the fourth edition, the Model State Constitution highlighted existing state and federal provisions that resembled its recommended provisions or from which they were purportedly derived. This change was more than cosmetic. The federal government's response to the Great Depression and its successful conduct of World War II had convinced state constitutional reformers that the federal Constitution provided a framework for effective government. Thus, this constitution—and state constitutions that resembled it—became the standard for constitutional reform.[84] Of course, few state constitutions measured up to that standard. This was implicit in the frequently voiced claim that the inadequacies of state governments had impelled citizens to take their concerns to Washington, where presumably they encountered no such obstacles to effective action.[85] Postwar reform publications, therefore, emphasized the disparities between the federal and state constitutions and urged states to emulate the federal Constitution in revising their charters.[86]

In endorsing this idealized federal model because of its promise of effective government, postwar constitutional reformers in effect embraced the efficiency strand of Progressive thought while abandoning the others. Progressives had campaigned for social justice for workers, but given the emphasis on eliminating constitutional legislation, this perhaps understandably had never played a significant part in the Model State Constitution.[87] What did figure prominently in the initial Model State Constitution but was abandoned by the postwar reformers was the Progressive concern for promoting direct democracy and correcting abuses of power. Indeed, by the publication of the sixth edition of the Model State Constitution, the legislative initiative and referendum, key elements of the Progressive agenda, had altogether disappeared.

The Model State Constitution that dominated postwar constitutional reform best fits what Daniel Elazar has labeled the "managerial pattern."[88] According to this view, the main problem facing state constitution-

[84] See, for example, Dishman, *State Constitutions; Model State Constitution*, 6th ed., viii; and Wheeler, *Salient Issues*. For similar sentiments from other constitutional reformers, see Commission on Intergovernmental Relations, *Report to the President*, 37–38.

[85] See, for example, Commission on Intergovernmental Relations, *Report to the President*, 37; and Sturm, *Thirty Years*, 2–4. The claim can be traced as far back as the beginning of the twentieth century. See Henry Jones Ford, "The Influence of State Politics in Expanding Federal Power," *Proceedings of the American Political Science Association* (Washington, D.C.: American Political Science Association, 1908).

[86] See, for example, Wheeler, *Salient Issues*; Graves, *Major Problems*; and John E. Bebout, introduction to *Model State Constitution*, 6th ed.

[87] The fourth edition of the Model State Constitution did contain a public-welfare article, which was retained in the fifth edition but excised from the sixth edition.

[88] See Elazar, "Principles and Traditions," 22. For elaboration of Elazar's point, see Hall, "Mostly Anchor," 407–10.

makers was structuring state government to act vigorously on the problems confronting the states. Such a proactive state government required "a flexible and adaptable instrument which helps us in the solution of today's problems" and which would be "flexible and adaptable, with only minor modifications, in managing tomorrow's tasks as well."[89] This flexibility and adaptability came from strengthening the executive and removing impediments to legislative action. In order to promote effective action by state executives, reformers proposed concentrating political authority in the hands of the governor by eliminating the independent election of other executive-branch officers, collecting the myriad independent boards and agencies into a manageable number of executive departments, and enhancing the governor's power over budgetary matters through the executive budget, the item veto, and other devices. In order to promote effective legislative action, reformers proposed abolishing virtually all procedural and substantive limits on legislative action. As the introduction to the sixth Model State Constitution put it, "The limitations on state and local government action were devised for the most part during an age when less was demanded of government than is the case today."[90] Insofar as they recognized abuse of power might pose a danger, the reformers seemed to assume that periodic elections were a sufficient check on such abuses. To constitutionalize limits on legislative power, according to one leading reformer, was "difficult to reconcile . . . with a real belief in democracy."[91]

The aim of state constitutional reformers, then, was to encourage the states to modernize their constitutions and their governments, thereby promoting a "resurgence of the states," enabling them to play the same positive role played by the federal government.[92] Even though voters rejected several proposed constitutions, the reformers achieved many of their goals. By the late 1970s forty-seven states had extended the gubernatorial term to four years, and many had strengthened the governors' appointment, personnel, and budget powers, although few had signifi-

[89] Grad, "The State Constitution," 4. See also David Fellman, "What Should a State Constitution Contain?" in Graves, *Major Problems*.

[90] *Model State Constitution*, 6th ed., ix.

[91] Frank M. Landers, "Taxation and Finance," in Graves, *Major Problems*, 225.

[92] The phrase is taken from Bowman and Kearney, *Resurgence of the States*. Other key sources dealing with this resurgence include John Kincaid, "The New Federalism Context of the New Judicial Federalism," *Rutgers Law Journal* 26 (summer 1995): 913–48; U.S. Advisory Commission on Intergovernmental Relations, *The Question of State Government Capability* (Washington, D.C.: Advisory Commission on Intergovernmental Relations, 1985); and Mavis Mann Reeves, "The States as Polities: Reformed, Reinvigorated, Resourceful," *Annals of the American Academy of Political and Social Science* 509 (May 1990): 83–93.

cantly reduced the number of separately elected state-level officials.[93] Several states had also professionalized their legislatures, consolidated their bureaucracies, and reformed their judicial systems.[94] Thus state governments were presumably equipped to assume a leadership role in policy development alongside the federal government.

A New Reform Agenda

Yet the timing of the reformers' success could hardly have been worse. They celebrated activist government at a time when citizens were becoming increasingly skeptical about the efficiency and effectiveness of governmental programs. They praised the professionalization of state government at a time when citizens were primarily concerned about the responsiveness of public officials and about their ties to special interests. And they encouraged state governments to emulate the federal government at a time when citizens increasingly rejected the idea of "their legislature [as] a 'little Congress,' their governor [as] a 'little president,' or their high court [as] a 'little Warren Court.'"[95]

Not surprisingly, then, the resurgence of state government promoted by the reformers prompted a reaction, an effort to curtail what were seen as overly expensive and powerful state governments that were insulated from popular concerns and popular control. Distrust of government in general and state legislatures in particular has, of course, provided an impetus for constitutional reform throughout American history. So in a sense the complaints of these "new reformers," as they might be called, were nothing new. However, the context in which they operated was quite different. Prior reformers had usually sought to make government more responsive by expanding the electorate, by changing the intrastate distribution of political power, or by restructuring government. But by the 1970s, with the extension of the franchise, the reapportionment of state legislatures, and the modernization of state executive branches, it was clear that such reforms could not dispel concerns about unresponsive government. This convinced the new reformers that representation did

[93] Thad Beyle, "Governors: The Middlemen and Women in Our Political System," in Virginia Gray and Herbert Jacob, eds., *Politics in the American States: A Comparative Analysis*, 6th ed. (Washington, D.C.: CQ Press, 1996); and Sabato, *Goodbye to Good-Time Charlie*, 61–63.

[94] Kincaid, "New Federalism Context," 927; and Advisory Commission on Intergovernmental Relations, *Question of State Capability*.

[95] Kincaid, "New Federalism Context," 929. On the decline of trust in government during the late 1960s and the 1970s, see Seymour Martin Lipset and William Schneider, *The Confidence Gap: Business, Labor, and Government in the Public Mind* (New York: Free Press, 1983).

not solve the problem of popular government. They therefore sought to lodge policymaking authority directly in the people, to reverse policies enacted by the established institutions of government, and to limit the powers and tenure of government officials.

Two aspects of this new reform agenda stand out. First, the emphasis on direct popular rule as a response to unresponsive government harkened back to Progressive thought, reemphasizing an aspect of that thought ignored by postwar reformers. Second, the new reformers' agenda was largely a negative one, concerned with preventing or combating impositions by government.[96] Given this focus, it is not surprising that the new reformers did not organize a nationwide movement for constitutional revision; indeed, they did not concern themselves with constitutional revision at all. Rather, what the new reformers produced was a series of state constitutional amendments that, taken together, fundamentally altered the character and powers of state governments by limiting the tenure of governmental officials, reducing their powers, and transferring policymaking responsibilities to the people.

The primary mechanism for accomplishing these changes was the constitutional initiative. The number of such initiatives has increased dramatically in recent years: from 1970 to 1979, only twenty-one state constitutional amendments were citizen initiatives, but from 1980 to 1989, thirty-three initiative amendments were ratified, and from 1991 to 1995, forty-two.[97] The new reformers relied on the initiative primarily in order to bypass state legislatures, which generally opposed their proposals.[98] In doing so, they vindicated the Progressives' hope that the initiative offered a means for circumventing entrenched political forces.[99] Yet the use of

[96] It is hardly surprising that during this era Ronald Reagan was twice elected president, campaigning on the idea that government was the problem, not the solution.

[97] These data are drawn from Albert L. Sturm, "State Constitutions and Constitutional Revision: 1978–79 and the 1970s," *Book of States, 1980–81,* 3, table B; Janice C. May, "State Constitutions and Constitutional Revision: 1988–89 and the 1980s," *Book of the States, 1990–91* (Lexington, Ky.: Council of State Governments, 1990), 30; and succeeding volumes of the *Book of the States.*

[98] Reformers have relied on the initiative because, as Thomas Gais and Gerald Benjamin have noted, "legislators resist fundamental revisions because many of the demands for reform are in fact *aimed* at state legislatures and threaten the interests of their members." See Gais and Benjamin, "Public Discontent and the Decline of Deliberation: A Dilemma in State Constitutional Reform," *Temple Law Review* 68 (fall 1995): 1298 and passim.

[99] Some critics have charged that these entrenched political forces are merely replaced by political entrepreneurs, who exploit the initiative process for their own purposes. For studies documenting the entrepreneurial character of the initiative process, see Candace McCoy, "Crime as a Bogeyman: Why Californians Changed Their Constitution to Include a 'Victims Bill of Rights' (and What It Really Did)," in Tarr, *Constitutional Politics in States,* and Rausch "Politics of Term Limitations." However, a large percentage of initiatives fail to make the ballot or are defeated at the polls—for data, see Magleby, "Direct

this "political outsider" approach limited reform primarily to the eighteen states that have instituted the constitutional initiative.[100]

If, as the new reformers believed, state government was unaccountable and beholden to special interests, then it was important to limit its power by constitutionalizing policy choices and circumscribing officials' freedom of action. Thus the new reformers initially sought to limit the funds that government could raise and spend.[101] In 1978 California adopted Proposition 13, which permanently limited property tax rates; and a year later, it curbed increases in state expenditures, tying them to changes in the rate of inflation and in the population.[102] In the decade after Proposition 13, reformers in other states also placed tax and/or expenditure limitations on the ballot, although few proposals were as radical as Proposition 13. They achieved some notable victories, such as Massachusetts' Proposition 2½, but suffered several defeats as well.[103] During the 1990s, a new wave of "plebiscitary budgeting" began, with initiatives in three states requiring a supermajority in the legislature for the enactment of tax increases, initiatives in two others tying increases in spending to the rate of inflation and population increases, and an initiative in Colorado (labeled by its proponents the Taxpayer's Bill of Rights) requiring voter approval for all new taxes.[104]

Legislation," 233, fig. 7-3. This suggests that only ballot proposals that tap into strongly felt dissatisfactions tend to succeed.

[100] Perhaps it is not coincidental that four states have adopted the constitutional initiative within the last three decades. For a listing of states with the constitutional initiative, see *Book of States, 1994–95*, 23, table 1.3.

[101] Limitations on revenues also had an effect on spending because state balanced-budget provisions prohibiting deficit spending, although the effectiveness of these provisions is open to question. See Richard Briffault, *Balancing Acts: The Reality behind State Balanced Budget Requirements* (New York: Twentieth Century Fund, 1996).

[102] For accounts of the origins and effects of Proposition 13, see Alvin Rabushka and Pauline Ryan, *The Tax Revolt* (Stanford, Calif.: Hoover Institution, 1982); Robert Kuttner, *Revolt of the Haves: Tax Rebellions and Hard Times* (New York: Simon and Schuster, 1980); David O. Sears and Jack Citrin, *Tax Revolt: Something for Nothing in California* (Cambridge: Harvard University Press, 1982); and William A. Fischel, "How *Serrano* Caused Proposition 13," *Journal of Law and Politics* 12 (fall 1996): 521–53. The pertinent provisions are California Constitution, arts. 13a and 13b.

[103] For a survey of these efforts, see John L. Mikesell, "The Path of the Tax Revolt: Statewide Expenditure and Tax Cutting Referenda since Proposition 13," *State and Local Government Review* 18 (1986): 5–13; Jack Citrin, introduction to Terry Schwadron, ed., *California and the American Tax Revolt: Proposition 13 Five Years Later* (Berkeley and Los Angeles: University of California Press, 1984); and Rabushka and Ryan, *The Tax Revolt*, 186–94.

[104] The supermajority requirements are found in Oklahoma Constitution, art. 5, sec. 33; Arizona Constitution, art. 9, sec. 22; and Nevada Constitution, art. 4, sec. 18. The spending limits are found in Colorado Constitution, art. 10, sec. 20; and Washington Revised Code, sec. 43.135.035 (1994). The requirement of popular approval for all new taxes is found in

This "tax revolt" involved more than a concern about taxes. As one leader of the revolt put it, "Our fight is not mainly about money. It's about control. They have to learn once and for all that it's our government."[105] To exert that control, the new reformers in the 1990s also imposed restrictions on the tenure and powers of state officials. In 1990 Oklahoma adopted a constitutional initiative limiting the length of legislative service to twelve years, and by 1994, twenty other states had also imposed term limits on state legislators. Eleven simultaneously imposed such limitations on governors, thereby reversing earlier reformers' efforts to ensure the indefinite reeligibility of the executive.[106] California complemented this attack on incumbency with the adoption of Proposition 140, which prohibited legislators from earning state retirement benefits and required major reductions in legislative agencies and staff.[107] And Texas and Oklahoma in 1990 constitutionalized ethics commissions that would investigate official misconduct.[108]

In the late nineteenth century, constitution-makers inserted policy provisions in state constitutions, because they did not trust state legislatures to represent the interests of the people. The adoption of the initiative has made it possible to circumvent representative institutions and enact constitutional legislation at any time, not just during constitution making. Yet the character of initiative politics is itself controversial. Popular majorities that have been stymied in the legislature have availed themselves of this option, in effect repudiating the notion that state constitutions should confine themselves to fundamentals. But so too have interest groups, which have used their resources to mount campaigns for their concerns. And so have aspiring politicians, who have encouraged initiatives as a way of advancing their careers. In recent years the focus of constitutional initiatives in several states has shifted from questions of governmental structure, responsiveness, and expense to questions of substantive policy. Highly contentious economic and social issues avoided by legislatures have come to dominate the agenda, exacerbating splits among the populace. Thus Florida has had initiatives on tort liability, gambling, the rights of gays, and the creation of an official language; Colorado on the rights of gays and parental rights; and California on

---

Colorado Constitution, art. 10, sec. 20. Interestingly, Colorado's "Taxpayer's Bill of Rights" was adopted in 1992 after being rejected in 1988 and 1990.

[105] Quoted in Citrin, introduction, 7.

[106] On the development of term limitations, see Gerald Benjamin and Michael J. Malbin, eds., *Limiting Legislative Terms* (Washington, D.C.: CQ Press, 1992); Rausch, "Politics of Term Limitations"; Samuel C. Patterson, "Legislative Politics in the States," in Gray and Jacob, *Politics in American States*; and Beyle, "Governors."

[107] California Constitution, art. 4, sec. 1.5.

[108] Texas Constitution, art. 3, sec. 24a; and Oklahoma Constitution, art. 29.

affirmative action and the rights of immigrants.[109] In addition, the new reformers in several states have used the constitutional initiative to reverse judicial rulings, illustrating the concern to check institutions that make policy but are perceived as outside popular control.[110] The proliferation of ballot questions during the 1990s suggests that constitutional reform by initiative will continue to be an important aspect of state constitutional development.

THE NEW JUDICIAL FEDERALISM

Among the most heralded constitutional developments in recent years has been state judges' increased reliance on state declarations of rights to secure rights unavailable under the U.S. Constitution.[111] This new judicial federalism, as it has been labeled, emerged during the early 1970s, following the appointment of Chief Justice Warren Burger to succeed Earl Warren on the U.S. Supreme Court, and was encouraged by Justice William Brennan, a stalwart of the Warren Court.[112] Thus, when state courts began to rely on their state constitutions, critics charged that they were merely attempting to evade Burger Court rulings and safeguard the civil libertarian gains of the Warren Court.[113] This criticism lost force,

[109] For a general discussion, see David Kohler and Robert M. Stern, "Initiatives in the 1980s and 1990s," *Book of the States, 1994–1995,* 279–93. For a case study of the changing use of the initiative in a single state, see Daniel R. Gordon, "Protecting against the State Constitutional Law Junkyard: Proposals to Limit Popular Constitutional Revision in Florida," *Nova Law Review* 20 (fall 1995): 413–35.

[110] Illustrative of this use of the constitutional initiative are California Constitution, art. 1, sec. 27, overruling *People* v. *Anderson,* 493 P.2d 880 (1972); California Constitution, art. 1, sec. 28, overruling a large number of defendants' rights rulings; Florida Constitution, art. 1, sec. 12, narrowing the state exclusionary rule; and Massachusetts Constitution, Declaration of Rights, art. 26, overruling *District Attorney* v. *Watson,* 411 N.E.2d 1274 (1980).

[111] For an early useful guide to the literature on the new judicial federalism, see Earl M. Maltz, Robert F. Williams, and Michael Araten, "Selected Bibliography on State Constitutional Law, 1980–1989," *Rutgers Law Journal* 20 (summer 1989): 1093–1113. For an examination of the legal community's response to the new judicial federalism, see Tarr, "Constitutional Theory," 843–50.

[112] Justice William H. Brennan Jr. initially endorsed the new judicial federalism in his oft-cited "State Constitutions and the Protection of Individual Rights," *Harvard Law Review* 90 (January 1977): 489–504.

[113] For criticism of the new judicial federalism as reactive and result-oriented, see Earl M. Maltz, "The Political Dynamic of the 'New Judicial Federalism,'" *Emerging Issues in State Constitutional Law* 2 (1989): 233–38; Steven J. Twist and Len L. Munsil, "The Double Threat of Judicial Activism: Inventing New 'Rights' in State Constitutions," *Arizona State Law Journal* 21 (winter 1989): 1005–65; and George Deukmejian and Clifford K. Thompson, "All Sail and No Anchor—Judicial Review under the California Constitution," *Hastings Constitutional Law Quarterly* 6 (summer 1979): 975–1010. Even some propo-

however, as the new judicial federalism spread, and courts in every state announced rulings based on the rights guarantees of their state constitutions.[114] Some state courts even indicated that they would henceforth address state constitutional claims first and consider federal constitutional claims only when cases could not be resolved on state grounds.[115] By the mid-1990s, then, the new judicial federalism had become an established feature of American federalism and, most likely, a permanent one.

The New Judicial Federalism in Historical Perspective

The judicial involvement in state constitutional development that has resulted from the new judicial federalism marks a major shift in the role of state courts.[116] For although state courts occasionally contributed to state constitutional development prior to the 1970s, state judges overall have been far less aggressive than their federal counterparts in promoting constitutional change. This reticence is particularly apparent in the civil-liberties realm. Some commentators have sought to portray the new judicial federalism as a "rediscovery" of state constitutions and state declarations of rights, insisting that until the 1930s state constitutions were necessarily the primary vehicle for protecting individual rights.[117] The claim

---

nents of the new judicial federalism viewed it as evasive. See the three articles by Donald E. Wilkes Jr., "The New Federalism in Criminal Procedure: State Court Evasion of the Burger Court," *Kentucky Law Journal* 62 (1974): 421–51; "More on the New Federalism in Criminal Procedure," *Kentucky Law Journal* 63 (1975): 873–94; and "The New Federalism in Criminal Procedure Revisited," *Kentucky Law Journal* 64 (1976): 729–52. For an early effort to develop standards for assessing the legitimacy for state judicial activism, see Porter, "State Supreme Courts." The criticism of state constitutional law as result-oriented and the responses to this charge are discussed in the next chapter.

[114] On the spread of the new judicial federalism, see Collins, Galie, and Kincaid, "State High Courts"; and John Kincaid, "State Court Protections of Individual Rights under State Constitutions: The New Judicial Federalism," *Journal of State Government* 61 (September–October 1988): 163–69. Annual surveys of state constitutional cases are found in the *Rutgers Law Journal*.

[115] These states include Oregon (*Sterling* v. *Cupp*, 625 P.2d 123 [Ore. 1981]); Washington (*State* v. *Coe*, 679 P.2d 353 [Wash. 1984]); Maine (*State* v. *Cadman*, 476 A.2d 114 [Me. 1984]); and Vermont (*State* v. *Badger*, 450 A.2d 336 [Vt. 1982]). This approach was championed by Justice Hans E. Linde of the Oregon Supreme Court; see his "Without Due Process."

[116] For further documentation of the argument of this section, see Tarr, "Past and Future," 64–69; and G. Alan Tarr, "The New Judicial Federalism in Perspective," *Notre Dame Law Review* 72 (May 1997): 1097–1118.

[117] The assumption of these scholars is that there were three eras of rights protection in the states. For the first 140 years of the nation's history, state courts served as the primary protectors of civil liberties. From the 1930s to the early 1970s, the incorporation of provisions of the Bill of Rights and increased federal judicial activism made federal courts the primary, almost exclusive, protectors of civil liberties. With the rise of the new judicial

has a certain plausibility. Until the 1930s state governments had more opportunities to invade rights, given the limited scope of the federal government, and federal remedies for such invasions were lacking because the protections of the Bill of Rights had not been incorporated, so the only legal recourse was to be found in state courts.

Unfortunately for those seeking a pedigree for state judicial activism, however, their claim is more edifying than accurate. Although conditions may have seemed ripe for the development of state civil-liberties law during the nineteenth and early twentieth centuries, no such development occurred. State constitutional litigation during this period was rare and seldom involved civil-liberties issues.[118] Although isolated civil-liberties rulings can be found (and have been cited over and over by advocates of the new judicial federalism), prior to the 1930s state courts failed to develop a coherent body of law relating to freedom of speech, religious liberty, the rights of defendants, or other civil-liberties concerns.[119] Contemporary state courts' failure to uncover early civil-liberties precedents on which to base their rulings underscores the point. Thus, until the advent of the new judicial federalism, state courts' contribution to developing constitutional protections for civil liberties was minimal.

This historical record raises two questions: why did state courts not play an important role in protecting rights prior to the new judicial federalism, and what changes led to the emergence of the new judicial federalism, to a more rights-protective role for state courts, in the 1970s? The key to answering these questions lies in the recognition that state constitutional interpretation occurs in the context of—and is influenced by—a broader American judicial tradition.[120] This is not to deny differences

federalism in the early 1970s, state and federal courts have shared the responsibility of protecting rights. For an account of the three eras focusing on criminal justice, see Abrahamson, "Criminal Law." For extension of this notion to civil liberties more generally, see Abrahamson and Gutmann, "The New Federalism"; and Abrahamson, "Divided We Stand." For my own ill-considered endorsement of the notion, see Tarr, "State Constitutionalism," 38–39. Nevertheless, some commentators on the new judicial federalism did recognize that, until recently, state constitutions never provided a major basis for protecting rights. See Judith S. Kaye, "Foreword: The Common Law and State Constitutional Law as Full Partners in the Protection of Individual Rights," *Rutgers Law Journal* 23 (summer 1992): 727–52.

[118] Two studies by Robert A. Kagan, Bliss Cartwright, Lawrence M. Friedman, and Stanton Wheeler confirm this: "Business of Supreme Courts"; and "The Evolution of State Supreme Courts," *Michigan Law Review* 76 (May 1978): 961–1005.

[119] Frequently cited cases include *Carpenter* v. *Dane,* 9 Wis. 249 (1859); and *State* v. *Sheridan,* 96 N.W. 730 (Iowa 1903). For a survey of state civil-liberties rulings prior to 1930, see Tarr, "Past and Future," 66–69.

[120] For an overview of this tradition, which recognizes the contributions of state judges to its development, see G. Edward White, *The American Judicial Tradition: Profiles of Leading American Judges* (New York: Oxford University Press, 1976). For a thoughtful

among states or among historical eras. Rather, the point is that the standards of appropriate judicial practice—best understood as prescribing a range of legitimate behavior rather than rigid rules governing judicial practice—change over time. State judges, like their federal counterparts, participate in creating those standards and respond to them. Gradually, judges become educated as to the prevailing standards; that is, they learn how to approach and interpret their state constitutions by watching how other courts (both federal and state) interpret their own charters.[121] Litigants also ensure that appropriate claims and arguments, pioneered in other judicial arenas, are brought before them. Thus, it was not surprising that in the late eighteenth and early nineteenth centuries, state courts looked to extratextual sources in interpreting their state constitutions; other courts were doing likewise.[122] Nor was it surprising that in the late nineteenth century, state courts began to invalidate legislation that trespassed on economic liberty; they had such a course urged on them by influential legal treatises and authorized by the example of sister courts.[123] Similarly, it was not surprising that, in the 1970s, state courts began to emulate the Warren Court in giving broad readings to their states' rights guarantees.

Put differently, the existence of state constitutional guarantees and the absence of federal involvement appeared to afford an opportunity for judicial initiatives prior to the 1930s, but this was not enough. What was missing was a model of how state judges could, even if they wished to, go about developing a civil-liberties jurisprudence. Because Americans had not come to rely on courts to vindicate civil liberties, state courts throughout the nineteenth and early twentieth centuries gained little ex-

---

analysis that links state and federal traditions, see Lawrence M. Friedman, "State Constitutions and Criminal Justice in the Late Nineteenth Century," in Finkelman and Gottlieb, *Toward a Usable Past*.

[121] These patterns of interaction between state and federal courts and among state courts have been labeled vertical judicial federalism and horizontal judicial federalism. See Porter and Tarr, introduction to *Policymakers*, xix–xxii; and Tarr and Porter, *State Supreme Courts in State and Nation*, chap. 1.

[122] On extratextualism in state constitutional interpretation, see Suzanna Sherry, "The Early Virginia Tradition of Extratextual Interpretation," in Finkelman and Gottleib, *Toward a Usable Past*; and Suzanna Sherry, "State Constitutional Law: Doing the Right Thing," *Rutgers Law Journal* 25 (summer 1994): 935–44. On extratextual interpretation of the federal Constitution, see Suzanna Sherry, "The Founders' Unwritten Constitution," *University of Chicago Law Review* 54 (fall 1987): 1127–77; Thomas Grey, "Do We Have an Unwritten Constitution?" *Stanford Law Review* 27 (February 1975): 843–93; and William E. Nelson, "The Impact of the Anti-Slavery Movement upon Styles of Judicial Reasoning in Nineteenth Century America," *Harvard Law Review* 87 (January 1974): 513–64.

[123] See Galie, "State Courts."

perience in interpreting civil-liberties guarantees. Nor could they look to federal courts for guidance in interpreting their constitutional protections. The federal courts too decided few civil-liberties cases, and their rulings often revealed little sympathy for rights claimants.[124] Only when circumstances brought a combination of state constitutional arguments, plus an example of how a court might develop constitutional guarantees, could a state civil-liberties jurisprudence emerge. Thus, when the Burger Court's anticipated—and to some extent actual—retreat from Warren Court activism encouraged civil-liberties litigants to look elsewhere for redress, the experience of the preceding decades had laid the foundation for the development of state civil-liberties law.

Paradoxically, then, the activism of the Warren Court, which has often been portrayed as detrimental to federalism, was a necessary condition for state judges becoming active in protecting civil liberties under state constitutions. The protection of civil liberties was not a zero-sum game, in which increased activity by one judiciary necessitated decreased activity by the other. Rather, the relationship between the federal and state judiciaries involved a sharing of responsibility and a process of mutual learning, such that a change in orientation by one set of courts was over time reflected in the other set of courts.

The Scope and Impact of the New Judicial Federalism

Writing in 1986, Justice William H. Brennan Jr. enthused that the "[r]ediscovery by state supreme courts of the broader protections afforded their own citizens by their state constitutions . . . is probably the most important development in constitutional jurisprudence in our time."[125] Brennan's claim is supported by the dramatic upsurge in state courts' reliance on state declarations of rights in civil-liberties cases over the past twenty-five years. From 1950 to 1969, in only ten cases did state judges rely on state guarantees to afford greater protection than was available under the

---

[124] In free-speech cases, "the Supreme Court, with one exception, uniformly found against free speech claimants." See David M. Rabban, "The First Amendment in Its Forgotten Years," *Yale Law Journal* 90 (January 1981): 520. For further documentation, see Russell B. Nye, *Fettered Freedom: Civil Liberties and the Slavery Controversy, 1830–1860* (Ann Arbor: University of Michigan Press, 1963); Norman L. Rosenberg, *Protecting the Best Men: An Interpretive History of the Law of Libel* (Chapel Hill: University of North Carolina Press, 1986); and Alexis J. Anderson, "The Formative Period of First Amendment Theory," *American Journal of Legal History* 24 (January 1980): 56–75. Whether or not correctly decided, the U.S. Supreme Court's religion rulings likewise reveal little sympathy for religious minorities. See, for example, *Reynolds v. United States,* 98 U.S. 145 (1878); and *Davis v. Beason,* 133 U.S. 333 (1890).

[125] *National Law Journal,* 29 September 1986, Special Section at S-1.

federal Constitution. However, from 1970 to 1986, they did so in over three hundred cases.[126] Most of these rulings dated from 1977 onward, revealing an increasing propensity to rely on state guarantees.[127] One also finds support for Brennan's claim if one examines the substance of the state rulings. Over the past quarter century, state courts have undertaken major initiatives involving school finance, exclusionary zoning, the rights of defendants, and the right to privacy. In several instances the state courts intervened because the U.S. Supreme Court had refused to grant relief, and thus the initiatives would have been impossible without the new judicial federalism.[128]

Yet this is not the whole story. If one is to assess the impact of this new state constitutional jurisprudence, one must also examine its overall effect on civil-liberties litigation. This includes how often litigants brought state constitutional claims before state courts, how often those courts based their rulings on state rather than federal law, and to what extent their reliance on state constitutions resulted in broader protections for rights than was available under the federal Constitution. The evidence on these issues cautions against blithe acceptance of Justice Brennan's assessment.

Proponents of the new judicial federalism have claimed that it increased challenges to state laws on state constitutional grounds in lieu of—or, at a minimum, in conjunction with—federal constitutional challenges. Although this is correct, a recent study revealed that litigants challenged state statutes solely on state grounds in only 22 percent of the

[126] Collins, Galie, and Kincaid, "State High Courts," 142, table 1; and Ronald K. L. Collins and Peter J. Galie, "Models of Post-incorporation Judicial Review: 1985 Survey of State Constitutional Individual Rights Decisions," *Publius* 16 (summer 1986): 111.

[127] During 1990, for example, state supreme courts decided over 140 civil-liberties cases based either exclusively on state protections of rights or on a combination of federal and state protections. See "Developments in State Constitutional Law: 1990," *Rutgers Law Journal* 22 (summer 1991): 906–1033.

[128] The pertinent Supreme Court ruling on education is *San Antonio Independent School District v. Rodriguez,* 411 U.S. 1 (1973). For a survey of state initiatives on school finance, see "Symposium: Investing in Our Children's Future: School Finance Reform in the '90s," *Harvard Journal of Legislation* 28 (summer 1991): 293–568. The Supreme Court's ruling on exclusionary zoning is *Warth v. Seldin,* 422 U.S. 490 (1975). For an analysis of state initiatives, see Tarr and Harrison, "Legitimacy and Capacity," 542–56. For surveys of Burger Court's rulings on the rights of defendants, see Richard Y. Funston, *Constitutional Counterrevolution?* (Cambridge, Mass.: Schenkman, 1977); and Vincent Blasi, ed., *The Burger Court: The Counter-revolution That Wasn't* (New Haven: Yale University Press, 1983). For state rulings, see Barry Latzer, *State Constitutions and Criminal Justice* (Westport, Conn.: Greenwood Press, 1991). On the right to privacy under state constitutions, see Mary Cornelia Porter with Robyn Mary O'Neill, "Personal Autonomy and the Limits of State Authority," in Friedelbaum, *Human Rights.* For an overview of state civil-liberties rulings, see Williams, *State Constitutional Law.*

constitutional cases coming before state supreme courts.[129] Most of these cases involved non-civil-liberties issues, such as restrictions on special legislation, spending and debt limitations, and the like. In over half the courts' civil-liberties cases, litigants continued to challenge state laws exclusively on the basis of the federal Constitution, and in only 17 percent of those cases did they challenge state laws exclusively on state constitutional grounds.[130] Thus, despite the new judicial federalism, litigants continue to rely primarily on the federal Constitution in framing their rights claims.

Proponents of the new judicial federalism have noted that state judges have increased their use of state constitutional guarantees to invalidate state statutes. Nonetheless, decisions based on state constitutions remain a rather small proportion of state criminal-justice and civil-liberties rulings. A study of state rulings from 1981 to 1985 found that less than 20 percent of criminal and bill-of-rights cases were decided exclusively on state law, and only 20 percent more on a combination of state and federal law.[131] Other studies, focusing on instances when state courts had an opportunity to rely on either federal or state guarantees, have reported similar findings. In a study of constitutional cases decided by six state supreme courts in 1975, Susan Fino found that only 17 percent were resolved on the basis of state law.[132] Her analysis of all equal-protection cases decided by state supreme courts from 1975 to 1984 found that less than 7 percent rested exclusively on state guarantees, and these were mostly cases involving traditional state concerns, such as bar regulation cases, Sunday-closing cases, inheritance cases, and the like.[133] In another article, Michael Esler discovered that despite the availability of analogous state and federal guarantees, state judges based their rulings exclusively on federal law in 78 percent of the self-incrimination cases they decided from 1981 to 1986.[134] Thus, even in recent decades, state judges have continued to rely primarily on federal law in resolving civil-liberties cases.

Finally, proponents of the new judicial federalism, following Justice Brennan, have assumed that reliance on state declarations of rights

[129] Craig F. Emmert and Carol Ann Traut, "State Supreme Courts, State Constitutions, and Judicial Policymaking," *Justice System Journal* 16 (1992): 37–48.

[130] Emmert and Traut, "State Supreme Courts," 44, table 2 (computed from "criminal rights" and "bill of rights" cases).

[131] Data in this paragraph are derived from Emmert and Traut, "State Supreme Courts," 42, table 1; 44, table 2; and 46, table 3.

[132] Fino, *Role of Supreme Courts,* 142.

[133] Fino, "Judicial Federalism and Equality," 61.

[134] Michael Esler, "State Supreme Court Commitment to State Law," *Judicature* 78 (July–August 1994): 25–32.

would result in greater protection for rights than was available under the federal Constitution. But if state judges conform their interpretations of state guarantees to federal precedent, then reliance on state grounds to decide cases need not translate into more rights-affirming decisions.[135] In a study of state supreme court rulings in criminal-procedure cases decided on the basis of state constitutions, Barry Latzer found that from the late 1960s to 1989 state judges routinely incorporated U.S. Supreme Court doctrines into state constitutional law—indeed, they adopted the Court's reasoning in over two-thirds of their criminal-procedure decisions.[136] Some of the states that were most willing to base their rulings on state constitutional guarantees, such as Connecticut and New Hampshire, were also among those most willing to endorse U.S. Supreme Court doctrine.[137] Meanwhile, California and Florida, two states that actively rejected Supreme Court doctrine, were "brought into line" during the 1980s by constitutional amendments that compelled conformity with federal law and, thereafter, substantially reduced their opposition.[138] Based on these findings, Latzer concluded that there was a "hidden conservatism" in the new judicial federalism because state judges, instead of independently developing state civil liberties law, tended to construe state and federal guarantees identically.[139]

In sum, when state judges began to turn to their state declarations of

[135] Proponents of the new judicial federalism have decried such a "lockstep" approach to state constitutional interpretation. On the undesirability of lockstep analysis, see Robert F. Williams, "In the Supreme Court's Shadow: Legitimacy of State Rejection of Supreme Court Reasoning and Result," *South Carolina Law Review* 35 (1984): 353–404. For a defense of lockstep analysis, see Earl M. Maltz, "Lockstep Analysis and the Concept of Federalism," *Annals of the American Academy of Political and Social Science* 496 (March 1988): 98–106. This issue is analyzed in chapter 6.

[136] Latzer, *State Constitutions,* 160–61, table 1. Unless otherwise indicated, data in this paragraph are drawn from that table.

[137] Latzer, *State Constitutions,* 165.

[138] The pertinent amendments are found in California Constitution, art. 1, sec. 28; and Florida Constitution, art. 1, sec. 12. For an in-depth analysis of the effects of the California amendment and of personnel changes that also contributed to the California Supreme Court's change in orientation, see Barry Latzer, "California's Constitutional Counterrevolution," in Tarr, *Constitutional Politics in States.*

[139] More impressionistic studies have supported Latzer's conclusion. Various commentators have noted the failure of most state courts to develop a broader protection for speech and press than is available under the federal Constitution. See Susan Davis and Taunya Lovell Banks, "State Constitutions, Freedom of Expression, and Search and Seizure: Prospects for State Court Reincarnation," *Publius* 17 (winter 1977): 13–31; and Simon, "Independent but Inadequate." A study of state rulings in speech and religion cases found that they "continued to reflect the assumption that consideration of these issues should begin and, in most instances, end with federal precedent" and that state courts "characteristically relied on federal precedent and doctrine in interpreting the state provisions" (Tarr, "State Constitutionalism," 39).

rights in the early 1970s, they were not recovering a tradition but creating one. Their unfamiliarity with state guarantees, the absence of a state constitutional jurisprudence, the easy availability of federal doctrine and precedent, and qualms about the legitimacy of judicial activism all worked against the development of state civil-liberties law. Yet, with the occasional encouragement of the U.S. Supreme Court and the example of a few pioneering state courts, state judges began to rely more frequently on state declarations of rights in deciding cases.[140] State law did not displace federal law: for most litigants and most state courts, federal constitutional law remained the primary protection for rights and the primary source of constitutional doctrine. But state law did serve as a complement to—and occasionally an antidote to—federal pronouncements. Even this intermittent reliance on state guarantees represented a major shift in state judicial practice. The reinvigoration of apparently obsolescent state constitutional provisions produced not only landmark rulings but also a changed judicial perspective.

In the future one can expect state judges to play an increasingly prominent role in state constitutional development. For one thing, the concern about the legitimacy of reliance on state constitutional guarantees, which plagued the early years of the new judicial federalism, has largely been put to rest.[141] For another, the expanding use of the initiative will likely encourage a defensive resort to state courts and state constitutions by the losers in this new majoritarian politics. Statutory initiatives may be challenged as violating state constitutions, and even constitutional initiatives may run afoul of state constitutional requirements governing such initiatives. The successful challenge to California's Proposition 115, which would have barred interpretation of the state constitution to extend rights to defendants beyond those found in the U.S. Constitution, reveals the potential payoff from such litigation.[142] Finally, the increasingly conservative direction of the U.S. Supreme Court under Chief Justice Rehnquist will promote an increased reliance on state constitutions, especially where distinctive state provisions promise a prospect of success. One likely area for the expansion of state constitutional litigation is church-state relations. Whereas the Rehnquist Court has signaled a new willing-

[140] For examples of encouragement by the U.S. Supreme Court, see *Prune Yard Shopping Center* v. *Robins*, 447 U.S. 74 (1980), and *Oregon* v. *Hass*, 420 U.S. 714 (1975); for less encouraging signals from the Court, see *Michigan* v. *Long*, 463 U.S. 1032 (1983), and *Pennsylvania* v. *Finley*, 481 U.S. 551 (1987).

[141] But cf. Robert F. Williams, "In the Glare of the Supreme Court: Continuing Methodology and Legitimacy Problems in Independent State Constitutional Rights Adjudication," *Notre Dame Law Review* 72 (May 1997): 1015–64.

[142] *Raven* v. *Deukmejian*, 801 P.2d 1077 (Cal. 1990). For discussion, see Latzer, "California's Constitutional Counterrevolution," 167–68.

ness to permit public aid that benefits religiously affiliated schools, most state constitutions contain stringent provisions banning such aid, thus encouraging litigants to mount state constitutional challenges to vouchers and other proposals to channel funds to parochial schools.[143]

CONCLUSIONS

Several sometimes-conflicting patterns emerge from our description of twentieth-century state constitutional development. Perhaps the most striking trend is toward the professionalization of state constitutional change. Illustrative of this shift is the decline of the constitutional convention. In the nineteenth century conventions served as a mechanism for popular influence on politics, often called by reluctant officials in response to popular pressures. But in the twentieth century far fewer conventions have been called, and their character has changed. Typically, it has been political elites and professional reformers who have campaigned for constitutional revision, with the populace reduced to rejecting convention calls and proposed constitutions to register its distrust of a process that it no longer feels it controls.[144] The professionalization of state constitutional change is also evident in the increasing use of constitutional commissions, expert bodies established without popular input, to set the agenda of constitutional change, identifying the problems that deserve attention and the appropriate solutions to those problems. Finally, the increased reliance on piecemeal change proposed by the legislature—constitutional amendment rather than constitutional revision—has also produced a shift in power to political professionals, who dominate this largely invisible process.

Yet countering this shift to the professionalization of constitutional change during the late twentieth century has been the renewed reliance on the constitutional initiative. One may well debate the wisdom of some of the changes introduced by constitutional initiative. Nevertheless, as the term-limits and tax-revolt movements demonstrate, the initiative does provide a mechanism for circumventing the power of political elites within state government, just as its early proponents had expected. Still, its effectiveness in ensuring popular rule should not be overstated. Less than half the states have adopted the constitutional initiative. Moreover, there is an ever-present danger that the initiative process may be captured

[143] For illustrative Supreme Court cases, see *Zobrest* v. *Catalina Foothills School District*, 509 U.S. 1 (1993); and *Agostini* v. *Felton*, 118 S.Ct. 40 (1997). For discussion of state constitutional provisions banning aid to religious schools, see Tarr, "Church and State"; and Friesen, *State Constitutional Law*, chap. 4.

[144] In recent years, of course, political elites have also ceased to campaign for constitutional conventions, presumably fearful of the radical changes that might result.

by interest groups or by entrepreneurial politicians backing (and some-times initiating) proposals and thus cease to reflect popular concerns.

A second major change during the twentieth century has been the in-creased influence of the federal Constitution and federal constitutional practice on state constitutionalism. In part, the greater importance of the federal Constitution has occurred through displacement. Constitutional issues that historically were matters of state concern, such as qualifications for the franchise, the apportionment of legislative power, and criminal procedure, are now largely controlled by federal constitutional standards. So too to a considerable extent are policy issues, such as economic regula-tion, that were traditionally state matters. These developments have ren-dered various state provisions either insignificant or superfluous. In part too, the greater federal influence has resulted from endorsement of the federal Constitution as the preferred model for state constitutional revi-sion. This elevation of the federal Constitution is reflected both in the later prescriptions for comprehensive revision of the National Municipal League and in specific reforms, such as the consolidation of state executive branches, sought by reformers. All states that have revised their constitu-tions during the twentieth century have moved closer to the federal model, and many states that did not revise their constitutions nonetheless inaugu-rated changes (e.g., consolidation of their executive branches) consistent with that model. Thus the structure of state constitutions over time has become more uniform. Finally, even as state judges asserted their power to interpret their constitutions independently of the rulings of the U.S. Su-preme Court, their approach to constitutional interpretation increasingly mirrored that of federal judges. This influence was particularly clear with regard to the new judicial federalism, which was spawned in reaction to the Burger Court and embodied the model of judicial activism pioneered by the Warren Court. Taken altogether, then these developments have fueled what Lawrence Friedman has described as "a trend toward a single legal culture—a trend that is persistent, genuine and significant."[145]

Yet just as the states' emulation of federal constitutional structure and practice has its limits, so too does the movement toward a common legal culture. These limits are reflected in the states' unwillingness to depart too much from existing institutions and practices, as demonstrated by popular refusal to authorize constitutional conventions, by voters' rejec-tion of several reform constitutions, and by the limited changes intro-duced by many charters that were adopted.[146] Even in the late twentieth

[145] Friedman, *History of American Law,* 663.

[146] For a discussion of the politics of state constitution-making as a conflict between reform and status quo forces, and for an analysis of the consequences of this for constitu-tional reform, see Cornwell, Goodman, and Swanson, *State Constitutional Conventions.*

century, few state constitutions mirror the Model State Constitution. The limits on state emulation of federal constitutionalism are also reflected in the recent shift in popular views about constitutional reform. The new state constitutional reformers did not get their ideas from the federal Constitution; rather, they disparaged that constitution or, at least, the government created by it. Instead, the constitutional reforms they pursued were designed to produce more chastened state governments. Ironically, during the 1980s and 1990s it was state constitutions that provided the model for proponents of national reforms such as the balanced-budget amendment, the line item veto, and term limitations. If federal and state constitutionalism are to grow closer, the movement may be on both sides rather than on the state side alone. Finally, the states have persisted in practices that are without federal analogue, such as their frequent recourse to constitutional amendment for constitutional change.

To some extent, the conflicting trends described in this chapter reflect the fact that state constitutional change in the twentieth century has been initiated in a variety of political arenas. The groups and perspectives behind constitutional changes initiated in one arena—for example, a state legislature—may well differ from those behind changes proposed by constitutional conventions, state supreme courts, or the initiative process. Whether the changes are comprehensive or piecemeal, necessary adjustments or shifts in policy will also depend on the arena in which they are introduced. Indeed, different understandings of state constitutional design may also, implicitly or explicitly, underlie changes undertaken in different arenas. For example, proponents of constitutional revision typically seek to adopt a brief framework for government that will promote vigorous government, whereas those supporting initiatives are attempting to include policy provisions in the constitution and thereby reduce legislative discretion.

These multiple inputs complicate the task of constitutional interpretation. Interpreters of the federal Constitution, whatever their differences in approach, share the belief that the document has a fundamental coherence, such that one can interpret individual provisions in the light of the overall constitutional design. For interpreters of a state constitution, given the document's multiple sources, constitutional coherence remains an open question. Other interpretive problems arise from the periodic revision of constitutions within individual states, from the multiplicity of state constitutions, and from the tendency of state constitution-makers to borrow provisions from other constitutions. It is to these distinctive problems of state constitutional interpretation that this volume now turns.

CHAPTER 6

State Constitutional Interpretation

THE EMERGENCE during the early 1970s of the new judicial federalism, the increasing reliance by state courts on state declarations of rights, co-incided with a revival of interest in jurisprudential concerns among constitutional scholars.[1] The conjunction of these developments might have proved fortuitous. Constitutional theory could have offered guidance to jurists and scholars as they undertook the task of interpreting state constitutions; while constitutional theorists could have benefited from expanding their focus beyond the United States Constitution. Unfortunately, the dialogue between constitutional theorists and state constitutional scholars never developed, however. State constitutional scholars have largely ignored constitutional theory, and constitutional theorists have continued to focus almost exclusively on the United States Constitution.[2]

This chapter bridges the gap between constitutional theory and state constitutional law by outlining an approach to the interpretation of state constitutions informed by the insights of constitutional theorists. In doing so, it demonstrates the usefulness for state constitutional interpretation of contemporary constitutional theories. At the same time, by identifying distinctive concerns and problems associated with the interpretation of state constitutions, it clarifies the limitations of those constitutional theories and thus serves a cautionary function. Initially, the chapter assesses challenges to the legitimacy of state courts relying on state constitutions to strike down governmental actions. Next, it responds to claims that it is impossible to develop a coherent state constitutional jurisprudence. Finally, it examines how the frequency of state constitutional change, the level of constitutional detail, the operation of horizon-

---

[1] Major contributions to the constitutional-theory literature include Ely, *Democracy and Distrust*; Robert Bork, *The Tempting of America* (New York: Free Press, 1990); Ronald Dworkin, *Takings Rights Seriously*, and *A Matter of Principle* (Cambridge: Harvard University Press, 1985); Perry, *The Constitution, the Courts*; Tushnet, *Red, White, and Blue*; Barber, *What the Constitution Means*; Levinson, *Constitutional Faith*; and Leslie Friedman Goldstein, *In Defense of the Text: Democracy and Constitutional Theory* (Savage, Md.: Rowman and Littlefield, 1991).

[2] Exceptions include Hans A. Linde, "E Pluribus—Constitutional Theory and State Courts," *Georgia Law Review* 18 (winter 1984): 165–200; David R. Keyser, "State Constitutions and Theories of Judicial Review: Some Variations on a Theme," *Texas Law Review* 63 (March–April 1985): 1051–80; and Tarr, "Constitutional Theory."

tal federalism, and a variety of other factors associated with the design and development of state constitutions create novel problems for state constitutional interpreters. In its examination of these problems, the chapter suggests an approach to state constitutional interpretation that is guided by, but not determined by, contemporary constitutional theories.

LEGITIMACY AND STATE CONSTITUTIONAL INTERPRETATION

The Legitimacy Issue in State Constitutional Law

Constitutional scholars have long devoted almost as much attention to legitimacy concerns (when may judges substitute their judgment for that of other constitutional interpreters, and with what deference to the views of those other interpreters?) as they have to substantive ones (what is the meaning of particular constitutional provisions?).[3] Concerns about the legitimacy of judicial rulings under the federal Constitution have arisen primarily when the U.S. Supreme Court has invalidated the actions of Congress or state legislatures, purportedly more democratic bodies, especially when the Court in doing so has arguably gone "beyond the value judgments established by the framers of the written Constitution."[4] However, this "counter-majoritarian difficulty" has been a less significant consideration in state constitutional law.[5] Perhaps this is because state judges have by and large been less aggressive than their federal counterparts in invalidating state legislation or because the relative ease of state constitutional amendment has made unpopular rulings easier to overturn. Or it may simply be that many state judges are popularly elected

[3] The classic account of the legitimacy issue dates from the nineteenth century: James Bradley Thayer, "The Origin and Scope of the American Doctrine of Constitutional Law," Harvard Law Review 7 (October 1893): 129–56. Subsequent accounts have tended to coincide with periods in which the Supreme Court has announced controversial rulings. See, for example, Alexander M. Bickel, The Least Dangerous Branch: The Supreme Court at the Bar of Politics (New York: Bobbs-Merrill, 1962); Eugene V. Rostow, The Sovereign Prerogative: The Supreme Court and the Quest for Law (New Haven: Yale University Press, 1962); Herbert Wechsler, "Toward Neutral Principles of Constitutional Law," Harvard Law Review 73 (September 1959): 1–35; and the works cited in note 1.

[4] Perry, The Constitution, the Courts, ix. Such rulings are controversial because of the widely shared belief that "society consents to be governed undemocratically [only] within defined areas by certain enduring principles believed to be stated in, and placed beyond the reach of majorities by, the Constitution." See Robert Bork, "Neutral Principles and Some First Amendment Problems," Indiana Law Journal 47 (fall 1971): 1–35.

[5] This is not to say that commentators have failed to raise the specter of countermajoritarianism. See, for example, Earl M. Maltz, "The Dark Side of State Court Activism," Texas Law Review 63 (March–April 1985): 995–1023; Paul S. Hudnut, "State Constitutions and Individual Rights: The Case for Judicial Restraint," Denver University Law Review 63 (1985): 85–108; and Twist and Munsil, "Double Threat."

and thus can claim to be at least somewhat accountable to the people.[6] Whatever the reason, debate about the legitimacy of state judicial rulings, at least in recent years, has focused on the relationship between state courts and the U.S. Supreme Court. The main issue has involved when state courts are justified in interpreting their state constitutions to reach results different from those obtained by the Supreme Court in interpreting the federal Constitution.[7] Just as advocates of judicial restraint at the national level have argued that judges should defer to the judgments of the people's representatives, so their counterparts at the state level have insisted that state judges should defer to the interpretations of the Supreme Court and construe state provisions in line with the interpretations that the Supreme Court has given to analogous provisions of the federal Constitution.

There are obvious parallels between the legitimacy debates in state constitutional law and in federal constitutional law. In both instances, the key issue is whether a presumption of validity should be given to the nonauthoritative constitutional judgment of a prior interpreter and, if so, how strong that presumption should be. In both instances as well, the justification offered for judicial deference emphasizes the position occupied by the prior interpreter. In federal constitutional law, the legislature that enacted the challenged statute can claim the mantle of popular sovereignty; in state constitutional law, the U.S. Supreme Court is recognized as the highest court in the land. Most importantly, the concern underlying the legitimacy controversy in both federal and state constitutional law is the same: to ensure that judgments are grounded in law rather than in the judges' policy preferences. When two sets of interpreters reach the same outcome in a constitutional case, this increases confidence that the

---

[6] Supreme court justices in twenty-three states are selected in either partisan or nonpartisan elections. Justices in twenty other states are chosen through "merit selection" and thus must run in retention elections after a period on the bench. For data on modes of judicial selection, see Tarr, *Judicial Process,* 67, table 3-1. In some states not only are judges elected but the state constitutions explicitly confer on them the power of judicial review. See, for example, Colorado Constitution, art. 2, sec. 15; Georgia Constitution, art. 1, sec. 2, par. 5; and North Dakota Constitution, art. 6, sec. 4.

[7] Major contributions to the literature on this problem include Robert F. Williams, "In the Shadow," "Methodology Problems in Enforcing State Constitutional Rights," *Georgia State University Law Review* 3 (fall–winter 1987): 143–77, and "Glare of Supreme Court"; Ronald K. L. Collins, "The Once and Future 'New Judicial Federalism' and Its Critics," *Washington Law Review* 64 (January 1989): 5–18; Hans A. Linde, "Without Due Process," "Are State Constitutions Common Law?" *Arizona Law Review* 34 (summer 1992): 215–29, and "E Pluribus"; Robin B. Johansen, "The New Federalism: Toward a Principled Interpretation of the State Constitution," *Stanford Law Review* 29 (January 1977): 297–321; Maltz, "Dark Side of Activism"; and Friesen, *State Constitutional Law,* chap. 1.

result is rooted in law rather than in will.[8] But when their interpretations diverge, two conclusions are possible. It may be that the issue is one on which there is no right answer, in which case advocates of judicial restraint at both the federal and state levels would, given the position of the initial interpreter, opt for deference.[9] Alternatively, it may be that one of the interpreters has interpreted the pertinent constitutional provision wrongly by mistake or by design in order to promote the interpreter's own value preferences. To ensure that the disagreement does not result from illegitimate judicial policy preferences, advocates of restraint would require later interpreters to provide persuasive arguments that an earlier interpretation was mistaken before overriding it. If the later interpreters were unable to do so, they would be obliged to defer to that interpretation. To do otherwise would fuel the suspicion that their interpretation was rooted in will rather than in judgment.

It is worth emphasizing that the main legitimacy debate in state constitutional law does not extend to all state constitutional rulings.[10] For this legitimacy problem to arise, state courts must be interpreting state provisions that are analogous to those in the federal Constitution or that constitutionalize principles, such as the separation of powers, that are implicit in the federal charter. Many state provisions—for example, those dealing with taxation or corporations or local government—have no federal counterpart, and thus their interpretation raises no issue of legitimacy. In addition, for the question of legitimacy to arise, the Supreme Court must have interpreted the pertinent federal provision prior to the state court being called upon to interpret the analogous state provisions.[11] If a state court had interpreted a state provision prior to the Supreme Court ruling on the analogous federal provision, and if deference to the Court's interpretation would require the abandonment of an

---

[8] See Robert M. Cover, "The Uses of Jurisdictional Redundancy: Interest, Ideology, and Innovation," *William and Mary Law Review* 22 (summer 1981): 639–82.

[9] Some constitutional theorists deny that there is no right answer, even in difficult cases. See, for example, Dworkin, *A Matter of Principle*, chap. 5. However, if there is no right answer, then the later interpreter has the discretion to impose additional requirements beyond those imposed by the initial interpreter. At this point, however, the argument for judicial restraint in order to allow a wider scope for popular government may also play a role. See Maltz, "Lockstep Analysis," 101–2.

[10] The secondary legitimacy issue in state constitutional law—whether state judges should overturn legislative enactments whenever they believe the enactments to be inconsistent with the state constitution or should defer to the judgment of the people's representatives—could arise in a wider range of cases. However, this paragraph ignores that issue to concentrate on the more fundamental legitimacy issue.

[11] Robert F. Williams has referred to such cases as "second-look" cases. See the discussion in Williams, "In the Shadow," 356.

established body of state law, presumably that would raise a rather different question.[12]

The conditions allegedly justifying deference to Supreme Court rulings are met most frequently when state courts are interpreting their state declarations of rights.[13] Indeed, the legitimacy debate in state constitutional interpretation emerged primarily because of changes in civilliberties litigation. The incorporation of various provisions of the federal Bill of Rights, which began in the 1920s and accelerated during the 1960s, transformed the Supreme Court's agenda and led it to elaborate constitutional doctrine on issues such as freedom of speech, equality, and the rights of defendants. The Court's receptivity to civil-liberties claims also encouraged litigants to direct their claims to federal rather than state tribunals, thereby decreasing opportunities to develop state civil-liberties law. Even when civil-liberties claims arose in state forums, as often they did in criminal cases, defendants tended to base their claims on the federal Bill of Rights, assuming that state protections at best merely duplicated federal guarantees. As a result, when state courts began to interpret their states' civil-liberties guarantees in the 1970s, they did not write on a blank slate. Rather, federal law "furnished the intellectual baggage, the doctrines and precedents, that state courts judges brought with them in confronting state constitutional guarantees.[14] Thus, the emergence of the new judicial federalism took place in the context of an existing body of federal civil-liberties law and an almost total absence of state civilliberties law.

Attacks on the Legitimacy of State Constitutional Rulings

Although it is not uncommon for dissenting justices or other commentators to attack judicial decisions as rooted in the political views of their authors rather than in the law, the attacks on state civil-liberties rulings have been particularly frequent and sharp.[15] In part, the novelty of the

[12] There have in fact been instances in which state courts have interpreted their state guarantees and later changed their interpretations to bring them into line with subsequent Supreme Court interpretations of federal provisions. See, for example, *Brown v. State*, 657 S.W.2d 797 (Tex. Crim. App. 1983), and *State v. Jackson*, 672 P.2d 255 (Mont. 1983). More typical, however, is the position taken by the New York Court of Appeals in *People v. Class*, 494 N.E.2d 444 (N.Y. 1986).

[13] Other analogous provisions are found in state executive and legislative articles. For a useful examination of the influence of federal constitutional law on state constitutional law in a non-civil-liberties field, see Levinson, "Decline of Legislative Veto."

[14] Tarr and Porter, *State Supreme Courts*, 21–22.

[15] Illustrative of state judicial opinions attacking reliance on state constitutional law are *State v. Miller*, 630 A.2d 1315, 1328 (Conn. 1993) (Callahan, J., concurring in part and

rulings explains this: state courts' recurrence to and reliance on state rights guarantees in the 1970s was, quite literally, unprecedented.[16] State courts had never developed a body of state civil-liberties law.[17] And for decades they had looked to federal law and federal precedent to resolve civil-liberties issues, either ignoring their state guarantees altogether or assuming without serious reflection that the protections conferred by those guarantees coincided with those available under federal provisions. Yet novelty alone cannot explain the reaction; for despite the proliferation of state constitutional rulings in the 1980s and 1990s, legitimacy concerns have remained and, according to some commentators, grown even more severe.[18]

Equally important in raising legitimacy concerns were the timing and the tenor of early state rulings under the new judicial federalism. State courts discovered state declarations of rights only after personnel shifts on the U.S. Supreme Court had changed—or threatened to change—the Court's orientation.[19] Indeed, most early new judicial federalism cases involved constitutional claims by defendants in criminal cases, an area in which the Burger Court gave early evidence of retrenchment.[20] Defendants urged state courts either to extend the precedents of the Warren Court or to circumvent the Burger Court's erosion of Warren Court precedents by interpreting state guarantees more broadly than the Burger Court had interpreted analogous federal protections. For example, after the U.S. Supreme Court in *Harris* v. *New York* (1973) permitted the introduction of illegally obtained confessions for impeachment purposes, defendants in ten states called on state courts to bar the introduction of such evidence under their state constitutions, and four state courts ac-

---

dissenting in part); *People* v. *Scott* and *People* v. *Keta,* 593 N.E.2d 1328, 1356 (N.Y. 1992) (Bellacosa, J., dissenting); *People* v. *Disbrow,* 545 P.2d 272, 283–84 (Cal. 1976) (Richardson, J., dissenting); *People* v. *Norman,* 538 P.2d 237, 245 (Cal. 1975) (Clark, J., dissenting); *People* v. *Cannon,* 310 N.E.2d 673 (Ill. 1974); and *State* v. *Florance,* 527 P.2d 1202 (Ore. 1974).

[16] For confirmation of the novelty of the new judicial federalism, see Tarr, "Past and Future," 64–69.

[17] For a state-by-state survey of selected aspects of civil-liberties law that confirms that assessment, see "Project Report: Toward an Activist Role for State Bills of Rights," *Harvard Civil Rights–Civil Liberties Law Review* 8 (March 1973): 323–50.

[18] Williams, "Glare of Supreme Court."

[19] On the anticipated and actual consequences of the shift from the Warren Court to the Burger Court, see James F. Simon, *In His Own Image: The Supreme Court in Richard Nixon's America* (New York: David McKay, 1973); Funston, *Constitutional Counterrevolution?* and Blasi, *The Burger Court.* Of course, state courts' new attention to state declarations of rights was a response to the arguments of litigants, who were fearful of Supreme Court review of their cases.

[20] See Latzer, *State Constitutions;* and Abrahamson, "Criminal Law."

cepted the invitation.[21] And after the Burger Court reversed Warren Court doctrine on issuing search warrants predicated on information from informants, courts in thirty states addressed the issue, with eleven rejecting the Burger Court position.[22] In cases not involving the rights of defendants, the arguments advanced by plaintiffs likewise had a liberal tenor, urging state courts to extend protections unavailable under the federal charter. Early rulings involving public-school finance and exclusionary zoning illustrate the point.[23] The consistently liberal thrust of rulings under the new judicial federalism led critics to charge that justices on state courts were relying on state law merely to advance a liberal policy agenda.[24]

These suspicions were fueled by the intermittent and reactive character of state courts' early reliance on state constitutions. Most state courts continued to rely on federal law to resolve most civil-liberties cases, reverting to state constitutional law only when it would yield a result unobtainable under federal law.[25] Even when ruling on state constitutional grounds, state courts seldom developed distinctive constitutional arguments, instead relying on federal precedents and federal doctrinal categories in interpreting state guarantees. Indeed, they not infrequently embraced the views of Court dissenters as the bases for their interpretation

[21] *Harris v. New York,* 401 U.S. 222 (1971). For a listing and discussion of these cases, see Latzer, *State Constitutions,* 91–92. Two of the states that rejected *Harris*—California and Pennsylvania—subsequently had their positions reversed by constitutional amendments.

[22] In *Aguilar v. Texas,* 378 U.S. 108 (1964), and *Spinelli v. United States,* 393 U.S. 410 (1969), the Warren Court announced a complex "two-pronged" test for determining the validity of a warrant issued based on information from an informant. In *Illinois v. Gates,* 462 U.S. 213 (1983), the Burger Court replaced this was a "totality of circumstances" approach. For a listing of state cases and discussion of them, see Latzer, *State Constitutions,* 58–59.

[23] The initial challenge to public school finance on state constitutional grounds was *Robinson v. Cahill,* 303 A.2d 273 (N.J. 1973). Reliance on state constitutions was necessary after the U.S. Supreme Court rejected a challenge under the equal protection clause in *San Antonio Independent School District v. Rodriguez,* 413 U.S. 1 (1973). For an overview of school finance litigation, see "Symposium: Investing in Children's Future."

The initial challenge to exclusionary zoning was *Southern Burlington County N.A.A.C.P. v. Township of Mount Laurel,* 336 A.2d 713 (N.J. 1975). Reliance on state constitutions was necessary after the Supreme Court's ruling in *Warth v. Seldin,* 422 U.S. 490 (1975), denying standing to sue to litigants complaining of exclusionary practices. See David L. Kirp, John P. Dwyer, and Larry A. Rosenthal, *Our Town: Race, Housing, and the Soul of Suburbia* (New Brunswick, N.J.: Rutgers University Press, 1995).

[24] See, for example, Maltz, "Political Dynamic."

[25] This is consistent with the position argued by many scholars and jurists, who have viewed state declarations of rights as supplementary to the federal Bill of Rights. See, for example, Stewart G. Pollock, "State Constitutions as Separate Sources of Fundamental Rights," *Rutgers Law Review* 35 (September 1983): 707–22. This "interstitial approach" is discussed below.

of state provisions, thus looking to federal rulings but using them to reach results different from those of the Supreme Court.

The legal literature extolling the new judicial federalism also prompted concerns that judicial reliance on state constitutions was opportunistic rather than principled. Many early advocates of the new judicial federalism were remarkably blatant in their result-orientation. Thus, Donald Wilkes applauded state courts' use of their state constitutions to "evade" Burger Court rulings, and articles in leading law reviews encouraged judges to turn to state provisions to reach desired rulings.[26] Even Justice William Brennan's famous endorsement of the new judicial federalism made clear that its purpose was an end run around conservative Supreme Court rulings.[27] In such circumstances, it was easy for critics to attribute to state judges the motives of the litigants and commentators who urged them to embrace state constitutional law.

Dealing with Legitimacy Concerns

THE LOCKSTEP APPROACH

Obviously, one way to banish legitimacy concerns is for state courts to eschew independent constitutional analysis and conform their rulings to federal precedent. According to its proponents, such a "lockstep approach" also has the advantage of promoting a desirable national uniformity and simplifying the task of officials seeking to understand and apply the law.[28] Florida by constitutional amendment in 1982 mandated just such a "lockstep approach" in search-and-seizure cases, requiring that the state guarantee "be construed in conformity with the 4th Amendment to the United States Constitution, as interpreted by the United States Supreme Court."[29] Even in the absence of similar amendments, some state

[26] Donald E. Wilkes Jr. presented his position in a series of three articles: "New Federalism," "More on New Federalism," and "New Federalism Revisited." The other relevant articles are "Project Report," 313–15; and "Note: Private Abridgment of Speech and the State Constitutions," *Yale Law Journal* 90 (November 1980): 165–88. A proponent of the new judicial federalism, nonetheless critical of this result-orientation, derided the use of state bills of rights as "little more than a handy grab bag filled with a bevy of clauses that may be exploited in order to circumvent disfavored United States Supreme Court decisions." See Ronald K. L. Collins, "Reliance on State Constitutions—Away from a Reactionary Approach," *Hastings Constitutional Law Quarterly* 9 (fall 1981): 2.

[27] Brennan, "State Constitutions," 503. For a critical assessment of Justice Brennan's view of federalism, see Earl M. Maltz, "False Prophet—Justice Brennan and the Theory of State Constitutional Law," *Hastings Constitutional Law Quarterly* 15 (spring 1988): 429–49.

[28] For a convenient summary of these arguments, see Friesen, *State Constitutional Law,* 13–17.

[29] Florida Constitution of 1968, art. 1, sec. 12. See Christopher Slobogin, "State Adop-

courts have concluded that state guarantees mirror analogous federal protections. In *Brown* v. *State* (1983), for example, the Texas Court of Criminal Appeals concluded that the search-and-seizure provisions of the Texas and federal constitutions "are, in all material aspects, the same."[30] And in *State* v. *Jackson* (1983), the Montana Supreme Court held that its state guarantee against self-incrimination "affords no greater protection than that of the Federal constitution" and that "[t]he opinions of the United States Supreme Court, therefore, delineate the maximum breadth of the privilege of self-incrimination in Montana."[31]

Yet absent a provision like Florida's linking state and federal interpretation, neither the desire to reduce legitimacy concerns nor prudential arguments for uniformity can justify the lockstep approach; for that approach is inconsistent with the nation's commitment to dual constitutionalism.[32] Under the system of dual constitutionalism, state supreme courts have the responsibility of providing the authoritative interpretation of their state constitutions, and they cannot legitimately delegate that responsibility to the Supreme Court by binding themselves to its rulings. In addition, the system of dual constitutionalism was originated to provide a "double security" for rights, and that security would be lost if states abdicated their responsibility to interpret their declarations of rights.[33] Obviously, some state guarantees mirror federal protections—it

---

tion of Federal Law: Exploring the Limits of Florida's 'Forced Linkage' Amendment," *University of Florida Law Review* 39 (summer 1987): 653–732. California attempted to adopt an even broader forced-linkage amendment, requiring thirteen separate guarantees to be interpreted no more broadly than the federal Bill of Rights, but that amendment was struck down by the California Supreme Court in *Raven* v. *Deukmejian*, 801 P.2d 1077 (Cal. 1990). For discussion of this provision, see Latzer, "California's Constitutional Counterrevolution."

[30] *Brown* v. *State*, 657 S.W.2d 797 (Tex. Crim. App. 1983).

[31] *State* v. *Jackson*, 672 P.2d 255, 260 (Mont. 1983). For a discussions of *Jackson*, see Abrahamson, "Criminal Law," 1166–68; and Collins, "Reliance on State Constitutions."

[32] The prudential arguments for uniformity of interpretation are questionable. Take, for instance, the claim that uniformity would simplify the task of officials, such as police officers, responsible for applying the law. The fact that legal standards are derived from two documents does not increase the difficulty of applying those standards. A single standard (the most rights-protective) is applied, whether its source is the state constitution, its federal counterpart, or both. In addition, state courts' adoption of the federal standard produces clarity only if the federal standard is by definition clearer than possible state standards. Yet there is little reason to believe that in theory or to expect that in practice, especially given the Supreme Court's well-documented difficulties in such fields as religious liberty and search-and-seizure. Responses to the other prudential arguments for the lockstep approach are summarized in Friesen, *State Constitutional Law*, 13–17.

[33] The importance of dual constitutionalism as a double security for rights is addressed in *Federalist* no. 51. On the danger of state abdication, see Collins, "Reliance on State Constitutions."

would be extraordinary if "independent state constitutions share[d] no principles with their federal counterpart."[34] Yet the lockstep approach renders state rights guarantees superfluous, a dubious result given the deliberate adoption of these guarantees by state constitution-makers, in some instances even after Supreme Court rulings had made clear that the federal Constitution protected against state violations of rights. In sum, dual constitutionalism obliges state supreme courts to conduct an independent inquiry to discover the principles embodied in their state constitutions before considering whether the state principles parallel those found in the federal Constitution. In undertaking this independent inquiry, a state court may of course consult how the Supreme Court has interpreted analogous federal provisions, just as it may consult how other state courts have interpreted their counterpart guarantees. But if a state court decides to conform its interpretation of a state provision to the Supreme Court's interpretation of an analogous federal provision, this decision has to be based on the persuasiveness of the Court's argument rather than on the Court's position in the legal hierarchy. Moreover, the state's interpretation of its constitution would presumably not change thereafter even if the Supreme Court altered its interpretation of the federal Constitution.[35]

THE SUPPLEMENTAL/INTERSTITIAL APPROACH

Equally unsuccessful in dealing with legitimacy concerns is a second approach to state constitutional interpretation, the supplemental or interstitial approach. This approach seeks to minimize legitimacy questions by limiting the frequency of rulings based on state declarations of rights. Thus, under this approach, when state laws or official actions are challenged on both federal and state grounds, state courts would address the federal claim first. Only if resolution of the federal claim did not resolve the case would the state supreme court supplement this inquiry into federal law with an examination of applicable state principles. The supplemental approach also seeks to allay legitimacy concerns by reducing the frequency of divergent interpretations of analogous state and federal provisions through a presumption of correctness for the Supreme Court's interpretation of federal guarantees. Under the supplemental approach, state departures from federal decisional law have to be justified; and in the absence of specific factors justifying such a departure, state courts are obliged to conform their interpretations to federal precedent. To ensure that such departures are principled rather than opportunistic, proponents

---

[34] Ellen A. Peters, "State Constitutional Law: Federalism in the Common Law Tradition," *Michigan Law Review* 84 (February–April 1986): 589–90.

[35] Abrahamson, "Criminal Law," 1169.

of the supplemental approach have identified criteria for divergence from federal rulings in those instances in which state courts address state constitutional issues, and they have committed to reaching divergent results in subsequent cases only when those criteria are met.[36]

This supplemental approach actually aggravates, rather than alleviates, legitimacy concerns. Recall that those concerns arose in part because courts relied on state guarantees intermittently, only when they sought to diverge from Supreme Court precedent. Yet the supplemental approach produces behavior indistinguishable from such reactive decision-making by encouraging courts to look to state guarantees only when a case cannot be resolved on federal grounds. In addition, the establishment of criteria justifying divergent interpretation does not eliminate disagreement and accusations of result-oriented rulings, because justices may still disagree about the application of those criteria in specific cases. All that the creation of criteria has done is imply that there is something dubious about independent interpretation of state constitutions. Finally, like the lockstep approach, the supplemental approach focuses attention on the relation between state and federal interpretations rather than on the more important question of the best interpretation of the state charter. As former Justice Hans Linde of the Oregon Supreme Court has observed: "[T]o ask when to diverge from federal doctrines is quite a different question from taking a principled view of the state's constitution; in fact, this supplemental or interstitial approach prevents coherent development of the state's law."[37]

THE PRIMACY/"FIRST THINGS FIRST" APPROACH

No such criticism can be made of the final approach, the primacy approach, since it largely ignores federal constitutional interpretations. Hans Linde, the foremost exponent of this approach, has noted that federal review of alleged state violations of rights typically arises under the due

[36] The New Jersey Supreme Court announced a set of criteria for divergence from Supreme Court rulings in 1982, and justices in at least six other states subsequently endorsed the supplemental approach. State cases in which justices have endorsed the supplemental approach include New Jersey: *State v. Hunt*, 450 A.2d 952 (N.J. 1982); Washington: *State v. Gunwall*, 720 P.2d 808 (Wash. 1986); Illinois: *People v. Levin*, 623 N.E.2d 317 (Ill. 1993), and *People v. Tisler*, 469 N.E.2d 147 (Ill. 1984); Kentucky: *Commonwealth v. Wasson*, 842 S.W.2d 487 (Ky. 1992); Michigan: *Doe v. Department of Social Services*, 487 N.W.2d 166 (Mich. 1992), and *Sitz v. Department of State Police*, 506 N.W.2d 209 (Mich. 1993); Massachusetts: *Guiney v. Police Commissioner of Boston*, 582 N.E.2d 523 (Mass. 1991), and *Commonwealth v. Amendola*, 550 N.E.2d 121 (Mass. 1990); and Connecticut: *State v. Geisler*, 610 A.2d 1225 (Conn. 1992), and *State v. Joyce*, 639 A.2d 1007 (Conn. 1994). For a thorough review of these cases and the difficulties with the supplemental approach, see Williams, "Glare of Supreme Court."

[37] Linde, "E Pluribus," 178.

process and equal protection clauses of the Fourteenth Amendment. These "state-failure" provisions authorize federal intervention only if a state fails to meet its constitutional responsibilities. Yet one cannot determine whether a state has failed to meet its responsibilities, has violated rights, until the state's action is completed. This entails not only the action of the state legislature or executive but also judicial review of the legitimacy of that action under the state constitution. Only when all pertinent organs of state government, including the courts, have approved the action is it appropriate to consider if the action is consistent with federal guidelines. Thus, Linde argues, state courts should *always* review challenged actions on the basis of state law, both constitutional and subconstitutional, before turning their attention to the federal Constitution.[38]

Although Linde has been described as the godfather of the new judicial federalism, few courts have adopted his rigorous primacy approach, and fewer still have adhered to it consistently.[39] This is unfortunate; for only the primacy approach encourages that independent interpretation of state constitutions which is appropriate to a system of dual constitutionalism. In addition, the primacy approach deals quite effectively with legitimacy concerns. The fundamental concern was that state judges would use state constitutions instrumentally, in order to pursue their policy goals. Under the primacy approach, however, the decision to consult the state constitution does not depend on the action of the U.S. Supreme Court or the judges' view of a particular case. In fact, the approach altogether eliminates state courts' discretion over whether to rely on state guarantees as an alternative to federal law. Recurrence to state law is an obligation, not a choice. Paradoxically, by requiring that state constitutions be interpreted more frequently, this approach allays concerns about state courts' reliance on state constitutions (though one may of course still disagree with a court's interpretations).

---

[38] Justice Linde's articles elaborating this approach include "Without Due Process" and "First Things First: Rediscovering the State's Bill of Rights," *University of Baltimore Law Review* 9 (spring 1980): 379–96. One critic of the primacy approach has argued that it would logically "preclude federal court jurisdiction until the challenged state action had been ratified by the state's highest court." See "Project Report," 288.

[39] This description initially appeared in Jeffrey Toobin, "Better Than Burger," *New Republic*, March 4, 1985, at 11. States that have embraced the "first-things-first" approach include Oregon (*Hewitt* v. *State Accident Ins. Fund Corp.*, 653 P.2d 970 [Ore. 1982]); Maine (*State* v. *Cadman*, 476 A.2d 1148 [Me. 1984]); and New Hampshire (*State* v. *Ball*, 471 A.2d 347 [N.H. 1983]). However, the consistency of their adherence to this approach has been questioned; see "Comment, Principled Interpretation of State Constitutional Law: Why Don't the 'Primacy' States Practice What They Preach?" *University of Pittsburgh Law Review* 54 (summer 1993): 1019–50. Of the courts that have endorsed "first-things-first," the New Hampshire Supreme Court has been the most consistent in adhering to that approach.

Nevertheless, the primacy approach seems to demand heroic efforts on the part of state constitutional interpreters. For instead of permitting courts to rely on convenient federal doctrine and precedent, the primacy approach requires them to begin anew, constructing a state constitutional jurisprudence that is faithful to the state's own charter rather than merely "replacing state constitutions with generic Supreme Court formulas."[40] This demands an attention to the specifics of text and history (among other matters), and because those specifics differ from constitution to constitution, it may produce considerable particularity in interpretation. Yet how to undertake this approach—and, indeed, whether such an approach is in fact possible or appropriate—are matters of considerable debate.

THE POSSIBILITY OF STATE CONSTITUTIONAL INTERPRETATION

Some commentators, most notably James Gardner and Paul Kahn, are skeptical about the prospects for independent state constitutional interpretation.[41] Gardner asserts that although state courts in recent decades have announced numerous decisions based on state constitutions, the courts' opinions have been largely devoid of coherent constitutional argument. In fact, he characterizes state constitutional law as "a vast wasteland of confusing, conflicting, and essentially unintelligible pronouncements."[42] For this failure to develop a coherent state constitutional jurisprudence, Gardner blames not state judges but state constitutions themselves. "A constitution, according to our legal and social conventions, is a document meant to identify a political community and to set out some of the most fundamental principles according to which the members of the community wish to live their lives."[43] Few, if any, state constitutions fit this description. Instead, according to Gardner, state constitutions typically are the products of compromise and logrolling rather than commitment to principle, and their provisions more often reflect mundane or trivial concerns than fundamental values. Properly speaking, they are not constitutions at all; and thus it is hardly surprisingly that these ersatz constitutions cannot sustain the "discourse of distinctiveness" that independent constitutional interpretation requires.[44] Perhaps surprisingly, Gardner concludes that this is fortunate: if

[40] Linde, "State Constitutions Common Law?" 225.

[41] Gardner, "Failed Discourse"; and Kahn, "Interpretation and Authority."

[42] Gardner, "Failed Discourse," 763.

[43] Gardner, "Failed Discourse," 769–70.

[44] The notion of state constitutions as ersatz constitutions is borrowed from Barry Latzer, "A Critique of Gardner's 'Failed Discourse,'" *Rutgers Law Journal* 24 (summer 1993): 1009.

state constitutions in fact embodied fundamental values inconsistent with national values, that would threaten national unity.

Several scholars have challenged Gardner's negative assessment of state courts' constitutional rulings, insisting that some state courts have developed a coherent constitutional jurisprudence.[45] The primary problem with Gardner's critique, however, is its unduly narrow view of constitutionalism. Although Gardner asserts that "our legal and social conventions" require that constitutions embody the political identity and fundamental commitments of a political community, one is left wondering to whom the "our" refers. For if state constitutions fail to meet this standard, then American political practice registers a diversity of views about what a constitution should be like. Furthermore, even the most detailed and frequently amended state constitution serves certain basic functions that one expects of a constitution. It establishes the institutions of government, distributes political power among them, defines their modes of operation, and limits political power.[46] It also likely enunciates basic principles and commitments of the state, albeit certainly not in all its provisions, thereby distinguishing itself from ordinary legislation. A state's declaration of rights, for example, defines the rights that the state deems fundamental and affirms the state's commitment to their preservation. Provisions on the franchise and on constitutional change reflect the state's commitment to popular government and popular sovereignty, while a state constitution's provisions on education and other aspects of public policy reflect the state's understanding of the needs of its citizens and its commitment to secure them. And so on.

Gardner also contends that constitutions that are not concise frameworks of government, that are frequently changed, include "statutory" provisions, and reflect the tug and pull of ordinary politics, cannot support independent interpretation. Yet even the U.S. Constitution, which Gardner holds up as a model, would fail his test, since it—like its state counterparts—was the product of compromise and political strife and contains constitutional legislation dealing with slavery, search warrants, the income tax, and other matters.[47] Failing grades would also have to be assigned to most other national constitutions, which resemble American state constitutions, far more than the federal Constitution, in their length

[45] See, for example, David Schuman, "A Failed Critique of State Constitutionalism," *Michigan Law Review* 91 (November 1992): 274–80; and Ronald L. Nelson, "Welcome to the 'Last Frontier,' Professor Gardner: Alaska's Independent Approach to State Constitutional Interpretation," *Alaska Law Review* 12 (1995): 1–41.

[46] See the discussions in Lutz, "Purposes of State Constitutions," and in chapter 1 of this volume.

[47] Earl M. Maltz, "James Gardner and the Idea of State Constitutionalism," *Rutgers Law Journal* 24 (summer 1993): 1019–24.

and level of detail.[48] Yet these alleged deficiencies have not prevented them from being recognized as constitutions or precluded the development of a constitutional jurisprudence in their countries.[49] In addition, as the earlier chapters on nineteenth- and twentieth-century state constitutional development have shown, the detail found in state constitutions has often reflected not a lack of skill or seriousness but rather a deliberate decision to remove important political decisions from the hands of untrustworthy state officials. State constitutions thus differ from the federal model primarily because their framers viewed that model as inadequate to deal with the distinctive problems confronting the states. Gardner claims that independent constitutional interpretation requires a document that resembles the federal Constitution, but the opposite seems true. A "discourse of distinctiveness" is possible only insofar as state constitutions are distinctive.

The second major critic of independent state constitutional interpretation, Paul Kahn, acknowledges that state constitutions contain some provisions that are of "constitutional dimension," as well as more prosaic provisions. The provisions of constitutional dimension include "the constitutional protections of liberty, equality, and due process, as well as the structuring of political institutions that aim simultaneously to realize these values and to represent constituent interests."[50] The text of these provisions varies from one constitution to another, but according to Kahn, such differences do not in and of themselves justify distinctive interpretation. Indeed, even the absence of a specific guarantee is not decisive: "[N]o state constitution is indifferent to the principle of equality, even if the state text does not have an equal protection clause."[51] Indeed, according to Kahn, the attempt to base divergent rulings on "unique state sources" is anachronistic in late-twentieth-century America, because Americans nowadays identify with a national community and share common fundamental values that are expressed in a common American constitutionalism.[52] Yet these common values do

[48] Daniel J. Elazar, "A Response to James Gardner's 'The Failed Discourse of State Constitutionalism,'" *Rutgers Law Journal* 24 (summer 1993): 975–84; and Goldwin and Kaufman, *Constitution Makers*. For the texts of these constitutions, see Albert P. Blaustein and Gisbert H. Flanz, *Constitutions of the Countries of the World* (Dobbs Ferry, N.Y.: Oceana, 1993).

[49] For a convenient collection of single-countries studies and pertinent bibliography, see C. Neal Tate and Torbjorn Vallinder, eds., *The Global Expansion of Judicial Power* (New York: New York University Press, 1995).

[50] Kahn, "Interpretation and Authority," 1159 n. 52.

[51] Kahn, "Interpretation and Authority," 1159–60.

[52] Kahn's argument here recalls Ronald Dworkin's distinction between "concept" and "conception" and is subject to the same criticisms. See Tarr, "Constitutional Theories," 101–4.

not lead him to endorse the lockstep approach. He is more sanguine than Gardner about state courts participating in the "interpretive enterprise," apparently because they are giving voice not to state values but to their "understanding of the values and principles of the national community."[53] "The diversity of state courts," he concludes, "is best understood as a diversity of interpretive bodies, not as a multiplicity of representatives of distinct sovereigns."[54]

Kahn's argument glosses over crucial differences between state and federal constitutions, substituting generic constitutional analysis for the interpretation of identifiable state constitutional provisions. His distinction between those features of state constitutions that are of constitutional dimension and those that are not is particularly revealing. Under Kahn's formulation, what is of constitutional dimension is what is found in both state and federal constitutions, namely, rights guarantees and provisions structuring governmental institutions. However, state constitutions' distribution of political power within the state is not of constitutional dimension. Neither is their structuring of the relationship between government and the economy nor their delineation of such constitutional aims as a thorough and efficient education or a clean environment nor their decision whether to institute the recall or the initiative or term limits. Likewise insupportable is Kahn's homogenization of state and federal guarantees under the rubric of shared national values. State constitution-makers debated among various formulations of rights, competing versions drawn from the constitutions of other states, because they expected their choice of language to make a difference. To speak of a national value forbidding cruel punishments, for example, ignores the fact that some states have chosen to ban "unduly harsh" punishments as well as "cruel and unusual" ones, while others have explicitly constitutionalized capital punishment. State constitution-makers have also debated whether to include particular guarantees. Yet Kahn's position would seem to make the adoption or nonadoption of, say, a "little ERA" irrelevant because "no state constitution is indifferent to the principle of equality." Finally, Kahn's premise of a national community with common values exaggerates the level of consensus on these values. Even on matters that Kahn deems of constitutional dimension, such as due process and equality, states in recent years have demonstrated a considerable range of opinion. Some states have adopted amendments restricting rights—Colorado's antigay amendment, Florida's limits on the exclusionary rule, and California's victims' rights amendment—while others

[53] Kahn, "Interpretation and Authority," 1168.
[54] Kahn, "Interpretation and Authority," 1148.

have rejected similar amendments.[55] These disparate outcomes suggest that one should be cautious in ascribing common values to all Americans.

Ultimately, Gardner and Kahn seem to be addressing the concerns of constitutional theorists rather than those of actual constitutional interpreters.[56] Nevertheless, they do identify features of state constitutions that complicate their independent interpretation and thus need to be addressed.

THE PRACTICE OF STATE CONSTITUTIONAL INTERPRETATION

The Diversity of State Constitutional Provisions

One complication for state constitutional interpretation stems from the diversity of state provisions. While state constitutions contain statements of broad principle, they also contain a range of other provisions of varying detail and specificity, including some that resemble statutes. This raises the question whether a single interpretive approach is appropriate for the disparate provisions. The problem is not unique to state constitutions. The federal Constitution too contains highly specific provisions dealing with such matters as qualifications for federal office and the enactment of legislation. Still, the problem is more serious at the state level. No one, for instance, would ever accuse the federal Constitution of being a "statutory bank vault within which favored schemes, phobias, and interests of the prevailing elite could be secured into the future beyond the reach of fickle legislatures and ungrateful governors."[57]

[55] Colorado Constitution, amendment 2 (adopted in 1992), invalidated by the U.S. Supreme Court in *Romer* v. *Evans,* 517 U.S. 620 (1996); Florida Constitution, art. 1, sec. 12; and California Constitution, Proposition 115 (adopted in 1990), invalidated by the California Supreme Court in *Raven* v. *Deukmejian,* 801 P.2d 1077 (Cal. 1990).

[56] Consider the perceptive criticism of Randall T. Shepard, "The Maturing Nature of State Constitutional Jurisprudence," *Valparaiso Law Review* 30 (spring 1996): 437. According to Chief Justice Shepard, "Kahn's strategy is to ratchet up the level of abstraction at which American constitutionalism is defined to a level which virtually assures similitude. Gardner's approach is to insist that legitimate constitutionalism be 'epic' or 'near-mythical' and then to dismiss all that state constitutional text without federal analog as the product of 'political deals among interest groups' about which one cannot 'plausibly claim a meaning rooted in political theory, or justice, or the framers' deliberations on fundamental principles.'" Their theories are thus subject to the same criticism that Robert F. Nagel has leveled against other "fundamental values" approaches to constitutional theory: "The exalted nature of the values is also a corollary to assumptions about constitutionalism itself: the Constitution necessarily must address the most serious public concerns and must achieve a result that can be seen as virtuous in order to be worthy of its fundamental status" (Nagel, *Constitutional Cultures: The Mentality and Consequences of Judicial Review* [Berkeley and Los Angeles: University of California Press, 1989], 111).

[57] Carleton, "Elitism Sustained," 561.

Some judges and constitutional scholars have proposed dealing with this problem through a dual approach to state constitutional interpretation.[58] Under this approach, the "great ordinances" of a constitution would receive different interpretive treatment than would those provisions that announced "no principle of government" but merely constitutionalized material that might ordinarily have appeared in a statute.[59] Presumably, the "great ordinances" would be interpreted as befits constitutional provisions, and a state constitutional jurisprudence built around them, while the other provisions would be interpreted like statutes.[60] Although a step in the right direction, this dual approach to state constitutional interpretation is too simple to solve the problem.

For one thing, dispensing with "lesser" provisions in building a state constitutional jurisprudence is highly questionable, because what a state chooses to include in its constitution is important evidence of the vision underlying the document. In addition, the sharp bifurcation of constitutional provisions reintroduces in another context Gardner's dubious distinction between what is truly constitutional and what is not. It is no coincidence that the most thoughtful exponent of this dual approach feels compelled to distinguish between provisions that are *constitutional* and those that are "merely constitutional."[61] Moreover, no simple dichotomy can do justice to the diversity of state constitutional provisions. While some state provisions can easily be placed in one category or another, a number of provisions cannot. Proponents of the dual approach have recognized this, proposing criteria for determining into which category to place those provisions that are "in the middle." Yet the proposed criteria differ from one commentator to another and have themselves been subjected to telling criticism.[62] The point is not that better criteria must be developed; rather, the dual approach itself needs rethinking.

In reconsidering their interpretive approaches, state constitutional interpreters should take their cues from those constitutional theorists who have already addressed this problem in the context of interpreting the

[58] The major case endorsing a dual approach to state provisions is *Vreeland v. Byrne,* 370 A.2d 825 (N.J. 1977). Compare also *Corum v. University of North Carolina,* 413 N.E.2d 276 (N.C. 1992), with *Kiser v. Kiser,* 385 S.E.2d 487 (N.C. 1989). The foremost scholarly exposition of this position is James Gray Pope, "An Approach to State Constitutional Interpretation," *Rutgers Law Journal* 24 (summer 1993): 985–1008.

[59] *Vreeland v. Byrne,* at 832.

[60] Schuman, "Failed Critique," 277–78.

[61] Pope, "Approach to Constitutional Interpretation," 986.

[62] The New Jersey Supreme Court in *Vreeland* bases its distinction on breadth of principle and constitutional subject matter. Pope rejects subject matter as a criterion and substitutes enactment by the people. For a telling criticism of Pope's criteria, see James A. Gardner, "What Is a State Constitution?" *Rutgers Law Journal* 24 (summer 1993): 1033 n. 38.

federal Constitution. Despite their many differences, these theorists agree that "constitutional provisions exist on a spectrum ranging from the relatively specific to the extremely open-textured."[63] Some are "drafted . . . in language admitting of only one interpretation," while others require "almost pure political judgment to interpret," and still others fall in between.[64] Given this diversity, the interpretation of state constitutions must respect each provision's character, rather than forcing the provision into a preexisting set of interpretive approaches.[65] Interpreters may differ as to where on the spectrum a particular provision fits, as scholarly debate on the meaning of the Eighth and Fourteenth amendments reveals.[66] Yet these disputes merely suggest the necessity of closer examination of the provision's text, generating history, and place in the constitutional design, the very factors proposed as bases for the independent interpretation of state constitutions.

Constitutional Coherence

Although constitutional theorists disagree about the nature of the United States Constitution, they largely agree that it embodies a coherent politi-

[63] Ely, *Democracy and Distrust,* 13.

[64] Ronald Dworkin, *Law's Empire* (Cambridge: Harvard University Press, 1986), 367 and 357.

[65] The character of most state provisions will encourage a narrow interpretation. As William Swindler has noted: "Because state constitutions are all too detailed and explicit, there is a built-in orientation toward strict construction in the majority of states" ("State Constitutions," 593).

[66] One basis for this dispute involves whether specific provisions are broad statements of principle or deserve narrow construction as "terms of art" or as a result of historical factors. Compare, for example, the contrasting interpretations of the Eighth Amendment's ban on cruel and unusual punishments offered by Ronald Dworkin and Raoul Berger: Dworkin, *Taking Rights Seriously,* and Raoul Berger, *Death Penalties: The Supreme Court's Obstacle Course* (Cambridge: Harvard University Press, 1982). This "level of generality" problem also explains much of the disagreement about the meaning of the Fourteenth Amendment. For varying perspectives, see Judith A. Baer, *Equality under the Constitution: Reclaiming the Fourteenth Amendment* (Ithaca, N.Y.: Cornell University Press, 1983); Raoul Berger, *Government by Judiciary: The Transformation of the Fourteenth Amendment* (Cambridge: Harvard University Press, 1977); Michael Kent Curtis, *No State Shall Abridge: The Fourteenth Amendment and the Bill of Rights* (Durham, N.C.: Duke University Press, 1986); Earl M. Maltz, *Civil Rights, the Constitution, and Congress, 1863–1869* (Lawrence: University Press of Kansas, 1990); William E. Nelson, *The Fourteenth Amendment: From Political Principle to Judicial Doctrine* (Cambridge: Harvard University Press, 1988); and Michael P. Zuckert, "Toward a Corrective Federalism: The United States Constitution, Federalism, and Rights," in Ellis Katz and G. Alan Tarr, eds., *Federalism and Rights* (Lanham, Md.: Rowman and Littlefield, 1996).

For a thoughtful treatment of this "level of generality" problem, see Tushnet, *Red, White, and Blue,* chap. 1.

cal theory and constitutional design.[67] Some theorists have discovered this coherence in the structure of the government that was created. Thus, many originalists view the Constitution as basically a majoritarian document and understand constitutional rights guarantees as exceptions to the document's primary emphasis on popular government.[68] Other theorists have also relied on the overall constitutional design, albeit to justify judicial protection of unexpressed rights.[69] Still others have appealed beyond the text of the U.S. Constitution, arguing that what unites the various provisions are certain unexpressed assumptions and value judgments about politics and political life. Walter Murphy, for instance, has argued that the Constitution "includes a tradition of ideals and practices that evidence values and principles as vital as those formalized in the actual document."[70] Thomas Grey has urged judges to consult "basic national ideals of individual liberty and fair treatment, even when the content of these ideals is not expressed as a matter of positive law in the written Constitution."[71] And Justice William Brennan has asserted that a concern for "human dignity" underlies the Constitution and should guide its interpretation.[72] For present purposes, what is important is not the source or character of the U.S. Constitution's coherence but the function that this notion of coherence serves in these diverse constitutional theories. If the Constitution embodies a particular political design or a set of shared values, then that design or those values can guide the interpretation of specific constitutional provisions and the elaboration of implied powers and/or unexpressed rights. Thus, constitutional theorists can interpret the parts in light of the whole, because they have concluded that the Constitution is truly a whole.

Previous chapters have described the political understandings underlying the state constitutions adopted in various eras. Nevertheless, it would be a mistake to assume that state constitutions embody the same coherence of perspective that one finds in the federal Constitution. As noted previously, many state constitutions include extensive "statutory" material. One would not expect to encounter a coherent political perspective

[67] William F. Harris II, "Bonding Word and Polity: The Logic of American Constitutionalism," *American Political Science Review* 76 (March 1982): 34–49.

[68] Bork, *The Tempting of America;* William Rehnquist, "The Notion of a Living Constitution," *Texas Law Review* 54 (May 1976): 693–706; and Berger, *Government by Judiciary.*

[69] Ely, *Democracy and Distrust;* and Charles L. Black, *Structure and Relationship in Constitutional Law* (Baton Rouge, La.: Louisiana State University Press, 1969).

[70] Walter Murphy, "An Ordering of Constitutional Values," *Southern California Law Review* 53 (January 1980): 705.

[71] Grey, "An Unwritten Constitution?" 706.

[72] William Brennan, "The Constitution of the United States: Contemporary Ratification," *South Texas Law Journal* 27 (fall 1986): 436.

in a body of statutory law enacted over a prolonged period, so it may also be unrealistic to expect it in a state constitution that incorporated over time a range of detailed policy prescriptions via amendments or successive revisions. Related to this is what might be called the "layering" in state constitutions. For most state constitutions, unlike the federal Constitution, it is inaccurate to speak of a single set of "founders" or even of a "founding epoch."[73] Rather, the states' frequent recourse to amendment, particularly during the twentieth century, undermines any notion of the state constitution as an organic whole; and the political perspective and aims of those amending the constitution may well differ from those of the constitution's initial ratifiers.[74] Indeed, previous chapters have documented the influence of disparate political movements, such as Jacksonian democracy and Progressivism, on the constitutional provisions adopted during various eras. The amendment process often involves neither deletion nor replacement but rather the addition of provisions; and like a geologist, a state constitutional scholar can study the various layers of provisions that have been incorporated into the document and the political movements that spawned them. Nor does constitutional revision altogether dispose of this difficulty. Because dissatisfaction with certain key features of a state's constitution usually provides the impetus for revision, constitution-makers focus on those features, often leaving untouched other provisions that have not excited controversy. Indeed, the attempt to change too much runs the risk of alienating diverse constituencies that could coalesce in opposition to a proposed constitution. As a result, even constitutions that have undergone revision typically retain "layers" of provisions, and this defeats—or at least complicates—the search for constitutional coherence.

Finally, one must consider the full implications of the fact that different eras of constitution-makers may have been motivated by quite different political theories and/or understandings of constitutionalism. Even if a state constitution initially embodied a principled constitutional perspective, it might—because of changes over time—come to contain key provisions reflecting distinct and perhaps inconsistent constitutional perspectives. For a judge seeking constitutional coherence, the task becomes

---

[73] Of course, although commentators often speak of a single set of founders for the federal Constitution, this is an oversimplification of the constitutional experience at the federal level as well. See Ackerman, *We the People.*

[74] This constitutional "layering" is related to the inclusion of "statutory" material in state constitutions, in that efforts by early constitution-makers to safeguard policies by constitutionalizing them have prompted amendments designed to replace those policies with others favored by subsequent majorities. However, "layering" may involve "constitutional" provisions as well, especially those constitutionalized by distinct political movements.

one of construction rather than discovery: transformational constitutional changes "fundamentally alter the terms of the interpretive problem," obliging judges to synthesize "the higher lawmaking efforts" of more than a single generation.[75] Bruce Ackerman has thoughtfully surveyed the difficulties involved in recasting the federal Constitution that were produced by the change in constitutional regime following the Civil War.[76] For state judges, the penetration of the state constitution by successive political movements makes the task of producing coherence even more difficult than it has been for federal judges seeking coherence in the federal Constitution.

Insofar as a state constitution does not reflect a single perspective, an interpreter cannot always look to the whole to illuminate the meaning of its various parts. Thus, one approach widely utilized by constitutional theorists in interpreting the federal Constitution seems inapplicable—or at least less frequently applicable—to state constitutions. Instead, something much closer to "clause-bound" interpretation is required, though exactly what the interpretive approach might be remains a question.[77]

Textualism, Originalism, and State Constitutions

THE ORIENTATION TOWARD TEXTUALISM AND ORIGINALISM

Those scholars and jurists who have supported the independent interpretation of state constitutions have argued for a close attention to the specifics of the constitutional text and to its generating history. So too have advocates of the supplemental approach. The arguments of both camps thus coalesce in support of a particular interpretive approach to state constitutions. If the distinctiveness of state constitutional guarantees justifies independent interpretation, then state jurists are encouraged to emphasize textual analysis and, more particularly, a textual analysis that operates at the level of the specific constitutional provision. If the distinctive origins or purpose of a provision justifies independent interpretation, then state jurists must pay particular attention to the intent of the framers and to the historical circumstances out of which the constitutional provision arose. Some commentators, it is true, have encouraged state judges to seek their own best interpretation of state provisions, even when an identity of language in state and federal guarantees suggests that

[75] Ackerman, *We the People,* 87 and 88.

[76] Ackerman, *We the People,* especially chap. 4.

[77] The distinction between "clause-bound" and broader originalism (or, as he calls it, "interpretivism") derives from John Hart Ely, who defines "clause-bound interpretivism" as giving content to a provision solely on the basis of its language and surrounding legislative history (*Democracy and Distrust,* 12).

they may share a common meaning.[78] Yet even these commentators recognize that this "best interpretation" is as likely to be found in the text as in extraconstitutional values—their concern is not to disparage textualism but to ensure that a fresh approach to the text is not precluded by the Supreme Court's interpretation of counterpart language. Thus, the justifications offered for independent interpretation, together with a need to be able to defend their rulings against accusations of illegitimacy, have oriented state judges toward a constitutional jurisprudence emphasizing textualism and original intent.

This textual emphasis should pose little difficulty—indeed, as one constitutional reformer put it, "[B]ecause state constitutions are all too detailed and explicit, there is a built-in orientation toward strict construction [i.e., textual analysis]."[79] Some constitutional theorists, however, have argued that proposals for an originalist jurisprudence face an insurmountable practical problem: the available historical materials do not provide an adequate basis for such a jurisprudence.[80] Focusing on the federal Constitution, they point out that the record of the Founders' views and of the history behind various provisions is at best incomplete.[81] Moreover, given the difficulty of determining collective as opposed to individual intent, even a detailed historical record would not necessarily dispel dispute about the intentions of the Constitution's framers (or ratifiers). Finally, even if one conceded that it was possible to discover the Founders' broad intentions, one could not determine their intentions about many of the specific problems faced today, because the Founders never addressed them.

Originalists have, of course, challenged the validity of this critique.[82] But whatever its validity with regard to the federal Constitution, the distinctive character and development of state constitutions suggest that the

---

[78] See, for example, Williams, "In the Shadow"; Linde, "E Pluribus"; and Kahn, "Interpretation and Authority."

[79] Swindler, "State Constitutions," 593.

[80] The foremost presentation of this position is Paul Brest, "The Misconceived Quest for the Original Understanding," *Boston University Law Review* 60 (March 1980): 204–54. Other major critiques include Dworkin, *Law's Empire,* chap. 10; Ely, *Democracy and Distrust,* chaps. 1–2; and Leonard W. Levy, *Original Intent and the Framers' Constitution* (New York: Macmillan, 1988).

[81] For an overview of the problems with the documentary record, see James H. Huston, "The Creation of the Constitution: The Integrity of the Documentary Record," *Texas Law Review* 65 (November 1986): 1–39.

[82] Gregory Bassham, *Original Intent and the Constitution: A Philosophical Study* (Savage, Md.: Rowman and Littlefield, 1992); Berger, *Government by Judiciary;* Bork, *The Tempting of America;* Richard S. Kay, "Adherence to the Original Intentions in Constitutional Adjudication: Three Objections and Responses," *Northwestern University Law Review* 82 (winter 1988): 228–92; and Maltz, *Rethinking Constitutional Law.*

critique does not apply—or at least does not apply with equal force—to efforts to develop an originalist interpretation of state constitutions.[83] For one thing, given the frequency of amendment and revision, many state constitutions and state provisions are relatively recent. The more recent a provision, the more likely that there is an extensive documentary record—preconvention studies, constitutional convention records, voters' pamphlets, and the like—bearing on its meaning; and the greater availability of these materials facilitates the discovery of the original intent.[84] In addition, the more recent the provision, the more likely it is that those who adopted it foresaw and discussed the constitutional issues currently arising under it. Thus, one may find in the historical material discussion not only of broad constitutional principles but also of how those principles would apply to contemporary problems.[85] Finally, the long-standing preference among state constitution-makers for detailed and specific language has the advantage of facilitating an originalist state jurisprudence. Indeed, state constitution-makers may have used clear and specific language in order to fix the meaning of provisions. Even where interpretation is required, the greater detail of state provisions often rewards attempts to use close textual analysis to discover original intent.

TAKING TEXTUALISM AND ORIGINALISM SERIOUSLY

But what would state constitutional interpretation based on textualism and/or originalism look like? To answer that question, we offer three examples of what such an approach might entail. The Oregon Supreme Court's approach to freedom of expression illustrates the potential of clause-bound interpretation of state constitutions; for the Oregon court

[83] Surprisingly enough, James Gardner is among those who contend that state sources are sufficient for an originalist state constitutional jurisprudence. See Gardner, "Failed Discourse," 811–12. It should be noted that the importance of state constitutional history does not depend on whether one subscribes to an originalist jurisprudence. As Stephen E. Gottleib has noted: "For those who reject a jurisprudence of original intent, constitutional history nevertheless helps us to preserve the lessons embodied in the drafting of the provisions at issues and to explore the consequences of the language chosen." See Gottleib, "Foreword: Symposium on State Constitutional History: In Search of a Usable Past," *Albany Law Review* 53 (winter 1989): 258.

[84] Pertinent state constitutional materials are cataloged in Cynthia Browne, *State Constitutional Conventions, from Independence to the Completion of the Present Union, 1776–1959: A Bibliography* (Westport, Conn.: Greenwood Press, 1973); and Bonnie Canning, *State Constitutional Conventions, Revisions, and Amendments, 1959–1976* (Westport, Conn.: Greenwood Press, 1977). A constitutional history for each state is contained in the volumes of the series Reference Guides to State Constitutions of the United States, likewise published by Greenwood Press.

[85] See, for example, Paul G. Cassell, "The Mysterious Creation of Search and Seizure Exclusionary Rules under State Constitutions: The Utah Example," *Utah Law Review* 1993:751–873.

has developed a distinctive jurisprudence based on the language and generating history of the state's guarantee of free expression.[86] The pertinent provision reads: "No law shall be passed restraining the free expression of opinion, or restricting the right to speak, write, or print freely on any subject whatever; but every person shall be responsible for the abuse of this right."[87] According to the Oregon Supreme Court, the provision on its face protects expression on all subjects equally, affording no special protection to political speech.[88] Instead of emulating the U.S. Supreme Court's balancing approach, the Oregon court has read the provision to prohibit laws against speech or expression as such, unless the restraint falls within a clear historical exception that was well established when the constitution was adopted and that the provision was not meant to eliminate.[89] On this basis, the Oregon court has invalidated statutes banning the dissemination of pornography, prohibiting the use of obscene language in public, and placing zoning restrictions on "adult businesses."[90] However, it has interpreted the provision to permit laws aimed at the injurious effects of communications rather than at the communications themselves, thus upholding laws against threats of violence, harassment, and intimidation.[91] According to the Oregon court, historical evidence reveals that the "responsible for the abuse" clause of the provision was inserted to preserve liability for defamation suits. Thus, speakers can be held responsible for the actual harms caused by their speech or expression. However, the clause limits responsibility to compensatory liability and does not authorize either punitive damages or criminal punishment for speech-generated harms.[92]

Utah's constitutional protection of water rights illustrates how the search for the original intent of state provisions can benefit from historical and comparative analysis. By its very terms, Utah's provision directs attention to the law affecting the ownership and use of water that existed at the time the constitution was adopted. It reads: "All existing rights to the use of any of the waters in this State for useful or beneficial purpose,

[86] Our analysis in this paragraph draws upon Friesen, *State Constitutional Law,* chap. 5; and Rex Armstrong, "Free Speech Fundamentalism: Justice Linde's Lasting Legacy," *Oregon Law Review* 70 (winter 1991): 855–94.

[87] Oregon Constitution, art. 1, sec. 8.

[88] *State v. Robertson,* 649 P.2d 569, 589 (Ore. 1982).

[89] *State v. Robertson,* at 576. The historically excluded classes of speech include perjury, fraud, and solicitation.

[90] *State v. Henry,* 732 P.2d 9 (Ore. 1987); *State v. Spencer,* 611 P.2d 1147 (Ore. 1980); and *City of Portland v. Tidyman,* 759 P.2d 242 (Ore. 1988).

[91] *State v. Moyle,* 705 P.2d 740 (Ore. 1985); *State v. Garcias,* 679 P.2d 1354 (Ore. 1984); *State v. Robertson,* 649 P.2d 569 (Ore. 1982); and *State v. Plowman,* 838 P.2d 558 (Ore. 1992).

[92] *Wheeler v. Green,* 593 P.2d 777, 788–89 (Ore. 1979).

are hereby recognized and confirmed."[93] The distinctive features of the existing law are clarified by contrasting them with the law in the eastern and midwestern states that had adopted the riparian doctrine governing water rights.[94] Comparison of Utah's provision with comparable provisions in surrounding states further clarifies its meaning. The delegates at the Utah convention had as potential models Colorado's 1876 constitution, which designated unappropriated water of natural streams as "the property of the public . . . dedicated to the use of the people of the State," and Wyoming's 1890 constitution, which declared water of natural streams the "property of the state." The delegates' rejection of both of those models underscores their commitment to ensuring the sanctity of the private right to water, and that commitment must therefore guide the interpretation of Utah's provision regarding water rights.

Finally, nineteenth-century state equality guarantees reveal the necessity of interpreting state provisions in light of the political theory underlying them.[95] These state equality provisions for the most part antedated the Fourteenth Amendment, with its emphasis on protecting minorities against majoritarian abuse. They can also be distinguished from eighteenth-century equality provisions, which recognized the natural equality of all men, and from twentieth-century guarantees of gender equality and prohibitions on discrimination in the exercise of civil rights. In contrast to the countermajoritarian equal protection clause, the state guarantees primarily served to protect the majority against legislative creation of special privileges or exemptions that destroyed equality under the law.[96] Thus, Ohio's 1851 constitution declared, "Government is instituted for . . . [all people's] . . . equal protection and benefit."[97] Oregon's 1859 constitution specifically banned legislative favoritism: "No law shall be passed granting to any citizen or class of citizens privileges or immunities which, upon the same terms, shall not equally belong to all citizens."[98] Constitutional prohibitions on special law and local laws, widely adopted during the nineteenth century, reflected a similar concern.

[93] Utah Constitution, art. 17, sec. 1. The analysis of this provision relies on Jean Bickmore White, *The Utah State Constitution: A Reference Guide* (Westport, Conn.: Greenwood Press, forthcoming).

[94] For an elaboration of the various approaches to water rights in the western states and their influence on state constitutions, see Donald J. Pisani, *To Reclaim a Divided West: Water, Law, and Public Policy, 1848–1902* (Albuquerque: University of New Mexico Press, 1992), chaps. 1–3; and Bakken, *Rocky Mountain Constitution Making*, chap. 6.

[95] The treatment of state equality provisions in this paragraph relies on the analysis in Williams, "Equality Guarantees." For a more detailed discussion of state equality guarantees, see Tarr, "Constitutional Theory," 859–61.

[96] Williams, "Equality Guarantees," 1205–7.

[97] Ohio Constitution of 1851, art. 1, sec. 1, par. 2.

[98] Oregon Constitution of 1859, art. 1, sec. 20.

And the mandate for a "thorough and efficient education" found in several constitutions served to ensure that all children would benefit equally from the system of public education, while the requirement of uniformity in taxation guarded against any citizen or group of citizens escaping the responsibility of contributing to the support of the state.

Some state judges, recognizing familiar equality language, have read the nineteenth-century state guarantees as miniature equal protection clauses.[99] However, such an ahistorical interpretation distorts their meaning: these state guarantees were designed to remedy or prevent different evils and were premised on a different understanding of the threats to equality.[100] That the guarantees had this character was hardly surprising; for most dated from the Jacksonian era, when war was being waged against pockets of entrenched privilege, or from the post–Civil War era, when popular distrust of legislatures was at its height.[101] What this example demonstrates, however, is that fidelity to the original intent of state provisions oftentimes requires attention to the political theory regnant at the time they were adopted. It also suggests that an interpretation faithful to that intent would have to be consistent with that understanding of equality.

Interpretation in a Universe of Constitutions

THE PERTINENCE OF OTHER CONSTITUTIONS

One distinctive aspect of state constitutional interpretation is that it occurs—and state judges perceive it as occurring—in the context of what might be called "a universe of constitutions." Although justices of the U.S. Supreme Court consult the Court's own precedents in interpreting the federal Constitution, they rarely pay close attention to how state judges have dealt with similar state provisions or to how foreign jurists have interpreted analogous provisions in their national constitutions.[102] Thus, the justices tend to act as if the text they are interpreting, and the

---

[99] See, for example, *Right to Choose* v. *Byrne,* 450 A.2d 925 (N.J. 1982). More generally, see Fino, "Judicial Federalism and Equality."

[100] Thus Hans Linde has noted that article 1, section 20 of the Oregon Constitution and the federal equal protection clause "were placed in different constitutions at different times by different men to enact different historic concerns into constitutional policy." See Linde, "Without Due Process," 141.

[101] See the discussion in chapter 4 of this volume.

[102] But see William J. Brennan Jr., "State Supreme Court Judge versus United States Supreme Court Justice: A Change in Function and Perspective," *University of Florida Law Review* 19 (fall 1966): 225–37; and J. Skelly Wright, "In Praise of State Courts: Confessions of a Federal Judge," *Hastings Constitutional Law Quarterly* 11 (winter 1984): 165–88.

interpretive problems they are confronting, are unique. In contrast, in interpreting state constitutional provisions, state judges regularly inquire into how sister courts, both state and federal, have interpreted similar provisions. As noted previously, the opinions of these sister courts are a prime source of constitutional doctrine, and their rulings often serve as persuasive precedent.[103]

This reliance on precedent from other jurisdictions is hardly surprising. For in looking beyond the state's borders for guidance in interpreting their state constitutions, state judges are merely extending to the realm of constitutional interpretation a mode of decision making that they have long employed in common-law cases. Yet differences in the interpretive project render this extension problematic. In elaborating the common law, state supreme court judges proceed without an authoritative legal text. The absence of an authoritative text permits judges to consult—and perhaps follow—the rulings of sister courts without risking slighting what is distinctive in the law of their own state. Moreover, the sense of participation in a common enterprise likewise encourages intercourt borrowing in the elaboration of the common law. But in interpreting a state constitution, a state court is interpreting a unique collection of provisions with a distinctive generating history. Borrowing from other states becomes more problematic, because even counterpart provisions from other states may differ in their language, the historical circumstances out of which they arose, or both. As Justice Hans Linde has put it, "[S]tate courts find themselves pulled between fidelity to the state's own charter and the sense that constitutional law is a shared enterprise."[104] The differences among state constitutions thus raise questions about the extent to which judges should borrow doctrine or rely on precedent from other jurisdictions in constitutional cases. If the U.S. Supreme Court's interpretations of counterpart federal provisions are not authoritative for state judges interpreting state constitutions, then one is tempted to conclude that neither are the interpretations by judges in other states of their counterpart state provisions.

The situation, however, is more complicated than it might initially appear. Interpretation in a universe of constitutions obliges state courts to accord particular weight to some constitutions and to the judicial rulings interpreting them. Most states have adopted more than one constitution,

---

[103] For studies of the use of precedent from other courts, see Peter Harris, "Difficult Cases and the Display of Authority," *Journal of Law, Economics, and Organization* 1 (spring 1985): 209–21, and "Structural Change in the Communication of Precedent among State Supreme Courts, 1870–1970," *Social Networks* 4 (September 1982): 201–22; and Gregory A. Caldeira, "The Transmission of Legal Precedent: A Study of State Supreme Courts," *American Political Science Review* 79 (March 1985): 178–93.

[104] Linde, "State Constitutions Common Law?" 228.

and the interpretation of a state's current constitution must take account of how current provisions relate to those in prior constitutions. In addition, most states in devising their constitutions have borrowed provisions from the constitutions of other states; and in interpreting those borrowed provisions, judges must take into account their origins in other state constitutions and judicial interpretation of those other constitutions. To these complications we now turn.

THE RELATION TO PRIOR CONSTITUTIONS OF THE STATE

In determining the meaning of a state constitution, one must first of all consider the relationship between that constitution and the state's past constitutions. Although the addition of altogether new provisions raises no unusual interpretive difficulties, both constitutional change and constitutional continuity raise perplexing issues.

When a state revises its constitution, one must examine how provisions have changed in order to interpret the current constitution. If the text was changed, one must assume that the change was introduced for a purpose. Occasionally, a change may merely involve constitutional housekeeping, an attempt to eliminate convoluted language or to deconstitutionalize essentially "statutory" provisions. In Louisiana in 1974, for example, constitution-makers substantially pared their charter by excising provisions and reenacting them as statutes.[105] More frequently, however, alterations in language are designed to produce changes in meaning. The meaning of a state constitutional text thus cannot be considered in the abstract; the meaning of the words is determined in part by what they have replaced. Thus, the constitution includes not only the current provision but also, as a reference point, the previous version of the provision and the interpretation given to that previous version.

Two examples serve to illustrate the point. The first involves New Jersey's guarantee that "[a]ll persons are by nature free and independent, and have certain natural and inalienable rights. . . ."[106] On initial inspection the guarantee seems no more than a recognition of natural rights, presumably introduced in the state's first constitution and carried over to its successors. However, when one compares this guarantee with its predecessor in New Jersey's 1844 constitution, one notes an important difference.[107] Whereas the 1844 version acknowledged that "men" possessed various natural rights, the 1947 version recognized that the rights

---

[105] Hargrave, *The Louisiana State Constitution,* 18.

[106] New Jersey Constitution, art. 1, sec. 1.

[107] The counterpart provision in New Jersey's 1844 constitution (art. 1, sec. 1) read: "All men are by nature free and independent, and have certain natural inalienable rights . . . ."

202 • Chapter 6

pertain to all "persons." By substituting the gender-neutral "persons" for the gendered "men," the constitution emphasized that women enjoyed the same rights as men.[108] However, looking at the 1947 provision in the abstract, one would hardly recognize that it was designed to protect women's rights.

The second example likewise involves gender equality. When Washington adopted a "little ERA" in 1972, the Washington Supreme Court might well have followed the lead of other courts that had interpreted similar provisions to establish gender as a suspect classification.[109] This, however, the court refused to do.[110] Instead, it noted that even prior to adoption of the amendment, Washington courts had already recognized gender as a suspect classification.[111] Since the constitution-makers would not have altered the constitution without purpose, the court concluded that the state's citizens, by ratifying the equal-rights amendment, must have sought to provide greater protection for gender equality than had existed previously.[112] In other words, the constitution included not only the text but the body of decisions within which the text fit. The court therefore ruled that the equal-rights amendment required a more stringent level of review than suspect classification.[113]

What often goes unrecognized, given the understandable attention devoted to constitutional change, is the extent of continuity between states' old and new constitutions. Several factors might account for the states' tendency to retain features and provisions from earlier constitutions— among them, the limited time and energy of most constitutional conventions, a general satisfaction with most aspects of the previous constitution, and the delegates' apprehension that too radical a change could endanger ratification by facilitating a coalition among those opposed to various elements of the proposed constitution. Whatever the reasons for

[108] Robert F. Williams, *The New Jersey State Constitution: A Reference Guide* (Westport, Conn.: Greenwood Press, 1990), 29; Karen J. Kruger, "Rediscovering the New Jersey E.R.A.: The Key to Successful Sex Discrimination Litigation," *Rutgers Law Journal* 17 (winter 1986): 253–81; and Robert F. Williams, "The New Jersey Equal Rights Amendment: A Documentary Sourcebook," *Women's Rights Law Reporter* 16 (winter 1994): 70–125.

[109] Washington's guarantee of gender equality is found in Washington Constitution, art. 31, sec. 1. The state's experience under that provision is discussed in Patricia L. Proebsting, "Washington's Equal Rights Amendment: It Says What It Means and It Means What It Says," *University of Puget Sound Law Review* 8 (winter 1985): 461–84. For surveys of state supreme court interpretation of state equal-rights amendments, see Tarr and Porter, "Gender Equality"; and Friesen, *State Constitutional Law,* chap. 3.

[110] *Darrin v. Gould,* 540 P.2d 882 (Wash. 1975).

[111] See, for example, *Hanson v. Hutt,* 517 P.2d 599 (Wash. 1973).

[112] *Darrin v. Gould,* 540 P.2d 882, 889.

[113] *Darrin v. Gould,* 540 P.2d 882, 893.

constitutional continuity, it poses unique problems for state constitutional interpreters. The nature of these problems can best be understood by considering analogous situations that arise in statutory interpretation.[114] When a court decides a case under a statute, it offers an interpretation of the statute's meaning. In theory, should the legislature believe the court's interpretation mistaken, it can correct the error by amending the statute to clarify how it should be interpreted. Some commentators and judges have argued that, given this opportunity to reverse the court's interpretation, the legislature's failure to amend the statute should be construed as agreement with the court's interpretation and should fix the meaning of the statute for subsequent litigation.[115] However, other commentators have maintained that, given the difficulties of enacting legislation and the array of issues demanding legislators' attention, one can draw no conclusions from legislative inaction.[116] Whatever the merits of the latter argument, the claim that the legislature has endorsed the judiciary's interpretation is undoubtedly strengthened when the legislature reenacts a statute after it has been interpreted by the judiciary, because the legislature has then acted affirmatively rather than merely failed to act. Thus, a standard source on statutory construction has concluded that "where the legislature adopts an expression which has received judicial interpretation, interpretation is prima facie evidence of legislative intent."[117] Yet other commentators have insisted that drawing conclusions from reenactment is unwarranted.[118]

When a constitutional provision has been carried over unchanged into a new constitution, the situation is in some respects analogous to the reenactment of a statute: in both instances the relevant governing authority has acted affirmatively. The question then becomes whether prior judicial interpretation of the "old" (and unchanged) provision determines

[114] The literature addressing the relation between earlier and later statutory enactments is extensive. See, inter alia, Reed Dickerson, *The Interpretation and Application of Statutes* (Boston: Little, Brown, 1975); William N. Eskridge Jr., *Dynamic Statutory Interpretation* (Cambridge: Harvard University Press, 1994); and Edward H. Levi, *An Introduction to Legal Reasoning* (Chicago: University of Chicago Press, 1949).

[115] See Norman J. Singer, *Sutherland Statutory Construction*, 5th ed. (Deerfield, Ill.: Clark Boardman Callaghan, 1992), sec. 49.10; Frank E. Horack Jr., "Congressional Silence: A Tool of Judicial Supremacy," *Texas Law Review* 25 (January 1947): 254–55; and Lawrence H. Tribe, "Toward a Syntax of the Unsaid: Construing the Sounds of Congressional and Constitutional Silence," *Indiana Law Journal* 57 (1982): 524–29.

[116] See Dickerson, *Interpretation and Application*, 179–83; Eskridge, *Dynamic Statutory Interpretation*, 241–52 and 309–15; Ernst Freund, "Interpretation of Statutes," *University of Pennsylvania Law Review* 65 (January 1917): 214–15; and John C. Grabow, "Congressional Silence and the Search for Legislative Intent: A Venture into 'Speculative Unrealities,'" *Boston University Law Review* 64 (July 1984): 740.

[117] Singer, *Sutherland Statutory Construction*, 69.

[118] See, for example, Eskridge, *Dynamic Statutory Interpretation*, 243–45 and 311–12.

the meaning of the "new" provision. If such reenactment constitutes endorsement of the judicial interpretation of the provision, then arguably the constitution not only includes the reenacted text of the provision but also makes authoritative the body of case law developed under the previous constitution. Moreover, inclusion of the unchanged provision would then fix its meaning so that neither judges nor other constitutional interpreters could legitimately diverge from the interpretation that had been ratified by reenactment.

There is some case law that supports this conclusion.[119] However, if one compares the political realities of legislating and revising a constitution, the analogy between reenactment of a statute and carrying over a constitutional provision breaks down. Indeed, the differences seem substantial enough to justify viewing prior judicial interpretations of a provision as not included in the new constitution. Because a statute embraces a single subject, and because of the level of specialization characteristic of state legislatures, it is reasonable to expect that those legislators most concerned with reenactment of a law will be familiar with its content, as well as with its implementation and its interpretive history. Therefore, drawing conclusions from reenactment may not be inappropriate. However, a constitutional convention does not have the professionalized membership, the established expertise deriving from specialization over time, or the institutional memory of a legislature. Unlike a legislature, a convention has only limited discretion in deciding what subjects to address—for example, a convention could hardly decide not to address local government in the constitution it was devising. Moreover, because the convention delegates must address a wide array of matters within a short time-frame, they are less likely to be knowledgeable about the meaning and interpretive history of all the provisions they consider. Certainly, what is true of the delegates is even truer of the ratifying public, those who give the constitution its authority.[120] Furthermore, even if citizens did possess such knowledge, they could not vote individually on specific constitutional provisions but instead have to accept or reject the constitution as a whole. Therefore, the ratification of a constitution does

---

[119] See, for example, *Reed v. Fain*, 145 So.2d 858 (Fla. 1962); *Gray v. Bryant*, 125 So.2d 846 (Fla. 1960); and *Hitchcock v. State*, 131 A.2d 714 (Md. 1957).

[120] As the New Jersey Supreme Court observed in *Gangemi v. Berry*, 134 A.2d 1, 9 (N.J. 1957), "[T]he Constitution derives its force, not from the Convention which framed it, but from the people who ratified it; and the intent to be arrived at is that of the people." The position taken by the New Jersey court is a standard one, at least on the rhetorical level, among constitutional interpreters and has an impressive lineage. See the remarks of James Madison on the floor of Congress in 1796: "As the instrument came from them [the delegates at the federal Constitutional Convention], it was nothing more than the draft of a plan, nothing but a dead letter, until life and validity were breathed into it by the voice of the people" (*Annals of Congress*, 5:776).

not have that character of active endorsement of specific provisions found in the reenactment of statutes. In sum, one cannot safely conclude that either delegates or ratifiers intended to include the judicial interpretation of a carried-over provision as part of the constitution. Yet it hardly seems reasonable to say that something is included in the constitution unless it was in some sense meant to be included. It therefore seems appropriate to treat prior judicial rulings interpreting the unchanged provision just as one would treat other precedents; namely, as entitled to considerable weight but not authoritative.

THE RELATION TO THE CONSTITUTIONS OF OTHER STATES

Earlier chapters have demonstrated that those who draft state constitutions have as often been borrowers—or even unabashed plagiarists—as creators. Indeed, it is precisely because of this that state constitutional commentators have placed such emphasis on textual differences.[121] If incorporation of provisions from other jurisdictions is the rule, then divergence from their formulations must signify something. Constitution-makers have frequently looked to the constitutions of sister states, perhaps because those states shared a similar heritage and political outlook or because they already had developed solutions from problems the constitution-makers confronted. However, the states have also on occasion looked to the federal Constitution, particularly to its institutional design, though the emulation of the federal model has been far from complete. Finally, the states have at times taken direction not from the text of the federal Constitution but from proposed amendments or from judicial decisions interpreting it. Thus, as noted earlier, several states drew inspiration for their "little ERAs" from the proposed amendment to the federal Constitution, and some states have redesigned their criminal-justice guarantees in light of Supreme Court rulings.[122] The fre-

[121] See, for example, Collins, "Reliance on State Constitutions," 18–19; Robert Dowlut and Janet A. Knoop, "State Constitutions and the Right to Keep and Bear Arms," *Oklahoma City University Law Review* 7 (summer 1982): 177–80; Pollock, "Constitutions as Separate Sources," 708–17; Williams, "In the Shadow," 369; and "Developments in the Law—Interpretation," 1359–62.

[122] On the relation between the federal equal-rights amendment and state guarantees of gender equality, see Lujuana Wolfe Treadwell and Nancy Wallace Page, "Comment: Equal Rights Provisions: The Experience under State Constitutions," *California Law Review* 65 (September 1977): 1087–88; and Tarr and Porter, "Gender Equality," 928–29.

From 1970 to 1985, six states adopted constitutional amendments reducing the size of trial juries in criminal cases, at least in part in response to *Williams* v. *Florida,* 399 U.S. 78 (1980), which held that there is no constitutional requirement for a twelve-person jury. In addition, Louisiana constitutionalized the warnings from *Miranda* v. *Arizona,* 384 U.S. 436 (1966), and Florida tied the interpretation of Florida's search-and-seizure provision to var-

206 · Chapter 6

quency and extent of this borrowing raises questions about exactly what is incorporated as part of a state's own constitution. In borrowing a provision from another constitution, does a state thereby adopt the meaning of that provision? Or, more to the point, does it endorse the meaning given to the provision by the originating jurisdiction, so that this interpretation becomes part of the state constitution?[123]

These questions have arisen most frequently when state courts have been called upon to interpret rights guarantees framed in the same language as found in the federal Bill of Rights. In such circumstances, advocates of the lockstep approach have suggested that state courts should conform their interpretations to those made by the U.S. Supreme Court. Such conformity, they have argued, accords with the "artificial canon of construction that identical language in two instruments should be interpreted identically" and protects against state judges writing their own political preferences into the law.[124] Moreover, such conformity seems consistent with the notion that in making another jurisdiction's provision its own, a state adopts not only the constitutional language but also its meaning. When that meaning is authoritatively elaborated by the Supreme Court, then state judges are obliged to accept the Court's determinations and rule accordingly.

This assumption that the states modeled their identical provisions on those contained in the federal Constitution is not altogether accurate: some state provisions antedated their federal counterparts.[125] Even where state and federal guarantees are identical, a state may have modeled its provision on one found in another state constitution. More fundamentally, even if the meaning of identical federal and state provisions is the same, it does not follow that state judges must treat the Supreme Court's interpretation of those provisions as controlling. As argued previously, this follows only if one assumes that the Supreme Court cannot err in its interpretation, or that the Constitution is merely what the Supreme Court says it is.[126] But once one accepts that constitutional provisions have meaning independent of how they have been interpreted, then state judges' obligation to follow the Supreme Court's rulings ceases. Instead,

---

ious U.S. Supreme Court rulings. See Louisiana Constitution, art. 1, sec. 13; and Florida Constitution, art. 1, sec. 12.

[123] See Fritz, "American Constitutional Tradition Revisited," 975–84.

[124] Keyser, "State Constitutions and Review," 1063.

[125] See Lutz, "State Constitutional Pedigree"; Williams, "Equality Guarantees"; and chapter 3 of this volume.

[126] This, of course, recalls Chief Justice Charles Evans Hughes's famous observation that "we are under a Constitution, but the Constitution is what the judges say it is." Quoted in Merlo J. Pusey, *Charles Evans Hughes*, 2 vols. (New York: Macmillan, 1951), 2:204.

they must determine whether the Court has arrived at the true meaning of the constitutional provision and follow the Court's interpretation only when they conclude that it is correct. Therefore, the Court's rulings do not constitute authoritative pronouncements but are merely accounts of constitutional provisions entitled to respectful consideration by state judges independently seeking the meaning of their state constitutions.

The situation is more complicated, however, when U.S. Supreme Court rulings—or in the case of borrowing from other states, state judicial pronouncements—antedate a state's adoption of a constitutional provision borrowed from another jurisdiction. In contrast with a state's reenactment of previously adopted provisions, where textual change requires more serious consideration than does no change, the initial decision to adopt a particular provision, usually from among several possible versions, involves a clear choice. Moreover, if decisions exist interpreting the provision, then a state in adopting the provision knows what the consequences of the choice are. One chooses not only the text but the consequences of that textual formulation, as indicated by the judicial decisions interpreting the text.[127] Thus, when Hawaii chose to model its guarantee of freedom of speech on the First Amendment, it thereby included within its constitution the rulings of the Supreme Court *to that point* interpreting the provision.[128]

Note, however, the proviso. In adopting a provision from another jurisdiction, a state adopts the same meaning of that provision. Where the meaning has not been elaborated, the state is free to develop its own independent interpretation of the provision. Where the borrowed provision has been authoritatively interpreted, the state is understood to have adopted the provision as interpreted, to have included within its constitution the authoritative interpretation of the meaning of the provision. However, no state can know how another state will interpret a provision in the future, and the borrowing state is not bound by whatever changes in interpretation might occur subsequent to ratification.

Although the analogy is not exact, state privacy provisions help to illustrate the point. When states began adopting privacy protections unconnected to search and seizure in the late 1960s, their understanding of the right to privacy was clearly influenced by the federal right to privacy, as elaborated in *Griswold* v. *Connecticut*.[129] Thus, in interpreting the

[127] State constitution-makers have sometimes expressly indicated their recognition that the provisions being borrowed came with a baggage of constitutional rulings elaborating their meaning. See Fritz, "American Constitutional Tradition Revisited," 983–84.

[128] Hawaii Constitution, art. 1, sec. 4.

[129] From 1968 to 1980, eight states—Alaska, California, Florida, Hawaii, Illinois, Louisiana, Mississippi, Montana, and South Carolina—amended their constitutions to incorporate an explicit right to privacy. In some instances, the scope of this right was exceedingly

state right to privacy in those states, *Griswold* can serve as the starting point. However, state guarantees, if adopted prior to 1973, do not necessarily include the right to terminate a pregnancy, the right recognized in *Roe v. Wade,* or exclude the right to be free of governmental interference in one's intimate relationships, the issue in *Bowers v. Hardwick.*[130] Nor, whether or not adopted after *Roe,* do they incorporate the restrictions that the Supreme Court subsequently placed on abortion rights.

CONCLUSION

The earliest proponents of the new judicial federalism were more inclined to extol the virtues of relying on state constitutions than to explain how one should go about interpreting them. This celebrational posture could not last, and in recent years state constitutional interpretation has been beset by naysayers. Contemporary constitutional theorists by their neglect have implicitly denied that state constitutional interpretation is worthy of serious attention. Critics of the new judicial federalism have condemned the independent interpretation of state constitutions as illegitimate or undesirable. Commentators such as James Gardner and Paul Kahn have denied that independent interpretation is possible.

These skeptics are wrong. Doubts about the viability of state constitutional jurisprudence have not prevented its development. State courts have continued, as in the past, to decide cases based on distinctive state provisions regarding taxes and finance, local government and schools. Although the interpretation of state declarations of rights has aroused more controversy, some states have begun to develop independent interpretations of their rights guarantees as well. This chapter focused on Oregon's interpretation of its constitutional safeguard for freedom of expression, but it could as easily have highlighted that state's distinctive approach to search and seizure or California's religious-liberty jurisprudence. Certainly, too many states continue to rely automatically on federal law when confronted with rights issues. Even when they interpret state guarantees, too many frame their analysis in federal doctrinal categories, making state constitutional law merely a poor relation, stuck with ill-fitting hand-me-downs. Yet over time the proliferation of independent

---

narrow—Mississippi's guarantee, for example, merely upheld victims' privacy rights by excluding the public from trials involving sex crimes. In some states—for example, Louisiana and South Carolina—the right was incorporated into provisions protecting against illicit searches. But in five states—Alaska, California, Florida, Hawaii, and Montana—the privacy guarantee was a "free-standing" protection. The federal ruling recognizing a right to privacy implicit in the penumbras of various constitutional guarantees was *Griswold* v. *Connecticut,* 381 U.S. 479 (1965).

[130] *Roe* v. *Wade,* 410 U.S. 113 (1973); and *Bowers* v. *Hardwick,* 478 U.S. 186 (1986).

state interpretations is likely to have a positive effect. Just as the diversity of state constitutional provisions enabled state constitution-makers to choose the model that best fit their needs, so the development of state constitutional doctrine can be expected to provide alternatives to the reflexive adoption of federal doctrine. Moreover, the necessity of choosing among these alternatives should stimulate state courts to examine more closely the text and history of their constitutional provisions, to determine which alternative—if any—best captures the meaning of the state's provision.

This is not to deny the difficulty of the enterprise of state constitutional interpretation. State constitutions are distinctive documents, and the approach to their interpretation must take account of that distinctiveness. Contemporary constitutional theory can assist in the development of a state constitutional jurisprudence, but state interpreters nevertheless confront a host of problems for which constitutional theorists supply no solutions. Yet these problems are not insuperable. Through attention to the text of state provisions, to their generating history, to their place in the state's overall constitutional design, and to their relation to earlier state provisions as well as provisions in other states, state interpreters can develop a body of law that reflects the distinctive traditions of state constitutionalism.

Bibliography

Abrahamson, Shirley S. "Criminal Law and State Constitutions: The Emergence of State Constitutional Law." *Texas Law Review* 63 (March–April 1985): 1141–93.

————. "Divided We Stand: State Constitutions in a More Perfect Union." *Hastings Constitutional Law Quarterly* 18 (summer 1991): 723–44.

Abrahamson, Shirley S., and Diane S. Gutmann. "The New Federalism: State Constitutions and State Courts." *Judicature* 71 (August–September 1991): 88–99.

Ackerman, Bruce. *We the People: Foundations*. Cambridge, Mass.: Belknap Press, 1991.

Adams, Willi Paul. *The First American Constitutions: Republican Ideology and the Making of the State Constitutions in the Revolutionary Era*. Chapel Hill: University of North Carolina Press, 1980.

Advisory Commission on Intergovernmental Relations. *The Question of State Government Capability*. Washington, D.C.: Advisory Commission on Intergovernmental Relations, 1985.

Alaska's Constitution: A Citizen's Guide. 3d ed. Juneau: Alaska Legislative Research Agency, 1992.

Allen, Robert S., ed. *Our Sovereign State*. New York: Vanguard, 1949.

Allen, Tip H., Jr., and Coleman B. Ransome Jr. *Constitutional Revision in Theory and Practice*. University: Bureau of Public Administration, University of Alabama, 1962.

Almond, Gabriel A., and Sidney Verba. *The Civic Culture: Political Attitudes and Democracy in Five Nations*. Princeton: Princeton University Press, 1963.

Amar, Akhil Reed. "The Bill of Rights as a Constitution." *Yale Law Journal* 100 (March 1991): 1131–1210.

————. "The Consent of the Governed." *Columbia Law Review* 94 (March 1994): 457–508.

Anderson, Alexis J. "The Formative Period of First Amendment Theory." *American Journal of Legal History* 24 (January 1980): 56–75.

Antieau, Chester J., Phillip M. Carroll, and Thomas C. Burke. *Religion under the State Constitutions*. Brooklyn: Central Book Company, 1965.

Armstrong, Rex. "Free Speech Fundamentalism: Justice Linde's Lasting Legacy." *Oregon Law Review* 70 (winter 1991): 855–94.

Baer, Judith A. *Equality under the Constitution: Reclaiming the Fourteenth Amendment*. Ithaca, N.Y.: Cornell University Press, 1983.

Bailyn, Bernard. *Ideological Origins of the American Revolution*. Cambridge, Mass.: Belknap Press, 1967.

Baisden, Richard N. *Charter for New Jersey: The New Jersey Constitutional Convention of 1947*. Trenton: New Jersey Department of Education, 1952.

Baker, Gordon E. *State Constitutions: Reapportionment*. New York: National Municipal League, 1960.

Bakken, Gordon Morris. *Rocky Mountain Constitution Making, 1850–1912*. Westport, Conn.: Greenwood Press, 1987.

Barber, Sotirios. *On What the Constitution Means*. Baltimore: Johns Hopkins University Press, 1984.

Bassham, Gregory. *Original Intent and the Constitution: A Philosophical Study*. Savage, Md.: Rowman and Littlefield, 1992.

Bastress, Robert M. *The West Virginia State Constitution: A Reference Guide*. Westport, Conn.: Greenwood Press, 1995.

Beeton, Beverley. *Women Vote in the West: The Woman Suffrage Movement, 1869–1896*. New York: Garland, 1986.

Belz, Herman. *Reconstructing the Union: Theory and Policy during the Civil War*. Ithaca, N.Y.: Cornell University Press, 1969.

Benedict, Michael Les. "Laissez-Faire and Liberty: A Re-evaluation of the Meaning and Origins of Laissez-Faire Constitutionalism." *Law and History Review* 3 (fall 1985): 293–331.

———. "The Problem of Constitutionalism and Constitutional Liberty in the Reconstruction South." In Kermit L. Hall and James W. Ely Jr., eds. *An Uncertain Tradition: Constitutionalism and the History of the South*. Athens: University of Georgia Press, 1989.

Benjamin, Gerald, and Melissa Cusa. "Constitutional Amendment through the Legislature in New York." In G. Alan Tarr, ed. *Constitutional Politics in the States*. Westport, Conn.: Greenwood Press, 1990.

Benjamin, Gerald, and Michael J. Malbin, eds. *Limiting Legislative Terms*. Washington, D.C.: CQ Press, 1992.

Berger, Raoul. *Death Penalties: The Supreme Court's Obstacle Course*. Cambridge: Harvard University Press, 1982.

———. *Government by Judiciary: The Transformation of the Fourteenth Amendment*. Cambridge: Harvard University Press, 1977.

Berkson, Larry Charles, and Susan B. Carbon. *Court Unification: History, Politics, and Implementation*. Washington, D.C.: Government Printing Office, 1978.

Besso, Michael. "Connecticut Legislative Power in the First Century of State Constitutional Government." *Quinnipiac Law Review* 15 (spring 1996): 1–56.

Beth, Loren P. *The Development of the American Constitution, 1877–1917*. New York: Harper and Row, 1971.

Beyle, Thad. "Governors: The Middlemen and Women in Our Political System." In Virginia Gray and Herbert Jacob, eds. *Politics in the American States: A Comparative Analysis*. 6th ed. Washington, D.C.: CQ Press, 1996.

Bickel, Alexander M. *The Least Dangerous Branch: The Supreme Court at the Bar of Politics*. New York: Bobbs-Merrill, 1962.

Binney, Charles C. *Restrictions upon Local and Special Legislation in State Constitutions*. Philadelphia: Kay and Brother, 1894.

Black, Charles L. *Structure and Relationship in Constitutional Law*. Baton Rouge: Louisiana State University Press, 1969.

Blasi, Vincent, ed. *The Burger Court: The Counter-revolution That Wasn't*. New Haven: Yale University Press, 1983.

Blaustein, Albert P., and Gisbert H. Flanz. *Constitutions of the Countries of the World*. Dobbs Ferry, N.Y.: Oceana, 1993.

Book of the States. Lexington, Ky.: Council of State Governments, various years.

Bork, Robert. "Neutral Principles and Some First Amendment Problems." *Indiana Law Journal* 47 (fall 1971): 1–35.

———. *The Tempting of America*. New York: Free Press, 1990.

Bowman, Ann O'M. "The Resurgence of the States: Laboratories under Pressure." In Franz Gress, Detlef Fechtner, and Matthias Hannes, eds. *The American Federal System: Federal Balance in Comparative Perspective*. Frankfurt am Main: Peter Lang, 1994.

Bowman, Ann O'M., and Richard C. Kearney. *The Resurgence of the States*. Englewood Cliffs, N.J.: Prentice-Hall, 1986.

Branning, Rosalind L. *Pennsylvania Constitutional Development*. Pittsburgh: University of Pittsburgh Press, 1960.

Brennan, William H., Jr. "The Constitution of the United States: Contemporary Ratification." *South Texas Law Journal* 27 (fall 1986): 433–46.

———. "State Constitutions and the Protection of Individual Rights." *Harvard Law Review* 90 (January 1977): 489–504.

———. "State Supreme Court Judge versus U.S. Supreme Court Justice: A Change in Function and Perspective." *University of Florida Law Review* 19 (fall 1966): 225–37.

Bresler, Kenneth. "Rediscovering the Right to Instruct Legislators." *New England Law Review* 26 (winter 1991): 355–94.

Brest, Paul. "The Misconceived Quest for the Original Understanding." *Boston University Law Review* 60 (March 1980): 204–54.

Briffault, Richard. *Balancing Acts: The Reality behind State Balanced Budget Amendments*. New York: Twentieth Century Fund, 1996.

Brown, Barbara A., Ann Freedman, Harriet Katz, and Ann Price. *Women's Rights and the Law*. New York: Praeger, 1977.

Brown, Robert E. *Middle-Class Democracy and the Revolution in Massachusetts*. Ithaca, N.Y.: Cornell University Press, 1955.

Browne, Cynthia. *State Constitutional Conventions, from Independence to the Completion of the Present Union, 1776–1959: A Bibliography*. Westport, Conn.: Greenwood Press, 1973.

Bruff, Harold H. "Separation of Powers under the Texas Constitution." *Texas Law Review* 68 (June 1990): 1337–67.

Bryce, James. *The American Commonwealth*. 2 vols. Chicago: Charles H. Seagal, 1891.

Buck, Arthur E. *The Reorganization of State Governments in the United States*. New York: Columbia University Press, 1938.

Busbee, George D. "An Overview of the New Georgia Constitution." *Mercer Law Review* 35 (fall 1983): 1–17.

Butler, David, and Austin Ranney, eds. *Referendums around the World: The Growing Use of Direct Democracy*. Washington, D.C.: American Enterprise Institute Press, 1994.

Cain, Bruce E., and Roger G. Noll, eds. *Constitutional Reform in California:*

Making State Government More Effective and Responsive. Berkeley, Calif.: Institute of Governmental Studies Press, 1995.

Caldeira, Gregory A. "The Transmission of Legal Precedent: A Study of State Supreme Courts." *American Political Science Review* 79 (March 1985): 178–93.

Canning, Bonnie. *State Constitutional Conventions, Revisions, and Amendments, 1959–1976.* Westport, Conn.: Greenwood Press, 1977.

Canon, Bradley C. Review of *Constitutional Politics in the States. American Political Science Review* 91 (March 1997): 200–201.

Carleton, Mark T. "Elitism Sustained: The Louisiana Constitution of 1974." *Tulane Law Review* 54 (April 1980): 560–88.

Cassell, Paul G. "The Mysterious Creation of Search and Seizure Exclusionary Rules under State Constitutions: The Utah Example." *Utah Law Review* 1993: 751–873.

Catalano, Michael W. "The Single Subject Rule: A Check on Anti-majoritarian Logrolling." *Emerging Issues in State Constitutional Law* 3 (1990): 77–86.

Changing Public Attitudes on Government and Taxes, 1988. Washington, D.C.: Advisory Commission on Intergovernmental Relations, 1988.

Changing Public Attitudes on Government and Taxes, 1991. Washington, D.C.: Advisory Commission on Intergovernmental Relations, 1991.

Citrin, Jack. Introduction to *California and the American Tax Revolt: Proposition 13 Five Years Later.* Ed. Terry Schwadron. Berkeley and Los Angeles: University of California Press, 1984.

Clinton, Robert L. *Marbury v. Madison and Judicial Review.* Lawrence: University Press of Kansas, 1989.

Colatuono, Michael G. "The Revision of American State Constitutions: Legislative Power, Popular Sovereignty, and Constitutional Change." *California Law Review* 75 (July 1987): 1473–1512.

Cole, Donald B. *Jacksonian Democracy in New Hampshire, 1800–1851.* Cambridge: Harvard University Press, 1970.

Collins, Ronald K. L. "Bills and Declarations of Rights Digest." In *The American Bench.* 3d ed. Sacramento: Reginald Bishop Forster and Associates, 1985.

———. "The Once and Future 'New Judicial Federalism' and Its Critics." *Washington Law Review* 64 (January 1989): 5–18.

———. "Reliance on State Constitutions—Away from a Reactionary Approach." *Hastings Constitutional Law Quarterly* 9 (fall 1981): 1–15.

Collins, Ronald K. L., and Peter J. Galie. "Models of Post-incorporation Judicial Review: 1985 Survey of State Constitutional Individual Rights Decisions." *Publius* 16 (summer 1986): 111–39.

Collins, Ronald K. L., Peter J. Galie, and John Kincaid. "State High Courts, State Constitutions, and Individual Rights Litigation since 1980: A Judicial Survey." *Publius* 16 (summer 1986): 141–62.

Colson, Dennis C. *Idaho's Constitution: The Tie That Binds.* Moscow: University of Idaho Press, 1991.

"Comment: California's Constitutional Amendomania." *Stanford Law Review* 1 (January 1949): 279–88.

"Comment, Principled Interpretation of State Constitutional Law: Why Don't the

'Primacy' States Practice What They Preach?" *University of Pittsburgh Law Review* 54 (summer 1993): 1019–50.

Commission on Intergovernmental Relations. *A Report to the President for Transmittal to the Congress.* Washington, D.C.: June 1955.

Committee for Economic Development. *A Fiscal Program for a Balanced Federalism.* Washington, D.C.: Committee for Economic Development, 1967.

———. *Modernizing Local Government.* Washington, D.C.: Committee for Economic Development, 1966.

———. *Modernizing State Government.* Washington, D.C.: Committee for Economic Development, 1967.

Conley, Patrick T. *Democracy in Decline: Rhode Island's Constitutional Development, 1776–1841.* Providence: Rhode Island Historical Society, 1977.

Connors, Richard J. *The Process of Constitutional Revision in New Jersey: 1940–1947.* New York: National Municipal League, 1970.

Cooley, Thomas. *A Treatise on Constitutional Limitations.* 8th ed. Boston: Little, Brown, 1927.

Cornwell, Elmer E., Jr. "The American Constitutional Tradition: Its Impact and Development." In Kermit L. Hall, Harold M. Hyman, and Leon V. Sigal, eds. *The Constitutional Convention as an Amending Device.* Washington, D.C.: American Historical Association and American Political Science Association, 1981.

Cornwell, Elmer E., Jr., Jay S. Goodman, and Wayne R. Swanson. *State Constitutional Conventions: The Politics of the Revision Process in Seven States.* New York: Praeger, 1975.

Corwin, Edward S. "The Extension of Judicial Review in New York: 1783–1905." *Michigan Law Review* 15 (February 1917): 281–313.

Cover, Robert M. "The Uses of Jurisdictional Redundancy: Interest, Ideology, and Innovation." *William and Mary Law Review* 22 (summer 1981): 639–82.

Coward, Joan Wells. *Kentucky in the New Republic: The Process of Constitution Making.* Lexington: University Press of Kentucky, 1979.

Cronin, Thomas E. *Direct Democracy: The Politics of Initiative, Referendum, and Recall.* Cambridge: Harvard University Press, 1989.

Crowley, Donald, and Florence Heffron. *The Idaho State Constitution: A Reference Guide.* Westport, Conn.: Greenwood Press, 1994.

Curry, Thomas J. *The First Freedoms: Church and State in America to the Passage of the First Amendment.* New York: Oxford University Press, 1986.

Curtis, Michael Kent. *No State Shall Abridge: The Fourteenth Amendment and the Bill of Rights.* Durham, N.C.: Duke University Press, 1986.

D'Alemberte, Talbot. *The Florida State Constitution: A Reference Guide.* Westport, Conn.: Greenwood Press, 1991.

Davis, Susan, and Taunya Lovell Banks. "State Constitutions, Freedom of Expression, and Search and Seizure: Prospects for State Court Reincarnation." *Publius* 17 (winter 1987): 13–31.

Dealey, James Q. *Growth of American State Constitutions from 1776 to the End of the Year 1914.* Boston: Ginn and Company, 1915; rpt. New York: Da Capo, 1972.

Deukmejian, George, and Clifford K. Thompson. "All Sail and No Anchor—

Judicial Review under the California Constitution." *Hastings Constitutional Law Quarterly* 6 (summer 1979): 975–1010.

"Developments in State Constitutional Law: 1990." *Rutgers Law Journal* 22 (summer 1991): 906–1033.

"Developments in the Law—the Interpretation of State Constitutional Rights." *Harvard Law Review* 95 (April 1982): 1324–1502.

Devitt, Daniel D. "State Action in Pennsylvania: Suggestions for a Unified Approach." *Emerging Issues in State Constitutional Law* 3 (1990): 87–114.

Devlin, John. "Toward a State Constitutional Analysis of Allocation of Powers: Legislators and Legislative Appointees Performing Administrative Functions." *Temple Law Review* 66 (winter 1993): 1205–68.

DeWitt, Benjamin Parke. *The Progressive Movement.* New York: Macmillan, 1915.

Dickerson, Reed. *The Interpretation and Application of Statutes.* Boston: Little, Brown, 1975.

Dillon, John Forest. *A Treatise on the Law of Municipal Corporations.* 5 vols. 5th ed. Boston: Little, Brown, 1911.

Dishman, Robert B. *State Constitutions: The Shape of the Document.* Rev. ed. New York: National Municipal League, 1968.

Dixon, Robert G., Jr. *Democratic Representation: Reapportionment in Law and Politics.* New York: Oxford University Press, 1968.

Dodd, Walter F. "The Functions of a State Constitution." *Political Science Quarterly* 30 (June 1915): 201–21.

———. "Implied Powers and Implied Limitations in Constitutional Law." *Yale Law Journal* 29 (December 1919): 137–62.

———. *The Revision and Amendment of State Constitutions.* New York: Da Capo, 1970.

Dowlut, Robert, and Janet A. Knoop. "State Constitutions and the Right to Keep and Bear Arms." *Oklahoma City University Law Review* 7 (summer 1982): 177–241.

Dubois, Philip L. *From Ballot to Bench: Judicial Elections and the Quest for Accountability.* Austin: University of Texas Press, 1980.

Dworkin, Ronald. *Law's Empire.* Cambridge: Harvard University Press, 1986.

———. *A Matter of Principle.* Cambridge: Harvard University Press, 1985.

———. *Taking Rights Seriously.* Cambridge: Harvard University Press, 1977.

Elazar, Daniel J. *American Federalism: A View from the States.* 3d ed. New York: Harper and Row, 1984.

———. *Cities of the Prairie: The Metropolitan Frontier and American Politics.* New York: Basic Books, 1970.

———. *Cities of the Prairie Revisited: The Closing of the Metropolitan Frontier.* Lincoln: University of Nebraska Press, 1986.

———. "Constitution-Making: The Pre-eminently Political Act." In Keith G. Banting and Richard Simeon, eds. *Redesigning the State: The Politics of Constitutional Change.* Toronto: University of Toronto Press, 1985.

———. "The Principles and Traditions Underlying American State Constitutions." *Publius* 12 (winter 1982): 11–25.

———. "A Response to James Gardner's 'The Failed Discourse of State Constitutionalism.'" *Rutgers Law Journal* 24 (summer 1993): 975–84.

———. "State-Local Relations: Reviving Old Theory for New Practice." In Stephanie Cole, ed. *Partnership within the States: Local Self-Government in the Federal System*. Urbana, Ill.: Institute of Government and Public Affairs, 1975.

Ely, John Hart. *Democracy and Distrust: A Theory of Judicial Review*. Cambridge: Harvard University Press, 1980.

Emmert, Craig F., and Carol Ann Traut. "State Supreme Courts, State Constitutions, and Judicial Policymaking." *Justice System Journal* 16 (1992): 37–48.

Erdman, Charles, Jr. *The New Jersey Constitution of 1776*. Princeton: Princeton University Press, 1929.

Eskridge, William N., Jr. *Dynamic Statutory Interpretation*. Cambridge: Harvard University Press, 1994.

Esler, Michael. "State High Court Commitment to State Law." *Judicature* 78 (July–August 1995): 25–32.

Fairlie, John A. "The Veto Power of the State Governor." *American Political Science Review* 11 (August 1917): 473–93.

Farrand, Max, ed. *The Records of the Federal Convention of 1787*. 4 vols. New Haven: Yale University Press, 1966.

Fehrenbacher, Don E. "Constitutional History, 1848–1861." In Leonard W. Levy, ed. *American Constitutional History*. New York: Macmillan, 1986.

———. *Constitutions and Constitutionalism in the Slaveholding South*. Athens: University of Georgia Press, 1989.

———. *Sectional Crisis and Southern Constitutionalism*. Baton Rouge: Louisiana State University Press, 1995.

Feldman, Jonathan. "Separation of Powers and Judicial Review of Positive Rights Claims: The Role of State Courts in an Era of Positive Government." *Rutgers Law Journal* 24 (summer 1993): 1057–1100.

Fellman, David. "What Should a State Constitution Contain?" In W. Brooke Graves, ed. *Major Problems in State Constitutional Revision*. Chicago: Public Administration Service, 1960.

Fernandez, Jose L. "State Constitutions, Environmental Rights Provisions, and the Doctrine of Self-Execution: A Political Question?" *Harvard Environmental Law Review* 17 (1993): 333–87.

Field, Phyllis F. *The Politics of Race in New York: The Struggle for Black Suffrage in the Civil War Era*. Ithaca, N.Y.: Cornell University Press, 1982.

Finkelman, Paul, and Stephen E. Gottlieb, eds. *Toward a Usable Past: Liberty under State Constitutions*. Athens: University of Georgia Press, 1991.

Fino, Susan P. "Judicial Federalism and Equality Guarantees in State Supreme Courts." *Publius* 17 (winter 1987): 51–67.

———. *The Michigan State Constitution: A Reference Guide*. Westport, Conn.: Greenwood Press, 1996.

———. "Remnants of the Past: Economic Due Process in the States." In Stanley Friedelbaum, ed. *Human Rights in the States*. Westport, Conn.: Greenwood Press, 1988.

———. *The Role of State Supreme Courts in the New Judicial Federalism*. Westport, Conn.: Greenwood Press, 1987.

Fischel, William A. "How *Serrano* Caused Proposition 13." *Journal of Law and Politics* 12 (fall 1996): 521–53.

Fischer, James M. "Ballot Propositions: The Challenge of Direct Democracy to State Constitutional Jurisprudence." *Hastings Constitutional Law Quarterly* 11 (fall 1983): 43–90.

Flango, Victor Eugene, and Nora F. Blair. "Creating an Intermediate Appellate Court: Does It Reduce the Caseload of a State's Highest Court?" *Judicature* 64 (August 1980): 74–84.

Flexner, Eleanor. *Century of Struggle: The Women's Rights Movement in the United States.* New York: Atheneum, 1971.

Foner, Eric. "From Slavery to Citizenship: Blacks and the Right to Vote." In Donald W. Rogers, ed. *Voting and the Spirit of American Democracy.* Urbana: University of Illinois Press, 1990.

———. *Reconstruction: America's Unfinished Revolution, 1863–1877.* New York: Harper and Row, 1988.

Force, Robert. "State 'Bills of Rights': A Case of Neglect and the Need for a Renaissance." *Valparaiso University Law Review* 3 (spring 1969): 125–82.

Ford, Henry Jones. "The Influence of State Politics in Expanding Federal Power." *Proceedings of the American Political Science Association.* Washington, D.C.: American Political Science Association, 1908.

Freund, Ernst. "Interpretation of Statutes." *University of Pennsylvania Law Review* 65 (January 1917): 207–31.

———. *Standards of American Legislation.* Chicago: University of Chicago Press, 1917.

Freyer, Tony A. *Producers versus Capitalists: Constitutional Conflict in Antebellum America.* Charlottesville: University Press of Virginia, 1994.

Fried, Margaret J., and Monique J. Van Damme. "Environmental Protection in a Constitutional Setting." *Temple Law Review* 68 (fall 1995): 1369–1401.

Friedelbaum, Stanley, ed. *Human Rights in the States.* Westport, Conn.: Greenwood Press, 1988.

Friedman, Lawrence M. *A History of American Law.* 2d ed. New York: Simon and Schuster, 1985.

———. "State Constitutions and Criminal Justice in the Late Nineteenth Century." In Paul Finkelman and Stephen E. Gottlieb, eds. *Toward a Usable Past: Liberty under State Constitutions.* Athens: University of Georgia Press, 1991.

Friesen, Jennifer. *State Constitutional Law: Litigating Individual Rights, Claims, and Defenses.* 2d ed. Charlottesville, Va.: Michie, 1996.

Fritz, Christian G. "Alternative Visions of American Constitutionalism: Popular Sovereignty and the Early American Constitutional Debate." *Hastings Constitutional Law Quarterly* 24 (winter 1997): 287–357.

———. "The American Constitutional Tradition Revisited: Preliminary Observations on State Constitution-Making in the Nineteenth-Century West." *Rutgers Law Journal* 25 (summer 1995): 945–98.

———. "Constitution Making in the Nineteenth-Century American West." In John McLaren, Hamar Foster, and Chet Orloff, eds. *Law for the Elephant, Law for the Beaver: Essays in the Legal History of the North American West.* Regina, Sask.: Canadian Plains Research Center, 1992.

————. "More Than 'Shreds and Patches': California's First Bill of Rights." *Hastings Constitutional Law Quarterly* 17 (fall 1989): 13–33.

————. "Rethinking the American Constitutional Tradition: National Dimensions in the Formation of State Constitutions." *Rutgers Law Journal* 26 (summer 1995): 969–92.

Froman, Lewis A., Jr. "Some Effects of Interest Group Strength in State Politics." *American Political Science Review* 60 (December 1966): 952–62.

Frug, Gerald E. "The City as a Legal Concept." *Harvard Law Review* 93 (April 1980): 1059–1154.

Funston, Richard Y. *Constitutional Counterrevolution?* Cambridge, Mass.: Schenkman, 1977.

Gais, Thomas, and Gerald Benjamin. "Public Discontent and the Decline of Deliberation: A Dilemma in State Constitutional Reform." *Temple Law Review* 68 (fall 1995): 1291–1315.

Galie, Peter J. *The New York State Constitution: A Reference Guide*. Westport, Conn.: Greenwood Press, 1991.

————. "Social Services and Egalitarian Activism." In Stanley Friedelbaum, ed. *Human Rights in the States*. Westport, Conn.: Greenwood Press, 1988.

————. "State Courts and Economic Rights." *Annals of the American Academy of Political and Social Science* 496 (March 1988): 76–87.

Gardner, James A. "The Failed Discourse of State Constitutionalism." *Michigan Law Review* 90 (February 1992): 761–837.

————. "What Is a State Constitution?" *Rutgers Law Journal* 24 (summer 1993): 1025–55.

Garnett, James L. *Reorganizing State Government: The Executive Branch*. Boulder, Colo.: Westview, 1980.

Geison, Gerald L., ed. *Professions and Professional Ideologies in America*. Chapel Hill: University of North Carolina Press, 1983.

Gettleman, Marvin E. *The Dorr Rebellion: A Study in American Radicalism, 1823–1849*. New York: Random House, 1973.

Gillman, Howard. *The Constitution Besieged: The Rise and Demise of Lochner Era Police Powers Jurisprudence*. Durham, N.C.: Duke University Press, 1993.

Gold, David M. *The Shaping of Nineteenth-Century Law: John Appleton and Responsible Individualism*. Westport, Conn.: Greenwood Press, 1990.

Goldberg, Richard A., and Robert F. Williams. "Farmworkers' Organizational and Collective Bargaining Rights in New Jersey: Implementing Self-Executing State Constitutional Rights." *Rutgers Law Journal* 18 (summer 1987): 729–63.

Goldstein, Leslie Friedman. *In Defense of the Text: Democracy and Constitutional Theory*. Savage, Md.: Rowman and Littlefield, 1991.

Goldwin, Robert A., and Art Kaufman, eds. *Constitution Makers on Constitution Making: The Experience of Eight Nations*. Washington, D.C.: American Enterprise Institute, 1988.

Gordon, Daniel R. "Protecting against the State Constitutional Law Junkyard: Proposals to Limit Popular Constitutional Revision in Florida." *Nova Law Review* 20 (fall 1995): 413–35.

Gormley, Ken, and Rhonda G. Hartman. "Privacy and the States." *Temple Law Review* 65 (winter 1992): 1279–1323.

Gottlieb, Stephen E. "Foreword: Symposium on State Constitutional History: In Search of a Usable Past." *Albany Law Review* 53 (winter 1989): 259–64.

Grabow, John C. "Congressional Silence and the Search for Legislative Intent: A Venture into 'Speculative Unrealities.'" *Boston University Law Review* 64 (July 1984): 737–66.

Grad, Frank P. "The State Constitution: Its Function and Form for Our Time." *Virginia Law Review* 54 (June 1968): 928–73.

Graves, W. Brooke, ed. *Major Problems in State Constitutional Revision.* Chicago: Public Administration Service, 1960.

Gray, Virginia. "Innovation in the States: A Diffusion Study." *American Political Science Review* 67 (December 1973): 1174–85.

Gray, Virginia, and Herbert Jacob, eds. *Politics in the American States.* 6th ed. Washington, D.C.: CQ Press, 1996.

Green, Fletcher M. *Constitutional Development in the South Atlantic States, 1776–1860: A Study in the Evolution of Democracy.* Chapel Hill: University of North Carolina Press, 1930.

Greene, Thurston. *The Language of the Constitution.* Westport, Conn.: Greenwood Press, 1991.

Grey, Thomas. "Do We Have an Unwritten Constitution?" *Stanford Law Review* 27 (February 1975): 843–93.

Griffin, Stephen M. *American Constitutionalism: From Theory to Politics.* Princeton: Princeton University Press, 1996.

Grimes, Alan P. *The Puritan Ethic and Woman Suffrage.* New York: Oxford University Press, 1967.

Grodin, Joseph R., Calvin R. Massey, and Richard B. Cunningham. *The California State Constitution: A Reference Guide.* Westport, Conn.: Greenwood Press, 1993.

Groot, Roger D. "The Effects of an Intermediate Appellate Court on the Supreme Court Work Product: The North Carolina Experience." *Wake Forest Law Review* 7 (October 1971): 548–72.

Gunn, L. Roy. *The Decline of Authority: Public Economic Policy and Political Development in New York, 1800–1860.* Ithaca, N.Y.: Cornell University Press, 1988.

Hall, Kermit L. "The Judiciary on Trial: Constitutional Reform and the Rise of an Elected Judiciary, 1846–1860." *Historian* 44 (May 1983): 337–54.

———. *The Magic Mirror: Law in American History.* New York: Oxford University Press, 1989.

———. *Major Problems in American Constitutional History,* 2 vols. Lexington, Mass.: D. C. Heath, 1992.

———. "Mostly Anchor and Little Sail: The Evolution of American State Constitutions." In Paul Finkelman and Stephen E. Gottlieb, eds. *Toward a Usable Past: Liberty under State Constitutions.* Athens: University of Georgia Press, 1991.

Hall, Kermit L., Harold M. Hyman, and Leon V. Sigal, eds. *The Constitutional Convention as an Amending Device.* Washington, D.C.: American Historical Association and American Political Science Association, 1981.

Handlin, Oscar, and Handlin, Mary Flug. *Commonwealth: A Study of the Role of Government in the American Economy: Massachusetts, 1774–1861*. Cambridge, Mass.: Belknap Press, 1969.

———, eds. *The Popular Sources of Political Authority: Documents on the Massachusetts Constitution of 1780*. Cambridge, Mass.: Belknap Press, 1966.

Hardy, Leroy, Alan Heslop, and Stuart Anderson, eds. *Reapportionment Politics: The History of Redistricting in the 50 States*. Beverly Hills, Calif.: Sage Publications, 1981.

Hargrave, Lee. *The Louisiana State Constitution: A Reference Guide*. Westport, Conn.: Greenwood Press, 1991.

Harris, Peter K. "The Communication of Precedent among State Supreme Courts." Ph.D. diss., Yale University, 1980.

———. "Difficult Cases and the Display of Authority." *Journal of Law, Economics, and Organization* 1 (spring 1985): 209–21.

———. "Structural Change in the Communication of Precedent among State Supreme Courts, 1870–1970." *Social Networks* 4 (September 1982): 201–22.

Harris, William F., II. "Bonding Word and Polity: The Logic of American Constitutionalism." *American Political Science Review* 76 (March 1982): 34–49.

Harrison, Lowell B. *Kentucky's Road to Statehood*. Lexington: University Press of Kentucky, 1992.

Hartz, Louis. *Economic Policy and Democratic Thought: Pennsylvania, 1776–1860*. Cambridge: Harvard University Press, 1948.

Havard, William C. "Notes on a Theory of State Constitutional Change: The Florida Experience." *Journal of Politics* 21 (February 1959): 80–104.

Heath, Milton S. *Constructive Liberalism: The Role of the State in Economic Development in Georgia to 1860*. Cambridge: Harvard University Press, 1954.

Heins, A. James. *Constitutional Restrictions against State Debt*. Madison: University of Wisconsin Press, 1963.

Heller, Francis H. *The Kansas State Constitution: A Reference Guide*. Westport, Conn.: Greenwood Press, 1992.

Henretta, James A. "Rethinking the State Constitutional Tradition." *Rutgers Law Journal* 22 (summer 1991): 819–39.

———. "The Rise and Decline of 'Democratic-Republicanism': Political Rights in New York and the Several States, 1800–1915." In Paul Finkelman and Stephen E. Gottlieb, eds. *Toward a Usable Past: Liberty under State Constitutions*. Athens: University of Georgia Press, 1991.

Herget, James E. "The Missing Power of Local Government: A Discrepancy between Text and Practice in Our Early State Constitutions." *Virginia Law Review* 62 (June 1976): 999–1015.

Hetherington, John A. "State Economic Regulations and Substantive Due Process of Law." *Northwestern University Law Review* 53 (1958–59): 226–51.

Hicks, John D. *The Constitutions of the Northwest States*. Lincoln: University of Nebraska University Studies, 1923.

Hill, Melvin B., Jr. *The Georgia State Constitution: A Reference Guide*. Westport, Conn.: Greenwood Press, 1994.

Hill, William C. *The Vermont State Constitution: A Reference Guide*. Westport, Conn.: Greenwood Press, 1992.

Hitchcock, Henry. *American State Constitutions: A Study of Their Growth*. New York: G. P. Putnam's Sons, 1887.

Hoar, Roger Sherman. *Constitutional Conventions: Their Nature, Powers, and Limitations*. Boston: Little, Brown, 1919.

Hoffman, Ronald, and Peter J. Albert, eds. *Sovereign States in an Age of Uncertainty*. Charlottesville, Va.: University Press of Virginia, 1981.

Hofstadter, Richard. *The Age of Reform: From Bryan to F.D.R.* New York: Alfred A. Knopf, 1968.

Horack, Frank E., Jr. "Congressional Silence: A Tool of Judicial Supremacy." *Texas Law Review* 25 (1946): 247–61.

Horowitz, Morton J. *The Transformation of American Law, 1870–1960: The Crisis of Legal Orthodoxy*. New York: Oxford University Press, 1992.

Horton, Wesley W. *The Connecticut State Constitution: A Reference Guide*. Westport, Conn.: Greenwood Press, 1993.

Hovenkamp, Herbert. *Enterprise and American Law, 1836–1937*. Cambridge: Harvard University Press, 1991.

Howard, A. E. Dick. *Commentaries on the Constitution of Virginia*. Charlottesville: University Press of Virginia, 1974.

———. *The Road from Runnymede: Magna Carta and Constitutionalism in America*. Charlottesville: University Press of Virginia, 1968.

———. "State Constitutions and the Environment." *Virginia Law Review* 58 (February 1972): 193–229.

Hudnut, Paul S. "State Constitutions and Individual Rights: The Case for Judicial Restraint." *Denver University Law Review* 63 (1985): 85–108.

Hurst, James Willard. *The Growth of American Law: The Lawmakers*. Boston: Little, Brown, 1950.

———. *Law and Social Order in the United States*. Ithaca, N.Y.: Cornell University Press, 1977.

———. *Law and the Conditions of Freedom in the Nineteenth-Century United States*. Madison: University of Wisconsin Press, 1956.

Huston, James H. "The Creation of the Constitution: The Integrity of the Documentary Record." *Texas Law Review* 65 (November 1986): 1–39.

Hyman, Harold M. *A More Perfect Union: The Impact of the Civil War and Reconstruction on the Constitution*. New York: Alfred A. Knopf, 1973.

Hyneman, Charles S., and Donald S. Lutz, eds. *American Political Writing during the Founding Era*. 2 vols. Indianapolis: Liberty Press, 1983.

Jameson, John Alexander. *A Treatise on Constitutional Conventions*. 4th ed. Chicago: Callaghan and Company, 1887; rpt. New York: Da Capo, 1972.

Johansen, Robin B. "The New Federalism: Toward a Principled Interpretation of the State Constitution." *Stanford Law Review* 29 (January 1977): 297–321.

Johnson, David Alan. *Founding the Far West: California, Oregon, and Nevada, 1940–1890*. Berkeley and Los Angeles: University of California Press, 1992.

Jones, Alan. "Thomas M. Cooley and 'Laissez-Faire' Constitutionalism: A Reconsideration." *Journal of American History* 53 (March 1967): 751–71.

Kagan, Robert A., Bliss Cartwright, Lawrence M. Friedman, and Stanton Wheeler. "The Business of State Supreme Courts, 1870–1970." *Stanford Law Review* 30 (November 1977): 121–56.

———. "The Evolution of State Supreme Courts." *Michigan Law Review* 76 (May 1978): 961–1005.

Kahn, Paul W. "Interpretation and Authority in State Constitutionalism." *Harvard Law Review* 106 (March 1993): 1147–68.

———. *Legitimacy and History: Self-Government in American Constitutional Theory.* New Haven: Yale University Press, 1992.

Kammen, Michael. *A Machine That Would Go of Itself: The Constitution in American Culture.* New York: Alfred A. Knopf, 1986.

Kay, Richard S. "Adherence to the Original Intentions in Constitutional Adjudication: Three Objections and Responses." *Northwestern University Law Review* 82 (winter 1988): 228–92.

Kaye, Judith S. "Foreword: The Common Law and State Constitutional Law as Full Partners in the Protection of Individual Rights." *Rutgers Law Journal* 23 (summer 1992): 727–52.

Keiter, Robert B., and Tim Newcomb. *The Wyoming State Constitution: A Reference Guide.* Westport, Conn.: Greenwood Press, 1993.

Keller, Morton. *Affairs of State: Public Life in Late Nineteenth Century America.* Cambridge, Mass.: Belknap Press, 1977.

Keller, Morton. "The Politics of State Constitutional Revision, 1820–1930." In Kermit L. Hall, Harold M. Hyman, and Leon V. Sigal, eds. *The Constitutional Convention as an Amending Device.* Washington, D.C.: American Historical Association and American Political Science Association, 1981.

Kelly, Alfred H., Winfred A. Harbison, and Herman Belz. *The American Constitution: Its Origin and Development.* 7th ed. New York: Norton, 1991.

Kenyon, Cecilia M. "Constitutionalism in Revolutionary America." In J. Roland Pennock and John W. Chapman, eds. *Constitutionalism.* New York: New York University Press, 1979.

Kesler, Charles R. *Saving the Revolution: The Federalist Papers and the American Founding.* New York: The Free Press, 1987.

Keyser, David R. "State Constitutions and Theories of Judicial Review: Some Variations on a Theme." *Texas Law Review* 63 (March–April 1985): 1051–80.

Kincaid, John. "The New Federalism Context of the New Judicial Federalism." *Rutgers Law Journal* 26 (summer 1995): 913–48.

———. "State Court Protections of Individual Rights under State Constitutions: The New Judicial Federalism." *Journal of State Government* 61 (September–October 1988): 163–69.

Kirby, James C., Jr. "Expansive Judicial Review of Economic Regulation under State Constitutions." In Bradley McGraw, ed. *Developments in State Constitutional Law.* St. Paul: West, 1985.

Kirp, David L., John P. Dwyer, and Larry A. Rosenthal. *Our Town: Race, Housing, and the Soul of Suburbia.* New Brunswick, N.J.: Rutgers University Press, 1995.

Kohler, David, and Robert M. Stern. "Initiatives in the 1980s and 1990s." In *The Book of the States, 1996–97.* Lexington, Ky.: Council of State Governments, 1996.

Kousser, J. Morgan. *The Shaping of Southern Politics: Suffrage Restrictions and* the *Establishment of the One-Party South, 1890–1910.* New Haven: Yale University Press, 1974.

Kruger, Karen J. "Rediscovering the New Jersey Equal Rights Amendment: It Says What It Means and It Means What It Says." *Rutgers Law Journal* 17 (winter 1985): 253–81.

Kruman, Marc W. *Between Authority and Liberty: State Constitution Making in Revolutionary America.* Chapel Hill: University of North Carolina Press, 1997.

Kuttner, Robert. *Revolt of the Haves: Tax Rebellions and Hard Times.* New York: Simon and Schuster, 1980.

Kynerd, Thomas E. *Administrative Reorganization in Mississippi Government: A Study in Politics.* Jackson: University Press of Mississippi, 1978.

Landers, Frank M. "Taxation and Finance." In W. Brooke Graves, ed. *Major Problems in State Constitutional Revision.* Chicago: Public Administration Service, 1960

Laska, Lewis L. *The Tennessee State Constitution: A Reference Guide.* Westport, Conn.: Greenwood Press, 1990.

Latzer, Barry. "California's Constitutional Counterrevolution." In G. Alan Tarr, ed. *Constitutional Politics in the States.* Westport, Conn.: Greenwood Press, 1996.

———. "A Critique of Gardner's 'Failed Discourse.'" *Rutgers Law Journal* 24 (summer 1993): 1009–18.

———. *State Constitutions and Criminal Justice.* Westport, Conn.: Greenwood Press, 1991.

Lee, Anne Feder. *The Hawaii State Constitution: A Reference Guide.* Westport, Conn.: Greenwood Press, 1993.

Lerner, Max. "Constitution and Court as Symbols." *Yale Law Journal* 46 (June 1937): 1290–1319.

Leshy, John D. *The Arizona State Constitution: A Reference Guide.* Westport, Conn.: Greenwood Press, 1993.

Levi, Edward H. *An Introduction to Legal Reasoning.* Chicago: University of Chicago Press, 1949.

Levinson, L. Harold. "The Decline of the Legislative Veto: Federal/State Comparisons and Interactions." *Publius* 17 (winter 1987): 115–32.

Levinson, Sanford. *Constitutional Faith.* Princeton: Princeton University Press, 1988.

———, ed. *Responding to Imperfection: The Theory and Practice of Constitutional Amendment.* Princeton: Princeton University Press, 1995.

Levy, Leonard W. *American Constitutional History.* New York: Macmillan, 1989.

———. *Emergence of a Free Press.* New York: Oxford University Press, 1985.

———. *The Establishment Clause: Religion and the First Amendment.* New York: Macmillan, 1986.

———. *Original Intent and the Framers' Constitution.* New York: Macmillan, 1988.

Libonati, Michael E. "Home Rule: An Essay on Pluralism." *Washington Law Review* 64 (January 1989): 51–71.

———. "Intergovernmental Relations in State Constitutional Law: A Historical

Overview." *Annals of the American Academy of Political and Social Science* 496 (March 1988): 107–16.

Linde, Hans A. "Are State Constitutions Common Law?" *Arizona Law Review* 34 (summer 1992): 215–29.

———. "E Pluribus—Constitutional Theory and State Courts." *Georgia Law Review* 18 (winter 1984): 165–200.

———. "First Things First: Rediscovering the State's Bill of Rights." *University of Baltimore Law Review* 9 (spring 1980): 379–86.

———. "When Is Initiative Lawmaking Not 'Republican Government'?" *Hastings Constitutional Law Quarterly* 17 (fall 1989): 159–73.

———. "Without 'Due Process': Unconstitutional Law in Oregon." *Oregon Law Review* 49 (February 1970): 125–87.

Link, Arthur S., and Richard L. McCormick. *Progressivism.* Arlington Heights, Ill.: Harlan Davidson, 1983.

Lipset, Seymour Martin, and William Schneider. *The Confidence Gap: Business, Labor, and Government in the Public Mind.* New York: Free Press, 1983.

Litwack, Leon F. *North of Slavery: The Negro in the Free States, 1790–1860.* Chicago: University of Chicago Press, 1961.

Lockhart, William B., Yale Kamisar, Jesse H. Choper, and Steven H. Shiffrin. *Constitutional Law: Cases—Comments—Questions.* 7th ed. St. Paul: West, 1991.

Loss, Richard, ed. *Corwin on the Constitution.* Vol. 1. Ithaca, N.Y.: Cornell University Press, 1981.

Lutz, Donald S. *The Origins of American Constitutionalism.* Baton Rouge: Louisiana State University Press, 1988.

———. *Popular Consent and Popular Control: Whig Political Theory in the Early State Constitutions.* Baton Rouge: Louisiana State University Press, 1980.

———. "The Purposes of American State Constitutions." *Publius* 12 (winter 1982): 27–44.

———. "The State Constitutional Pedigree of the U.S. Bill of Rights." *Publius* 22 (spring 1992): 19–45.

———. "Toward a Theory of Constitutional Amendment." *American Political Science Review* 88 (June 1994): 355–70.

———. "The United States Constitution as an Incomplete Text." *Annals of the American Academy of Political and Social Science* 496 (March 1988): 23–32.

Lynd, Staughton. *Intellectual Origins of American Radicalism.* Cambridge: Harvard University Press, 1982.

Magleby, David B. "Direct Legislation in the American States." In David Butler and Austin Ranney, eds. *Referendums around the World: The Growing Use of Direct Democracy.* Washington, D.C.: American Enterprise Institute Press, 1994.

———. "Let the Voters Decide? An Assessment of the Initiative and Referendum Process." *University of Colorado Law Review* 66 (1995): 13–46.

Main, Jackson Turner. *The Sovereign States, 1775–1783.* New York: Franklin, Watts, 1973.

———. *The Upper House in Revolutionary America.* Madison: University of Wisconsin Press, 1967.

Maltz, Earl M. *Civil Rights, the Constitution, and Congress, 1863–1869.* Lawrence: University Press of Kansas, 1990.

———. "The Dark Side of State Court Activism." *Texas Law Review* 63 (March–April 1985): 995–1023.

———. "False Prophet—Justice Brennan and the Theory of State Constitutional Law." *Hastings Constitutional Law Quarterly* 15 (spring 1988): 429–49.

———. "James Gardner and the Idea of State Constitutionalism." *Rutgers Law Journal* 24 (summer 1993): 1019–24.

———. "Lockstep Analysis and the Concept of Federalism." *Annals of the American Academy of Political and Social Science* 496 (March 1988): 98–106.

———. "The Political Dynamic of the 'New Judicial Federalism.'" *Emerging Issues in State Constitutional Law* 2 (1989): 233–38.

———. *Rethinking Constitutional Law: Originalism, Interventionism, and the Politics of Judicial Review.* Lawrence: University Press of Kansas, 1994.

Maltz, Earl M., Robert F. Williams, and Michael Araten. "Selected Bibliography on State Constitutional Law, 1980–1989." *Rutgers Law Journal* 20 (summer 1989): 1093–1113.

Marritz, Donald. "Making Equality Matter (Again): The Prohibition against Special Laws in the Pennsylvania Constitution." *Widener Journal of Public Law* 3 (1993): 161–215.

Matheson, Scott M., Jr. "Eligibility of Public Officials and Employees to Serve in the State Legislature: An Essay on Separation of Powers, Politics, and Constitutional Policy." *Utah Law Review* 1988:295–377.

May, Janice C. "Constitutional Amendment and Revision Revisited." *Publius* 17 (winter 1987): 153–79.

———. "The Constitutional Initiative: A Threat to Rights?" In Stanley Friedelbaum, ed. *Human Rights in the States.* Westport, Conn.: Greenwood Press, 1988.

———. "State Constitutions and Constitutional Revision, 1988–89 and the 1980's." In *The Book of the States, 1990–91.* Lexington, Ky.: Council of State Governments,

———. "State Constitutions and Constitutional Revision, 1992–93." In *The Book of the States, 1994–95.* Lexington, Ky.: Council of State Governments, 1994.

———. *The Texas Constitutional Revision Experience in the '70s.* Austin, Tex.: Sterling Swift Publishing, 1975.

———. *The Texas State Constitution: A Reference Guide.* Westport, Conn.: Greenwood Press, 1996.

McBeath, Gerald. *The Alaska State Constitution: A Reference Guide.* Westport, Conn.: Greenwood Press, 1997.

McCarthy, Sister M. Barbara. *The Widening Scope of American Constitutions.* Washington, D.C.: Catholic University of America, 1928.

McCormick, Richard L. *From Realignment to Reform: Political Change in New York, 1893–1910.* Ithaca, N.Y.: Cornell University Press, 1981.

McCormick, Richard P. *The Second American Party System: Party Formation in the Jacksonian Era.* Chapel Hill: University of North Carolina Press, 1966.

McCoy, Candace. "Crime as a Bogeyman: Why Californians Changed Their Constitution to Include a 'Victim's Bill of Rights' (and What It Really Did)." In G. Alan Tarr, ed. *Constitutional Politics in the States*. Westport, Conn.: Greenwood Press, 1996.

McDaniel, Ralph Chipman. *The Virginia Constitutional Convention of 1901–1902*. Baltimore: Johns Hopkins University Press, 1928.

McGoldrick, Joseph D. *Law and Practice of Municipal Home Rule, 1916–1930*. New York: AMS Press, 1967.

McGrane, Reginald. *Foreign Bondholders and American State Debts*. New York: Macmillan, 1935.

McGraw, Bradley, ed. *Developments in State Constitutional Law*. St. Paul: West, 1985.

McKay, Robert B. *Reapportionment: The Law and Politics of Equal Representation*. New York: Twentieth Century Fund, 1965.

McMillan, Malcolm C. *Constitutional Development in Alabama, 1798–1901: A Study in Politics, the Negro, and Sectionalism*. Chapel Hill: University of North Carolina Press, 1955.

Meller, Norman. *With an Understanding Heart: Constitution-Making in Hawaii*. New York: National Municipal League, 1971.

Merritt, Deborah Jones. "The Guarantee Clause and State Autonomy." *Columbia Law Review* 88 (January 1988): 1–78.

———. "Republican Governments and Autonomous States: A New Role for the Guarantee Clause." *University of Colorado Law Review* 65 (1994): 815–33.

Meyers, Marvin. *The Jacksonian Persuasion: Politics and Belief*. Madison: University of Wisconsin Press, 1956.

Miewald, Robert D., and Peter J. Longo. *The Nebraska State Constitution: A Reference Guide*. Westport, Conn.: Greenwood Press, 1993.

Mikesell, John L. "The Path of the Tax Revolt: Statewide Expenditure and Tax Cutting Referenda since Proposition 13." *State and Local Government Review* 18 (1986): 5–13.

Miller, William Lee. *The First Liberty: Religion and the American Republic*. New York: Alfred A. Knopf, 1986.

A Model State Constitution. New York: National Municipal League, 1924.

Model State Constitution. 4th ed. New York: National Municipal League, 1941.

Model State Constitution. 6th ed. New York: National Municipal League, 1968.

Monsell, Margaret E. " 'Stars in the Constellation of the Commonwealth': Massachusetts Towns and the Constitutional Right of Instruction." *New England Law Review* 29 (winter 1995): 285–309.

Moore, Michael C. "Constitutional Debt Limitations on Local Government in Idaho—Article 8, Section 3, Idaho Constitution." *Idaho Law Review* 17 (fall 1980): 55–85.

Morgan, Edmund S. *Inventing the People: The Rise of Popular Sovereignty in England and America*. New York: Norton, 1988.

Mowry, George E. *The California Progressives*. Chicago: Quadrangle Books, 1951.

Murphy, Walter F. "An Ordering of Constitutional Values." *Southern California Law Review* 53 (January 1980): 703–60.

Murphy, Walter F., James E. Fleming, and Sotirios A. Barber. *American Constitutional Interpretation*. 2d ed. Westbury, N. Y.: Foundation Press, 1995.

Nagel, Robert F. *Constitutional Cultures: The Mentality and Consequences of Judicial Review*. Berkeley and Los Angeles: University of California Press, 1989.

Nelson, Ronald L. "Welcome to the 'Last Frontier,' Professor Gardner: Alaska's Independent Approach to State Constitutional Interpretation." *Alaska Law Review* 12 (1995): 1–41.

Nelson, William E. *Americanization of the Common Law: The Impact of Legal Change on Massachusetts Society, 1760–1830*. Cambridge: Harvard University Press, 1975.

———. *The Fourteenth Amendment: From Political Principle to Judicial Doctrine*. Cambridge: Harvard University Press, 1988.

———. "The Impact of the Anti-Slavery Movement upon Styles of Judicial Reasoning in Nineteenth Century America." *Harvard Law Review* 87 (January 1974): 513–64.

Neuborne, Burt. "State Constitutions and the Evolution of Positive Rights." *Rutgers Law Journal* 20 (summer 1989): 881–901.

Nevins, Allan. *The American States during and after the Revolution*. New York: Macmillan, 1924.

Newhouse, Wade J. *Constitutional Uniformity and Equality in State Taxation*. 2d ed. Buffalo: William S. Hein, 1984.

"Note: Private Abridgment of Speech and the State Constitutions." *Yale Law Journal* 90 (November 1980): 165–88.

Novak, William J. *The People's Welfare: Law and Regulation in Nineteenth-Century America*. Chapel Hill: University of North Carolina Press, 1996.

Nye, Russell B. *Fettered Freedom: Civil Liberties and the Slavery Controversy, 1830–1860*. Ann Arbor: University of Michigan Press, 1963.

Oberholtzer, Ellis Paxson. *The Referendum in America*. New York: Da Capo, 1971.

Olin, Spencer C., Jr. *California's Prodigal Sons: Hiram Johnson and the Progressives, 1911–1917*. Berkeley and Los Angeles: University of California Press, 1968.

Orth, John V. "Forever Separate and Distinct: Separation of Powers Law in North Carolina." *North Carolina Law Review* 62 (October 1983): 1–28.

———. *The North Carolina State Constitution: A Reference Guide*. Westport, Conn.: Greenwood Press, 1993.

Palmer, Robert C. "Liberties as Constitutional Provisions: 1776–1791." In William E. Nelson and Robert C. Palmer, eds. *Liberty and Community: Constitution and Rights in the Early American Republic*. New York: Oceana, 1987.

Pangle, Thomas L. *The Spirit of Modern Republicanism: The Moral Vision of the American Founders and the Philosophy of John Locke*. Chicago: University of Chicago Press, 1988.

Patterson, Samuel C. "Legislative Politics in the States." In Virginia Gray and Herbert Jacob, eds. *Politics in the American States: A Comparative Analysis*. 6th ed. Washington, D.C.: CQ Press, 1996.

Perman, Michael. *The Road to Redemption: Southern Politics, 1869–1879*. Chapel Hill: University of North Carolina Press, 1984.

Perry, Michael J. *The Constitution, the Courts, and Human Rights*. New Haven: Yale University Press, 1982.

Peters, Ellen A. "State Constitutional Law: Federalism in the Common Law Tradition." *Michigan Law Review* 84 (February–April, 1986): 583–93.

Peters, Ronald M., Jr. *The Massachusetts Constitution of 1780: A Social Compact*. Amherst: University of Massachusetts Press, 1978.

Peterson, Merrill D., ed. *Democracy, Liberty, and Property: The State Constitutional Conventions of the 1820's*. Indianapolis: Bobbs-Merrill, 1966.

Pisani, Donald J. *From the Family Farm to Agribusiness: The Irrigation Crusade in California and the West, 1850–1931*. Berkeley and Los Angeles: University of California Press, 1984.

———. *To Reclaim a Divided West: Water, Law, and Public Policy, 1848–1902*. Albuquerque: University of New Mexico Press, 1992.

Pocock, J. G. A. *The Machiavellian Moment: Florentine Political Thought and the Atlantic Republican Tradition*. Princeton: Princeton University Press, 1975.

Pole, J. R. *Political Representation in England and the Origins of the American Republic*. New York: St. Martin's, 1966.

Pollock, James K. *The Initiative and Referendum in Michigan*. Ann Arbor: University of Michigan Press, 1940.

Pollock, Stewart G. "State Constitutions as Separate Sources of Fundamental Rights." *Rutgers Law Review* 35 (September 1983): 707–22.

Pope, James Gray. "An Approach to State Constitutional Interpretation." *Rutgers Law Journal* 24 (summer 1993): 985–1008.

Porter, Mary Cornelia. "State Supreme Courts and the Warren Court: Some Old Inquiries for a New Situation." In Mary Cornelia Porter and G. Alan Tarr, eds. *State Supreme Courts: Policymakers in the Federal System*. Westport, Conn.: Greenwood Press, 1982.

Porter, Mary Cornelia, with Robyn Mary O'Neill. "Personal Autonomy and the Limits of State Authority." In Stanley Friedelbaum, ed. *Human Rights in the States*. Westport, Conn.: Greenwood Press, 1988.

Porter, Mary Cornelia, and G. Alan Tarr, eds. *State Supreme Courts: Policymakers in the Federal System*. Westport, Conn.: Greenwood Press, 1982.

Press, Charles. "Assessing the Policy and Operational Implications of State Constitutional Change." *Publius* 12 (winter 1982): 99–111.

Proebsting, Patricia L. "Washington's Equal Rights Amendment: It Says What It Means and It Means What It Says," *University of Puget Sound Law Review* 8 (winter 1985): 461–84.

"Project Report: Toward an Activist Role for State Bills of Rights." *Harvard Civil Rights–Civil Liberties Law Review* 8 (March 1973): 323–50.

Pusey, Merlo J. *Charles Evans Hughes*. 2 vols. New York: Macmillan, 1951.

Rabban, David M. "The First Amendment in Its Forgotten Years." *Yale Law Journal* 90 (January 1981): 514–95.

Rabushka, Alvin, and Pauline Ryan. *The Tax Revolt*. Stanford, Calif.: Hoover Institution, 1982.

Ragosta, John A. "Free Speech Access to Shopping Malls Under State Constitutions: Analysis and Rejection." *Syracuse Law Review* 37 (1986): 1–42.

Rahe, Paul A. *Republics Ancient and Modern: Classical Republicanism and the American Revolution.* Chapel Hill: University of North Carolina Press, 1992.

Rankin, Robert S. *State Constitutions: The Bill of Rights.* New York: National Municipal League, 1960.

Rausch, John David, Jr. "The Politics of Term Limitations." In G. Alan Tarr, ed. *Constitutional Politics in the States.* Westport, Conn.: Greenwood Press, 1996.

Reeves, Mavis Mann. "The States as Polities: Reformed, Reinvigorated, Resourceful." *Annals of the American Academy of Political and Social Science* 509 (May 1990): 83–93.

Rehnquist, William H. "The Notion of a Living Constitution." *Texas Law Review* 54 (May 1976): 693–707.

Reid, John Phillip. *The Concept of Representation in the Age of the American Revolution.* Chicago: University of Chicago Press, 1989.

Rivlin, Alice M. *Reviving the American Dream.* Washington, D.C.: Brookings, 1992.

Rodgers, Daniel T. *Contested Truths: Keywords in American Politics since Independence.* New York: Basic Books, 1987.

Rohlfing, Charles C. "Amendment and Revision of State Constitutions." *Annals of the American Academy of Political and Social Science* 181 (September 1935): 180–87.

Rose, Carol M. "The Ancient Constitution vs. the Federalist Empire: Anti-Federalism from the Attack on 'Monarchism' to Modern Localism." *Northwestern University Law Review* 84 (fall 1989): 74–105.

Rosenberg, Norman L. *Protecting the Best Men: An Interpretive History of the Law of Libel.* Chapel Hill: University of North Carolina Press, 1986.

Rosenthal, Alan, and Maureen Moakley, eds. *The Political Life of the American States.* New York: Praeger, 1984.

Rossum, Ralph A., and G. Alan Tarr. *American Constitutional Law.* 4th ed. New York: St. Martin's, 1995.

Rotunda, Richard J., John E. Nowak, and J. Nelson Young. *Treatise on Constitutional Law.* St. Paul: West, 1986.

Rowe, G. S. *Embattled Bench: The Pennsylvania Supreme Court and the Forging of a Democratic Society.* Newark: University of Delaware Press, 1994.

Ruud, Millard H. "No Law Shall Embrace More Than One Subject." *Minnesota Law Review* 42 (January 1958): 389–452.

Sabato, Larry. *Goodbye to Good-Time Charlie: The American Governorship Transformed.* 2d ed. Washington, D.C.: CQ Press, 1983.

Rebecca Mae Salokar, "Creating a State Constitutional Right to Privacy: Unlikely Alliances, Uncertain Results." In G. Alan Tarr, ed. *Constitutional Politics in the States: Contemporary Controversies and Historical Patterns.* Westport, Conn.: Greenwood Press, 1996.

Sanford, Terry. *Storm over the States.* New York: McGraw-Hill, 1967.

Scheb, John M., and John M. Scheb II. "Making Intermediate Appellate Courts Final: Assessing Jurisdictional Changes in Florida's Appellate Courts." *Judicature* 67 (May 1984): 474–85.

Scheiber, Harry N. "Federalism and the American Economic Order, 1789–1910." *Law and Society Review* 10 (fall 1975): 57–118.

Schiesl, Martin J. *The Politics of Efficiency: Municipal Administration and Reform in America, 1800–1920*. Berkeley and Los Angeles: University of California Press, 1977.

Schlam, Lawrence. "State Constitutional Amending, Independent Interpretation, and Political Culture: A Case Study in Constitutional Stagnation." *DePaul Law Review* 43 (winter 1994): 269–378.

Schmidt, David D. *Citizen Lawmakers: The Ballot Initiative Revolution*. Philadelphia: Temple University Press, 1989.

Schouler, James. *Constitutional Studies: State and Federal*. New York: Da Capo, 1971.

Schuman, David. "A Failed Critique of State Constitutionalism." *Michigan Law Review* 91 (November 1992): 274–80.

———. "The Right to a Remedy." *Temple Law Review* 65 (winter 1992): 1197–1227.

Schwartz, Bernard. *The Great Rights of Mankind: A History of the American Bill of Rights*. New York: Oxford University Press, 1977.

Sears, David O., and Jack Citrin. *Tax Revolt: Something for Nothing in California*. Cambridge: Harvard University Press, 1982.

Selsam, J. Paul. *The Pennsylvania Constitution of 1776: A Study in Revolutionary Democracy*. Philadelphia: University of Pennsylvania Press, 1936.

Shepard, Randall T. "The Maturing Nature of State Constitutional Jurisprudence." *Valparaiso Law Review* 30 (spring 1996): 421–57.

Sherry, Suzanna. "The Early Virginia Tradition of Extratextual Interpretation." In Paul Finkelman and Stephen E. Gottlieb, eds. *Toward a Usable Past: Liberty under State Constitutions*. Athens: University of Georgia Press, 1991.

———. "The Founders' Unwritten Constitution." *University of Chicago Law Review* 54 (fall 1987): 1127–77.

———. "State Constitutional Law: Doing the Right Thing." *Rutgers Law Journal* 25 (summer 1994): 935–44.

Simon, James F. *In His Own Image: The Supreme Court in Richard Nixon's America*. New York: David McKay, 1973.

Simon, Todd F. "Independent but Inadequate: State Constitutions and the Protection of Freedom of Expression." *University of Kansas Law Review* 33 (winter 1985): 305–43.

Singer, Norman J. *Sutherland Statutory Construction*. 5th ed. Deerfield, Ill.: Clark Boardman Callaghan, 1992.

Skover, Robert. "The Washington Constitutional 'State Action' Doctrine: A Fundamental Right to State Action." *University of Puget Sound Law Review* 8 (winter 1985): 221–82.

Slobogin, Christopher. "State Adoption of Federal Law: Exploring the Limits of Florida's 'Forced Linkage' Amendment." *University of Florida Law Review* 39 (summer 1987): 653–732.

Smith, Chuck. *The New Mexico State Constitution: A Reference Guide*. Westport, Conn.: Greenwood Press, 1996.

Snowiss, Sylvia. *Judicial Review and the Law of the Constitution*. New Haven: Yale University Press, 1960.

Snyder, Sheryl G., and Robert M. Ireland. "The Separation of Governmental

Powers under the Constitution of Kentucky: A Legal and Historical Analysis of *L.R.C. v. Brown.*" *Kentucky Law Journal* 73 (1984–85): 165–233.

Stewart, Frank Mann. *A Half Century of Municipal Reform: A History of the National Municipal League.* Berkeley and Los Angeles: University of California Press, 1950.

Storing, Herbert J., ed. *The Complete Anti-Federalist,* 7 vols. Chicago: University of Chicago Press, 1981.

Story, Joseph. *Commentaries on the Constitution of the United States.* Durham: Carolina Academic Press, 1987.

Strumm, Philippa. *The Supreme Court and "Political Questions": A Study in Judicial Evasion.* University: University of Alabama Press, 1974.

Sturm, Albert L. "The Development of American State Constitutions." *Publius* 12 (winter 1982): 57–98.

———. "State Constitutions and Constitutional Revision: 1978–79 and the 1970's." In *The Book of the States, 1980–81.* Lexington, Ky.: Council of State Governments, 1980.

———. *Thirty Years of State Constitution-Making: 1938–1968.* New York: National Municipal League, 1970.

Suber, Peter. *The Paradox of Self-Amendment: A Study of Logic, Law, Omnipotence, and Change.* New York: Peter Lang, 1990.

Sukol, Robert M. "Developments in State Constitutional Law, 1992: Legislative Branch Reapportionment: Decennial State Constitutional Controversies." *Rutgers Law Journal* (summer 1993): 1106–32.

Summers, Mark W. *Railroads, Reconstruction, and the Gospel of Prosperity: Aid under the Radical Republicans, 1865–1877.* Princeton: Princeton University Press, 1984.

Swindler, William F. *Court and Constitution in the Twentieth Century: The Old Legality, 1889–1932.* Indianapolis: Bobbs-Merrill, 1969.

———, ed. *Sources and Documents of United States Constitutions.* 10 vols. Dobbs Ferry, N.Y.: Oceana, 1979.

———. "State Constitutions for the Twentieth Century." *Nebraska Law Review* 50 (summer 1971): 577–99.

Swisher, Carl Brent. *American Constitutional Development.* Boston: Houghton Mifflin, 1943.

———. *Motivation and Political Technique in the California Constitutional Convention, 1878–1879.* New York: Da Capo, 1969.

"Symposium: Investing in Our Children's Future: School Finance Reform in the '90s." *Harvard Journal of Legislation* 28 (summer 1991): 293–568.

"Symposium: Policy Diffusion in a Federal System." *Publius* 15 (fall 1985): 1–132.

"Symposium on the Guarantee Clause." *University of Colorado Law Review* 65 (1994): 709–946.

Tarr, G. Alan. "Church and State in the States." *Washington Law Review* 64 (winter 1989): 73–110.

———. "Constitutional Theory and State Constitutional Interpretation." *Rutgers Law Journal* 22 (summer 1991): 841–61.

————. "The Effect of Court Unification on Court Performance: A Preliminary Assessment." *Judicature* 64 (March 1981): 356–68.

————. *Judicial Process and Judicial Policymaking.* St. Paul: West, 1994.

————. "The New Judicial Federalism in Perspective." *Notre Dame Law Review* 72 (May 1997): 1097–1118.

————. "The Past and Future of the New Judicial Federalism." *Publius* 24 (spring 1994): 63–79.

————. "State Constitutional Politics: An Historical Perspective," in Tarr, *Constitutional Politics in the States.* Westport, Conn.: Greenwood Press, 1996.

————. "State Constitutionalism and 'First Amendment' Rights." In Stanley Friedelbaum, ed. *Human Rights in the States.* Westport, Conn.: Greenwood Press, 1988.

————, ed. *Constitutional Politics in the States.* Westport, Conn.: Greenwood Press, 1996.

Tarr, G. Alan, and Russell S. Harrison. "Legitimacy and Capacity in State Supreme Court Policymaking: The New Jersey Supreme Court and Exclusionary Zoning." *Rutgers Law Journal* 15 (spring 1984): 514–72.

Tarr, G. Alan, and Mary Cornelia Porter. "Gender Equality and Judicial Federalism: The Role of State Appellate Courts." *Hastings Constitutional Law Quarterly* 9 (summer 1982): 919–73.

————. *State Supreme Courts in State and Nation.* New Haven: Yale University Press, 1988.

Tate, C. Neal, and Torbjorn Vallinder, eds. *The Global Expansion of Judicial Power.* New York: New York University Press, 1995.

Thach, Charles C. *The Creation of the Presidency, 1775–1789: A Study in Constitutional History.* Baltimore: Johns Hopkins University Press, 1922.

Thayer, James Bradley. "The Origin and Scope of the American Doctrine of Constitutional Law." *Harvard Law Review* 7 (October 1893): 129–56.

Thompson, Barton H., Jr. "Environmental Policy and the State Constitution: The Role for Substantive Policy Guidance." In Bruce E. Cain and Roger G. Noll, eds. *Constitutional Reform in California: Making State Government More Effective and Responsive.* Berkeley, Calif.: Institute of Governmental Studies Press, 1995.

Thompson, Michael, Richard Ellis, and Aaron Wildavsky. *Cultural Theory.* Boulder, Colo.: Westview, 1990.

Tinkle, Marshall J. *The Maine State Constitution: A Reference Guide.* Westport, Conn.: Greenwood Press, 1992.

Treadwell, Lujuana Wolfe, and Nancy Wallace Page. "Equal Rights Provisions: The Experience under State Constitutions." *California Law Review* 65 (September 1977): 1086–1102.

Tribe, Lawrence H. *American Constitutional Law.* 2d ed. Mineola, N.Y.: Foundation Press, 1988.

————. "Toward a Syntax of the Unsaid: Construing the Sounds of Congressional and Constitutional Silence." *Indiana Law Journal* 57 (1981–82): 515–36.

Tushnet, Mark A. *Red, White, and Blue: A Critical Analysis of Constitutional Law*. Cambridge: Harvard University Press, 1988.

Twist, Steven J., and Len L. Munsill. "The Double Threat of Judicial Activism: Inventing New 'Rights' in State Constitutions." *Arizona State Law Journal* 21 (winter 1989): 1005–65.

Utter, Robert F., and Edward J. Larson, "Church and State on the Frontier: The History of the Establishment Clauses in the Washington State Constitution." *Hastings Constitutional Law Quarterly* 15 (spring 1988): 451–78.

Vile, M. J. C. *Constitutionalism and the Separation of Powers*. Oxford: Clarendon Press, 1967.

Vose, Clement. "Discussion of 'The American Constitutional Tradition: Its Impact and Development.'" In Kermit L. Hall, Harold M. Hyman, and Leon V. Sigal, eds. *The Constitutional Convention as an Amending Device*. Washington, D.C.: American Historical Association and American Political Science Association, 1981.

Walker, Jack L. "The Diffusion of Innovations among American States." *American Political Science Review* 63 (September 1969): 880–99.

Wechsler, Herbert. "Toward Neutral Principles of Constitutional Law." *Harvard Law Review* 73 (1959): 1–35.

Welch, Stephen. *The Concept of Political Culture*. New York: St. Martin's, 1993.

Wheeler, John P., Jr. *Magnificent Failure: The Maryland Constitutional Convention of 1967–1968*. New York: National Municipal League, 1972.

———. *Salient Issues of Constitutional Reform*. New York: National Municipal League, 1961.

Wheeler, Marjorie Spruill, ed. *One Woman, One Vote: Rediscovering the Woman Suffrage Movement*. Troutdale, Ore.: NewSage Press, 1995.

White, G. Edward. *The American Judicial Tradition: Profiles of Leading American Judges*. New York: Oxford University Press, 1976.

White, Jean Bickmore. *The Utah State Constitution: A Reference Guide*. Westport, Conn.: Greenwood Press, forthcoming.

Wiebe, Robert H. *The Search for Order, 1877–1920*. New York: Hill and Wang, 1967.

Wiecek, William M. *The Guarantee Clause of the U. S. Constitution*. Ithaca, N.Y.: Cornell University Press, 1972.

Wilkes, Donald E., Jr. "More on the New Federalism in Criminal Procedure." *Kentucky Law Journal* 63 (1975): 873–94.

———. "The New Federalism in Criminal Procedure: State Court Evasion of the Burger Court." *Kentucky Law Journal* 62 (1974): 421–51

———. "The New Federalism in Criminal Procedure Revisited." *Kentucky Law Journal* 64 (1976): 729–52.

Williams, Robert F. "Are State Constitutional Conventions Things of the Past? The Increasing Role of the Constitutional Commission in State Constitutional Change." *Hofstra Journal of Public Policy* 1 (1996): 1–26.

———. "Comment: On the Importance of a Theory of Legislative Power under State Constitutions." *Quinnipiac Law Review* 15 (spring 1996): 57–64.

———. "Equality Guarantees in State Constitutional Law." *Texas Law Review* 63 (March–April 1985): 1195–1224.

———. "In the Glare of the Supreme Court: Continuing Methodology and Legitimacy Problems in Independent State Constitutional Rights Adjudication." *Notre Dame Law Review* 72 (May 1997): 1015–64.

———. "In the Supreme Court's Shadow: Legitimacy of State Rejection of Supreme Court Reasoning and Result." *South Carolina Law Review* 35 (spring 1984): 353–404.

———. "The Influence of Pennsylvania's 1776 Constitution on American Constitutionalism during the Founding Era." *Pennsylvania Magazine of History and Biography* 112 (January 1988): 25–48.

———. "Methodology Problems in Enforcing State Constitutional Rights." *Georgia State University Law Review* 3 (fall–winter 1987): 143–77.

———. "The New Jersey Equal Rights Amendment: A Documentary Sourcebook." *Women's Rights Law Reporter* 16 (winter 1994): 70–125.

———. *The New Jersey State Constitution: A Reference Guide*. Westport, Conn.: Greenwood Press, 1990.

———. *State Constitutional Law: Cases and Materials*. 2d ed. Charlottesville, Va.: Michie, 1993.

———. "State Constitutional Law Processes." *William and Mary Law Review* 24 (winter 1983): 169–228.

———. "State Constitutional Limits on Legislative Procedure: Legislative Compliance and Judicial Enforcement." *Publius* 17 (winter 1987): 91–114.

Williamson, Chilton. *American Suffrage: From Property to Democracy, 1760–1860*. Princeton: Princeton University Press, 1960.

Williamson, Joel. *The Crucible of Race: Black-White Relations in the American South since Emancipation*. New York: Oxford University Press, 1984.

Winkle, John W., III. *The Mississippi State Constitution: A Reference Guide*. Westport, Conn.: Greenwood Press, 1993.

Witte, Harry L. "Rights, Revolution, and the Paradox of Constitutionalism: The Processes of Constitutional Change in Pennsylvania." *Widener Journal of Public Law* 3 (1993): 383–476.

Wood, Gordon S. *The Creation of the American Republic, 1776–1787*. New York: Norton, 1969.

———. *The Radicalism of the American Revolution*. New York: Alfred A. Knopf, 1992.

Wright, J. Skelly. "In Praise of State Courts: Confessions of a Federal Judge." *Hastings Constitutional Law Quarterly* 11 (winter 1984): 165–88.

Zimmerman, Joseph F. "State Mandate Relief: A Quick Look." *Intergovernmental Review* 28 (spring 1994): 28–31.

Zuckert, Michael P. *Natural Rights and the New Republicanism*. Princeton: Princeton University Press, 1994.

———. "Toward a Corrective Federalism: The United States Constitution, Federalism, and Rights." In Ellis Katz and G. Alan Tarr, eds. *Federalism and Rights*. Lanham, Md.: Rowman and Littlefield, 1996.

Index

Ackerman, Bruce, 23n76; on constitutional change, 194
Adams, John: on stratification, 86
Adaptability, 156
Admission of states, 41; requirements for, 41–55; vote on, 40
Admonitory language, 76, 78
Agenda, state constitutional, 99–101
Alabama Constitution (1819), amendments to, 35
Alabama Constitution (1875), 132n175; corporate aid and, 114; legislative control and, 125; ratification and, 35n23; on unnecessary offices, 132
Alabama Constitution (1901): amendments to, 24; white supremacy and, 144
Alaska Constitution, Model State Constitution and, 153, 154, 154n81
Amar, Akhil Reed: civic republicanism and, 64n16; on popular authority, 74n55
Amendments, 29, 53, 59, 60, 94n2, 174, 196; adjustment-by, 144; average number of, 24; constitutional length and, 38; local, 142n28, 143; by petition, 141n22; piecemeal transformation by, 139; politics of, 142; procedures for, 17n46, 23, 26n86, 35, 37, 62; proposal of, 36, 57, 140n12; rate of, 35–36, 36n24, 37, 38n36, 140, 141, 141n25; ratification of, 26–27, 32, 32n11, 36, 36n26, 74, 139, 139n11, 140, 141; rejection of, 32n11, 36n26, 143–44; reliance on, 31, 38, 141; resubmission of, 143–44; state legislatures and, 25, 143; voter knowledge about/interest in, 32. *See also* Constitutional changes
Anti-Federalists, state government and, 90
Apportionment, 45, 46, 82n93, 86n107, 93, 102–5, 129, 136; formulas for, 102, 145; judicial supervision of, 147; problems dealing with, 103–4, 145–46; taxation and, 86. *See also* Reapportionment
Aristocracy, 85, 100n20

Attitudinal explanations, constitutional changes and, 30–34
Authority: assumption of, 67–69; problem of, 67–71. *See also* Popular authority

Baker v. *Carr* (1962), 42
Balanced-budget amendment, 172
Bankruptcy, 30, 77
Benjamin, Gerald: on reformers/initiatives, 158n98
Berger, Raoul: on Eighth Amendment, 191n66
Bills of rights, 13, 24; judicial federalism and, 180n26; labor, 148; state law and, 167. *See also* Federal Bill of Rights
Blacks: disenfranchisement of, 106, 131, 144; political rights for, 101, 101n23, 131n172; rights for, 97
Black suffrage, 95, 95n6; limiting, 107; struggle for, 106
Borrowing, 65, 66, 68, 70, 98, 201; constitutional, 51, 52–53, 54; extent/character of, 54; interpretation and, 206, 207–8
Bowers v. *Hardwick* (1986), 208
Brennan, William H., Jr., 161; on human dignity/Constitution, 192; judicial federalism and, 166, 167–68, 180; on state supreme courts/constitutions, 165
Brown v. *Heymann* (1972), 15n37
Brown v. *State* (1983), 181
Bryce, James, 4; on constitutionalization of politics, 133–34; on 19th-century constitutions, 98
Budgets: plebiscitary, 159; reducing, 131–32
Burger, Warren, 161
Burger Court: civil-liberties cases and, 161, 165; *Illinois* v. *Gates* and, 179n22; judicial activism and, 171; retrenchment by, 178; on search warrants, 179; state constitutions and, 180; state guarantees and, 178

California Constitution: Article 10B of, 21; on eight-hour workday, 21; on judi-

Tocqueville, Alexis de, 134; on constitution-makers, 118–19; on federal Constitution, 118n108; on state constitutions, 118n108
Transportation, developing, 110
Twenty-Fourth Amendment, 45
Twenty-Sixth Amendment, 45, 45n65

U.S. Constitution. *See* Federal Constitution
U.S. Supreme Court: on districting decisions, 146–47; divergence from, 183, 183n36, 187; federal guarantees and, 182; interpretations by, 171, 174n3, 177n12, 182, 199, 206–7; judicial federalism and, 166; judicial rulings and, 174; lockstep approach and, 181n32; state courts and, 175
Unfunded mandates, curbing, 20
Unicameral legislature, 65n19, 153
Upper houses: establishment of, 85–86; property qualifications for, 85n104

Vermont Constitution (1793): amendments to, 35n18; length of, 10; on senatorial terms, 89
Vetoes: gubernatorial, 123, 130, 156; line item, 172
Victims' rights amendments, 53, 188
Vile, M. J. C.: on constitutional doctrine, 88n115
Virginia Constitution (1830), amendments to, 35n18
Virginia Constitution (1851): amendments to, 35n18; corruption and, 112; on free blacks, 129n160; legislative restrictions in, 121
Virginia Constitution (1902), white supremacy and, 144
Virginia Declaration of Rights, 12, 63n12, 75, 75n57, 76; borrowing from, 66, 81; on freedom of the press, 77; on political power, 74

Virginia Supreme Court, legislative control by, 124
Vose, Clement: on constitutional amendments, 37
Voting, 45; requirements for, 69, 82, 85, 85n102, 93, 105, 106–7, 127, 147; secret, 108. *See also* Disenfranchisement; Elections; Franchise; Suffrage
Voting Rights Act (1965), federal supervision and, 45–46

Wagner Act, 148
Warren, Earl, 161
Warren Court: civil-liberties cases and, 161, 165; judicial activism and, 171; on search warrants, 179; state guarantees and, 164, 178
Warth v. *Seldin* (1975), 179n23
Washington Supreme Court, on little ERAs, 202
Water rights, protection of, 197–98
West Virginia Constitution, on bond sales, 141
West Virginia Court of Appeals, on separation of powers, 15
Whig theory, 92n124; Federalist theory and, 92
Wilkes, Donald: on state constitutions/Burger Court, 180
Williams, Robert F.: on second-look cases, 176n11
Williams v. *Florida* (1980), 205n122
Wilson, James: on popular rule, 71n39
Woman suffrage, 45, 101, 101n23; campaign for, 108–9, 144–45
Wood, Gordon: on aristocracy, 85; on civic republicanism, 64n14
Workingmen's Compensation State Fund (Wyoming), 148
Wyoming Constitution (1889): inspector of mines and, 116; inspiration for, 98; on water rights, 198

Zoning restrictions, 166, 179, 197; challenges to, 179n23

ABOUT THE AUTHOR

G. ALAN TARR is Professor of Political Science and Director of the Center for State Constitutional Studies at Rutgers University at Camden. He is the author or editor of seven books, including *Constitutional Politics in the States, Judicial Process and Judicial Policymaking,* and *State Supreme Courts in State and Nation.*